Unity 3D and PlayMaker Essentials

Essentials

Game Development from Concept to Publishing

Unity 3D and PlayMaker Essentials

Game Development from Concept to Publishing

Jere Miles

CRC Press
Taylor & Francis Group
Boca Raton London New York

CRC Press is an imprint of the
Taylor & Francis Group, an **informa** business

AN A K PETERS BOOK

CRC Press
Taylor & Francis Group
6000 Broken Sound Parkway NW, Suite 300
Boca Raton, FL 33487-2742

© 2016 by Taylor & Francis Group, LLC
CRC Press is an imprint of Taylor & Francis Group, an Informa business

No claim to original U.S. Government works

Printed in India by Replika Press Pvt. Ltd.

Printed on acid-free paper
Version Date: 20160414

International Standard Book Number-13: 978-1-138-92177-1 (Paperback)

Library of Congress Cataloging-in-Publication Data

Names: Miles, Jere, author.
Title: Unity 3D and PlayMaker essentials : game development from concept to publishing / Jere Miles.
Description: Boca Raton : Taylor & Francis, CRC Press, 2016. | Includes bibliographical references and index.
Identifiers: LCCN 2016000972 | ISBN 9781138921771 (alk. paper)
Subjects: LCSH: Computer games--Programming. | Video games--Design. | Unity (Electronic resource) | Three-dimensional display systems.
Classification: LCC QA76.76.C672 M5395 2016 | DDC 794.8/1536--dc23
LC record available at https://lccn.loc.gov/2016000972

Visit the Taylor & Francis Web site at
http://www.taylorandfrancis.com

and the CRC Press Web site at
http://www.crcpress.com

This work is dedicated to my wife, Raylene Miles, for putting up with the long nights and Sundays while I sat in the office and typed and typed and typed. This is also dedicated to my children, Sergei and Steven, for the long discussions and early prototyping of the Sancho Panza idea during the morning drives to school.

Contents

Preface xv
Acknowledgments xxiii

SECTION I   Background

Chapter 1: Introduction 3
   1.1 Who Plays Games? 4
   1.2 How Are Games Made? 6
       1.2.1 AAA Studios 6
       1.2.2 The Indie Studio 7
   1.3 Who Can Make Games? 7
       1.3.1 Skills and Jobs 8
       1.3.2 Working in the Industry 8
   1.4 What Types of Games Are There? 10
       1.4.1 Role-Playing Games 10
       1.4.2 Adventure Games 11
       1.4.3 Platformer Games 12
       1.4.4 Shooter Games 13
       1.4.5 Action Games 14
       1.4.6 Strategy Games. 15
       1.4.7 Simulation Games 16
       1.4.8 Sports Games 17
       1.4.9 Puzzle Games 18
       1.4.10 MMO Games 18
   1.5 Summary 19
   Vocabulary 20
   Review Quiz 20
   Exercises 20
   Design Document 21

Chapter 2: Design Document 23
   2.1 Introduction to the Design Document 24
       2.1.1 Do We Need a Design Document? 25
       2.1.2 Methods of Design 26
       2.1.3 Logical Design versus Descriptive Design 27
       2.1.4 Mission and Vision 28
   2.2 Sections of the Design Document 29
       2.2.1 Game Concept 30
       2.2.2 Game Characters 33
       2.2.3 Game Story. 34

	2.2.4	The Game World	35
	2.2.5	Game Audio	36
	2.2.6	Game Interface	37
2.3	Summary		37
Vocabulary			38
Review Quiz			38
Exercises			39
Design Document			39

Chapter 3: Using Unity and PlayMaker **41**

3.1	Installing Unity	42
3.2	Unity's Interface	44
3.3	Using Unity	52
3.4	Installing PlayMaker	60
3.5	PlayMaker's Interface	63
3.6	State Machines	65
3.7	Using PlayMaker	70
3.8	Summary	85
Vocabulary		85
Review Quiz		85
Exercises		86
Design Document		86

SECTION II   Building Blocks

Chapter 4: Characters **89**

4.1	The Purpose of Characters		90
4.2	Do Games Need Characters?		90
4.3	Traditional Character Types		91
	4.3.1	The Hero	93
	4.3.2	The Shadow	93
	4.3.3	The Mentor	94
	4.3.4	The Ally	95
	4.3.5	The Herald	95
	4.3.6	The Trickster	95
	4.3.7	The Shapeshifter	96
	4.3.8	The Threshold Guardian	96
4.4	Game Character Types		97
	4.4.1	Merchants	97
	4.4.2	The Quest Giver	98
	4.4.3	Information	98
4.5	Character Design		99
4.6	Character Asset Design		102

4.7 Importing Assets in Unity. 105
   4.7.1 Back to Projects 105
   4.7.2 Importing 3D Assets 107
   4.7.3 Settings for Imported 3D Assets. 111
   4.7.4 From 3D Assets to Player Controllable Assets . . . 120
4.8 Character Control Systems with PlayMaker 122
   4.8.1 Designing the Character Response System 123
   4.8.2 Getting Input through Unity 126
   4.8.3 Building State Machines in PlayMaker 126
      4.8.3.1 Moving Sancho 127
      4.8.3.2 Rotating Sancho. 138
      4.8.3.3 Jumping Sancho 140
      4.8.3.4 The Camera Follows Sancho 145
4.9 Summary 147
Vocabulary. 147
Review Quiz. 148
Exercises 149
Design Document. 149

Chapter 5: Non-Player Characters 151
5.1 What Is Artificial Intelligence?. 152
5.2 Some Different Types of Artificial Intelligence 152
   5.2.1 Scripted Behavior. 152
   5.2.2 Random Behavior 154
   5.2.3 Expert Systems 156
   5.2.4 Mathematical Behavior Modeling 157
   5.2.5 Evolutionary Systems 159
5.3 Selecting an Artificial Intelligence System 161
5.4 Designing a Threshold Guardian 162
5.5 Implementing the Threshold Guardian. 167
   5.5.1 The Controller 168
   5.5.2 Patrolling. 171
   5.5.3 Spotting the Player 180
   5.5.4 Attacking the Player 184
   5.5.5 Hurting the Player 190
   5.5.6 Connecting the Attack and Health States. 194
   5.5.7 Final Tweaks. 196
5.6 Prefabs. 199
5.7 Summary 200
Vocabulary. 200
Review Quiz. 201
Exercises 201
Design Document. 202

Chapter 6: Story. 203
6.1 What Is a Story? 204
6.2 Does My Game Need a Story?. 204

6.3   How to Tell a Story 205
6.4   The Building Blocks of a Story......................... 206
    6.4.1   Characters..................................... 206
    6.4.2   Setting 206
    6.4.3   The Problem................................... 207
    6.4.4   The Plot 209
    6.4.5   The Solution................................... 209
    6.4.6   The Theme 210
6.5   Aristotle and the Greeks 211
    6.5.1   Plot 212
    6.5.2   Characters.....................................214
    6.5.3   Thought.......................................215
    6.5.4   Diction 215
    6.5.5   Melody..216
    6.5.6   The Spectacle 216
6.6   The Return of Joseph Campbell..........................217
    6.6.1   The Ordinary World.............................219
    6.6.2   Call to Adventure 219
    6.6.3   Refusal of the Call..............................219
    6.6.4   Meeting the Mentor 220
    6.6.5   Crossing the Threshold 220
    6.6.6   Tests, Allies, and Enemies 220
    6.6.7   Approaching the Cave 221
    6.6.8   The Ordeal 221
    6.6.9   The Reward 221
    6.6.10 The Road Back................................ 222
    6.6.11 Resurrection.................................. 222
    6.6.12 Return with Elixir 222
6.7   Story Design 222
    6.7.1   The Theme 223
    6.7.2   Characters.................................... 224
    6.7.3   Setting and Backstory 225
    6.7.4   The Problem.................................. 226
    6.7.5   The Plot 227
    6.7.6   The Solution.................................. 228
    6.7.7   Dialogue 228
6.8   Putting the Story into the Game 231
    6.8.1   Voice-Over Narration 232
    6.8.2   Written Text 235
    6.8.3   Character Dialogue 238
    6.8.4   Journal Systems 255
6.9   Summary 256
Vocabulary.. 256
Review Quiz... 257
Exercises 257
Design Document.. 257

Chapter 7: Environment **259**

7.1   Environments for Stories 260

7.2   Environments for Games 261

     7.2.1   Controlling the Player.......................... 261

     7.2.2   Informing the Player 263

     7.2.3   Challenging the Player......................... 264

     7.2.4   The Final Design 265

7.3   Creating the Terrain in Unity 269

     7.3.1   Settings 271

     7.3.2   Terrain Collider 273

     7.3.3   Height Tools................................. 274

7.4   Dressing a Terrain with Standard Content 279

     7.4.1   Painting Textures 279

     7.4.2   Adding Water................................ 288

     7.4.3   Adding Trees 289

     7.4.4   Adding Grass 296

7.5   Adding Imported Assets............................. 301

7.6   Lighting the Environment 307

7.7   Boundaries....................................... 307

7.8   Summary 310

Vocabulary...311

Review Quiz..311

Exercises 312

Design Document..312

Chapter 8: Mechanics.. 313

8.1   What Are Game Mechanics? 314

     8.1.1   The Core Mechanics 314

     8.1.2   Victory and Loss Conditions....................315

     8.1.3   Balance Mechanics 316

     8.1.4   Story Mechanics..............................316

     8.1.5   System Mechanics 317

8.2   Where Do Mechanics Come From?....................317

8.3   Designing Our Mechanics 318

     8.3.1   The Checkpoint System........................319

     8.3.2   Respawning Sancho 320

     8.3.3   Sancho and Water 321

     8.3.4   Sancho's Collection System 323

8.4   Implementing Our Mechanics 325

     8.4.1   The Checkpoint System........................ 325

     8.4.2   Sancho and Water 330

     8.4.3   Respawning Sancho 333

     8.4.4   Sancho's Collection System 338

8.5   Summary 343

Vocabulary 344

Review Quiz 344

Exercises. 345

Design Document 345

SECTION III   Bringing It Together

Chapter 9: **Audio** **349**

9.1   How Audio Is Used in Games 350

    9.1.1   Music. 350

    9.1.2   Ambience 352

    9.1.3   Sound Events. 354

9.2   Finding Audio. 354

9.3   Introduction to Audacity 356

    9.3.1   Cutting Up an Audio File 357

    9.3.2   Applying Effects to Audio 360

    9.3.3   Adjusting Volume Levels 364

9.4   Audio in Unity. 364

    9.4.1   2D Audio 366

    9.4.2   3D Audio 369

    9.4.3   Playing Ambient Audio 371

    9.4.4   Playing Background Music 375

9.5   Using PlayMaker to Play Audio. 375

    9.5.1   Background Music 376

    9.5.2   Ambient Sounds. 379

    9.5.3   Effects for Events 382

9.6   Summary 386

Vocabulary 387

Review Quiz 387

Exercises. 388

Design Document 388

Chapter 10: **The User Interface** **391**

10.1   The Types of User Interfaces 392

    10.1.1   Menu-Based Systems 392

    10.1.2   Heads-Up Display Systems and Overlays. 392

10.2   User Interface Design. 393

    10.2.1   HUD Design 394

    10.2.2   Menu Design 397

    10.2.3   Basics of Color Theory 398

10.3   The User Interface System of Unity. 402

    10.3.1   Building Blocks of uGUI 402

    10.3.2   Constructing the Main Menu. 404

    10.3.3   Constructing the HUD Overlay 412

    10.3.4   Polishing the Dialogue Work 418

10.4 Updating the User Interface with PlayMaker. 420

      10.4.1 Responses on the Main Menu 421

      10.4.2 Updating the Overlay 430

      10.4.3 Integrating the Dialogue System 440

10.5 Summary 444

Vocabulary 445

Review Quiz 445

Exercises. 446

Design Document 447

Chapter 11: Testing, Tweaking, and Publishing 449

11.1 What Is Testing?. 450

      11.1.1 Hunting Bugs. 452

      11.1.2 Play-Through Testing 453

      11.1.3 Unit Testing. 454

      11.1.4 Break Testing 457

11.2 Fixing and Tweaking 457

      11.2.1 Fixing the Following Sheep 458

11.3 Building the Game 460

      11.3.1 Game Development Life Cycle 462

      11.3.2 Build Options in Unity. 463

      11.3.3 Creating a Stand-Alone Build. 465

11.4 Summary 470

Vocabulary 471

Review Quiz 472

Exercises. 472

Design Document 472

Index **473**

Preface

As we begin the process of looking into how to use Unity and PlayMaker to create video games, we need to ensure that we are all on the same page, pardon the pun. It is important that you know what this book is about and what this book isn't about. It is also important to be aware of the expected skills and skill levels as we begin this book together.

What This Book Is About

The focus of this book is to introduce you to game development. Through this book you will get an overview of how to create video games. The process of creating a video game includes developing scripts and programmed behavior for the objects that are within the game to be played. As far as the development of programmed behaviors, we will be able to ease the transition into this process through the use of the PlayMaker visual scripting plugin, which will allow us to bypass all the syntax and technical aspects of programming and instead focus solely on the logical construction of a program or behavior script. When it comes to developing a game, it is created through the programming of the game, and the other parts (the graphics, for instance) define what the game looks like, not how it is played or how it behaves. As an example we could create a platform game with nothing but colored blocks running around the game world jumping over empty areas. The game would have all of the behaviors and playability of a platformer; however, it would not look nearly as cool as the platformer games that are currently on the market. The wonderfully cool graphics and animations of video games are *not* what we will be creating in this book.

Who This Book Is For

The concept for this book originated as a textbook for an introduction to a game development course (SGD 111) taught at Wilkes Community College in North Carolina. As a result, the target audience for this book is anyone who is interested in learning about game development and how to create games. It is assumed that the reader does not actually already know how to create video games. For instance, if you have extensive experience using another game engine such as Game Maker, you may be ready for a slightly more advanced book than this one. However, if you have not worked with any other game engine or if you have tried working with a couple but just could not seem to get the hang of it, then this book should be a good starting point to get you up and going with the Unity game engine.

Likewise, if you have extensive experience writing code in Java or C++ or some other language, you may be better suited to find a book that works with the C# scripting language within Unity. This being said, PlayMaker can be a very powerful tool for quickly prototyping an idea to see how things work, in which case it can be useful to add PlayMaker to your skill set. However, if you do have extensive programming experience, then you may find the pace of this book a little slow as the target audience is for those who have no experience with programming or those who have tried programming but are a little fuzzy on it.

If you are an artist that would like to learn how to put your artwork into Unity and get it to work with some game ideas of your own, then this book should be very helpful in getting you started with the game engine and also accomplishing the behaviors that you want associated with the art content so that you can demonstrate your own game concepts and even fully develop them into final products.

How This Book Is Organized

Each chapter of this book is laid out to focus on a specific topic with the topics building on each other so that by the end of the book we will have looked into all of the topics relevant to creating a game of our own. The chapters each begin with a theory section, discussing the background and various approaches to the given topic. Following the theory section, the chapter will work on designing components for the game project based upon the theories that were just presented. Finally, the chapter text will conclude with an implementation section in which the created designs will be built within Unity and PlayMaker to bring the theory of the topic to life within our game project. Each chapter also ends with a set of review questions that you can use to test your understanding of the concepts, and a set of exercises that are intended to expand upon the examples presented in the text of the chapter.

The idea of a design document will also be discussed during the course of the book with each chapter adding to the design document for a game idea of your own creation. By the end of the book, you should be able to take your design document and create the game that you have designed. Within each chapter, there are download boxes where you can get the version of the game project that is within the book or other content to add to the project as well as any video tutorials that have been developed to supplement the chapter contents.

Book Content

Section I: Background

- **Chapter 1—Introduction**
  - *Theory*: Students will be introduced to the overall process of game development including a discussion of the tools used, the skills needed, the various jobs within the industry, and the vocabulary of

game development. A brief overview of the various genres and their characteristics is also provided.

- **Chapter 2—Design Document**
  - *Theory*: The design document is introduced, placing emphasis on the rationale behind each section and the role that each section plays in the overall development process of a video game project. While much of this content is covered in the chapters that follow, it is important for the reader to recognize the role of design, as it forms the foundation for the vision of a game project.
  - *Design*: We will introduce the overall vision of the Sancho Panza project, which we will be working on during the course of the book while encouraging the reader to begin the design work on a game idea of their own by focusing on the primary game concept with respect to the targets and vision of the game.
  - *Implementation*: Based on the information from the chapter, we will begin the creation of our design document that will cover the Sancho Panza project and continue to add to it with each chapter.

- **Chapter 3—Using Unity and PlayMaker**
  - *Theory*: We will introduce the tools that the book will focus on, detailing how to download and install the software and providing overviews of the user interfaces for both applications. A discussion of the resources that are available on both websites is also included.
  - *Design*: The discussion focuses on what a finite state machine (FSM) is and how to construct one based upon the plain English description of what is intended to occur. Creating state machines to accomplish examples are presented in the practical section.
  - *Implementation*: We will demonstrate how to place objects within Unity and move them around and manipulate other primary components. Import assets and packages are discussed. Readers will learn how to develop state machines to alter the properties of various game objects placed within a scene. Through these state machines we will dynamically make the changes that were originally done as static changes in the previous demonstration of moving and manipulating objects within Unity.

Section II: Building Blocks

- **Chapter 4—Characters**
  - *Theory*: We provide a background discussion of characters focusing on the Jungian character types and their roles within a story and how they interact with one another. The chapter also discusses the other components of a character such as background, physical appearance, emotional construction, psychological construction, environment, and so on.
  - *Design*: We will create algorithms (plain English) to define the controller behaviors that our character should have based upon

decisions we made as the character idea was developed through the theory discussion. From the algorithms, we will demonstrate how to sketch state machines for these functionalities.

- *Implementation*: We will introduce the lead character of our book's example project, Sancho Panza, and demonstrate how to bring him into Unity, and through the use of PlayMaker turn him into a character that the player can control and play. The PlayMaker FSMs developed will be the implementation of those constructed during the design phase.

- **Chapter 5—Non-Player Characters**
  - *Theory*: Based upon the characters that were developed in the last chapter, we will look at how we can bring those characters to life within our game project and begin to populate the world around Sancho Panza. We will explore artificial intelligence (AI) by developing our own definition of it and looking at the major types of AI that can be developed and eventually deployed.
  - *Design*: Based upon our work with the player character and the needs of the project, we will design the behavior system that will govern the decision-making process of a threshold guardian character during the game so that they will be able to respond to events and actions that occur as the player plays our game.
  - *Implementation*: We will use PlayMaker to get our design working with a spider added to the Sancho Panza project that will attack and eventually kill the player character. This spider will have a rudimentary AI system that will give it the abilities we need for this project. These same basic principles will be applicable to any other non-player character (NPC) within the game.

- **Chapter 6—Story**
  - *Theory*: We will provide background information on the story, such as the theme, plot and devices, backstory, premise, and so on. This chapter includes a discussion of Aristotle's ideas about stories. We will also discuss the Hollywood 3-act structure and how it helps to guide a story along. Joseph Campbell's "Journey of a Hero" will also be demonstrated as a potential blueprint for story creation.
  - *Design*: This chapter covers the development of the backstory and other story components for a game project. While much of this design work may not make a direct appearance within the game, we need to know the story of the game in order to know what will happen during game play. We will also create potential quest systems based upon the story and dialogue trees between the NPC and the player character.
  - *Implementation*: We will construct the basis for a quest system for Sancho as well as an elementary dialogue between Sancho and his wife Teresa. In addition, we will add a narrative introduction to the game based upon the game's backstory, explaining who the player is and why they are on the island that they are on.

- **Chapter 7—Environment**
  - *Theory*: We provide an overview of the level design including the theme, atmosphere, and purpose. We focus on the level design as an episodic structure, specifically as a chapter of the overall story that is being told within the game. By recognizing the level as a chapter in the story, it becomes more apparent what purpose the level must serve and therefore what we as developers must do to keep our players on track within the story.
  - *Design*: Based upon the game design document and an understanding of the purpose of a level, we will sketch out a first-level environment for Sancho Panza to be dropped into. This level will consist of the island that the story is going to take place on.
  - *Implementation*: We demonstrate how to construct a level out of standard assets within Unity as well as importing external assets. The standard assets will be utilized to construct an exterior terrain for the game world while the provided assets will build the town and other props, all based upon our design work for this island.

- **Chapter 8—Mechanics**
  - *Theory*: Mechanics are the underlying rules that govern the behaviors of games; we discuss the guiding principles of these mechanics within video games by placing them within different categories to see how they impact the games that we play and ultimately the games that we design.
  - *Design*: Based upon the components and uses of game mechanics, we will determine and plan various obstacles for Sancho to deal with in the level that was constructed during the previous chapter. We will demonstrate several different game mechanics within this design.
  - *Implementation*: With a working Sancho Panza from previous chapters, we will add things for Sancho to interact with (collecting various objects, for instance) and tweak his controller system to provide for the game mechanic functionality as depicted in the design phase just completed based upon the original design document.

Section III: Bringing It Together

- **Chapter 9—Audio**
  - *Theory*: What role does audio play within a game? We introduce the different types of audio that can be utilized and their specific purpose within the overall game-play experience: music, ambience, effects, and voice-overs.
  - *Design*: We create an audio list that can be used within the project that has been developed thus far. Along with this list, we will sketch out locations of audio sources and potential areas of impact; the purpose of this design component is to check for dead and overpopulated areas within our overall audio scheme and plan "what and where" before trying to add it.

- *Implementation*: We will add various audio to our Sancho Panza example game and learn how Unity 3D handles and works with audio. Along with the audio being added, we will demonstrate how to use PlayMaker to script when audio will play and when it will not, so that user feedback (theoretical component) can be understood. A section incorporating the use of Audacity (a free audio editing application) for tweaking the audio files used in the game is also included.

- **Chapter 10—The User Interface**
  - *Theory*: Without a user interface, the player is very limited in what they know of the game world. We discuss the various uses of the system interfaces, ranging from menus to heads-up displays and how to consider the impact of these components, both positive and negative, to the overall game-play experience of the player.
  - *Design*: We will create sample sketches of how the user interface could look within our game. The purpose of designing the interface through sketching is to consider what information should be provided to the player and how to lay it out in a functional manner. In addition, we will create menu systems, which means that we will need to consider what options should be provided to the player of the game.
  - *Implementation*: We will add graphical user interface (GUI) components to our Sancho Panza game project including a menu system and heads-up display to provide information during game play. PlayMaker will be used to update the GUI information and also to respond to user interaction on the menu system.

- **Chapter 11—Testing, Tweaking, and Publishing**
  - *Theory*: We will explore the various types of testing and how to approach the testing of a game project with a specific focus on our Sancho Panza game project. In addition, we will look at the different stages of a life cycle of a video game project, concentrating on the types of content that should be emerging from each of the stages.
  - *Design*: We will need to take into account the target platform from our initial design and determine how to best build a deliverable of our game for that system. It is also important to consider the potential similarities between other builds. Finally, we will design solutions to the bugs that we find through our methodical testing of the Sancho Panza project.
  - *Implementation*: We will demonstrate how to deploy our Sancho Panza game as a stand-alone Windows deliverable, focusing on the various settings that we can customize. In addition, we will discover bugs within the project and properly document their cause in order to repair them from the developer's perspective.

Companion Website

Over the course of this book, we will be utilizing many resources that are not included with the default installation on Unity 3D. These resources include models, sounds, and textures. All of these can be obtained from the companion website that has been created to accompany this book. The website also includes links to video tutorials to enhance the content of the book and a complete version of the project developed over the course of the many examples. This project file includes the full and final project, but scene files have been created to correspond with each chapter and section as needed. The companion website also includes content for instructors such as PowerPoints for each chapter and a set of sample test questions for each chapter. Finally, the design documents developed through this book are also available on the website: http://www.darkglass-studio.com/Unity_PlayMaker_Essentials.

Acknowledgments

Wilkes Community College Simulation and Game Development students for serving as a test bed for the development of the content and the flow of the material.

Sean Connelly at Focal Press for editing my rambling writing and putting up with my incessant e-mails.

Unity Creative magazine, unfortunately no longer in print, for the availability of the animated knight character for free use (Issue #3, September–October 2010).

Alex Chouls at Hutong Games for getting us into the Beta for version 1.8 of PlayMaker.

Steve Finney at Arteria3D for the wonderful medieval town and the characters that are used over the course of the example project.

Timothy Bivans at Enlitanment Studios, LLC, for some early feedback and general advice on this project and then stepping up to do a full review of the content of the book.

SECTION I
Background

CHAPTER 1

Introduction

Welcome to the essentials of game development with Unity and PlayMaker. In this chapter, we will lay the basic groundwork for the game development process by focusing on the tools and skills used as well as looking into who plays games and what types of games there are to play. These topics may, at first glance, seem to be obvious to all of us. However, there is a specific vocabulary that is used within the game industry, and it is important that we make sure we are all on the same page with these terms and with these concepts. Game development is a wonderfully entertaining industry to get into; however, it is not necessarily for everyone, and it is through this chapter that we intend to help clarify some aspects of the industry and dispel some potential myths, beginning with the idea that playing games and making games are not the same thing.

- Who Plays Games?
- How Are Games Made?
- Who Can Make Games?
- What Types of Games Are There?

1.1 Who Plays Games?

Historically, this would have been considered to be teenage boys in their bedrooms on Saturday nights. Interestingly enough, this classic misconception of who plays video games is just as common today as it was back in the 1980s. Many average people consider video games to be the activity and hobby of the socially awkward teenage male. It is not our goal here to argue the merits one way or the other with this view of gamers; we are just stating how gamers are generally viewed by non-gamers. But what exactly is a non-gamer? Given today's society of smartphones, mobile technology, Facebook, gamification, and the emergence of virtual reality and augmented reality, it is very difficult to find someone that is an active member of our society that genuinely does not play video games. Games today can be used for training, education, scientific visualization, advertising, and, of course, entertainment. Table 1.1 outlines the actual statistics of who is playing video games today as compiled by the Entertainment Software Association in 2014. As can be seen from this information, the average video gamer is most definitely not the stereotype. Keep in mind that these statistics are only for American gamers.

The idea of judging gamers and placing them within cute little boxes is not only one that non-gamers engage in, but even gamers themselves want to label each other and specifically label themselves to differentiate from other gamers. This has led to the distinction of gamers as casual or hard core. Originally, hard-core gamers were ones that invested a lot of time in the games that they play and became experts at those games, knowing all of the tricks and intricacies of their games. A casual gamer, on the other hand, was one that played from time to time and did not take gaming seriously. A casual gamer would play a game until it became too difficult and would then quit, not wanting to invest the time required to become skilled enough at the game to advance past those stages. However, with the birth of the social gaming scene, the idea that a hard-core gamer is one that invests a tremendous amount of time in the games they play, meant that the millions of people investing hours into a game like *Farmville* were hard-core gamers,

TABLE 1.1 Video Game Players in 2014

59% of Americans play video games	Average of two gamers in each game-playing household
51% of American households own a dedicated game console	Average household has at least one game-playing device: 68% play on a console 53% play on a smartphone 41% play on a wireless device
Average age of gamer is 31	29% of gamers are under 18 32% of gamers are 18–35 39% of gamers are over 36 52% of gamers are male, 48% female

Source: ESA, 2014 Sales, Demographics, and Usage Data, Entertainment Software Association, http://www.theesa.com/wp-content/uploads/2014/10/ESA_EF_2014.pdf, 2014.

not casual gamers. As a result, the label hard-core gamer has shifted in recent years to be those gamers that play games on consoles, or specifically those gamers that do not play social games. But, once again, which of us does not play a game on our smartphone from time to time? These traditional labels are becoming more difficult to easily apply to a broad range of game players. Thankfully, this need to label gamers as either hard core or casual is beginning to fade as the amount of gamers and the types of games that we play continues to grow and to cross traditional boundaries. More important than whether we are casual or hard core, are the motivations behind why we play, or to put it another way, what we do when we play games.

A researcher named Richard Bartle looked into the ways that people played MUDs (multi-user dungeons) and discovered that there are essentially four distinct player classifications or motivations as shown in Figure 1.1. As we move to the left on this graph, players are more interested in the other players that are in the game, while moving to the right leads to players that are more interested in the environment. In today's vernacular, we are looking at the distinction between the PvP (Player versus Player) players and the PvE (Player versus Environment) players. However, as we can see with Bartle's characteristics, those who are interested in other players in the game world may not necessarily want to kill them, the player Killers in the top-left quadrant, they may just want to hang out with them and chat, the Socializers of the bottom-left quadrant. Swinging back the other way, we have players who want to conquer the environment—the Achievers in the top-right quadrant who want all the achievements and unlocks, with the those who just want to explore the vast game world, their only reward is knowing that they have seen what is just over the horizon—the Explorers in the bottom-right quadrant.

At first glance, this may seem like a bunch of academic babble about why people play games. However, knowing why people play games will help us create games that they will enjoy playing, it is not enough to copy the features and mechanics of other successful games, we need to understand what it is about those games

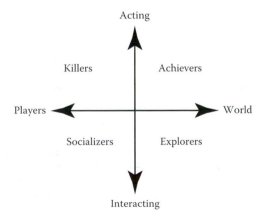

FIG 1.1 The Bartle player types.

that the players enjoyed. In order to create rich and diverse video games, it will be necessary for us to expand our gamer experience and try different things; in fact, we may even need to try to figure out why these other gamer types exist and what exactly they are getting out of playing the games that they do. As gamers, we have our favorite games and genres, as gamers we play games for fun. But, as developers we play games for work, we play games for research, and to be fair on occasion we play our favorite games for fun. As developers, we need to move out of our typical gaming experience and start looking at some different types of games, what can we learn from them as developers and what can we learn about the players of those games as developers.

> **Note**
> You are encouraged to look at the work of Jason VandenBerghe—he started with the work of Bartle and expanded upon it to include more extensive psychological modeling based upon the OCEAN personality traits and merged those with player motivations to be able to map personalities to games.

1.2 How Are Games Made?

There are essentially two approaches to the development of video games, from an industry perspective. These include the AAA studio and indie studio viewpoints. The way that these two approach the development of video games has some similarities, but also some distinct differences that can be attributed to scope of the game project and target audience. The scope of the project refers to the size of the project as well as the amount of features to be included. A game such as *World of Warcraft* has a much larger scope than does a game such as *Farmville*. Notice that the scope of the game had nothing to do with the success of a game; this is a vital concept for us early on as it is easy for us to think that we need to build enormous game worlds in order to be successful at game development. Success in game development is ultimately measured differently by different people based upon your goals. If your goal is to create a *WoW* killer, then unless your project passes *World of Warcraft*, the project will be a failure. However, if your goal is to build a game that you and your friends can play together then you will be a success if you can get the project finished and into your friend's hands. This may make it seem as though the second example would be easier to be successful at, but as we break these two approaches down, we will see that they are both equally challenging.

1.2.1 AAA Studios

AAA studios are what many of us think of when we consider the game development industry; these are the big names that create the big titles. Companies, such as Electronic Arts, BioWare, Bethesda, and Insomniac, are all examples of AAA studios. With this approach to game development, large teams are created for each project with the responsibilities divided among the various team members. This type of approach creates an environment of very deep specializations, with each team member only responsible for their small portion of the project.

AAA studios may easily spend 2 to 4 years with over 200 developers working to bring a project to the market. Along with the time and personnel, there may also be an enormous monetary investment into the project. This investment means that the game must be successful enough as a commercial project in order for the parent company to recoup the initial money invested, it is just basic business. If it is necessary to maximize the likelihood of getting a certain amount of money back once the game has been released, then it is less likely that you would be willing to experiment and try new things that may not work. Rather, you would be more interested in looking at what has been successful and trying to leverage that within your own project; once again this is just basic business. This is not to say that big studios do not develop amazing games, as they most definitely do, we are simply pointing out that the bigger the studio the more business decisions there are that must be made. We are also not trying to imply that AAA studios do not innovate, as many of them do, we are only pointing out that there are times when decisions must be made with a business perspective as opposed to a game design or game-play perspective.

1.2.2 The Indie Studio

The indie studio is a relatively newcomer to the game development process, at least as a viable business venture for individuals. With the release of powerful game engines such as Unity and Unreal, the average person can develop video games using the same tools and technologies as the big studios. Also, with the rise of digital delivery mechanisms, it is easier for a small studio to get their games to market and find buyers, especially with the rise of the mobile systems as a gaming platform. Indie studios are usually small operations with less than 50 people working on projects, though many independent studios have fewer than 10 people toiling away on a given video game. With this smaller approach to game development, there are many things that the indie studio simply cannot do as the skills available to the studio are limited to those possessed by the few employees or those that may be purchased through contract workers. It is very common for an indie studio to divide the labor up very differently from the AAA studio approach; one or two programmers will be responsible for all of the coding, and one or two art people will be responsible for all of the three-dimensional work including animations and one person may be handling all of the two-dimensional work. Indie studios can develop some amazing games; however, due to the number of people working on the projects, there are business decisions that these smaller studios will have to make as well, namely the size and scope of the projects that they work on.

1.3 Who Can Make Games?

As technology has changed over the years, the creation of games is no longer limited to only those that can program a computer. With the introduction of tools such as PlayMaker, we can start making games without having to focus on the intricacies of programming languages. This is freeing up the possibility for many people to begin to make video games. We have worked with kids as young as fifth graders and on into the collegiate years and beyond. The only trick to making video games is that it will require a commitment of time on your part, a willingness to work through some very challenging and at times frustrating topics and skills until you have mastered them to a level that you can use to make what you would like to make. The bottom line is that if you are interested and if you are willing to practice then you can make games. If, however, you are not willing to put the game controller down to practice your game development skills then being a game developer is not a good fit for you. It is best to be completely honest with yourself and to recognize that if you want to be a game developer, you will have to work at it and practice it; parts of it will be very challenging to master. You will not become a great game developer in a weekend, or a week, or a month, or even after reading this book. To become a great game developer will take time, dedication, patience, and practice. You will learn something new with every project that you work on which is part of what makes this field so exciting and fun to work in.

1.3.1 Skills and Jobs

There are a wide range of skills needed to create video games, though it is not necessary for one person to possess all of these skills in order to work within the game industry. For our task, we will focus on the types of skills needed in order to create games and the software tools that can be used to practice those skills. It is not our goal to advertise or sell a specific application over any of the others; however, there are some that are industry standard, and as such if your goal is to work within the game industry as a content creator or game developer, you would be well served to go ahead and learn those tools rather than the alternatives, though we have included alternative applications with our list of recommended software. We are not going to list every single skill that could exist; rather it is our goal to focus on a high view of the skills. Table 1.2 lists the skills as well as the potential software tools and job titles that could be associated with these skills. As can be seen from this list, to create a game requires a lot of different skills, meaning that we as individuals may be able to find our niche within the industry without necessarily knowing all of the skills, then again it would be fun to be able to do it all, especially if you are an indie developer. However, for AAA studios, focusing on a couple of these skills that you most enjoy would be the way to go as far as preparing yourself for potential employment at a major studio.

1.3.2 Working in the Industry

The first step is to decide if you want a job in the industry or if you want to be a game developer. In order to get a job as a game developer, you will need to develop the skills to do the work. There are no magic degrees to guarantee that a studio will hire you. In order to develop the skills, however, you may want to experiment with the different aspects of game development to find

TABLE 1.2 Skills and Some of the Associated Job Titles

Skill	Description	Software	Jobs
Three-dimensional modeling	Creation of all three-dimensional mesh content: characters, props, environments, etc.	3ds Max Maya zBrush Blender	Character modeling Prop modeler Environment modeler Hard-surface modeler
Three-dimensional animation	Building animation sequences to provide motion for three-dimensional meshes.	3ds Max Maya Blender	Character animator Character rigger Three-dimensional animator
Texture artist	Creation of two-dimensional graphical content to be used as textures on three-dimensional meshes or as skins of user interfaces.	Photoshop Illustrator GiMP	Texture artist UI artist
Concept artist	Develop sketches of worlds and characters in order to assist the modelers with their job.	Photoshop	Concept artist
Programming	Develop the scripts to get the game and content to behave and respond the way that it should.	C++ C#	AI programmer System programmer UI programmer
Level design	Combine the graphical assets within a game engine in order to create playable levels for the game.	Unity Unreal CryEngine	Level designer Environment designer
Audio editing	Create and edit audio for use in video games including both music and sound effects.	Audition Vegas Audacity	Sound engineer Music composer

an area that really excites you and that you enjoy—this is where college programs in game development can be enormously beneficial in providing guidance and training into the various aspects of the industry. In order to get the skills needed, you will need to work very hard at making games. It is the goal of this book to introduce you to the process of creating a game, but not the processes of creating the assets that go into the game, that is, an entirely different topic for another book. The game industry essentially has three major categories: business, content creation, and game creation. The business component is all of the financial, marketing, and legal kinds of things that go into having a business in today's global economy; this is a very important aspect, and this would be a job within the game industry.

Generally speaking, though, when we say that we want to work in the game industry, we mean that we want to make games. This brings us to the other two categories: content creation and game creation. Content creation involves all of the skills needed to create the many things that we see and hear when playing a game. Music, sounds, characters, buildings, lights, and so on—all of the content that is in a game must be created by someone as mentioned previously; we will not be focusing on these skills. The game creation process generally involves the programming and compiling of the assets that have been created; it is this process that we intend to introduce through the course of this book to help you to decide if making games is for you or not.

There is a final way of looking at working within the game industry and that is making games as a hobby. There is nothing wrong with making some games on the side for you and your friends to knock around with. The goal is simply to make a few games that you have fun playing with your friends or other people. In many ways, being a hobby game developer is far easier as there is no restriction on what you can or cannot do, you are limited only by your imagination and the amount of time that you are willing to put into the various ideas that you have.

1.4 What Types of Games Are There?

Types of games are defined and categorized as genres. A game genre provides an outline of a specific game as far as how the game might look as well as the essential game-playing elements. Game genres are important to us as developers as they assist us in defining game types but also help us to communicate basic game features to help streamline some components of the design process. For instance, if we were to say that we have a cool idea for a platform game, the people that we are talking to will immediately picture the basic elements of platform games, thereby saving us from having to describe all of those details. There is a flipside to this, however, in that our gamers will have certain expectations from our game as well, and it is difficult for us to break out of those expectations. As another example, players of a first-person shooter game expect to have some information on the screen informing them how many bullets they have left and how healthy they currently are. This may seem fine, but what if we want to create a hyperrealistic shooter in which the player needs to either count the rounds they fire or check the clip to see how many shots are left. While that example is technically still a first-person shooter, it will not be matching the gamer's expectations of games within that genre. The following sections will detail these genres.

1.4.1 Role-Playing Games

Role-playing games are ones which allow the player to create a character representation of themselves within the game. The created character may be one that closely matches the real person or may have nothing at all in common with the player of the game. The character will be defined by a set of attributes and skills which they can perform; and how well the character does certain actions within the game will be determined by these skill values. Over the course of game play, the player will be able to level this character by performing actions that will grant experience points; these experience points may then be applied to the character to improve skills or acquire new skills.

FIG 1.2 *Skyrim* by Bethesda, is an example of a role-playing game.

Players can also acquire items to equip their character with, such as armor and weapons to help the character be more successful within the game world.

These games have their origin in the heritage of the pencil and paper role-playing games such as *Dungeons & Dragons* but have matured on their own within the video game world. These games may be played in either a first-person perspective, in which the game is viewed through the eyes of the character, or a third-person perspective, in which the game character is visible. Bethesda is famous for making role-playing games such as *Skyrim* (shown in Figure 1.2) or *Fallout*.

1.4.2 Adventure Games

Adventure games had their heyday in the 1980s and 1990s, especially under the guidance of studios like Sierra. There are a couple of types of adventure games that we will look at: the traditional point and click and the text adventure. Generally speaking, this style of game lacks violence and is not dependent on the reflex abilities of the game player; rather the focus of game play is on solving puzzles and riddles, some of which may be incredibly obtuse. With the point and click variety, the player is presented with a scene and they are able to click items within the scene to interact with things, for instance, clicking a roll of tape will pick up the tape and add it to the player's inventory. As the player interacts with objects on the screen, they can solve potential puzzles that are presented to them. For instance, in *The Book of Unwritten Tales: The Critter Chronicles* (shown in Figure 1.3), it is the player's responsibility to figure out how to get the human character away from the monster (at least in the depicted scene). The player has various hints and clues within the scene and as they click on things and combine objects in their inventory they can solve the puzzle that the developers have created.

FIG 1.3 *The Book of Unwritten Tales: The Critter Chronicles* developed by KING Art.

Text adventures, on the other hand, do not utilize any graphics at all so there is nothing to point and click. These games commonly called interactive fiction are entirely in text with the world being verbally described and the player entering commands through a text prompt. The systems of these games can be extremely picky about the exact words that they recognize, leading the player's to sometimes have to solve the riddle of how the system wants them to word a specific command aside from the other puzzles and riddles that are presented. This genre was once a very large genre in the PC world when graphics were not very powerful; however, today this is a niche genre at best. Still, for narrative developers, the text adventure genre can be an excellent place to spread your wings and experiment on story ideas without having to focus on graphics and other content.

1.4.3 Platformer Games

Traditional and classic arcade games from the golden era of the arcade are members of the platform genre. These games include such classics as *Pac-Man* and *Donkey Kong*. Games of this genre are defined by the player being required to complete certain tasks that require reflexes or quick thinking in order to avoid being destroyed by something within the game. While there may be enemies that challenge the player and that can be destroyed by the player, these confrontations are not the primary focus of the game; the game play is more centered on solving puzzles and challenges through reflex skills than on fighting and violence. Even the fighting that does occur, such as boss battles at the end of levels, require a degree of problem solving in order to discover the boss' pattern and counteract it. These games generally have a life system in which the player has so many lives and after they have lost those lives the game is over. The game play is entirely dependent on the game

FIG 1.4 *Super Mario Galaxy* by Nintendo.

player's skill with pushing buttons and other control mechanisms. While the examples thus far have been two-dimensional games, we can create platform style games within the three-dimensional game world as well; *Super Mario Galaxy* (shown in Figure 1.4) is an example of a three-dimensional platformer game as it contains all of the elements of this style of game.

1.4.4 Shooter Games

Shooter-based games revolve around the player fighting with and destroying bad guys. When we hear the genre shooter, we immediately think of guns; however, a shooter game could be created without using a gun as the primary weapon for the main character. Keep in mind that these genres are intended to provide a generic outline of the game play and game experience, not necessarily a literal perspective of those. A shooter game can be either a first-person perspective, in which the player sees the game world through the eyes of the in-game character; or a third-person perspective, in which the character controlled by the player is visible. In either case, the player will be given a wide variety of weapons to use as they attempt to defeat the enemy of the game. The game's enemy may be alien invaders, in the case of *Halo*, or a terrorist organization, in the case of *Call of Duty*, or it may even be other players in the case of *Team Fortress 2* (shown in Figure 1.5). With shooter-type games, there are no puzzles to solve, or if there are they are rudimentary in nature. The only challenge presented to the player is the number of enemies that are trying to destroy the player and the limited ammunition and health that the player has for the current level. These games can exist in single-player or multiplayer modes and can also have complex story lines for the players to experience or no story at all except for what the player creates during their game play.

FIG 1.5 *Team Fortress 2* developed by Valve.

1.4.5 Action Games

The action genre of games is almost a catchall in that it contains so many games that could almost fit into other categories. Racing games, for instance, could be labeled as a simulation or a sports game, but are many times thrown in with action games. The same goes for what has become known as the action–adventure genre—games such as *Assassin's Creed IV: Black Flag* (shown in Figure 1.6) have much in common with the shooter genre but also much in common with the platform genre. Fighter games

FIG 1.6 *Assassin's Creed IV: Black Flag* developed by Ubisoft Montreal.

such as *Street Fighter* and *Mortal Kombat* also fall into this action genre of games. Essentially, an action game is a game in which there are many things for the player to do or a conflict type of game in which there are attack combinations and other rapid button sequences. Game play varies slightly depending on the specific game, but as a hybrid type of genre, the game play can be heavily influenced by the other genre that the specific game is drawing upon. At its core, the action genre requires fast reflexes from the player as well as knowledge of the different button combinations and sequences possible with the controllers.

1.4.6 Strategy Games

Strategy games have two subcategories that need to be considered: real-time strategy and turn-based strategy. In either case, the central feature of a strategy game is the player's ability to process data and information in order to determine the best potential way to beat opponents. Strategy games can be played against artificial intelligence (AI) opponents or against other human players or can be played in teams (against other teams of humans or computer-controlled teams). Strategy games require resource management as there are limited quantities of resources within games that must be utilized for the construction of other game units needed to become more powerful or in some other way expand your side's advantage over the other side. Examples of strategy games include *Civilization V* and *Europa Universalis IV* (shown in Figure 1.7). Turn-based strategy games allow the game play to pause between turns as each player develops a plan of action for their side to perform during the next turn sequence. Generally speaking, the player is allowed to take as long as they want to formulate a strategy during a turn-based game making these very mental and completely independent

FIG 1.7 *Europa Universalis IV* by Paradox Interactive.

of the gamer's reflexes or memorization of shortcut keys. Real-time strategy, on the other hand, has all of the players taking their turns at the exact same time with no pause in the game action. Whichever player can locate and get a worker to that treasured pile of wood is the player that gets to keep it, unless the other players come flying in with massive troops and kill the initial player's lone worker. Either type of strategy game presents the player with a view of the game world with some parts of it hidden until the player has discovered those regions. The player makes the best choices that they can with the information that they have available to them at the time that a choice must be made.

1.4.7 Simulation Games

The goal of a simulation game is to mimic, as closely as possible, some real-world system. We can create games that are simulations of the business world such as *Capitalism Plus* or simulations of city management such as *Sim City*. It is common for simulation games of those types to get somewhat confused with strategy games due to the strategic elements of the game. However, the games are simulating a real-world system. Whatever is simulated, we must get the game to not only act like that thing, such as an airplane in *Microsoft Flight Simulator X* (shown in Figure 1.8), but the game must also accurately simulate the appearances of the control mechanisms for what is being simulated, such as a crane. These types of games have often been viewed as a niche market due to the level of expertise and knowledge that the player is required to obtain in order to play the game successfully; however, with the rise of gamification, which is using game technology to create applications that are not explicitly a game, these types of games are becoming more popular outside of the gamer world,

FIG 1.8 *Microsoft Flight Simulator X* developed by Microsoft Game Studios.

thereby making them a more popular type than they used to be. Just as these games are very demanding on the player, they are equally demanding on the developer as we must become extremely knowledgeable in the subject matter that we are simulating in order to know what should happen and why so that we can properly develop the software to generate that required behavior.

1.4.8 Sports Games

Sports gamers are an interesting hybrid genre. They are a hybrid because many of them will utilize the reflex systems of a platform game by requiring the player to click the correct button at the proper time in order to throw or hit a ball in combination with the simulation genre as the goal of these games is to get as close to the real sport as possible. Within the sports genre, there are entire simulation systems that do not utilize any direct player control during the games, such as *Out of the Park Baseball* or *Football Manager*. These games have a very strong simulation engine at their core and through statistical modeling are able to provide the gamers with a simulation of these sports and the businesses of these sports. On the other side of the sports genre are games such as *Madden* or *FIFA* in which the player takes direct control of a participant within the sport and through reflex button presses can take an active role in determining the outcome of each individual game played. These games are attempting to provide the player with an experience that is as close to the real sport as possible, and it will be very interesting to see how these games utilize virtual reality over the next few years (Figure 1.9).

FIG 1.9 *R.B.I. Baseball 15* developed by MLB.com.

1.4.9 Puzzle Games

With the explosion of Facebook and mobile gaming, the puzzle category of games has found a new home and is enjoying a huge popularity at the moment. Puzzle games revolve around requiring the player to find a solution to a specific puzzle before them. Unlike adventure games, there is no story or reason for the puzzle per se; it is just a puzzle that the player must solve to win. Hidden object games are puzzle-type games as players try to find the objects that are hidden among other objects on the screen within a specified time limit. Matching games such as *Bubble Pop* or *Bejeweled 3* (shown in Figure 1.10) are also puzzle games in which the puzzle is to figure out how to move your pieces around in order to create a match of at least three of a kind. Due to their quick play nature, these games are very good choices for mobile gaming and can even be inserted into other genres to provide the player with a puzzle to solve in order to advance within a level. Stories can be added to the game experience to provide a background for why the player is solving the puzzles; however, the story is not necessary to the experience of the game as the player's focus is to score as many points as possible within the small amount of time that is allotted for each game-play session.

1.4.10 MMO Games

Online games provide players with the opportunity to explore the virtual game worlds as an individual or with groups of players. Players are given the opportunity to create a character that will be their representation within the game world, just like with role-playing games, and through the game-play experience allow these characters to grow and become better at performing

FIG 1.10 *Bejeweled 3* developed by PopCap Games, Inc.

FIG 1.11 *Star Trek Online* developed by Cryptic Studios.

certain tasks. The game play itself is generally of the action–adventure game style combined with the role-playing style along with the added benefit of being able to play the game with small or large groups of other players, including playing against those players. Traditionally speaking, MMO games charged a monthly subscription fee, but in recent years there has been a trend toward a free-to-play model in which gamers can get and play the game for free, but there are certain cosmetic features which will cost money if a player desires those additions in their game. These games also have large story lines with many quests along both the primary story and also along other side story lines that may involve the player's selected class or character race. It is interesting to note that while these games are very popular, according to the Entertainment Software Association (ESA), among online games that are played, only 4% of the online games played are MMOs, most of them are casual or puzzle games, once again due to the explosion of Facebook and mobile gaming (Figure 1.11).

1.5 Summary

Throughout this chapter, we looked at game development from a bird's-eye type of perspective. It was not our goal to get into the nuts and bolts of game development and come out of this chapter with a full knowledge of how to create a game. Rather, we have emerged with an understanding and realization that games, gamers, and game developers are a wide range of areas with different specializations and preferences. Now that we have a basic foundation for the background of the video game industry and how things theoretically work in this world, we are ready to continue and begin the process of designing a game of our own. We have come face to face with the reality that playing games and making games are two very different things and that our vast experience as game players may help give us ideas to draw upon as game developers. We have also taken a look at the many different skills that are used when creating a video game, and while this book will only focus on a specific subset of those skills, we are aware that what we will learn and practice throughout this book is part of the larger family of game development skills.

Vocabulary

Gamification
Role-playing game
Hybrid
Simulation game
Strategy game
Adventure game
Text adventure game
Sports game
Puzzle game
Action game
Shooter game
Platformer game
Genre
AAA studio
Indie studio
Casual gamer
Hard-core gamer
Real-time strategy game
Turn-based strategy game

Review Quiz

1. What are the differences in the Bartle character types?
2. What are the differences between an AAA and an indie studio?
3. What is the average age of a gamer?
4. Approximately how many Americans play video games?
5. What software can be used to create character models?
6. What software can be used to create levels for games?

Exercises

1. What types of games do you like to play?
   a. Why do you like to play these games?
2. Given the two options of an AAA studio or indie studio, which route would you be more interested in pursuing and why?

3. Considering your favorite genre of games, what could you add to it to make it a hybrid with another genre?

4. Considering the games that you like the least, try playing games from those genres with the goal of discovering what those players get from the game. Keep in mind that the goal is not the cliché answer defining the genre characteristics; rather the goal is to actually try to understand these games and gamers.

Design Document

Throughout this book, we will be demonstrating the design document for the Sancho Panza project that is built during the writing of this book. Each chapter will add a new section to the document, and in each chapter, you will be working on a design document for your own game idea, whatever that may be. The next chapter will introduce you to the design document and get this process started; for now, take a deep breath and let's start making a game.

CHAPTER 2

Design Document

Generally speaking, once we have a cool idea for a game, we are all in a rush to get to our computers and start building the game. However, as we will see in this chapter, it is important for us to take some time and think our game idea through more thoroughly and make sure we are ready to build this game. Design documents are an interesting aspect of game development as they are often overlooked, but at the same time, they are very difficult (if not impossible) to fully develop without. This leads to a chicken-and-egg type of situation in which we need to create a design document in order to build a game, but in order to create the design document, we need to know how to build a game. We will address this throughout the book by building our own design document as we go along and also by having you work on your own design document as you learn new concepts and skills. Rather than create a full design document in one go, we will only create the pieces that we are ready for and finish with a full document by the end of this book. In this chapter, we will introduce the design document and why we should use one.

- What Is a Design Document?
- Do We Actually Need a Design Document?
- Are There Other Ways We Can Make a Design Document?
- What Are the Parts of the Game That We Should Design?

2.1 Introduction to the Design Document

The design document is often an intimidating aspect of game development. Throughout software development the role of the design document serves as a guiding light for the project that is under development. During the development of a design document, developers force themselves to focus on both the small and the big picture of the project at hand, including a game project. Before we sit at our computer and begin to implement a game idea, we need to know what it is that we are going to be building; otherwise, we will have issues with continuity and consistency within our game idea.

This may be better illustrated through a couple of quick examples. Consider that your friend calls you up and says "Hey, wouldn't it be really cool if we made a game where the player could have infrared vision?" Our immediate response may be to agree that this would be cool and to charge over to the nearest computer and start creating some textures in Photoshop to mimic objects as they may appear when viewed with infrared light. However, as you have probably already noticed, we actually do not know what objects to create, so should we just start creating anything that comes to mind or should we spend a little more time with this idea and flesh out some more details to get a better idea of exactly what this game could possibly be and if we should even continue working on it. Other questions that come up may include whether the infrared vision is a constant or something that the player can turn on and off. If it can be turned on and off, then we will also need to create textures for the noninfrared versions of the objects. This infrared idea may be a great start for a game concept, but we are going to need to know quite a bit more about the game before we are ready to start building it and this is where the design document comes into play.

Design documents should contain as much information and detail about your game idea that you can think of, even if it is not going to show up in the game. This document is your repository of every thought that you have had about your game. It should also include any sketches or pictures that carry some significance for the game whether it be an exact concept of what you want something to look like or just some really cool building that you saw somewhere that could be a good inspiration for something in your game. We also need to consider how the game is going to be built, the logical flow of how these ideas will go from abstract cool things to functioning behaviors within our game world. The more detail and the more thought that we put into this design process, the less time we will spend doing unnecessary activities once we begin the actual implementation process of our game.

2.1.1 Do We Need a Design Document?

The short answer to this question is "Yes, we do need it." But the longer answer to this question is a little more interesting. We need a design document, but our design document does not need to be your design document, necessarily. More importantly, we need to quickly recognize that the design document is intended to be a guideline for the game project and that each game project is unique and somewhat different than previous projects. There have been many games that have been released that have also had a design document appear on the Internet. In these cases, we can see that the final product of the game does not always match what was specified in the original design document; the game *Neverwinter Nights* is an interesting example of this. As long as we remember that the design document is a guideline for the project and not the final word on any aspect of the project, we should not have any difficulties. Always remember that the most important parts of a game are whether it is playable and whether it is fun. If there is an idea within the design document that turns out to not be fun, then the idea should be dropped. At the same time, if something is in the document that just does not work within the game itself, the idea should be dropped or be seriously reconsidered as to how it is being implemented and working within the game. For instance, consider the previous thought of a character with infrared vision, if implementing that concept suddenly makes it difficult for the player to differentiate between a wall and a door, because they are the same temperature, and as a result of this difficulty, the player cannot figure out how to get out of a room, then this infrared idea needs to be reworked and might even be dropped from the game altogether.

The bottom line is that we need to spend some time designing our game before we ever try to build the game. We need to make sure that we understand what it is we will be building before the implementation begins. There is a trend in the game industry at the moment to move away from this formulistic approach to a more fluid and agile style of development. However, even with this trend, there is still some level of design that is going on prior to any building. Another example may help to bring this idea home. We have decided to hire a 3D modeler and animator to help with our current game project. After hiring the new modeler, we sent the modeler an e-mail letting them know that we need four new characters created with animation sequences by next month. To which the modeler responds by e-mail asking what characters they need to make. At this point, it would be wonderful to send them a design document of some sort so that they could see what we need; and it would not be good if our response was something along the lines of "well, we're not really sure yet, but we are going to have infrared vision in the game, so, you know something like that." Design is very important; it tells us where we are going; however, we may not take the exact path we documented to get there, but we do need to know where it is that we are going.

2.1.2 Methods of Design

Thus far, we have been referring to the design document; however, this wording brings certain images to mind and those images may cause us to restrict our thinking of how to create a design document. The first step, even though A Word document is being used and even though we have included a Microsoft Word document with this chapter as an example, does not mean that it actually needs to be something that is formally typed and entered into a computer. Our preferred method of design documentation is actually a composition journal that can be picked up at almost any store. We tend to keep the journal and pen in our backpack, which is with us wherever we go and as a result if a thought or idea comes up, it can be quickly written down before it is forgotten.

Perhaps typing and writing is not your thing, in which case feel free to use a sound recorder on your cell phone and dictate your design ideas, or buy a whiteboard and keep it in your room to jot down ideas. We have even known someone that bought whiteboard-type paint to paint the walls in one of his rooms with this special material that can be written on and erased, with this approach the whole wall became his design document for various projects.

There are some pros and cons to be aware of and to consider, but ultimately the documentation choice that works best for you is the one that you should use. A computer document is nice as it can provide one source or location where all of your game design ideas are located. Any pictures or sketches that you may have can easily be added to your document rather than being stored in some other location. However, a potential problem with the computer document approach is that we tend to spend a lot of time worrying about layout and how it looks, which can end up making the documentation process very frustrating and annoying. If something is frustrating, we are less likely to do it.

Using a pen and paper journal, on the other hand, is easy and convenient as well as very quick to use. It is very easy to quickly sketch some concept idea into your journal without having to worry about scanning it or using some 2D art program to create a rough sketch. But organization can become an issue with the pen and paper journal approach as pages are filled up we have to use other pages at other places within the journal for any new ideas and sometimes ideas can get lost because we do not remember where in the journal they were written down. We generally use the pen and paper approach, as previously mentioned, but then add any information from that journal into a computer document later when we have time and access, although with the growth of mobile devices we can also use a cell phone to quickly pull up a design document and make additions or changes to it.

2.1.3 Logical Design versus Descriptive Design

As a general rule, the more descriptive that you can be about a character or an object within your game world, the more likely you are to get that out of your head and into the game exactly as you want it to be. This descriptive aspect is easily overlooked as we tend to make assumptions about details. We see or are aware of details within our heads, but fail to share those details with others because we work under the assumption that the information is common knowledge. A good rule of thumb is to have a friend read what you have so far and see if they have any questions. Encourage your readers to ask those questions and if you already know the answer then add them to the document, if you do not know the answer, then it is time to figure it out. It is easier to remove details later than it is to try to come up with more details and more information.

Along with the descriptive aspect of a design document, we also need to consider the logical needs for the implementation of behaviors within the game project. It is through the design of the logical side of the game that we start to find dependencies as well as recognize the needs of the things in our game projects. By this we mean, for instance, that if we are going to allow a player character to have checkpoints that they can activate during a specific level, this in turn means that we will have to have a variable somewhere that will store the location of the last checkpoint that the player touched. It also means that we will need to make sure that the initial value of that variable is not outside of the game world somewhere just in case the player dies before finding another checkpoint and they try to respawn to that initial value. The player character is also going to need to have a method of determining whether they have contacted one of these checkpoints or not. That information may have seemed trivial to us as gamers; however, that kind of information can easily slip through the cracks when designing and then later when building the game project that error will continue into the functional game. Eventually, this problem should be detected, through testing; however, the bug within the game may not be immediately obvious to us by that point in time, especially if the game code has become quite complex. Descriptive text works best for describing levels, characters, stories, dialogues, and events; however, it is oftentimes better to create some logical diagram to depict the flow of the behaviors that we are going to develop. Figure 2.1 shows a logical diagram of this same checkpoint type of system that we have described. Notice that it contains the same information, but through this diagram style display, it is easier to follow how this system could be constructed once we know how to do such things. It is also easier to understand the checkpoint system as the descriptive version was somewhat confusing.

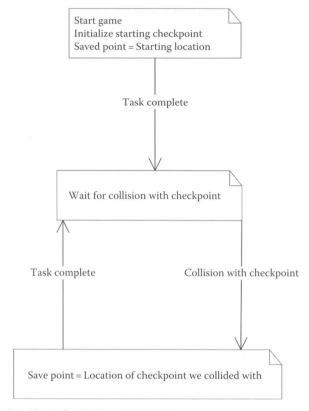

FIG 2.1 The logical diagram for a checkpoint respawn system.

> **Note**
> The more information that we provide in our design document, the easier it will be to construct our game later. We can always drop some of the detail and information if needed.

2.1.4 Mission and Vision

The last thing that we would like to mention in regard to the reasoning behind a design document is this idea of mission and focus. Within the business world, a mission statement is something that defines the goal of the business. Businesses spend large amounts of money hiring consultants to help with the development of a mission statement. These statements allow everyone working for the company understand what their goal is, why the business is there, and how the business will go about reaching its goal. For example, part of the mission of Dark Glass Studio, our indie game development studio, is to create games that do not rely on mature content to deliver the story and experience. This is not to say that mature games should not be developed, it is just part of the mission of our studio to make games without that. Knowing this mission, knowing this method of game development, helps those that work with us to recognize the type of content that will be developed for each game. This example can be extended with the following question: Which game studio would you like to work for and why? Most likely, the answer for this question is going to be because you enjoy the games that that studio makes and if the studio were to suddenly start making completely different games you probably would not be interested in working for them. While the type of games they make may not be an inherent part of their mission statement, this does illustrate the idea of understanding how the company works or how the game will be constructed. Design documents help us to get this mission of the game across by listing and describing so much of the game that it is clear what will be included within the game as well as what will not be included in the game.

The other aspect is the vision of the game. Where the mission is how and what will be done by a business or game, the vision is more of an inspirational guide for where the business may be in a few years, think of this as goals for the business to accomplish. We can apply this to a game project by asking the question why we are making this game. What do we want people to get out of this game? The answers to those questions are the vision of the game. Now, to be realistic and honest, this type of question is most commonly answered with two specific answers: we want the players to have fun playing our game and we want to be able to sell the game and make money. There is absolutely nothing wrong with those as a vision for the game, but sometimes, every now and then, a game project comes along that has a different vision. An example of a game vision being something other than players having fun and making money is an ongoing project that we are working on with students at Wilkes Community College, which is a Facebook-based game developed for a local horse rescue ranch. The vision of the game, why it is being developed, is to provide students with an opportunity to work on something that is not just a "school project" and to also help raise awareness in our community about the game development program. The project is also being developed to meet the needs of the horse rescue ranch, raising awareness of the plight for abandoned and abused animals while giving their financial donors something interesting to do rather than just mailing a check. Vision—why we are making a game is very important and it is something that everyone on the team needs to be aware of and be onboard with.

2.2 Sections of the Design Document

There are many design document templates available online. Google Docs has one listed and there is also the very thorough template developed by Chris Taylor, which is also available online. These templates form wonderful starting points for the development of a design document as oftentimes the first question is where to even begin with such a seemingly daunting task. However, both of these templates have a depth of information that we have opted to avoid in this introductory look at the design document and at this process in general. We have provided a much stripped down and streamlined version that is available from the companion website for this text.

Before we jump into the document and start editing it for our great game idea, however, we need to look at what each section is about and why we even need to consider thinking about such sections. Some of these sections will immediately strike us as so obvious that we would do just fine by skipping over them and not even worrying about them; however, as we will see, the design document not only describes the game we are creating but also defines the overall vision of the game, and it is vital that everyone working on the project be on the same page and working toward the same goal.

2.2.1 Game Concept

Our design document should begin with a concise discussion of the game itself. This section should not be very long, a page or two should be more than enough. The goal in this section is for the reader to get the mission and the vision of the game right away, rather than having to wade through many pages of information to try and figure it out. If this section cannot be done in under two pages or if it is extremely difficult to write, then we are not yet sure what the game is that we want to make. Essentially, this section is the traditional high concept or elevator speech portion of a design document. We should be able to knock this part out pretty quickly.

This section begins with the game description, which is what the game is about. If we need 15 minutes to tell someone what a game is about, then, in actuality, we do not even know what it is about. As an example, what is *Super Mario Bros.* about? It is about the main character, Mario, rescuing Princess Toadstool from Bowser and his stooges in the Mushroom Kingdom. Notice that the description of the game does not go into what all the players can do or even how it is the player does anything, it is just a quick sentence or two describing what the point of the game is. Even modern games can be described in a couple of sentences, no matter how complex the game may be. For instance, *Civilization* by Sid Meier, is about the player leading their society from a nomadic lifestyle all the way through the space race. How the player does this is not the point at all.

Following the description of the game, we have the opportunity to expand on the game concept by providing some target information for the game. Who are the players for our game? This may seem like a question that is not very important or we may want to whitewash it by saying the target audience is whoever will buy our game. But we need to consider it a little more carefully than that as the target audience of the game, as well as target genre, rating, and platform, will have an impact on many decisions later, and remember this is the vision and mission of the game. Consider creating a first-person shooter game for military use versus creating one for kids that enjoy water gun fights. Both games are first-person shooters, but the behaviors of the weapons, as well as the weapons themselves, will be drastically different between the two. Going along with this is the genre or style of game that we want to make. When we say that we are making a first-person shooter, there are certain things that all of us picture in our heads that go with a first-person shooter. These things range from the camera perspective of the game to the activities involved in the game to the in-game user interface. However, if we were to say that we are going to create a strategy game, suddenly what we have in our heads looks completely different. Remember the primary goal of a design document is to make sure that everyone on the development team is on the same page, the more information we know about the game the better off we will be.

In our targeting section, we also have the Entertainment Software Rating Board (ESRB) rating and the type of system that the game will run on. These both are very important as a game created for the WII will have a very different control scheme than a game created for the PC or a game created for a mobile device. We need to know what type of system we are targeting to make sure that what we are building is suitable and also to take advantage of the various aspects of the system. As an example, constructing a text adventure game for a mobile device would not be the best of ideas, sure it can be done, but as soon as someone reads our target platform and target genre they should ask if that specific genre is best suited for that platform. There are always times and reasons to break genre stereotypes, but there are also reasons to stay within the expectations of players and the playability of the devices.

The ESRB ratings, as shown in Table 2.1, help us understand the type of content we will be developing to incorporate into our game. For instance,

TABLE 2.1 Current Entertainment Software Rating Board Rating System

Rating	Meaning	Type of Content
eC	Early Childhood	The content is specifically intended for young children.
E	Everyone	The content is suitable for anyone. May contain minimal mild violence including cartoon or fantasy violence, or infrequent use of mild language.
E10+	Everyone 10+	Anyone over the age of 10. May contain mild violence, or violence in cartoon or fantasy depiction, mild language, or minimal suggestive themes.
T	Teen	Suitable for anyone over the age of 13. May contain violence, suggestive themes, crude humor, blood (in small amounts), gambling with fake money, or occasional strong language (profanity).
M	Mature	Suitable for those over the age of 17. May contain strong violence, blood, gore, sexual content (not explicit), or strong language (profanity).
AO	Adults Only	Only suitable for adults 18 and up. May contain long scenes of intense violence, explicit sexual content, or gambling with real money.

if we know that the game is going to be E or T rated, then we also know that there will not be any gore spatter or profanity in the game. If we want to include those components, then we need a different rating for the game. Likewise, if I want to work on a game with mature content, then perhaps this project is not one that I would want to consider being a team member on. We are returning to that idea of mission and vision and making sure that everyone is on board. Granted in mainstream industry, it is a job and we do what is required of the job, but as an indie developer, we have the flexibility to explicitly pick the projects that we want to work on.

The features of the game provide a list of all the player can do during the game and what can be done to the player. It is not necessary that this list be exhaustive and all inclusive, but the reader should be able to read through this list and know what the player can and cannot do during a typical game-play session. As an example, if the player has the ability to see in infrared then this should definitely be listed as a game feature. Be careful of feature creep, which is the process of new features being added to a game project during the development process. While it is important for our game designs to be flexible and adaptable to what is playable and fun in the game, it is also important that new features do not keep getting added to the project; otherwise, we will never get it finished. Another issue with feature creep is that some features actually cannot be added without doing a major rework of the underlying game system. Flying is an example, if we were to decide that it would be wonderful if our Sancho Panza character could fly then we will need to return to the model and create an animation system for this. We will also need to rework our control scheme to allow the player to activate this feature and then redo our level layouts as currently there is nothing in the sky for him to do, not to mention that he could fly right over the artificial boundary systems we have constructed.

Whenever we are introduced to a game, our first questions tend to go in the following order: what is the game about, what can I do in the game, and how do I win the game. We have already addressed the first two questions and now it is time to take on the third. For instance, Mario can win by rescuing Princess Toadstool, and the player in *Civilization* can win by being the first to be in space or destroying all the other civilizations. Generally speaking, this category is fairly straightforward and easily derived from the description of the game, but once again, it is important to make sure that we know exactly where we are going with this game. Along with this are the similar games, these are games that may be inspirational to the current project. For instance, our horse rescue ranch game, mentioned earlier, may be similar to Farmville, PetCity, and Zoo World. We are not saying that we are copying these games or even that the project will have the same features as these, only that these are similar to it and perhaps we would like to incorporate some components from those games into our project.

With this section of the design document complete, we should now have a pretty solid understanding of the game that we would like to make.

We should have a good idea of how it is going to behave based on the game features and the target genre. We should also have a strong idea of what it is going to contain based on the ESRB rating, audience, and similar games. All of these put together have given us a strong concept of the mission and vision of this game, and the pages that will follow in the design document will all relate back to this quick introduction to the game.

2.2.2 Game Characters

Most games have characters; there are notable exceptions to this, but generally speaking, games have characters that are either representations of the player within the game world or are something that the player can interact with during game play. We need to consider the characters of our game and get to know them as well as we possibly can. This section will include both verbal descriptions as well as concept art to go along with these characters. The more that we put into this, the more that we know about the characters within the game, the closer we can get the game versions of these characters to the initial ideas in our head. Another interesting aspect of this section is that we also need to start considering how these characters behave within the game world. This varies from how the player can control their main character to what the other characters in the game can do and how they make these decisions. As you may have noticed, it is difficult to design the logical flow for this if we do not know how to program. We could view this as trying to make a blueprint for a house without knowing how a house is built; for instance, things like load-bearing walls are pretty important in the design of the house.

When creating characters for a game, there are essentially two main categories of characters. The first are the primary characters which include not only the player's character but also the main characters that the player will interact with during game play. For instance, in our Sancho project, we will be adding in a character to serve as his wife, Teresa, which will be the primary source of quests and objectives for the game. We will also be adding in a spider character that will be there for the sole purpose of trying to bite and kill Sancho. Here in the design document, we need to describe these characters: their background, their personality, why they are in the game, what they want, and also how they do whatever it is that they do within the game. The more detail, the easier it will be for us to construct these characters. The other group of characters are window dressing, or characters that are in the game but just do not really do all that much. An example of such a character for Sancho will be the sheep that he can go around and gather. All they do is stand there, eat grass, and follow Sancho around after he has found them. They do not fight anything and nothing fights them. Once Sancho has returned them to their pen they just stay there and eat grass. Not an overly exciting life, but that is what we need them to do.

We will hit this section pretty hard when we get to our chapters on the player character and non-player characters. However, before we leave this section, notice also that we need to begin to consider the art assets that will have to be developed for all of the characters for the game. Not only do we need to construct the models and animations for the characters, but also any other objects that they may need to use. For instance, if we were to decide that Sancho Panza could swing a sword as part of the player control system, then that means that we will need to construct the model of a sword for Sancho to hold and also an animation system of him swinging that sword. This information is very important for the art team of any project to know, we need to know what exactly it is that the developers need built for the game project—remember our example from earlier about hiring a 3D modeler and asking them to build some characters by next month. When working on this section do not expect to sit down and run through the whole thing in one go, there are characters that may be added as the game continues to develop, but we really do need to get the primary characters down as quickly as possible.

2.2.3 Game Story

After developing our game characters, or perhaps before creating them depending on our preference, we need to determine the story of our game. There are many games that do not contain stories and that do not need stories at all. However, if we consider a story at its most basic level, it is nothing more than what the game is about in a little bit more detail. For instance, our Sancho Panza project is about the main character, Sancho Panza, returning peace and tranquility to an island kingdom called Barataria. That is what the game is about; however the story of the game is far more than just that. As we read the description of this game, we should have questions that pop into our heads. Questions such as:

- Where is this island of Barataria?
- Why is it not peaceful?
- Where was Sancho before the island?
- How did Sancho get to the island?
- How did Sancho hear about the island?
- Why does Sancho want to save this island?

There may be other questions that come to you, but these serve as a strong starting point. All of these questions can and should be answered by the story of the game. The backstory or background will provide the information as to what has happened prior to the game starting whereas the story itself will provide the information of what happens during the game. The interesting thing about this story stuff is that the plot within the story ends up becoming the challenges and obstacles that our character must overcome during the game, or more specifically the things that the player must accomplish in order to beat the game. Remember that beating the game is a victory condition, so while we have already specified the victory condition the story may describe how the main character gets from the beginning of the game to that victory condition, assuming that the player performs the required tasks with the needed skill level.

The story section also allows us to provide a descriptive account of what this world is like, the basic questions of who, what, when, where, why, and how are all generally answered through the story of the game. While the game description and victory conditions may provide a hint to this information, the game story fleshes out those details. It is interesting to note that in all probability much of our story work may not even show up in the game itself for various reasons, at any rate we will get into this in much detail with our chapter on story and development.

2.2.4 The Game World

The game world is the environment in which the game actually takes place. While the story section describes what occurs as well as a solid foundation for the environment of the story, the game world is more focused on the artistic aspect as well as game-play components for our game project. It is important for us to have a clear understanding of what our game world looks like artistically; there is a vast difference between a cartoony cel-shaded game world and a gritty photo-realistic one, and we need to know what it is we are trying to create before we start creating anything. This is a great place to gather concept images, which are images and photos that give ideas about what this world would look like. These images do not have to be exact, they are just inspirational for the eventual art work that will go into constructing the various game levels and world.

While the appearance and styling of the game world is very important, from a game-play perspective, it is more important for us as developers to know what the levels actually look like and what the players can do within the levels. A top-down map sketch of each level is very beneficial so that when it comes time to start building these levels we know exactly where it is that we need to put all of the various pieces that have been made. We also need to consider what the player can and cannot do within each level; for instance, Sancho cannot run off the island and go find mainland Europe, we just are not going to allow that mainly because we do not want to have to build all of that stuff on the off chance that some player decides to see what is out there. Being aware of this, our descriptions and concept sketches for the island will contain barrier information to keep Sancho locked on the island itself.

We should also consider how each level ties back into the story itself. As we will discover later, stories tend to be episodic in nature, that is to say, that they tend to have chapters. As it turns out, games tend to have separate and distinct levels that correlate very nicely into episodes or chapters of our story. So, each level may correspond to a specific part of the story that we have developed for the game, we need to know this information as the challenges from that portion of the story should be incorporated into the level design in some way. We are not saying that each level must exactly match a part of the story, only that they should represent a part of the story. How much of that story component is included in the level will ultimately depend on the playability and fun factor of that level as we will see in our chapter on game worlds and environments.

2.2.5 Game Audio

Game audio, as we will discover in Chapter 9, is an easily overlooked aspect of game development. It is very easy for us to think that we will just grab a couple of music files from here or there and a couple of sound effects from here or there and the audio will be done, it will be easy. The irony here is that audio actually is quite easy to implement within a game project, especially in Unity; however, it tends to take a whole lot longer to both find the correct audio and to tweak it in the game than we expect. This is where design can come in to save the day. It is surprising how just making a list helps us to realize that a given task is going to require more effort than initially thought. For instance, consider the following statements, "I need you to pick up a couple of things from the grocery store" versus "I have a list for you next time you go to the grocery store." Notice that in both examples the amount of things to get is not specified and for all we know the amount is exactly the same. However, as soon as someone says they have a list for us we immediately imagine all of this work we have to do. How many times have you looked at a list and responded with "Oh, well this isn't too bad, I can do this."

The primary purpose of the audio section in our design document is to force us to start thinking about the audio in our game and start gathering those assets. Music is surprisingly tricky due to copyright and legal issues. Finding the music that exactly matches what we want and having the legal rights to use the music is going to take some time; the sooner we get started on it the better off we will be. If we wait until we are ready for the music to be thrown into the game, the search becomes frustrating instead of fun as the music really does help to define the overall feeling of our game. By describing the music that we want and providing some quality examples of it, this task of getting the music can then be delegated to someone and what they come back with later should match what we want, or at least be close enough that we are good with it.

The same thing goes for sound effects within a game. We do not fully realize how many events and actions in our game we want sounds for until we start making a list. Many of those actions that we put into the character control systems will need sounds to go with them. This includes seemingly simple things; for instance, consider a character jumping:

- Do they make a sound, grunt maybe, when they jump?
- Do they make any sounds when they are in the air?
- Do they make a sound when they land?
- Do they make any sounds while they are falling?
- Do they make different sounds based on the surface they land on?

If we wait until later in the game, we are more likely to decide that feature X is not really that important because we are burned out looking for sounds and just want to advance the game project and get it finished. This brings us back to the role of a design document, to help keep us on track and help keep us focused. If we have already gathered a whole bunch of audio files that we think we might want to use for various actions in the game, then when we start implementing those it goes much smoother and the game feels like it is really coming together instead of starting to fall apart at that point in time. We will spend a chapter on the audio and implementing it within our game project.

2.2.6 Game Interface

The final section for our version of a design document is the interface system that we will be using within the game. This is another area that can be viewed as really easy until we start to do it. Many times the creation of a user interface, whether a menu system or an in-game overlay system, is going to involve quite a bit of 2D art work. If we do not have the art work available when we get to those stages, then the project can slow down drastically as we go off and work on that. Also, if we have not considered the overall layout as far as colors, fonts, and positioning, then we will spend quite a bit of time trying different ideas until we figure out what it is that we want to do with the game. We have returned, once again, to the idea that the design document should serve as a guideline for our game project; it keeps us on track and helps us to know where it is we are going and possibly even how we will get there in the case of many of the sketches and diagrams that are developed. If we are utilizing menu systems in our game, what role they serve and how the player interacts with them are just as important to consider as what the systems will actually look like. Many times during this questioning and designing stage of game development we will discover aspects of the game that we did not even realize we were going to have to create or we may even discover parts of the game that really just do not fit after we think about them some more.

Fonts are a tricky thing and we need to make sure that we have the legal rights and licenses to use any fonts that we are incorporating into our game projects. When working on noncommercial projects there is a lot of legal leeway with what we can do; however, as soon as we start selling a game or trying to make money from a game, the legal landscape changes drastically and these are issues that we should consider while designing the game, not after it has been released. We will focus on the various interface systems available in Unity and how to update them through PlayMaker later in the book.

2.3 Summary

Throughout this chapter, we looked at the design document for a game project. We have focused on the initial section of the design document, the game concept, and will fill in the other sections as we go through this book. At first glance, we may overlook the design document as something of drudgery that we really do not want to do or perhaps something that we will do after we have built the game, but after this chapter, we can see how having a guideline and direction for where we are going will have a very positive and beneficial influence on the rest of the game development process. While it is definitely not necessary to focus on a formal document within a computer word processing program, some kind of documentation should be done for our game projects; otherwise, we will forget some of our great ideas and may even lose focus during the development of our project. This document helps us to stay on track and as we will see throughout the rest of this book there are many diversions and detours during game development that can send us off on wild goose chases and prevent us from finishing our game. The best way to learn game development and to become better at it is to finish games, starting a game and not finishing it really does not help us and the design document can help us to finish a project, which is a good thing.

Vocabulary

Design document
Mission statement
Vision statement
Descriptive design
Logical design
Target audience
Target platform
Target ESRB rating
eC
E
E10+
T
M
AO

Review Quiz

1. How can the expression "a picture is worth a thousand words" be applied to a game design document?
2. What is the difference between a rating of E and a rating of T?
3. Are we required to use a computer and word processor for the creation of a design document?
4. What is the primary role of a design document?
5. Can we create a game without a design document?
6. Why would we need to know what system we are building a game for?
7. What is the difference between a game genre and a target audience?

Exercises

1. Consider one of your favorite games:
   a. What is that game about?
   b. What are the features of the game?
   c. What other games are similar to the game?
      i. In what ways are they similar and what ways are they different?
   d. What is the rating of this game and what would have to be changed to go to a rating of T (if the game is currently M) or M (if the game is currently not M)?
      i. Would this positively or negatively impact the game? Why?
2. Consider your favorite game platform:
   a. What advantages does it have over other platforms?
   b. What disadvantages does it have over other platforms?
   c. If you were to design a game for this platform, how would you try to leverage the advantages and minimize the disadvantages?

Design Document

In this addition to the *Sancho Panza* design document, we have started the work on our design document by filling out the title pages as well as the game concept section.

Download
The updated version of the *Sancho Panza* design document can be downloaded from the companion website within the Design Document archive, this chapter's document is named: "Design Document_Chapter 2."

Take some time to consider one of the many amazing game ideas that you have had over the years. As you think about these, pick one to focus on during the course of this book as a design document exercise and start constructing your design document for that idea. Add the following to it:

1. Name of the game, this can be changed later or even skipped for now.
2. Your name.
3. Game concept section.
   a. Game description, what is your game about?
   b. What and who are you targeting with your game?
      i. Why are those the target?
   c. What features will you put into the game?
      i. This section can most definitely be expanded as we continue, but you may want to jot down some initial ideas.
   d. How does the player win or lose your game?
   e. What other games are like this one or what games have inspired you to want to make this game?

CHAPTER 3

Using Unity and PlayMaker

Now that we have some background information on the various development tasks that need to be done and a basic overview of how to approach these, it is time to get our development environment configured and get to know our way around it. It is a common mistake to try to learn every aspect of a development tool in one go; as a result, in this chapter, we will focus on the basics that we need to know in order to get started with our game project. As we need to know more about either Unity or PlayMaker we will add to our knowledge base at that time, rather than try to get our heads around all of it right now. Just as creating games is an iterative development process, so too is learning the tools and techniques. Each new piece of knowledge will stand on the foundation of some previous piece that we have already gotten a good grip on. With these ideas in mind, in this chapter, we will focus on

- Getting and Installing Unity 3D
- The User Interface of Unity 3D
- Game Objects and Their Components
- Projects and Scenes

- Getting and Adding PlayMaker to Our Project
- The User Interface of PlayMaker
- Finite State Machines in Design and Implementation

3.1 Installing Unity

Before we can install the Unity game engine, it will have to be downloaded from the Unity website: http://www.unity3d.com. While at the website, it is worth it to take a few moments and browse around the links that are available in the top-level site navigation as seen in Figure 3.1. Unity provides a showcase gallery to view other products that have been made with Unity; they also have a hashtag (#madewithunity) for use with any Twitter posts to help get the word out not only on the Unity game engine but also on any project that you may be working on. Through this showcase link on the main page, you can browse through all of the games that have been posted with this hashtag. Browsing through this directory will reveal many interesting titles, and it is an encouraging process to play what others have made with Unity as it can help us stay focused and also realize that what we are trying to do is possible, if we stick with it.

The Community link will give you access to the Unity forums and a Q&A knowledge base. Both of these are very active with questions and solutions being posted on a regular basis. It is reassuring to know that if we run into any problems with Unity during development that there is a community willing to help find solutions. Not only can questions be posted about Unity issues specifically, but also implementation questions can be posted here as well; these would be questions specific to how to get something working the way that we want within our game project. For instance, if we were trying to figure out how to create an explosion with the Shuriken particle system we could post a question and get help from someone that would either solve the problem or guide in the right direction so that we can build our own solution.

Unity also provides a Learn link that serves as a starting page for many tutorials with the game engine. Long gone are the days of game development being a cryptic and secretive practice. The developers of Unity want you to know how to use the tools that are being placed at your fingertips. The more that you know about Unity, the more that you can do with Unity. It is a win–win situation for everyone involved and this tutorial resource can be very valuable in the learning process. Along with the tutorials, there are also links to both the Unity manual and the Unity scripting API. While the scripting API may not be overly relevant to this book, it is of significance to note that the actions we will be using within PlayMaker are derived directly from the

FIG 3.1 Top-level site navigation on the Unity 3D website.

scripting API; in fact, they even use the same names. This means that through learning PlayMaker, we will also become familiar with many aspects of the scripting API without even knowing that we are learning that content.

The final stop on the top-level navigation is the Get Unity or download page. From this page, we can get the current free version of Unity or a previous version if for some reason we need an earlier release of the application. It is also possible to look at the system requirements for the Unity game engine. It is important to ensure that your system meets these requirements prior to attempting to install the engine and developing a game with it. Having a computer that does not meet these specifications will create a very frustrating development experience. There are also links to a license comparison, release notes, and patch downloads. The license comparison provides valuable information in helping you to decide when and if you will need to purchase the Professional version of the software. For the project that we will be working on in this book and many other game projects as well, the Personal Edition of Unity has all of the features that will be needed.

> **Note**
>
> As of the release of Unity 5, the free version has been named the Personal Edition and includes all of the engine features that were originally available only in the Professional version. These features include the advanced lighting system, advanced water, and advanced shadows along with others. And the Personal Edition is royalty free until you reach an income level of $100,000 with your Unity projects.

Now that we have looked around their website some and ensured that our computer can handle running Unity, go ahead and download the newest version of Unity available from their download page and begin the installation process. While installing Unity, you will be greeted with several screens asking for clarification from you. All of the default options will work, including the option to install the example projects, although we will not be looking at that project, during your reading of this book it may prove to be a useful reference. After Unity has completed installing, a link on your desktop as well as a start menu shortcut will appear. With the completion of the installation process, we can launch the Unity development environment and move forward to the next section.

> **Note**
>
> The version of Unity used during the writing of this book is Unity 5.0.0. While there will undoubtedly be many exciting new features added during the 5.x version, all of the content of this book should be compatible throughout the lifespan of Unity 5.

3.2 Unity's Interface

When we launch Unity, the screen that will appear is the Project Wizard, the default version of which is depicted in Figure 3.2. There are two tabs at the top left and two buttons at the top right within the Project Wizard browser. Beginning with the tabs to the left, the Projects tab allows us to select a previously loaded Unity project to launch and continue working with (if you have downloaded and installed the Example Project then it will be listed here). The "Get started" tab will present a short video introducing Unity as well as some of the resources we mentioned in the previous section. With the Open Other button, located at the top right of the Project Wizard we can browse to a location where another project is located and open it. Keep in mind that when opening a project through the Open Other project browser what you will be pointing Unity toward is the project directory or folder, not to a specific file. This point can cause some confusion when first using Unity as we are used to using applications to open files, but with Unity we direct it to a folder that contains the project that we want to open. This is a point that we will return to when we discuss using Unity in the next section. The last button is the New Project button, which will begin the process of creating a new project. Go ahead and click the New Project button as we currently do not have a project to open and would like to begin our *Sancho Panza* game project.

Creating a new Unity 3D project is accomplished by selecting the Create New Project tab and providing the required information for the new project to be created; the view of this tab is shown in Figure 3.3. When creating a new project there are two aspects that need to be considered: the first is where

FIG 3.2 Default Project Wizard browser.

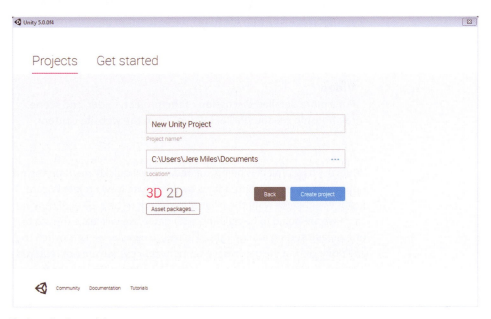

FIG 3.3 The Create New Project dialogue screen.

the project will be located and the second is what the name of the project will be. By default, Unity likes to create new projects within the Documents\ Unity Projects (on a Windows machine) folder. This is the default location that Unity would like to store the projects; in fact, you will find the Standard Assets Example Project folder here. This is a good location for our project, and it is vital that we remember where it is in case we need to back it up, share it with another developer or if we plan on utilizing a version control system. Or we could opt to save our new project in a different location, Unity will always remember where we have saved this project and it will be an option for us to open when we launch Unity until we delete or move the project's folder.

When providing a name for our project, we are also providing the name of the folder that the project will be stored within. This can be an element of slight confusion, as we tend to think that the project is an individual file as we mentioned earlier, when in actuality the project is a folder that contains all of the individual files required for the project. Remember, the project is simply a folder that is storing all of the individual components that build the game we are working on; therefore, renaming the folder does not do any damage to the content of the folder. We cannot rename the folder while Unity is open and that project is currently loaded though, as that would create a sharing violation with the files that are open by Unity. If we did rename the project's folder, the next time that we launch Unity it would be necessary to use the "Open Other" button to browse to the new project folder. By default, Unity names each new project "New Unity Project" as can be seen in the location bar for the new project, in Figure 3.3. For now, go ahead and leave it with the default name and location. We will change this later and reinforce the idea of projects and folders. Click the "Create project" button and Unity will create a new project for us with the folder name location that we specified earlier. The "Back" button will return us to the starting point in the Project Wizard.

> **Video**
> For a more detailed discussion of the project, folder, and scene relationship see the "Project Video" from the website content.

While the new project is being created, we will quickly mention the other options that were presented to us by the Create New Project Wizard. The first is whether we want the project to default to be a 2D or 3D environment. Since we are going to be building a 3D game, we will leave this set to 3D (the default setting as highlighted in red). However, we can switch to 2D at any point during the game development process, we are not required to start a brand new project if we to switch to a 2D game, although there may be a fair amount of asset reworking that may need to be completed. With Unity, 2D can be done in two different approaches: the first is a traditional 2D style game using 2D sprites, and the other is a pseudo 2D in which we will actually use 3D assets but only present the game from a 2D perspective, which is a very interesting approach if you consider the possibilities of that route (for instance, the ability to toggle from 2D to 3D during game play).

The other setting for us to look at is the Asset Packages importer, which allows us to include standard assets at the start of our project. For this particular project, we are not going to import any packages at the beginning; however, if we wanted to (or knew for certain that we would need certain packages later in the development process) we could have selected to import any or all of the assets that are available. In order to view the asset packages that are available, click the Asset Packages button and a new selection dialogue window will appear. This dialog includes both standard asset packages that ship with the Unity development system as well as any new packages that you purchase through the Asset Store. There are many methods of getting assets into a project and just because we do not include a particular package at the creation stage, it does not prevent us from being able to add that package later. The standard asset packages that ship with Unity 5 are detailed in Table 3.1.

Depending on the speed of your machine, we should not have to wait too long for the full Unity environment to appear with a brand new project ready for us to start working on. At first glance, the Unity interface may seem overwhelming because it appears so empty with no indication of what to do next. However, that is also one of the things that we particularly like about Unity's interface is its simplicity. The interface is not cluttered with unneeded icons and buttons, and everything that we do need is readily accessible. Let's begin with the generic Unity interface as depicted in Figure 3.4.

Section 1 of Figure 3.4, shows the Scene Editor pane within Unity. It is within this pane that we are given a 3D view of the game world that we

TABLE 3.1 Standard Asset Packages within Unity 5

2D	This package includes many assets that could be used in the creation of a 2D game. The content includes a fully animated sprite, RobotBoy, which could be used as a character in your game.
Cameras	Includes several different camera controller rigs that are ready to be dropped into your project, although they may require tweaking to get the exact behavior you are after.
Characters	A collection of character controller systems to incorporate into your project. The controllers also include graphics, animations, and audio. However these may need to be changed for your specific project.
CrossPlatformInput	Scripts to provide input functionality in different platforms, this package is also included in many of the other packages where input is needed.
Effects	Scripts and shaders to provide special lighting effects to the environments that we create. These effects range from new materials to light shafts and light flares.
Environment	Contains components that could be used in the construction of terrains and outdoor environments. Sample trees are included for SpeedTree as well as textures to use as bases for terrain materials.
Fonts	Four open-source sans serif fonts that we can use including bold, light, regular, and a semi-bold.
ParticleSystems	Standard particle systems for inclusion in your project ranging from explosions to dust storms. These have been created with the Shuriken particle system making them a valuable resource for understanding how to create our own particle effects.
PhysicsMaterials	Unity utilizes physics materials to define the friction and bounce when two game objects collide. This package has several different materials, including rubber and wood, as well as different friction types to quickly adjust the physics collision properties of our game objects.
Prototyping	Various assets and scripts that could be utilized to quickly prototype a game concept to test for playability and provide a fast demo. Prototyping game ideas allows us to test the mechanics of a game idea prior to investing a large amount of time in the creation of graphical content as this is very useful and oftentimes overlooked.
Utility	Scripts and sprites that could fall into a miscellaneous category, such as a FollowTarget or FPSCounter script. This collection is included as a part of most of the other packages as well.
Vehicles	An airplane and car control system including audio and animation can serve as a useful starting point for creating your own vehicle control system.

are creating. As you can tell, there is nothing in the current world except for some lines, an oddly shaped white thing, some type of yellow-looking sun thing, and a kind of box with colored cones coming out of it in the top right corner. The oddly shaped white thing is the default camera object that is always added to a new scene, within Unity we need a camera in order to be able to see the game world when running the game. We can select this game object by left-clicking on it within the Scene Editor, or by selecting it from the Hierarchy panel (which we will discuss shortly with Section 4 in Figure 3.4). The white box in the top right corner is a quick

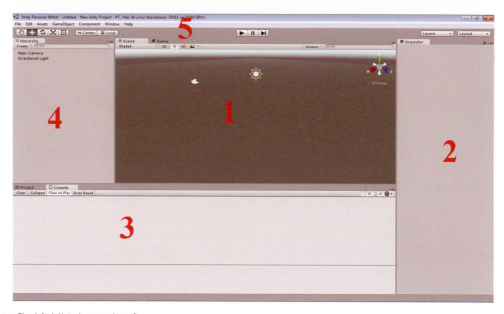

FIG 3.4 The default Unity layout and interface.

snap tool that we can use to align the Scene Editor camera along any of the axis. We can also quickly toggle between isometric and perspective modes by left-clicking on the white box in the middle. Go ahead and experiment a little by left-clicking the cones protruding from the central box to see how they change your view within the Scene Editor. The lines provide us with a grid system that we may use for positioning objects within the game world. This grid display can be toggled on and off from the Gizmos drop-down menu along the top of the Scene Editor window, as depicted in Figure 3.5. Finally, the small sun object is a default directional light that Unity adds to our scene for us. Unity includes four different types of light objects, the directional light is one that is intended to mimic the lighting provided by the sun in the real world. It will cast light in one direction toward our environment. The other three types of lights will be discussed when we get to Chapter 7, on building the environment for our game project.

> **Note**
> The view of the scene in the Scene Editor is NOT the same as the way that the game will look through the game camera(s). Moving your view around within the Scene Editor will not have any impact on the player's view of the game during game play.

FIG 3.5 The configuration options for the Scene Editor.

There are times when it will be necessary to view a scene in different styles or to only view certain parts of the scene. These configurations are all available within the options along the top toolbar of the Scene Editor (see Figure 3.5). You can remove the grid lines by left-clicking the Gizmos drop-down dialogue and toggling the Show Grid on or off. While you are there, you may notice that there is a long list of other things that can be turned on or off. We are not going to go over each one at this time, but this is a nice list to be aware of. Continuing from right to left, after the Gizmos drop down is a similar selection system for the Effects that may be within the scene. The Effects drop down allows us to disable skyboxes, fog, flares, and animated materials. However, disabling these graphical effects is only disabling them in the Scene Editor not in the game itself.

Note
A scene within Unity is the same as a level within a game, so when we are referring to a specific scene we are referring to the level of the game as well.

The next two icons allow us to toggle the display of sound on or off within the Scene Editor and to toggle between the lighting rig that we have built within the scene and the default environment lighting of Unity. The difference in the lighting can make a huge difference while you are working on your levels. There are many times when we are trying to get a certain feeling or mood with the lighting that we build for the scenes; however, once we have achieved the effect that we are after the scene is now too dark or too heavily colored for us to be able to easily discern the placement of game objects. It is for this reason that it may be best to leave the lighting of your levels until after the rest has been completed, but even then there are times that we need to return to the scene and tweak something within it. Toggling to the default Unity lighting can make it a lot easier to see what we are working on.

Next to the Lighting toggle is the ability to quickly transition between 2D and 3D mode. So, if at some point during our game development project, we decide that we would like to switch to a 2D system for the game we can simply click that button and change our scene view to the orthographic style of a 2D game. However, doing this does not convert the game itself to a 2D game (or 3D) or even change the way that the game appears during game play, we are only changing the way that it appears within the Scene Editor itself. If you go ahead and click the 2D button, you will notice that the Scene Editor rotates to an orthographic view and that the quick movement cube disappears, as there is no multiple axis for us to snap the camera to on a 2D orthographic view, the view is only a perpendicular view toward the game world. Go ahead and switch back to 3D now so we can continue with the rest of the settings for the Scene Editor.

The next drop-down menu item is labeled "Shaded" and can be used to modify how the scene is displayed to us. The first three options deal directly with the draw mode and can be either textured, wireframe, or both. With shaded selected, we essentially see the scene as it will appear while the game is running, within reason. Wireframe mode, on the other hand, will display the edges of the meshes without any texturing on the surfaces (edges are the individual lines within a 3D mesh that connect points, called vertices). This can be especially beneficial when we are trying to get objects to line up with each other. The default shaded mode is perhaps the most commonly used of these options. The options below these are more useful when we get to optimizing our game project.

The final thing to mention in regard to the Scene Editor is the tab selector along the top of it, which was previously depicted in Figure 3.5. There are two tabs present, the Scene view and the Game view. The Scene view is the one that we have been working with thus far, but we can select the Game view tab to see the game from the player's perspective; remember that this perspective is most likely not the same perspective as shown in the Scene view. This is not a useful tab unless the game is running or we are constructing interface systems, as we cannot modify anything from within this view.

At this point, we need to mention that all the panels within Unity are dockable. This means that by clicking with the left mouse button and holding the mouse button down on the tab for the panel, we can grab the panel and move it to wherever we want it to be. For instance, we could grab the Game view tab and move that panel somewhere else. Or, as in the example shown in Figure 3.6, we can put the Game view side by side with the Scene view. Having multiple monitors also allows us to move any of these panels to one of the other screens. Practice moving these panels around a bit to get the hang of it, if your display gets really messed up, you can reset it back

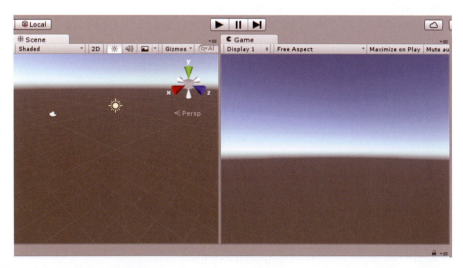

FIG 3.6 Side-by-side display of Scene and Game views.

to default by clicking the Layout drop-down list in the top right corner and selecting "Revert Factory Settings."

Section 2 in Figure 3.4, is the Inspector panel. This panel is used to view and modify the properties of game objects. Anything that is within a scene is referred to as a Game Object by Unity. Currently, the Inspector panel is blank; however, if we click the directional light within the Scene Editor, the Inspector will change to show the properties of that specific object. We will go into more detail about the Inspector panel in the following section on Using Unity. At this point, just keep in mind that the Inspector panel can be used to modify a game object's properties and also to add new components to the object. A component can be anything from a behavior script to a Collider to an Audio Source. All game objects have a Transform component which governs the position, rotation, and scale of the object. If the game object did not have this Transform component, then it would not exist within the scene.

The next section to look at is section 3, which is our Project panel. The Project panel contains a list of all of the assets that are a part of the current project. This view is the exact same view that we would use, if we were using a file explorer to browse the folder that we created for this project during the creation stage earlier. Anything added to or removed from the Project panel is also added to or removed from the project folder itself. When we want to add an asset to a scene, we can drag it from the Project panel and drop it into our scene, at which point it will be added to the Hierarchy panel.

The Hierarchy panel is found in Section 4 of Figure 3.4. Within this panel, we will find a list of all the game objects that are currently within our scene, be aware of the distinction between the scene and the project. Notice that there are two objects listed: Main Camera and Directional Light, the same two objects that we discussed when looking at the Scene Editor panel. We begin to recognize that information is presented to us in multiple fashions by the Unity editor and that the information is consistent. Earlier, we selected the Directional Light from the Scene Editor in order to view the properties of the object, this time select the Main Camera from within the Hierarchy panel. Notice that the Inspector panel has changed to show the properties for the selected camera object. Also, notice that within the Scene Editor the transform gizmo (the red, green, and blue arrows) has moved to now be centered on the camera object there as well. One final point on the Hierarchy Panel, in the top left corner of it, is there is a drop-down menu labeled Create. Clicking this allows us to create new game objects to add to our scene (they will not be added to the Project panel, however, but we will discuss that in more detail later when looking into Prefabs). The options available in the Create drop-down menu are the exact same options available in the GameObject menu bar option along the top of the Unity window.

The last section to look at is the Toolbar, number 5 in Figure 3.4. The toolbar begins on the left-hand side with the transform gizmo toggle buttons. Earlier we mentioned that all Game Objects within a scene must have a Transform component and that the Transform component controls the position, rotation, and scale of the object. These buttons allow us to switch the transform gizmo between these different modes. The hand icon allows us to pan the view in the scene editor. The next two buttons are for the placement of the transform gizmo (either the center of the object or the pivot point of the object) and the alignment of the transform gizmo (aligned to the game world or the local axis of the game object itself).

The middle of the Toolbar section is dominated by three buttons: Play, Pause, and Step. These control the executing of our game. The Play button will start the game running and the Pause button allows us to pause it, which can be extremely useful for making adjustments to properties of Game Objects. To stop the game, while it is running, simply click the play button for a second time. The Step button will allow us to advance the game forward one refresh cycle. At the far right of the toolbar are two drop-down menus. The Layers menu allows us to specify which layers are visible within the Scene Editor. We can assign Game Objects to different layers, you can notice this at the top right of the Inspector panel for a selected object, and then toggle the visibility of those layers on or off. The Layout drop down is to select predefined layout configurations or to return to the factory default setting as was discussed earlier. It is also possible to save our current layout from this menu.

3.3 Using Unity

It is now time to play around a little with Unity and to put what we just learned about its interface to use. We will create a very simple scene to get used to placing objects and using the different transform gizmos. We will also utilize the Inspector panel to make some changes and additions to our game objects within our scene. This scene will go on to be our test development scene for the character system of the next chapter.

The first thing that we will add to our scene will be a cube that we will use as a ground object for our game world. Select GameObject → 3D Object → Cube from the menu bar at the top of the Unity editor. A Cube Object will appear in both the Scene Editor view and the Hierarchy view and the Inspector panel will populate with the properties of this Cube Object. Finish creating the Ground Object by completing the following steps:

1. Position the object at the center of the world by changing the transform Position values to 0, 0, 0.
   a. This can be done by moving the arrows within the Scene Editor or by entering the values directly within the X, Y, Z boxes of the Position part of the Transform component.
2. Change the scaling of the object so that it will be a good size for the ground. Set the Scale values to 30, 1, 30.
   a. The Y value of 1 indicates the "height" of the ground, this can be any value that we want, however, there is no need to make it particularly thick as the player should always be on top of it anyway.

We now have an object that can serve as the ground, at least temporarily. Now we will make some housekeeping changes to this object that will prove to be a beneficial habit to get into. The first is to change its name. While "Cube" is an adequate name for the object in a small testing scene such as this, if we were to add 30 more cubes to the scene, which cube would be which? It is a very good idea to get into the habit of naming your objects something relevant so that while reading the Hierarchy panel you will be able to quickly know which object is which. There are two methods that we can use to change this name. The first is to select the Cube object within the Hierarchy panel and press F2 on our keyboard, now we can change the name from Cube to something more descriptive such as Ground. The other approach to changing the name is to click on the text box with the name at the top of the Inspector panel and to change it there.

Directly beneath the name of the object in the Inspector panel are drop-down lists for Tag and Layer. The Layer list is used to specify what layer we want an object to be a member of and can then make that layer visible or not as we discussed earlier. The Tag list is used to give the object a tag that can be referenced from within a script to access that object, which will be very important later, especially for collisions between Game Objects. For instance, we may want the player to die or be hurt when impacted by an arrow. To accomplish this, in broad terms, when the collision occurs between the two objects we would have the player object check the tag of what it collided with and if that tag were "arrow" (for instance) we would cause damage to the player, but a different amount of damage than if the tag were "racing bus." If we select either the Tag or the Layer we can see the default options that are available, while it is fine to use these, it will not take long before we need others or more descriptive ones. As a result, we are going to go ahead and create both a custom layer and a custom tag.

Select the Layer drop-down list followed by the Add Layer option. The Inspector panel now changes to depict the list of layers within our current project. The built in layers are listed at the top and are greyed out, indicating that they cannot be modified. Select the text box of the first available layer and enter a name for this layer; in this case, we will name this new layer "base." To return to the properties of the Ground object that we were working with select it in either the Scene editor or the Hierarchy view. Generally, we find it easier to select objects from the Hierarchy panel as it prevents accidental clicks on other things. With that object selected, we can once again choose the Layer drop-down list and this time our new layer is available for us to select. Repeat this process for the tag, you can use the same name "base" although we will be tagging this object as "ground." This tag will be used later to indicate objects that the player can walk on. This time when you select Add Tag, you are presented with the view as depicted in Figure 3.7 below. Select the plus sign in the bottom right to add a new tag to the list of custom tags and provide the name for this tag. Do not forget to return to the game object and change its tag within the Inspector.

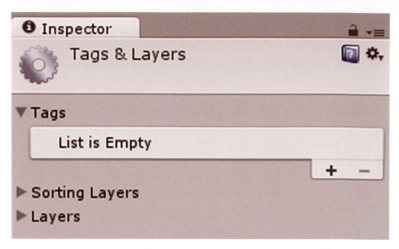

FIG 3.7 The new tag list display in the Inspector panel.

Now that we have looked at the top two sections of the Inspector panel for this and all other Game Objects, we will go through the remainder of the standard components for many Game Objects. The section immediately below the Transform component is the Mesh Filter part. This component defines what mesh, or 3D shape, is drawn as a representation of this particular Game Object. Currently, the selected Mesh is a Cube, but if we click the circle icon to the right of the text box, we will get a browser window allowing us to select any other mesh currently included in our project, of which there are not many only the default meshes. We can go ahead and change this mesh from a cube to a sphere, for instance, and see how that changes what is displayed in the scene editor, this change can be seen in Figure 3.8. Notice that the sphere mesh does not exactly look like a sphere. This is because the sphere mesh is being placed within the transform properties that we have defined, including the scale settings. Now we have a squished sphere where we did have a cube. If we wanted the sphere to appear proper again, we could just change our scale settings back to a uniform value, such as 30, 30, 30. But we actually do not want a sphere, so go ahead and return the mesh back to the cube that it was.

The next section in the Inspector panel defines the Collider component for the Game Object. Colliders are an important element of every Game Object and have several interesting parts to them. For now, we are going to gloss over these, but they will be reinforced in upcoming topics. A box collider has been applied to this particular object and Box Colliders are the cheapest of the available colliders. By cheap, we are referring to the cost of using the collider from the perspective of the CPU or GPU depending on the system. A box collider, as depicted in Figure 3.9, is comprised of six sides. When calculating collisions, this means that the CPU (or GPU depending) only has to check each of the six sides to know if a collision has occurred. In comparison, a sphere collider, also depicted in Figure 3.9, contains eight surfaces that must be checked for collisions. The fewer surfaces that we are checking for

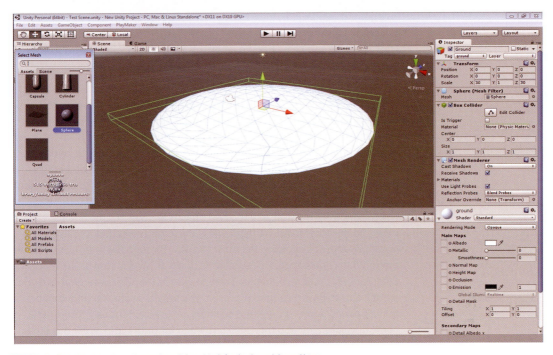

FIG 3.8 The Cube Mesh has been changed to a Sphere Mesh for the Ground Game Object.

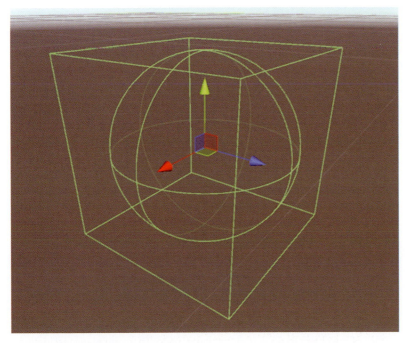

FIG 3.9 A sphere collider inside of a box collider.

collisions, the quicker that we can cycle through all of the colliders within our scene, and therefore, the faster and smoother the game will run. This is a key concept to keep in mind when we are working with Game Objects and assigning colliders to them and we will return to this in more detail in upcoming chapters.

Within the options of a collider component, we can specify a Physics Material to define the friction and bounce when other objects collide with it. There is also a check box to change the collider into a trigger volume or back to a rigid collider. Triggers are a unique type of collider in that they allow us to detect when a collision has occurred without preventing the colliding object from passing through. A standard collider will not allow the objects to pass through each other, consider placing your hand against a concrete wall. Your hand has collided with the wall, and the two objects are now resting against each other. On the other hand, a trigger will allow us to detect that a collision has occurred while still allowing the object to pass through the area. Consider the motion detection systems for automatic doors at various stores. The motion detector gets triggered when you collide with its range of detection, but you are still able to pass through; otherwise, you would be stuck trying to get to the opened door. Triggers and colliders are used extensively throughout game development, and there will be a need for both types at various times.

We can also modify the center position of the collider and its size. It may not be immediately obvious why we would want to do such things, but consider the following example. We have a character that can run around in our game world. We give it a collider to know when it hits walls or when bad things hit it. However, we would also like to know when the character's feet hit the ground during each step. We can do this by adding colliders to the character and positioning them where the feet are and changing the size to only include the foot itself. Finally, if we turn those foot colliders into triggers, then we will know exactly when each foot strikes the ground and can then play a footstep audio effect or perhaps a little puff of dust particle effect.

Directly below the box collider component is the Mesh Renderer component. Throughout this book, we will generally ignore this component as there is not much reason to change away from the default options. However, the check box immediately to the left of Mesh Renderer will allow us to turn the renderer on or off (there is a check box for the box collider as well). By turning the renderer off, we are making the object invisible. There are many times during the course of a game that we want something to be invisible for various reasons including making a cube invisible but allowing its trigger collider to still exist within the game world. All of these properties can be accessed when the game is running through behavior scripts which we will develop within PlayMaker.

The last component we are going to look at, for now, is the Material component. All Game Objects have a Material component assigned to them. Materials, or shaders as they are also referred to, define how light reacts when it hits the surface of the object. That is to say, the material defines how the surface of the object looks within the game world. There are many fascinating things that we can do with materials, however an in depth exploration of shaders is not an introductory topic. For the moment, we will say that materials are comprised of textures (or solid colors) and that a mathematical algorithm is applied to these textures to determine how the light of the game world should behave when hitting these surfaces. Textures are image files and can be either photographs, drawn images, or computer generated images.

Unity 5 introduces the new physically based shading system that much more closely mimics the way that light interacts within the real world. This, in turn, makes our game objects look better and more realistic. To take a very quick look at this shading system, we are going to create a new material to apply to our ground object. In the Project panel, click the drop-down menu labeled Create and select Folder from the top of the list. While this is not a material, it is very important that we keep our project as organized as we can, this will make it easier for us to find things as the project grows during the natural development cycle. This new folder, name it Materials; this is where we will store all of the custom materials that we create for use in our game. Double-click the Materials folder, to make sure that we are within that newly created folder, and select the Create drop down again, this time choose Material. We will name this new material ground. Figure 3.10 depicts the default properties of a standard material.

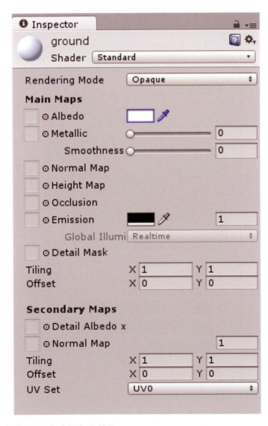

FIG 3.10 Properties for a standard shader in Unity.

We are not going to define each of these pieces at this time, rather we are going to create a simple green material to serve as our ground surface. Under the main maps section, the first item listed is Albedo. This is essentially the traditional Diffuse channel, not quite but for our purposes, we can leave it at that. Albedo defines how the surface of the object would appear in standard diffuse lighting with no shadowing details on it at all. Diffuse lighting is dependent on the direction of the light, this means that parts of the object's surface that are facing the lighting source will appear brighter than will the parts facing away from the light source. This is a mimic of how surfaces appear in the real world. There are other lighting models; however, such as ambient lighting which applies light equally to all surfaces of an object, regardless of whether the surface is facing the light source or not. Therefore, what we put in the Albedo channel is going to define how the surface of this object looks normally. We have two options here, the first is to apply a texture map to this channel and the second is to apply a color to the channel. For this example, we are going to apply a greenish color to this channel by selecting the white box next to Albedo and grabbing the color that we want within the color swatches. Select any color that you like, our selection is shown in Figure 3.11. We will finish this material by dragging it into the scene editor and dropping it onto our ground object thereby applying the material to that object.

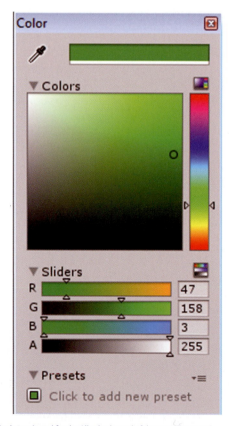

FIG 3.11 The green shade is selected for the Albedo channel of the ground material.

TABLE 3.2 Navigating a Scene within Unity

Press and hold middle mouse button or ALT key plus the middle mouse button	Pan the camera around the scene. This is not moving the game camera or changing how the game actually looks, this is only moving yourself around the scene to have a better view.
Press and hold the right mouse button or ALT key plus the left mouse button	Rotate the camera around the scene. This is very useful in conjunction with panning so that you can move around objects that may be blocking your view.
Scroll middle mouse button or ALT key plus the right mouse button	Zoom in and out of the scene.
When a game object is selected in the scene editor, ALT key plus left mouse button	Rotate around the selected object as opposed to rotating the camera view from where it is.

Now that we have an interesting game object out in our world, we will look into navigating around our scene. Table 3.2 depicts the standard navigation methods. It is strongly recommended that you go ahead and practice moving around your scene with these combinations to become familiar with them. An important one to note the distinction is the ALT key plus the left mouse button. If no game object is selected, then this will behave the same as the right mouse button action; however, if a game object is selected then the behavior is quite different and there will be many times that you will need exactly this behavior as you are working with your scene.

Now that we have a basic scene constructed, go ahead and add some more objects to it. We will use these objects to test standard collisions as well as jumping when we build our character in the next chapter. For our version, we are going to add some more cubes to the scene with various scale factors and place them near each other using the techniques that we have learned thus far. We will also go ahead and add new materials to these objects to differentiate them from the ground itself. However, the layer and tag for these new cubes will both be set to ground and base just as we did for our actual ground object. The final version of our scene is depicted in Figure 3.12. Before we leave this section, we need to make sure to save our scene so that we will be able to access it again later. Create a new folder in the Assets section of our Project (not in the Materials sub-folder of the project). This new folder will be called Scenes, and we will save all of our scenes within this folder to make them easier to find. Finally, save the scene by selecting File from the menu bar and Save Scene As. Browse to the folder that we just created and name the scene something like "test scene" as this will serve as a testing platform for many of the things that we build.

Select the main camera in the scene and notice that a new window appears in the bottom right-hand corner of the Scene editor pane. This window is displaying what the camera can see and, consequently, what the player can see since this is the only camera in the scene. The main camera will default to the player's view when the game is run, go ahead, and click the Play button in the toolbar to verify that what you see when the game is running is the same as what you see through the preview pane of the main camera.

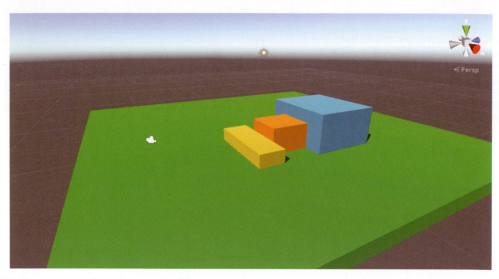

FIG 3.12 A basic testing scene for our character, nothing fancy.

Practice moving objects around some more by moving the camera in such a way that you have a better view of the boxes that you have placed into your scene. It may be necessary to use the rotation tool to rotate your camera to get your camera in a view that you are happy with.

Select the directional light and notice the direction of the movement gizmo arrows on the default setting of local. Up, the green or Y-axis, is not actually pointing up, but rather in a diagonal kind of direction. This is caused by the rotation of this directional light. Notice in the Rotation settings for this object that it has been rotated 50° on the X-axis and −30° on the Y-axis. As a result of this rotation, the direction that the light thinks is up, its local alignment, is not the same direction that the world thinks is up. Therefore, if we wanted to pull this light straight up to get it further from the surface of the ground, we would have some difficulty moving it in the exact direction we want. However, if we were to change from Local to Global, by clicking the button in the toolbar section, the alignment of our movement gizmo now matches that of the world and not the object itself, making it much easier to move the object straight up and away from the surface of the ground. There are times when we will want to use the global alignment, and other times when the local alignment will be the best to provide what we need.

3.4 Installing PlayMaker

PlayMaker is a visual scripting interface developed by Hutong Games. The idea behind PlayMaker is to allow the development of games with complex behaviors and interactions without having to spend a tremendous amount of time developing the programming skills and sophistication to script those behaviors in either javascript or C#. In order to get the functionality out of your projects as you envisioned them, you will need to create this functionality, it is not sitting on the shelf just waiting for you to rename it and use it in your game. Through the use of PlayMaker, we can focus on the logical underpinning of programming without getting bogged down in the syntax of specific languages. This is an exciting possibility for us as we embark on our own game development projects, as the skills that we learn in PlayMaker are the same logical skills that we will need in order to master a programming language. To add even more benefit, the actions that we will be using within PlayMaker are derived directly from the Unity API (Application Programming Interface). What this means is that we are also learning our way around the standard methods of the Unity API, while we are learning the logical underpinnings required to become expert game programmers.

There are two different methods we can use in order to obtain your own copy of PlayMaker. The first is to utilize the Unity asset store mentioned in the previous section in which case once we have bought the package it will now be available for adding to our future projects through the package import tools within Unity. The other available option for getting PlayMaker is directly from their website: http://hutonggames.com/. Whether you purchase the plugin through the asset store or directly from the developer's website, you will have a Unity package that can now be imported into your projects. It is strongly recommended that you visit their website and especially take a look at the forums that they provide (http://hutonggames.com/playmakerforum/index.php). These forums are a wonderful resource for finding answers to questions that you may have. While it is our hope that this book will answer nearly all of the questions that you will have in regards to using PlayMaker, the reality is that you will at some point in time try to do something not directly covered within this book. These forums can provide an excellent resource for you to ask questions and to get help with resolving any problems that you may encounter. These forums are specific for PlayMaker; Unity specific questions should be addressed to the Unity forums mentioned earlier.

> **Note**
> As of this writing, the current release version of PlayMaker is 1.7.8. However, throughout this book we will be using the 1.8.0 Beta (RC20). This will allow the techniques in the book to be applicable to the first release version of PlayMaker for Unity 5, which will be 1.8.0. While there may be some minor changes between the current Beta and the final release of PlayMaker, these changes should only add features and stability, not remove anything we do here.

Installing PlayMaker into our project is different from installing other applications in the sense that it is not a stand-alone program that we can run independently. What this means is that the process of "installing" PlayMaker is actually the process of importing the PlayMaker package into a project that we are working on. There are two methods that we can use to import the PlayMaker package into our current project. For the first method, we have to have purchased PlayMaker through the Unity Asset store in which case the

FIG 3.13 The Importing Package dialogue window.

package is added to the Standard Packages that we can select from to import into our project. To access these packages, once a project is loaded select Assets from the menu bar followed by Import Package. The pop up selection list should include PlayMaker (if you had purchased it through the Asset Store as mentioned), if the PlayMaker package is not listed, select the Custom Package option and browse to the location where the PlayMaker package is stored on your computer. The other method of importing a package into a Unity project is to drag the package (a. unitypackage file) from whatever folder it is currently located in and drop it into the Project Pane. Whichever approach is selected, a dialogue will appear after the package file has been decompressed, as seen in Figure 3.13, allowing us to select which parts of the package that we would like to import. As a general rule, we want to import all of the pieces of a package; however, there will be times during a project when we might only want to import a small portion of a package, a specific model or audio file for example. We will need all of the parts of the PlayMaker package, so click the Import button to bring the package into our current project.

> **Note**
>
> With PlayMaker 1.8.0, as used in this text, an Update Warning dialogue box that will appear. PlayMaker 1.8.0 is compatible with both Unity 4 and Unity 5; however, there are some functions in Unity 4 that were removed in Unity 5, hence the warning. Unity will convert the functions to the newer versions, and there should not be any issues.

3.5 PlayMaker's Interface

The PlayMaker interface is as streamlined and easy to use as is Unity itself. To begin, adding PlayMaker to our project only made two immediately noticeable changes to our project. The first is that some new folders have been added to the Project Pane. These folders are required for various PlayMaker functionalities, a breakdown of the contents may be found in Table 3.3. The second change is a subtle change to the menu bar, a new item has been added titled PlayMaker. Listed within the PlayMaker menu item is the PlayMaker Editor, this is the window from which we will do the vast majority of our work with PlayMaker.

The first time that the PlayMaker editor is launched, it will open with a "Welcome to PlayMaker" dialogue providing quick links to sample scenes, tutorial videos, online documentation, and the forums. These are all very valuable resources for us to look at, in the case of the sample scenes, or for us to find help with as we discussed earlier with the forums and documentation. Once past the welcoming screen, we will be confronted with the PlayMaker editor as depicted in Figure 3.14. This screen is divided into two distinct panels: the state machine view and the properties panels. The state machine view, the left-hand portion of the window, is where we can edit the overall logic of our state machine in a visual interface. The properties portion allows us to adjust the properties of our state machine, the individual states of the machine, the events within the state machine, and the variables available to the state machine. This is somewhat analogous to the Inspector pane within the Unity editor and we will dive into more detail with these views shortly. In order to continue working with PlayMaker, we will need to select a GameObject from the current scene.

Events in a state machine define what causes a transition from one state to another. A simplistic example would be that I am currently in the state of

TABLE 3.3 Folder Structure of the PlayMaker Package

Gizmos	The icons that will appear throughout the Unity editor when necessary to display. This includes icons that will appear directly within the Scene Editor and the Inspector Pane.
iTween	iTween is an extension for the Unity editor that adds in the construction of animation through the use of interpolation. More information is available at: http://itween.pixelplacement.com/index.php
Plugins	This folder contains any plugins that are created or will be created for PlayMaker. Version 1.7.8 includes plugins for both the WebGL and Windows Phone 8 deployments. It is expected that the release version of 1.8.0 will include this as well. Expect a plugin for the new networking system UNET at some point during the 5.x life.
PlayMaker	This folder contains the necessary C# scripts that are the backbone of PlayMaker. It will not be necessary for us to do anything with this folder, however, if we lose it we will also lose PlayMaker within our project.

FIG 3.14 The default PlayMaker editor screen.

being alive; however, as soon as I am crushed underneath a massive asteroid that strikes the earth (a rather catastrophic event not only for me personally but potentially for everyone else as well) I will cease being in the state of being alive and move over to the state of being dead. The events tab in the PlayMaker editor will allow us to create our own custom events, such as the asteroid striking the earth, to use within the currently active state machine. Other state machines do not have access to the states or the events of different state machines; they are all encapsulated inside of themselves.

When we create scripts we oftentimes need to store data for use at a later point in time either as a comparison check for something or as a setting for an object. Data are stored within variables, which we can manage from the variables tab within the PlayMaker editor. We have two types of variables that we can create: global and local. Global variables are ones that are visible and available to all state machines within a scene. At first glance this may seem like a good idea, for instance, making the player's score available to everything. However, this also means that any state can modify the value stored within the global variable, which in turn may lead to very difficult to find errors and odd behavior within the FINISHED scene. For instance, our player's score may be jumping by 10 points at various times during game play and we are not entirely certain why as all of the state machines have access to that variable. Therefore, to find the problem, we will need to look through each state machine within our scene until we find the one that is changing our player's score by 10. As it turns out, we can do the same thing with local variables it is just far more difficult, which in turns makes them safer to use. Local variables are only available within the state machine that they were created in. It is possible to make the values of these variables visible to other state machines; however, doing so will require the use of more action commands, thereby making it more difficult for us to accidently change the value of the variable. We will be returning to variables in the next chapter.

State machines are scripted behaviors that can only be applied to Game Objects; the state machines do not exist in a vacuum they are an integral part of the object that we want to be able to give commands too. Go ahead and click on one of the blocks from the current test scene and notice how the PlayMaker editor changes. The text is no longer directing us to select a Game Object, rather we can now right-click and add a state machine to the selected object. But, before we do that, we need to define state machines in more detail than we have thus far.

3.6 State Machines

State machines provide a method for us to visually design a script. There are several techniques that software engineers use to diagram a solution to a system, or program, and state machines are one of the tools that they have available. Figure 3.15 depicts the concept of a state machine with the simplified example of starting a car. State machines are comprised of three key elements: a state, a sequence of actions, and transitions. A state is depicted by the white boxes in Figure 3.15, and you can see that we have two states in this machine; one is labeled "State 1" and the other "State 2." Labeling states is a very important step, as it allows us to look at the state and guesstimate what function it may serve; in the case of this example, the labels currently selected are bad choices as in order to know what either state is doing we need to read through the list of actions and determine what function they perform. It may seem as though reading through the actions is a good approach to determining what a state does; however, as the list of actions within a state grows in detail and intricacy it becomes more difficult to easily detect why the state is there and what it does.

Actions, as they have been referred to above, refer to a list of things that the state does. This list will contain specific actions to be performed and they are performed sequentially. By this we mean that once we enter a state, the actions are performed from top to bottom and in order. So in the example of "State 1" from Figure 3.15, the first thing to be done when entering this state is to get in the car. The key is not put into the ignition until after we have gotten into the car. At this point that may seem like an obvious distinction, but as we move forward and build more complex logic with PlayMaker we will need to keep this in mind and remember that the actions are performed from top down. This will extend to some special actions,

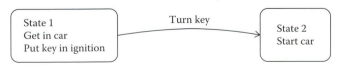

FIG 3.15 Example of a state machine.

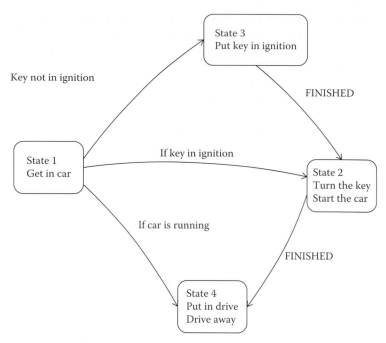

FIG 3.16 A more complex version of the starting car state machine.

conditional checks, which may cause us to leave the state that we are in. PlayMaker provides a list of actions that we can add to each state that we create. This list is directly derived from the Unity API, what this means is that if Unity can do it then so can PlayMaker. The trick, for us, will be to determine which action it is that we need at which point in time. But we will look at some tips that we can use to help us make the correct decisions, or at least good guesses.

The last core component of a state machine is a transition. The transition is depicted in Figure 3.15 as a line ending with an arrow head. The line and arrow indicate which state we are coming from and which state we are going to. While it is possible for a single state to have multiple transitions going to different states, consider the slightly more complex state machine of Figure 3.16, it is not possible for a single transition to go to multiple states. Each transition has a specific starting and ending state. The label above the transition indicates what event causes the transition to occur. In the case of Figure 3.15, the event that causes us to leave "State 1" and go to "State 2," where we happen to perform the action of starting the car, is to turn the key after it has been placed into the ignition.

State machines can be constructed directly from our plain English list of things that we want something to do. Consider the following list of things that I want to happen in order to start a car:

Get into the car and put the key into the ignition. When you turn the key, go ahead and start the car.

We have added some color coding to the text so that you can more easily visualize the distinctions in our plain English instructions. This cannot be stressed enough, before you ever begin to write any code or develop a state machine, you must take a few minutes to write down what you want to happen. Make sure that you can explain to yourself, in your language, what you want the computer to do before you ever attempt to tell the computer in its language what you want it to do. In this example, the actions have been color-coded with blue. So, we can easily see that at one point in time we want to perform the actions of getting into the car and inserting the key into the ignition. These actions can be performed at the same time. Now, by that we do not mean simultaneously as one would expect, but rather that these two actions can be performed sequentially with each other and do not require anything else to occur. Consider the example of the action "start the car"; in order to perform that action, something else has to have occurred first, specifically the red-colored "turn the key." As a general rule, if your list of actions include the words "when" or "if," you have found a transitional event. Another indicator of a transitional event can be seen in the plain English version of our more complex example as follows:

> Get into the car. If the key is already in the ignition go ahead and turn the key to start the car. Otherwise, put the key into the ignition and then turn the key to start the car. But, if the car is already running, put it into drive and drive away.

We still have some very obvious actions (blue text), to perform, such as: "get into the car." But the events that cause us to transition from one state to another become a little more fuzzy as we start to introduce conditions, the "if" statements. The purpose of conditions is to control the flow of the actions. For instance, if the key is already in the ignition then not only is there no point in putting the key into the ignition, but it is actually impossible to do so (without removing the key first). Remember, in an earlier discussion, we mentioned that the actions are performed within a state sequentially from top to bottom. Well, if we want to short circuit this behavior and only perform the remaining list of actions under certain conditions, then we can incorporate a conditional check that will cause the execution to switch to another state if the specified condition is met. Writing in plain English, as has been done in the current examples, is not always the most beneficial approach however. As a general rule, I will create a bulleted list of what needs to happen and from that list, I will look for those hot words which will tell me where the actions are and what the events are that cause the transitions to the new states to occur. Based on this, the earlier example could be written as follows:

- Get in the car
- Check to see if the key is in the ignition
- If it is then turn the key and start the car
- If it is not then put the key in the ignition and turn the key to start the car
- Check to see if the car is running
- If it is running then put it in drive and drive away

This approach to thinking through our state machine is quite a bit easier to visualize the actions, states, and events. There is another major advantage to this approach, by looking at it we pick up on some logical issues that many of you may have already noticed, but that were not immediately obvious to begin with. Specifically, the "check to see if the car is running" should occur before "checking to see if the key is in the ignition." After all, based on what we know about state machines already, there is no way that our flow of actions will ever get to the "check to see if the car is running." Consider this for a moment before moving on to the next paragraph, when we "check to see if the key is in the ignition" there are only two possible outcomes: it is in the ignition or it is not in the ignition. If both of these outcomes lead to transitions out of this state, then the actions that come after the comparison action are never executed. Earlier we mentioned that the top-down sequential execution of actions is important and something that should not be overlooked; here, we can see an example of it causing us a problem and it would be an annoying problem to debug because it is not immediately obvious why it is not "checking to see if the car is running." This is the same as the plain English sentence structure version; however, it is easier to dissect and convert to the state machine that we saw in Figure 3.16. Also, note that this bulleted list approach helps us to pick up on repeated actions. This indicates multiple avenues to the same state and may not have been quite as obvious to us through the other plain English sentence approach.

There is one further special type of transition that we would like to mention before bringing all of this together into a final example. This transition is the "FINISHED" event. This event occurs when all of the actions within a state have completed their execution and are finished. As a result of those actions being completed, we may want to transition to another state. This event is an overlooked but very powerful tool to add to our tool belt when building state machines as there will be many times when we want a sequence of actions to occur and when those are done go do something else, but the something else is not logically part of the same state. There are two primary types of states that we will be interested in creating: ones that loop continuously until something happens causing them to go do something else and those that will only execute their list of actions one time before going on to do something else. Remember, a state encapsulates a set of actions that are logically a part of each other. You can see an example of the FINISHED event in Figure 3.16 when we transition from starting the car to driving the car. This transition event could be named "when car starts" or "when you have finished starting the car." For the moment, we are ignoring the very real possibility that the car does not start due to some mechanical issue. We will leave error checking and handling for later.

OK, let's build an example from scratch. As I sit here typing on a cold winter morning, I have been enjoying sipping from a mug of hot green tea; however, it is now empty and I would like some more. Let's create

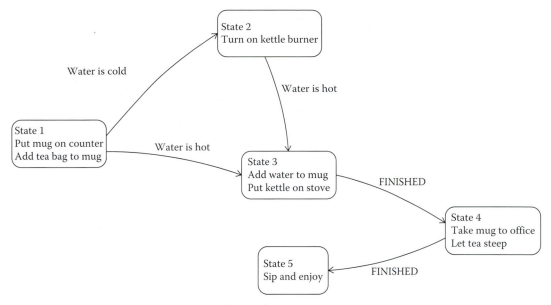

FIG 3.17 A state machine to have my computer make a mug of green tea for me, or at least a starting point.

a state machine that would, if the technology permitted, allow my computer to make the tea for me so that I would not have to get up and make a new mug. We will begin by creating a bulleted list of what it needs to do and from that see if we can find some states, actions, and transitions. I have intentionally left out the color-coding on this example to give you the opportunity to try to come up with it on your own prior to building that actual state machine itself, which can be seen in Figure 3.17.

- Put mug on kitchen counter
- Add tea bag to mug
- Check tea kettle
- If water is still hot add water to the mug and put tea kettle back on stove
- Take mug to office
- Let tea steep (subtle, but notice this is one time and next is a loop?)
- Sip and enjoy
- Otherwise turn on the burner for the tea kettle
- Wait (but don't watch because a watched pot never boils)
- When water starts to boil
- Turn off burner
- Add water to mug and put kettle pot back on stove
- Take mug to office
- Let tea steep
- Sip and enjoy

3.7 Using PlayMaker

Now that we have a good starting understanding of the PlayMaker interface and state machines, we will combine the two and create some state machines inside of PlayMaker to modify some basic behaviors in our testing scene. We are going to go ahead and add another 3D game object to our current test scene and apply some PlayMaker state machines to it. That way we can easily remove the object and the scripts if we want to at some later time. For the moment, I have opted to add a sphere to the current scene and placed it in a viewable area as can be seen in Figure 3.18. We are going to create some basic state machines and attach them to this object to get our feet wet with PlayMaker before moving on to characters and character controllers. Make sure to create a new material for our little sphere, as we did in the earlier section. One other note about our sphere, the collider that has been automatically added to it is what Unity will use in order to detect if we are clicking on it or if the mouse is over it. If we were to remove the collider from the object, then the events would no longer work as there would be no way for Unity to detect if the mouse has intersected with the sphere or not, in fact we will test this to verify later.

This sphere object is going to allow the user to click on it and then have different things happen. We will begin by having the sphere change colors when the mouse is hovering over it and maybe have it get larger as well. Then we will add the ability to change colors of other objects by clicking on

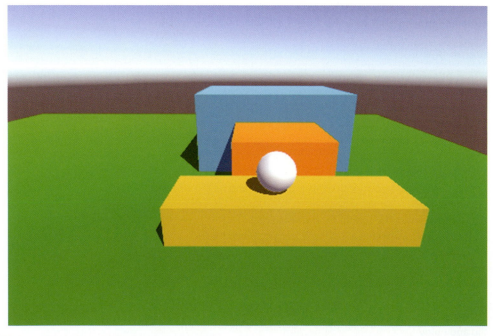

FIG 3.18 A new sphere has been added to the scene.

the sphere. To begin we need to put our state machine into a nice bulleted list to make sure that we understand what it is doing:

- Set the color to a default value
- When the user moves the mouse over the object
    - Change the color to a new color
    - When the mouse moves away from the object
        - Set the color back to default and repeat
    - If the user clicks on the sphere
        - Set one of the blocks to be the color of the sphere

At first glance, this may seem simplistic in comparison to our green tea example; however, the green tea example was a hypothetical one, whereas this will be implemented. Also, let's ensure that we can spot the actions and the events clearly before building systems that are overly complex. In this example, there are three distinct events: when the user moves the mouse over the object, when the mouse moves away from the object, and when the user clicks on the object. For the development of the state machine itself, we will go straight into PlayMaker now that we have a nice list of the actions and events that we need to worry about.

Make sure that the sphere is the currently selected game object and open the PlayMaker editor, if it is not already open. Beginning with the blank editor window, right-click in the state machine editor pane to add a new state machine to this object, the sphere. We can add multiple state machines to each object and this is a very useful thing to keep in mind as we progress and begin to construct more complex behaviors; we do not need to try to figure out how to cram everything into one state machine. After selecting "add FSM" your editor should have changed to appear as it does in Figure 3.19.

Notice that not only has a small state machine appeared in the left-hand panel, but the right-hand information panels have changed as well. In the right-hand panel, we now have PlayMaker's equivalent of the Inspector Pane as it pertains to the currently selected state, highlighted with the blue border. We can change the name of the state, currently "State 1," to something a little more appropriate. We can also add a brief description of the state that will appear directly beneath it within the editor view. Between good descriptions and descriptive names, there should not be any problems for others to know what each state does within our machine. Or more importantly, there should not be any difficulty for us to know what each state is *supposed* to be doing when we return to it for debugging purposes. Go ahead and change the name of the state to "Waiting" and give it a suitable description to explain that it is waiting for the user to do something.

While it is still early in the creation of our state machine we should go ahead and click on the FSM tab to give this machine a quality name and description. We need to try to be deliberate about the development of our

FIG 3.19 The PlayMaker editor after adding a state machine to the current object.

PlayMaker machines. By this I mean that we should avoid creating machines when we do not know what they are going to do or what they will be needed for. New programmers often make the mistake of throwing random code at a problem hoping that the problem will magically solve itself. While we may eventually stumble onto a solution through this approach, we will not know why the solution works, or more importantly how to add content to the solution so that it will be able to do bigger and greater things. This same mistake can occur with PlayMaker when we just start creating state machines in the hope that throwing some states and actions into it will give us the functionality we are trying to develop. Slow down, force yourself to name things, force yourself to give things descriptions. What you are doing is making sure that *you* understand what should happen before trying to convince the computer to do what you want it too. In this case, I have named my state machine "Color Changer" and gave it an adequate description. Take a look at Figure 3.20 and notice that the name and description of the state machine is not only visible within PlayMaker, but it also appears within the Inspector panel for the sphere game object, this is very nice as if we ever want to disable a state machine, we will not be forced to guess which one is which, we can read which is which directly in the Inspector for the object.

Now that we have the basics of our state machine out of the way we can add some actions to our state. To begin, we will take a look at how to move around within the Editor viewport. Holding the Middle mouse button down allows us to pan our view of the state machine. Currently, it looks as though

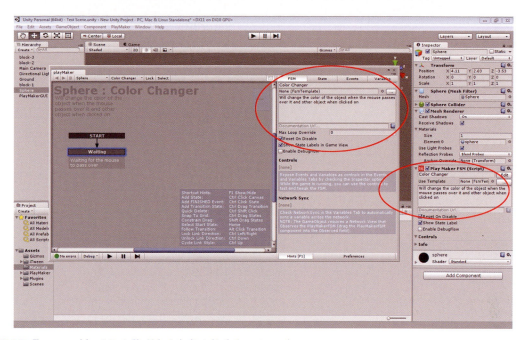

FIG 3.20 The name and description in PlayMaker is duplicated in the Inspector panel.

we are actually moving the state machine itself, but we are in fact panning our view of it as we will see when our machine has more states within it. In the bottom right portion of the State inspector view is a button labeled "Action Browser." By clicking this button, we will be greeted with a browser to search through all of the available actions within PlayMaker (see Figure 3.21). This is a daunting and intimidating list at first. However, it is not necessary to memorize the list, or to even memorize the categories per se, as we can use the search bar at the top to try to find actions.

When we select an action from within the Action Browser, a description of the action will appear in the bottom as well as a prototype indicating what the action needs and what it can use. For example, let's add an action to change the color of a material to our current state. Since we are not sure what it is called, we will type "color" in the search box and see what pops up. There are a bunch of options that appear and scrolling through them reveals many that sound interesting but still pretty fuzzy as to exactly what it is that we want. Before panicking, we will pause and consider things for just a moment. In order to change the color of a game object, what did we have to do? We created a material, added the material to the game object and then gave it whatever color we wanted within the material. So, if we want to change the color of this object, it would stand to reason that we might need to do something to the material of it. As a result of this, we may want to check in the category for Material and see if there is anything that our "color" search found. As it turns out there is a "Set Material Color" and if we select it we can see the description for it in the bottom of the Action Browser. According to the description, this

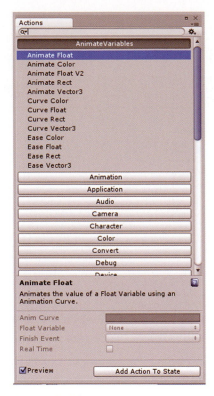

FIG 3.21 The default action browser in PlayMaker.

action should set a color to the game object's material that sounds like exactly what we want, let's see what will happen. Go ahead and click the "Add Action To State" button at the bottom. Conversely, you could also double-click the action to add it, or drag the action from the browser into the state inspector panel. Figure 3.22 depicts the State inspector with this new action added to it.

We are going to take a moment here to look through what we are seeing to make sure that we understand the basic properties of actions within PlayMaker. It begins with the Game Object selection. This is used to select which Game Object we want this action to be performed on. As a general rule the default value of "use owner" is exactly what we want. What that means is for this action to be performed on the object that this state machine is attached to, the owner of the state machine. However, there will be times that we want the action to be performed on some other object. For instance, in our current example when the player clicks on the sphere we will want to change the color of some other object instead of the sphere.

Every action within PlayMaker will begin with the Game Object selection. The options that come below will be different for each action, though after looking at a few actions we will begin to get the hang of them. In the case of the "Set Material Color" action, the next property is the Material Index.

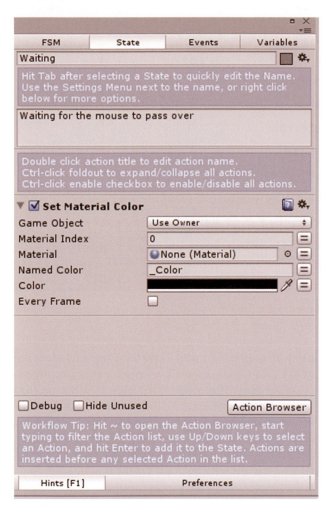

This is referring to which material from the Game Object selected in the preceding property we want to modify. The list of materials applied to a specific Game Object can be accessed through the Mesh Renderer component in the Inspector panel. As it turns out, the sphere only has one material applied to it and that material is located in Element 0, as seen in Figure 3.23. Therefore, Material Index 0 in the Set Material Color action will refer to Element 0 from the Materials list in the Mesh Renderer of the owner Game Object.

Following the Material Index component is a Material property. With this option, we can specify a material from the Project pane by dragging the material into this slot. An interesting effect of doing this would be to change the color on that base material and thereby change it on all objects that have that material assigned to them. This needs a moment of clarification, for this is subtle but very powerful stuff. If we modify the

FIG 3.23 The Mesh Renderer component of the sphere Game Object, notice Material Element 0 is the material we created earlier for the sphere.

color property of the material that is located in Element 0 of our object (it happens to be the sphere material), we are *only* changing the color of the instance of the material attached to this object; we are not changing the color of the original sphere material. However, if we drag the sphere material into the Material property for our Set Material Color action, we will be changing the color of the base material, which will in turn change the color for all objects that have that material associated to them. Let's demonstrate this concept very quickly, by making some minor changes to our scene:

1. Select the sphere material from the Assets → Materials section in the project pane.
2. Drag this new material onto the ground object in the Scene Editor, notice that it is now the same color as the sphere.
3. Play the game and notice the results:
   a. Our PlayMaker script is executed and the sphere turns black, but the ground stays white; we have changed the color of the material instance on the sphere, but not the base material.
4. OK, now in PlayMaker modify the properties of our action such that we drag the sphere material from the Assets → Materials section of the Project pane onto the Material property.
   a. Now run the program again and observe what happens. Both the ground and the sphere are black, because the color of the base material has been changed.
5. Go ahead and return this to what we had by replacing the sphere material on the ground with its original material.

6. To reset the Material property of the Set Material Color action, click the little circle icon to the left of the text box. This brings up an asset browser from which we can select an appropriate asset in either the Scene or the Project (this is another way of applying the material without dragging it from the Project pane). Browse to the top of the selector and select the "None" option to return our Material property to none.

At first glance, that may have seemed like an interesting if somewhat irrelevant little diversion in our exploration of PlayMaker and Unity. However, we were just introduced to an enormous principle of modern programming and as a result game development, object-oriented programming. We have a material; let's call it sphere that is defined in our Project. This is the parent, or the base, or the class, from which we can derive materials to put into our game. As we drag the material onto an object in our scene, we are creating an instance of that original class. This process is referred to as "instantiating an object." The instance of the material, or the child, will inherit all of the properties of its parent, but can then have new properties or modified properties that differentiate it from the parent. We will see this in much more detail when we start building our game world.

Following the Material property are two properties that are easily confused as at first glance they seem as though they accomplish the same task. But, they are actually quite different. The first property, Named Color, is allowing us to determine which color property within the material we want to change. As has been mentioned this is not really a book on shaders and materials, so without going into a large amount of detail we will simply state that the default value of "_Color" is what we want. This value refers to the main color of the material. Other color values that could be altered within the default shaders would include specular, emission, and reflection colors.

The next property is labeled Color and this one will specify which color we want to change the material to. We have two methods of selecting the color, though we will add a third in a few moments. We can click the color bar, which is black by default, and then use the color selector that we used earlier to determine which color we want to use. The other approach is to select the eyedropper icon which will allow us to pull the color values from something and use that for the new color. This eyedropper tool is very powerful as we can pull the color from a Game Object in the scene or even from a rendered Game Object while the game is playing to be able to match colors. This approach is often done when working with shaders to get the various colors the way that we want them. For now, I am going to leave the Color property at the default value of black. As we have already seen, if we run this game then the sphere will change to a black color, so we know that our state machine is currently working. It is strongly encouraged that you get in the habit of testing your scripts as you are working on them piece by piece to make sure that each component is doing what you want it to do at that point in time. This is referred to as iterative development, building a small piece, testing it, fixing it (if needed), and building the next piece. This is also a form of unit testing as we will encounter later when we explore testing and building.

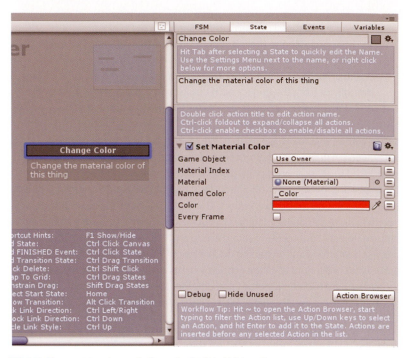

FIG 3.24 The new state and properties for another Set Material Color action.

There are two more elements that we need to discuss in the state properties before moving on. The box with two lines in it to the right of each property is the variable toggle. If we click that box then the selection for that property will change to a drop-down list from which we can select a variable that is appropriate for that particular property. The other option to look at is the "Every Frame" check box at the bottom. This toggle will determine whether this specific action is to be performed every frame, which is every time that the screen refreshes or updates, or if we only want to do it one time. Having Every Frame turned off for our current example, though in the next chapter we will see the power of that toggle.

With our starting state constructed and an understanding of the components that are within it, we are going to go ahead and add a new state to our machine. Do this by right-clicking within the state machine editor pane and selecting the option "Add State." Following what we did above we are going to complete the following steps with this new state (Figure 3.24 depicts the final version of this new state that I created).

1. Give it an appropriate name and description
2. Add the Set Material Color action to it
3. Make sure the properties are set correctly
4. Change the new color to something other than black

Hopefully, as you were working through the above steps you noticed something very interesting when you were adding the Set Material Color action to the state. In the Action Browser, there was a number in brackets next to the action. That number indicated how many times that particular action was currently being used by the state machine. This can be helpful, because there will be times when we are looking through the possible actions and the description of something sounds like what we want so we select it. After adding this different and unknown action to our machine, we then spend a fair amount of time trying to figure out why it is not working like the other one did. An example of this is the Audio Play and Play Sound actions; they seem like they are the same, but in actuality are slightly different leading to different behavior during the execution of the game. If we had already used one of these actions, then it would be indicated with a number within the bracket and during our next selection we would be able to recognize which action we used before.

We now have our two states created and just need to add an event to these things to get our scripted behavior working. If we refer back to our original bulleted list, we will see that the event that will cause a transition to the Change Color state is when the mouse comes over the object, and then we will transition back after the mouse leaves the object. Select the "Waiting" state and right-click to bring up a context sensitive menu from which we can select "Add Transition." This pop-out menu includes all of the default events available within PlayMaker. Notice that one of the events is the "FINISHED" event that we mentioned in our earlier discussion. While we can create custom events, if there is a default event that does what we want, we can save time and work by using it. If we point the cursor to the "System Events" section, we will get a pop-out for several default events generated by the system that we can utilize. These are specifically generated by the MonoBehaviour class and are messages that it sends out when certain things happen while the game is running. In our case, we are interested in leveraging these mouse events that it includes and these messages are sent out whenever the mouse has interacted with the collider of the owner object. A full list of these mouse messages is available in Table 3.4.

TABLE 3.4 Listing of the Default Mouse Event Messages Generated by Unity

MOUSE DOWN	Left mouse button has been pressed over the owner object.
MOUSE DRAG	Player has clicked on the owner object and is still holding the button down while moving the mouse.
MOUSE ENTER	Mouse cursor has entered into the area covered by the collider of the owner.
MOUSE EXIT	Mouse cursor has left the area covered by the collider of the owner.
MOUSE OVER	Called every frame that the mouse is hovering over the collider of the owner.
MOUSE UP	Player has released the mouse button.

For our problem, it appears as though we have two options that will satisfy our needs. We could select either the MOUSE ENTER or the MOUSE OVER event and in this case either one will work. Let's begin by using the MOUSE ENTER event, once you select that notice that the event has been added to a box in the state and that we now have a red exclamation point, error message, at the top left of the state. The error message is informing us that we have an event that is not actually transitioning anywhere. This is a common message to see as we are constructing our machines and one that we can ignore at the moment. But as our machines get more complex, spotting those red exclamation points can help us zero in on the areas of our state machines that should be causing the problems. To make this event lead to a transition to another state, simply drag from that event to the state that we want to transition too. Let's test this, iterative development, and see if the color of the sphere changes when we mouse over the sphere object. It looks as though we have the behavior that we wanted, when I moved the mouse over the sphere it turned red. So, let's finish this part of our state machine off by adding a MOUSE EXIT event to our Change Color state and connecting this event to the Waiting state.

Congratulations! You have created your first behavior script is based entirely on the logical structure of a state machine. It may not be the most exciting behavior, but then again it is a solid starting point. A couple of notes before we complete this section; did you notice what happens in the PlayMaker editor window while the game is running? There is a green box around the currently active state, and as you moved the mouse around you could see the activity occurring within the PlayMaker editor; this helps us to see exactly where our scripts are and what they are doing. The last thing to notice is that the state label displayed over the object while the game is running. There are many times that it can be very useful to be able to see exactly which state a given object is in; however, as we complete state machines or as we prepare to publish and release our game we will no longer want those state labels to appear. To remove the state labels, turn off the Show State Label option in the state machine section of the Inspector panel for the owner object (see Figure 3.25).

To complete our original vision for this state machine, we only need to add a couple more pieces. We will need a new state that will be changing the color of some other object. Since we are changing the color of a different object, we will want to specify the object rather than use the default of "Use Owner." Notice that when we do this we get a new box where we can tell the action exactly which object we want to use. We can either drag the object from the Hierarchy panel into this box or use the circle selection option to bring up the Asset Browser to find the object. One warning at this point, be careful to ensure that you are using an object from the scene (either the Hierarchy panel or the Scene tab if using the browser). Selecting an object from the Project pane is perfectly acceptable; however, be aware that this means we will be modifying the object that is in the Project, not the instance of the object that is actually in the scene. With our new state created, we just need to connect it to everything. I will do this with a MOUSE DOWN event connected from Change Color to the new state and a FINISHED event connected from the new state back to the original Waiting state.

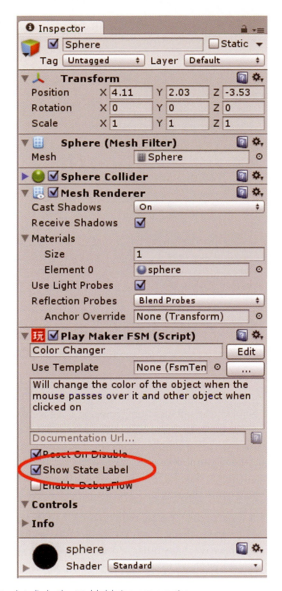

FIG 3.25 The toggle to display the state label during game execution.

Figure 3.26 displays the finished version of this state machine. By left-clicking on one of the states we can drag them around in our editor pane to make them easier to view, especially those transition arrows. A quick play through will show that we have the behavior that was initially described in our problem.

Our current solution to this problem is "hard coded." This means that the values, such as new colors and which objects to modify, are specified within the actions themselves. Therefore, if we ever wanted to go back and change it so that the sphere changes to a different color we would have to go into the state machine itself and make those changes. At the moment, that does

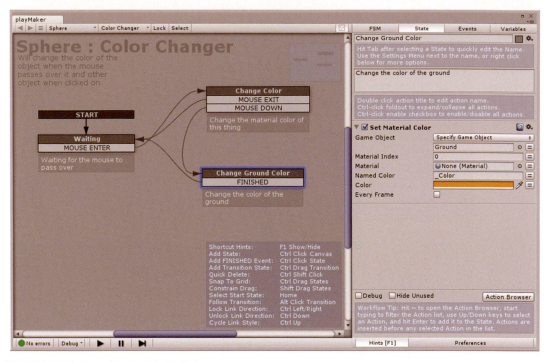

FIG 3.26 FINISHED state machine as initially described.

not seem like it would be a huge problem; however, if we were to consider a larger game it quickly becomes more efficient to use variables and then when we want to make a change we simply modify the value of the variable and that change will cascade throughout our state machines. In the next chapter, we will look at variables in detail when we construct the character controller system for our main game character.

We have one final topic to cover before moving on. When it comes to using PlayMaker, we are limited to the actions that are included within our installed PlayMaker package. If we want any other actions than what is available within the Action browser, we will have to create our own, or we could add custom actions to our installed PlayMaker package (these are actions that other people within the PlayMaker community have created). A nice graphical package and action browser has been developed for use with PlayMaker called "Ecosystem," which we are going to go ahead and download and add to our current project just in case we ever need any other actions that are not included within the default package later. The Ecosystem download is located at https://hutonggames.fogbugz.com/?W1181 and can be downloaded by clicking the link labeled "EcosystemBrowser Package." Once the package file has been downloaded, go ahead and locate the location where it was saved on your computer and drag this package into the Project pane of Unity as shown in Figure 3.27. Once the package is released into the Project pane, Unity will decompress the package and give us the option as to which components we would like to import into our project (see Figure 3.28).

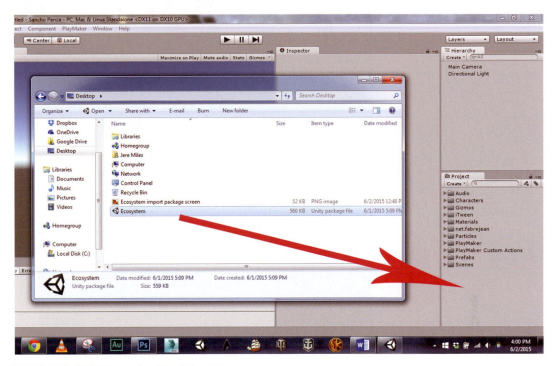

FIG 3.27 Adding the Ecosystem package to our Unity project.

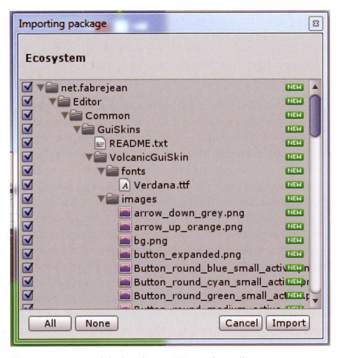

FIG 3.28 The Import components dialog box when importing a package to Unity.

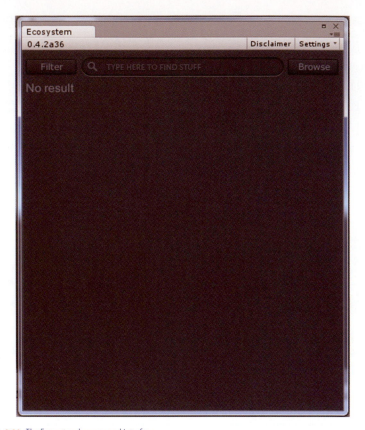

FIG 3.29 The Ecosystem browser and interface.

For our case, we are going to leave all of the components. This is the same process we went through to add PlayMaker to our project initially.

The Ecosystem browser is a very powerful tool that will enable us to search for new actions to import into our project if we need. The browser will automatically handle downloading, importing, and rebuilding PlayMaker for anything that we decide to add to it. The reason for the rebuild is that the actions utilized by PlayMaker are written in the C# language and in order for them to be utilized by PlayMaker, Unity will need to compile them after they are imported into the project. Once the new actions have been added, they will be available through the Action browser that we have used thus far. To launch the Ecosystem browser select PlayMaker from the toolbar followed by Addons → Ecosystem. The first time it launches you will be greeted with a disclaimer and an option to watch a YouTube video providing a quick introduction to the system. The orange button at the bottom will exit the disclaimer and open the browser itself as depicted in Figure 3.29. We will worry about actually searching for and installing any new actions later if it becomes necessary.

3.8 Summary

In this chapter, we looked at how to obtain copies of both the Unity 3D game engine and the PlayMaker visual scripting system so that we can begin to make our own games. We also got to know the user interfaces for both, while they are daunting at first, we have gained a solid understanding of the basic elements and the core components that we need at this point in time. State machines have changed from an abstract concept to a logical construct that we can use to build the behavior of the objects within our game worlds. While we may not have put a game together just yet, we have the basic understanding of these building blocks such that we are now ready to go to the next step and begin adding a character into our game project.

Vocabulary

Project
Scene
Package
Scene Editor
Game view
Inspector pane
Component
Project pane
Hierarchy pane
Transform component
Transform gizmo
Game object
Layer
Tag
Mesh filter component
Collider component
Physics material
Mesh renderer
Material component
Shader
State machine
State
Transition or event
Action
Variable
Object oriented
Ecosystem

Review Quiz

1. What is the difference between a Unity Project and a folder?
2. What key combination is used to pan the camera around a Unity scene?

3. What key combination is used to rotate a camera around a specific object in a Unity scene?
4. What is the least expensive type of collider to use on a Game Object?
5. Who is the developer of PlayMaker?
6. What is a state?
7. What is a transition or event?
8. Which folder within a Unity Project contains all of the content that we create and add to our game?
9. In a PlayMaker action, what would the owner object refer to?
10. How can we pan the view in the PlayMaker machine editor view?
11. What does the Every Frame toggle do in a PlayMaker action?
12. Which built-in event could be used to know when the player has released the mouse button?
13. What add-on is used to add new actions to an installed PlayMaker package?

Exercises

1. Modify the test scene that you created in this chapter to include some platforms in the air for the player to jump onto and run along.
2. Create two new Game Objects in the scene, have one of them change the color of objects to yellow and have the other reset the colors to the original color, both work when the player clicks them.
3. Consider the following problem, create a bulleted list from this that could be used as the first step in creating a state machine to control this behavior (NOTE: focus on constructing the logical version of the state machine, rather than implementing it within PlayMaker):
   a. We will create a game in which the player is represented by a ball. There will be four buttons on the screen with arrows to represent which way the ball can go. When the player clicks on one of the buttons the ball will move in the direction indicated by the arrow on the button.
4. Modify the scene and state machine that we created in this chapter such that when the user holds the mouse button down the color will change as we created it to, but when the user releases the mouse button the color returns to what it was.

Design Document

> **Download**
> The Design Document that we created in the last chapter has not been updated with any information from this chapter, therefore there is nothing to download.

We do not have any new information to add to our design document, so what was done in the last chapter will hold through until we get to the end of the next chapter. Although, many times in a design document there is a section that specifies which tools will be used during the project as well as file format and version specifications.

SECTION II
Building Blocks

CHAPTER 4

Characters

Now that we have some solid concepts on game development under our belts, we are going to start laying the foundation for our game. Characters play a pivotal role in some games. However, as we will shortly discuss, not all games rely on characters. For our project at hand, we are going to need to understand characters, after all the game does star Sancho Panza, in order to better design our player character and any others that may appear during the game. Even if you are building a puzzle or strategy game, see Chapter 1 for a discussion of these different genres, characters can play an intriguing role by providing a context for the game, not that this is necessary, but it is an option to consider. If you are considering building a role-playing or story-driven game, then the characters will be vital to your project. There is a tremendous overlap between characters and stories which will cause the next chapters to blur together in some aspects. In this chapter, we will explore the following concepts as they pertain to characters and video games.

- Purpose of Characters
- Do Games Need Characters?
- Traditional Character Types

- Game Character Types
- Character Development
- Character Design
- Importing Models in Unity
- Character Control System in PlayMaker

4.1 The Purpose of Characters

Characters provide us, as the audience, with a reference within the story. The characters that we develop for our audience become the perspective that our audience experiences things through or with. Characters also provide a means for distributing information, usually to other characters and therefore to the audience indirectly, although it could be direct through the breaking of the concept of the fourth wall. The characters of a story allow the audience to explore the questions and dilemmas of the story from a safe vantage point; for instance, I may enjoy exploring the depths of human bonding and loyalty through war movies such as *Band of Brothers*, however, that does not mean that I have any interest in actually serving during the frigid nights of the Battle of the Bulge of World War II. Stories cannot exist without characters; they are the framework that the story hangs upon. After creating characters, we can develop stories by throwing our characters into interesting situations and exploring various questions of morality or friendship or just aspects of being alive. It is through the implementation of characters within a story that we can create tension and emotional connectedness.

4.2 Do Games Need Characters?

The short answer to this question is "No, games do not need characters in them." We can create many great and fun games that do not contain any characters. Games of chance or strategy can be created with no characters within the game and also with essentially no story to the game. Consider many of the board games that you may play, the only characters within those games are the human players themselves. Consider the exciting strategy game *Clear Tactic* (Figure 4.1), developed by Enlitanment Studios. While this game does not provide characters in this traditional sense, it still provides a fun and challenging game-play experience with a high replay value. In fact, a strong argument could be made that games can have higher replay values without characters due to an increase in the flexibility of the game-play experience. Through playing a game such as *Clear Tactic*, the traditional roles of characters, specifically the hero and shadow as we will discuss shortly, is taken on by the human players themselves. This makes the game-play experience dynamic and different each time that the game is played.

We need to pause for a moment to differentiate between avatar and character. An avatar in a game is a physical representation of a player. For instance, the player piece that you may select for a game of *Monopoly* is your avatar on the board, this is not a character. A character, on the other

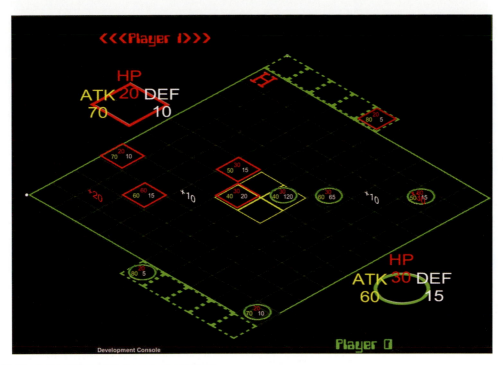

FIG 4.1 *Clear Tactic* by Enlitanment Studios as played on Facebook.

hand, may incorporate an avatar for the player, but more than that in order to be a character it must contain its own goals and motivations within the game. Consider a computer-based role-playing game (CRPG), as game developers, we need to provide a customizable avatar for the player to represent themselves within the game world and we must provide a flexible story for the player to interact with; however, the player's motivations for doing what they do will be entirely defined by the player themselves, within the confines that we provide inside of the story. On the other hand, if we create a third-person shooter in which the player plays the role of a SWAT team member fighting crime in some fictional city, we as the game developers have created a character and avatar for the player, why the player is doing what they are doing is defined by the motivations and desires of the character that we have created. This may be a subtle distinction, but it is very important for us to grasp. Video games must have some form of avatar to represent the player within the game world, the moveable pieces from Enlitanment Studio's *Clear Tactic* for instance, but they do not need to contain characters, unless we require characters because of the story that we wish to tell through the game-play experience.

4.3 Traditional Character Types

Through the history of storytelling and drama, a rich heritage of character types has developed. While it is not necessary for each game, or indeed even any game, to contain all of these different characters, it is nice to know what we have available to us in the traditional arsenal, especially when we get into creating stories. Over the years, many people have studied the traditional stories that societies tell looking at how they are constructed and the characters that appear within them. A full book could easily be dedicated to a solid study of characters and character development, both in and out of games. As an introduction to this topic, however, we have selected the character types developed by Christopher Vogler in his work *The Writer's Journey: Mythic Structures for Writers*.

A little background is in order before going on into the character archetypes. Christopher Vogler's work was developed as a blueprint for the adaption of Joseph Campbell's *The Hero with a Thousand Faces* to the creation of screen writing. Joseph Campbell spent most of his life studying mythology from all cultures and utilized the theories of Carl Jung and Sigmund Freud in his analysis of these legends and myths. Over the course of this study, he began to notice a certain pattern emerging. This pattern would go on to become known as the hero's journey or journey of the hero. We will look at this pattern in more detail in the next chapters as it specifically pertains to stories and the events within a story. But, for now, what we are interested in is that Joseph Campbell noticed that within this hero's journey, there were specific character types needed to fulfill specific roles, and Christopher Vogler has provided a solid guideline for the use of these character archetypes. Throughout the following discussion on the character archetypes, we will reference the classic work *The Lord of the Rings* by J.R.R. Tolkien as an example of these character types in action. This particular story was created prior to the work of Joseph Campbell and yet because Tolkien was a scholar of old English and Nordic legends, his characters incorporate the same archetypes. Table 4.1 displays an overview of the character types that we will be looking at.

TABLE 4.1   Christopher Vogler's Character Archetypes and Examples from *The Lord of the Rings*

Archetype	Story Purpose	Example
Hero	Protagonist, main character of the story	Frodo
Shadow	Antagonist, main villain of the story	Sauron
Mentor	Trainer and teacher for the hero	Aragorn
Ally	Helper and assistant to the hero	Samwise
Herald	Beacon pointing the hero in the correct direction	Gandalf
Trickster	Comic relief and general mischief	Mariadoc and Peregrin
Threshold Guardian	Obstacle before the hero can pass into new knowledge	Shelob, among others
Shapeshifter	Character with seemingly changing loyalties and views	Gollum

4.3.1 The Hero

Every story must have a central character, a primary and pivotal character around which the whole story revolves. It is through this central character that the audience will experience the story. Not only will the audience experience the story through this character, but the audience will also perceive the story through this character. This central character is the hero of the story. In a video game, the hero is also the player character; after all, very few of us would want to play a video game in which we were not the pivotal character of the game, though this may be an interesting concept to incorporate into a game idea. A traditional view of the hero character is a character that has a willingness to protect others that are not able to protect themselves. This protection provided by the hero character may even involve the sacrifice of the character in some way. However, the game industry has begun to experiment with this model by casting the main character of the game in a morally ambiguous context. While the exploration of morality within a story and game experience is an exciting opportunity for us to explore, keep in mind that in order to follow these classic models of storytelling, the hero should follow those more traditional guidelines.

The hero for *The Lord of the Rings* is Frodo Baggins. He was a typical Hobbit that could so easily be identified with by the audience even though the audience did not actually consist of any Hobbits. He cared for the other Hobbits and Middle Earth in general but would much prefer to be left alone. However, his character is such that he is willing to do what must be done to protect those that cannot protect themselves, to the ultimate willingness of sacrificing himself if it were to become necessary.

4.3.2 The Shadow

The opposite of the hero is the shadow character. It is the job of the shadow to challenge the hero in various ways. Generally speaking, the shadow should be a character of similar qualities to the hero in order to provide conflict for the characters in the story and also to provide challenges for the player in the game. The shadow could, and generally should, be stronger than the hero at the beginning to allow for character growth; however, by the conclusion, they should both be fairly evenly matched, consider Luke Skywalker and Darth Vader at the end of *Return of the Jedi*. Within the context of a video game, the shadow character is the boss of the game or in some cases of the level depending on the construction of the game itself. A well-designed shadow character should be a mirror of the hero, not only in skills but also in world outlook as it is through this difference between the primary characters that conflict can so easily be created and nurtured. It is of interest to note, however, that the shadow does not have to be a character in the traditional sense that we may consider one. The essential purpose of the shadow character is to provide a physical form to oppose the hero, and this opposition may come in the shape of an inanimate object just as easily as an animate character, it depends on the needs of the story (or in our case the game).

The shadow from Tolkien's work is Sauron. This character perfectly embodies the darkness of the story and presents the hero with his ultimate challenge. In Sauron, we can also see an example of a shadow character that does not necessarily have a physical form in the traditional sense. Rather, Sauron spends the trilogy growing in power and manipulating others, but always without actual form. His presence and challenge to Frodo is not merely in the physical sense, but also in a deeper mental and spiritual sense as the two opposites struggle for ultimate control of the ring of power. This essential conflict between the hero and shadow is one that we will return to when we explore the development of stories and conflict.

The hero and the shadow form the two primary characters required. It is not necessary to have any other characters involved. Many fighting games, for instance, are based entirely around the conflict between two characters, one being the player's character (or the hero) and the other being the player's challenger (or the shadow). We can even look at many classic video games such as *Donkey Kong* or *Ms. Pac-Man*, while they definitely do not have complex story lines, they do have story lines nonetheless and within those stories are characters. For *Donkey Kong,* there are three characters, a hero played by Jumpman (the player), a shadow played by Kong (the computer AI); the other character we will not worry about at the moment. Likewise, *Ms. Pac-Man* has a small cast of characters that can essentially be boiled down to the heroine as Ms. Pac-Man (the player, once again) and the shadow which has four physical representations in the ghosts (again, the computer AI). Many wonderful and fun games can be created with no more of a cast than the hero and the shadow because we have provided a player character within the hero and an obstacle to the player within the shadow and at its core this is all that is needed for fun games.

For the construction of more complex and engaging stories, however, more characters will be necessary. As Christopher Vogler points out, these characters are not just filler and stage dressing, well some may be, but these other characters have very specific roles to fulfill within the story and therefore within the game as well. The remaining character archetypes that we will look at are: the mentor, the threshold guardian, the herald, the shape-shifter, the ally, and the trickster. We are not required to have a representative of each of these archetypes within our games, and we may have more than one of certain archetypes, for instance the ally.

4.3.3 The Mentor

The mentor is a character type that appears early in the story to provide assistance to the hero. Not only does the mentor provide help, but the mentor will also train the hero many times in some fashion to prepare the hero for the road ahead of him. Generally speaking, the mentor tends to be some aged character with a seeming overabundance of wisdom; in fact, the mentor may even have hints of divinity to them. Whatever conflict is planned between the hero and the shadow, it is not the mentor's job to fight this battle, but only to get the hero out the door, so to speak, and send them down the proper path with the proper skill set, or at least a solid start to obtaining that skill set. At first glance, we may throw Gandalf the Grey, from Tolkien's work, into this role as mentor. This would seem reasonable as Gandalf is older, is wise, and does appear as divine in many ways. However, the ultimate role of the mentor is to train the character, to get them going in the right direction. While we could still make an argument that Gandalf fulfills this role, a better fit for the mentor character archetype would be Aragorn or even the fellowship as a unit body.

4.3.4 The Ally

Speaking of helpers for the hero, these are found in the character archetype labeled as ally. The purpose of the ally character is to travel with the hero, to provide assistance to the hero. This assistance may be in the form of combat by fighting alongside the hero, or it may be in the form of taking care of the hero's basic needs, such as cooking dinner. Ally characters also provide someone for the hero character to talk to during the story. Without conversations, the audience will never know what is going on inside of the hero's head and therefore what the hero thinks or feels about certain events that occur within the story. Granted, we could provide such character insight through the use of voice-over narration of what the hero is thinking, but it is far more engaging for the audience to have interaction between the hero and some other characters. It is also interesting to note that many times these ally characters go on to become some of the most beloved characters of stories. Frodo's ally throughout *The Lord of the Rings* is the ever faithful Samwise Gamgee. Throughout his journey, Frodo can always rely on Samwise being there to help him in either large ways or smaller ways. Samwise also provides someone for Frodo to talk to and to help bear the burden that Frodo is stuck with.

4.3.5 The Herald

Another vital character archetype is one that Christopher Vogler has labeled as the herald. The role of the herald, quite simply put, is to announce the coming of change. As a general rule, these character types will appear very early in the story to inform the hero that something is coming and to issue a challenge to the hero to start the story rolling. Heralds will also reappear throughout the story to remind the hero character of what it is that they are supposed to be doing, to encourage them along the path, and to keep them from going too far off track. Given this new character archetype, we can see how Gandalf the Grey from *The Lord of the Rings* so easily fits into this role. He was there at the start of the story to get the ball rolling, so to speak, with Frodo and would reappear from time to time, always reminding Frodo of what his task was.

4.3.6 The Trickster

Most stories can do with some comic relief, or some characters that are there just to express some desire for change, either good or bad. These character types are the trickster characters. Their role is comic on the one hand, but it is also one of keeping egos in check. Through the trickster characters, the hero's ego can be kept from getting too far out of control. For *The Lord of the Rings*, the hobbits, Meriadoc Brandybuck and Peregrin Took, Merry and Pippin, are the trickster characters. They routinely provide a comic backdrop to lighten more serious moments as well as a humble perspective. They are ultimately driven into the story through their own desire for change and to see new things, nothing more.

4.3.7 The Shapeshifter

Whereas the tricksters can be used to lighten a story, the shapeshifter character can be utilized to keep the audience guessing and to keep the hero on their toes. Shapeshifters are characters that may change their mood or opinions at the drop of a hat and oftentimes keep the hero unsure as to exactly what their motives may be. Because the loyalty and goals of the shapeshifter are always somewhat in question and can seem to go either way, these characters can provide an opportunity to introduce new plot elements, something that we will discuss later. Gollum is a shapeshifter character archetype. He continually flips back and forth between good and evil, constantly fighting his own battle of desire for the one ring. This flip-flopping nature of Gollum allows the relationships within the story to become so tense that Frodo places more trust in Gollum than he does in Samwise, despite all the reasons not to do so.

4.3.8 The Threshold Guardian

Threshold guardians are fascinating character types and ones that we can find very useful within game development. As a hero journeys through the story, they will reach moments of growth or discovery. These moments will be thresholds into a new portion of the story, into a new depth of understanding and knowledge for the hero which in turn would mean new information for the player as well. As the hero nears these points, there needs to be a guardian there to prevent the hero from just waltzing through to the new knowledge. These guardians can come in a wide range of individual characters or obstacles. For instance, the hero may have to overcome their own fear of the dark in order to sprint through the darkened hall in order to get the key that will open a door. However, emotional or psychological guardians are very difficult for us to implement within a video game for reasons that we will discuss later, although with the rise of virtual reality, the doors are beginning to open in this area in some exciting and intriguing ways. Threshold guardians can also be traditional physical characters, but are never the actual antagonist or shadow of the story, that confrontation is saved for the conclusion. J.R.R. Tolkien provided many threshold guardians for Frodo to deal with throughout the story, perhaps one of the more obvious one being Shelob, the spider that guarded the entrance into Mordor, and the threshold into that portion of the story. Threshold guardians within video games are the level bosses at the end of each level or section.

TABLE 4.2 Character Archetypes Used within Games

Archetype	Game Use	Example
Hero	Player character	Lloyd Irving
Shadow	Endgame boss	Mithos Yggdrasill
Mentor	Tutorial system and trainers	Raine Sage
Ally	Other players in co-op modes or non-player characters (NPCs)	Genis Sage
Herald	Character to be rescued or objective markers	Colette Brunel
Trickster	Comic relief	Zelos Wilder
Threshold Guardian	Level or section boss	Temple guardians and others
Shapeshifter	Character that the player is unsure of	Kratos Aurion

With these eight character archetypes, we can build a diverse and deep story for our games. However, as discussed previously, we are not required to create detailed and thought provoking stories for our games, after all we are the Game Makers, we can create whatever games we want to make and should always use game playability as the final benchmark for any decisions involving the game. With that said, we can use the character archetypes to quickly flesh out a basic game idea by recognizing how the types interact with each other and depend on each other. See Table 4.2 for a summary of how these character archetypes can be utilized within a game system and example characters from *Tales of Symphonia* developed by Namco.

4.4 Game Character Types

As previously noted, games do not necessarily need to have characters within them; however, for games that do utilize characters, there are some additional types from those that Christopher Vogler has described. These extra character types are exclusive to games, as they are not necessarily required components for stories, but may very well be required in order to develop the game-play systems and features that are desired. It is very possible to double up these character types with those found within the main character archetypes, but it is not necessary.

4.4.1 Merchants

We will consider the example of a computer role-playing game or an MMO. In either case, we plan on developing a story for the player to experience through the eyes of the hero character and within this story will be utilizing many, if not all, of the character archetypes that

Christopher Vogler has outlined. However, we are also going to need merchant character types for the player to interact with. These characters generally will have no value to the story itself, but without which the player will become severely limited in the actions that they can perform. The merchants will allow the player to buy and sell goods and treasure that has been gathered on their journey. They will also be able to rent rooms to heal, or buy fragments of maps, or even random food and drink items from a local tavern within the game world. These interactions are in no way required for the telling of the story, but they are very necessary for the immersion of the player. This immersion is something that we will discuss in more detail in Chapter 7 on creating game worlds. But, for now, immersion is how invested the player becomes within the game that we have created. Our goal is for the players to lose themselves within the games that we create, though probably not literally, but we definitely want them to have fun.

4.4.2 The Quest Giver

Another important game character for these styles of games is the quest giver. At first glance, it would seem as though the quest giver and the herald would be the same character and perhaps they could be, at least for main story line quests. However, for all of the side quests that we as players enjoy so much, we will need characters to provide those quests. We will need characters within our games with question marks and the exclamation points hovering over their heads so that players will know that there is some random quest to be had with some new piece of loot to add to their collection. It is possible to merge this quest giver character with the merchant character for some of the quests, but we will also want just everyday random NPCs to provide these opportunities to our players.

4.4.3 Information

The final game-specific character type we would like to mention is an informational character. The purpose of this character is to provide a source of information to the player, not the hero per se. For instance, upon entering a new town, the player may need to know where the nearest tavern is in order to go heal from the battles along the road. Many times, there will be an NPC somewhere near the entrance of the town that the player can interact with and obtain this basic information. This interaction does not advance the story in any way but is important information that the player will need in order to play the game. Once again, this character type could be combined with a merchant, perhaps a street vendor peddling their wares at the city gates, or it could be a stand-alone character, perhaps a town guard on duty at the entrance. As developers, we can find other methods of delivering this information to the player, but utilizing a character of this type is a definite option and one that has been used many times in the past.

We have taken a quick look at three additional types of characters that are not required by the primary story that we are telling, but could prove to be very important to the player playing our game. Just because these character types exist, does not mean that we need to figure out a way to shoe horn them into every game that we create. On the contrary, we must always be considering the playability of the game that we are working on first and foremost. If adding a character, of any type, detracts from the playability and the fun of the game, then that character must be removed, no matter how important the character is to us personally; at least, it must be removed until we can figure out a better way to use it. Do not look at these character types and archetypes as components that your game absolutely must have, for it is very possible to make wonderful and engaging games with no characters at all. However, if you are interested in exploring the possibilities of deep and engaging story lines with large game worlds, then you had better consider these character types and how they could fit into your game world.

4.5 Character Design

In this section, we are going to apply the theories that we have discussed in this chapter. We have some advantages in our chosen game design in that through the selection of a book, many of the characters have already been created for us. Miguel Cervantes has already done the background work of character creation for us. All we have to do is to drop the characters into the roles that we want them to fulfill and flesh out any missing details; we should also consider altering the characters from the book to better fit the needs that we have within our game. It is at this point that we may have a moment of hesitation as we balk at the idea of altering the previously created characters. Generally speaking, alterations to previously created characters are slimming of the character, dropping some details and background in order to make a more simplified personification. While it is true that our goal is to create deep and vibrant characters for our games, we must always remember that we are making games and that our primary goal is to create something that is both playable and, if we are fortunate, something that is fun.

When creating a character, we should begin by asking ourselves some very basic questions to get started as depicted in Table 4.3. As we answer each question, the following ones become relevant or not for us. This type of approach can help to keep us on track while creating characters and keep us from getting too side tracked. One other thought, before we start looking at this process, if we get stuck on a particular question for a character and just do not know the answer at the moment, make a note somewhere and come back to it later. The processes involved in creation are often not the straightest path to a solution. The creative process can wander at times, and it is OK to do this, as long as we reel it back in before it goes too far off track. Recognizing when we are getting too far off track is something that takes time and practice to pick up on, for me when I jump to a new and blank page in my idea book that is a sign that I have probably gone off track of the current project. Maybe make a quick note of the thought that lead us there, but then immediately get back on target.

TABLE 4.3 Basic Character Description Template

Character Description
What is the role in the story/game?
What is the character's name?
How old is the character?
What does the character look like?
What does the character sound like?
How does the character move?
What careers has the character had? How did they get them?
What knowledge does the character have? How did they get it?
What skills does the character have? How did they get them?
Where is the character from?
What does the character think about the world around them? Why?
What does the character think about themselves? Why?

The first question we should address when creating a character is what is the character's role in the story or game. If the character is the hero or the shadow then we are going to need to delve into this character; however, if the character is some cool quest giver, we thought of that lives on a plywood platform in a tree, she may not need quite as much depth as the primary characters do. An interesting thought on this though, is that the more depth we do give those seemingly bit characters, the more real our game will feel to the players. But there is a balancing act to this, as the more detail each character has, the more unique each character is, the more time that must be spent in creating the graphical assets and programming the interactions for these characters. Let's take a look at the other questions that we should consider for our characters.

During the process of constructing our characters, consider the questions from Table 4.3. While not all of them need to be answered for each character, the more that are answered, the more we will know about that character. As you work on answering the questions and getting to know the character better, be careful to avoid stereotypes. It may seem like an easy shortcut to use racial, ethnic, or religious stereotypes. Do not do it. The only good use of stereotypes would be if it were the goal of your game to be exploring these stereotypes through the story that you have developed.

Note
Many times when creating games, we will create this wealth of detail and background that never makes it into the game itself, for various reasons. This is OK, as it is much better to drop extra detail from a game than to have a game that lacks detail and depth because we had not considered such.

While creating characters, consider answering the questions for yourself to get the hang of it. You will notice that while the questions seem somewhat simple, the answers tend to lead to either new questions or more information that you had not considered. All of us are a collection of our life experiences, and how we view the world is directly related to those experiences.

Consider the possibility of wanting to create a straightforward character as our hero for an action–adventure type of game. This character will be a former military member, however, due to the loner nature was unable to stay within the military for a full career. Rather, the character left the military and has been living a solitary life on their ranch until a former commanding officer contacts them for a special mission. Now, each of us has a picture of this character in our heads based solely on these words that have been used to describe them. But pause for a moment and consider that image in your head, why do you picture the character the way that you do? If we could do a show of hands, most would raise their hands that the character is male, probably muscular, and most likely over six feet tall. Why? What part of the description from above stated that the character was male, or muscular, or tall? We realize that the description states military so therefore we drew a conclusion that they must be muscular, but that is not necessarily the case. What each one of us did was to inject our own personal bias into that description, even though that bias was not actually a part of the description to begin with.

This exercise was a very enlightening one for us to consider. At first glance, the description that was provided for the hero character seemed adequate, but now we recognize that there was so much information left unsaid about the character, so much information that was left as assumed. It would be much better for us to take a few minutes and to flesh out the characters, force ourselves to answer the questions rather than assuming that the other details were understood. It is best to let your imagine run as you develop characters for your games early on as it can be extremely difficult to add new things to the characters later in the development process. Remember, it is your game, you have the final say on what goes into the game and what does not, but the more ideas you start with the better. And any ideas not used with this character may be used with another character inside of the game or even a different game altogether.

One final thought on character creation before we move on. Even for a bit character such as a merchant, you can still ask yourself the questions from the list, though how much detail is provided is entirely up to you. But, give the character a reason for existing. Give the character a view of the world. While this may seem somewhat pointless for say a street vendor character that is just going to be standing there selling random trinkets, by going through this process you may accidentally discover a cool little side quest for the story, a cool little snippet to add in to the game and give it some more flavor. At the same time, if you are planning a game with many characters, you are going to have to content yourself with some cookie cutter characters at some point in time; it is just the nature of the beast.

4.6 Character Asset Design

The process of creating your character assets for use in a game are beyond the scope of this book, at least in any level of useable detail. However, it is important for us, as we are learning about the overall processes involved in the development of games, to consider the steps that would be required for the creation of these characters. The creation of character assets works through the following steps: prototype and concept, 3D mesh, animation sequences, UV unwrapping and texturing, and finally exporting and importing the asset.

Working together, the story writer and concept artist will develop an initial look for the character. This process is extremely fluid as the artist may be inspired by the verbal description of the character or the writer may become inspired by the sketches of the character. At any rate, the inspiration flows back and forth and is dependent on a willingness to show initial work to other people. It is too often that we as creative people are unwilling to let other people see what we are working on because "it is not finished." Showing unfinished work to other people will oftentimes lead to a fresh take on what we are developing after the reviewer provides us with some feedback on it. Do not be afraid to show your work to others; however, there is a difference between constructive criticism and bashing someone's work. Through this process, a full sketch of the character will eventually emerge including multiple views so that the modelers can create the 3D version of the character, see Figure 4.2.

The concept images of the character are handed off to the modelers to create a 3D mesh. Depending on the size of the studio, the modeler may fulfill multiple roles. Creating the model of the character is not merely a task of tracing the concept art within a 3D application. The modeler is responsible for the topology of the object which means that the surfaces

FIG 4.2 An example of concept art for a character.

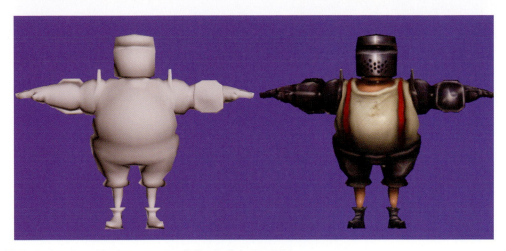

FIG 4.3 The *Sancho Panza* model without texture maps (left), and with the maps (right).

of the character must flow in a fluid and consistent manner such that when the animation is constructed there will be no tears and distortions within the model. With the model constructed, there are final chances to make any major tweaks to the appearance of the character, for once it is animated and textured the base model cannot easily be changed. Figure 4.3 demonstrates a character model with and without texture maps applied to it.

Animating a character involves the process of creating a skeletal rig for the model to hang on. The bones are associated with various parts of the model through a process referred to as skinning. As the bones are moved and animation sequences are created, the connected portions of the model will move and deform with the animation. The animation sequences can either be stored in one file, such as the case with our *Sancho Panza* example, or they may be stored in separate files. At any rate, it is important to maintain a clear list of what animations are what and in the case of a single file make sure to list when each animation starts and ends, Table 4.4 demonstrates the list of animations found in the file for *Sancho Panza*.

There are times during the animation process that portions of the model may need to be tweaked to help smooth out various animation sequences. Once the mesh is finalized, it will need to be UV unwrapped. This is the process of associating X, Y coordinates in a 2D image to X, Y, Z coordinates within a 3D mesh. The easiest way to think of this is to consider a soda bottle and to cut the label such that it can be peeled off of the surface of the bottle. This label can now be laid flat on a 2D surface and manipulated in whichever way we might like. However, once the 2D work is complete, the 2D image can be wrapped back around the 3D mesh to provide a texture for the object, Figure 4.4 demonstrates a UV unwrap template and the associated texture map.

TABLE 4.4 Animation Frame List for the *Sancho Panza* Character

Animation Name	Start Frame	End Frame
idle	0	29
idle1	30	90
idle2	90	150
run-start	150	159
run	160	180
jump-all	185	231
jump-fly	196	210
jump-start-to-fly	185	195
bonk	235	264
boxing	265	285
self-hit	285	310
die	315	355

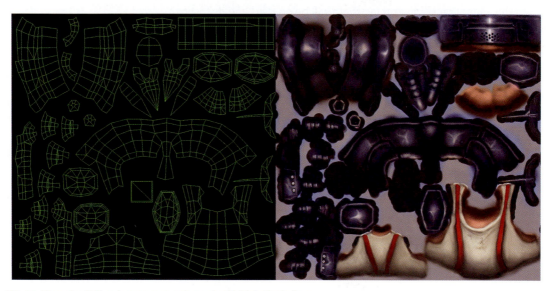

FIG 4.4 UV template (left), and a texture map on the template (right), for *Sancho Panza*.

Finally, the model is ready to be brought into the game engine. The FBX file format has become the most widely used for exporting and importing files. This format can store all the information for the model including the model, the animations, and the texture maps. Interestingly, Unity can utilize the default file format for many modern 3D applications, which makes it appear as though it would be easier to just stay in the native file format. The catch to this process is that Unity will actually convert the file from the native format to FBX in order to use it, so once the model is completed, you might as well export as an FBX file and bring that into your Unity project. The native file version of the asset can also be saved with other native content for the game project.

4.7 Importing Assets in Unity

Bringing assets into a Unity project is a fairly straightforward process. But, when the asset that you are importing is going to be used as a character or as a player controlled object, we will need to do some tweaking to it before the asset will be ready to be used in that sense. Also, if the asset we are importing will include any animations, then we will need to configure those as well. It is not necessary to configure the animations right away, but then again, there is also no real reason not too (unless we are mass importing a whole bunch of assets for our level such as doors, windmills, and such).

Download
You can continue with your project from the end of Chapter 3 or use our scene found in the final project package: "Chapter4_part1." Be aware that this download is for a Unity package file which will need to be imported into your project *after* you have imported PlayMaker into your project.

Video
You can view the "Importing Final Project" video on the companion website for a full demonstration of how the full project package has been organized and how to use it.

4.7.1 Back to Projects

We are now ready to bring our Sancho Panza character into our game project that we began in the previous chapter. However, before we start Unity, we are going to go ahead and rename our project from New Unity Project to something more meaningful to what we are working on, perhaps Sancho Panza. To do this browse to the location where your project was created and stored in the previous chapter and rename the project folder to whatever name you wish to give this game project, as mentioned, we will be calling ours Sancho Panza.

Note
The default location on a Windows machine for the Unity projects to be stored is: C:\Users\<User Name>\Documents\Unity Projects; where <User Name> would be your user name on the machine. Browsing to the Documents folder will bring you to the same location.

Now that the project folder has been renamed, we are ready to launch Unity. Once Unity has initialized, we will be greeted with the project

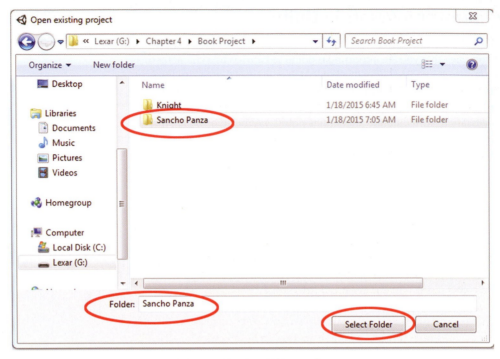

FIG 4.5 The open project browser, note the Select Folder button and the selected folder, not a file.

selection window. Since we just renamed our project from New Unity Project to Sancho Panza, Unity's project browser is blank as it is not aware of any projects that we can open. Click the "Open Other" button near the top right of the window and browse to where our new Sancho Panza project is located. It is not necessary to open the Sancho Panza folder, however, as the whole folder is the project. Rather, just select the folder and click the Select Folder button in the browser window, as depicted in Figure 4.5. This is a bit unusual as we are accustomed to that button being an Open button, which it is, but it is opening a Unity Project, not an individual file. So, by looking at the label on the button, Unity is trying to help us recognize exactly what it is that we are looking for, a folder not a file. This is an area where new users to Unity can have some issues; if you always open your projects through the project browser within Unity, you will not have any problems. We can follow these steps to rename our project as many times as we might like.

After Unity loads with our project, go ahead and close it out and restart it again. This time you will notice that the project browser has been populated with the project that we just opened and we can easily select which project it is that we want to work with. Go ahead and select the Sancho Panza project to let Unity load it once again and we will get started.

4.7.2 Importing 3D Assets

Browse to the Scenes folder in the Project pane and load the Test Scene that we built in the previous chapter. You can do this by double-clicking the scene file within the Project Pane or by selecting the Test Scene and clicking Open inside of the Inspector Pane. Once the scene loads, we will save it out as a different file name. We are essentially making a copy of this scene, the reason for this is that we will not be needing the Sphere object in the scene any longer; however, it might be nice to hold on to this test scene in case we want to be able to come back and reference it at some point in the future. Save the scene as "Character Test" using the save scene as dialogue found in the File menu; make sure to save it in the Scenes directory as well so that it will be easy to find again.

Select the Sphere object from the Hierarchy pane and delete it so that we are left with the cubes, the ground, the camera, and the light. This will serve as our test bed for getting our character working in our game and moving around correctly. This is a very good practice to get started as you develop games. Create scenes that you can use for testing basic components and basic interactivity before dropping those objects into the full game. By following this technique, if you have tested your object's behavior by itself and it worked, then any problems you have are going to be in how the object is interacting with the scene, at least generally speaking, and this can help you to troubleshoot bugs during your development.

Download
Get the "Knight.zip" file from the companion website and unzip the file on your local machine in order to have the necessary files for the upcoming sections.

Importing assets into Unity can be done through three different methods. The first method is to drag the object being imported from a file explorer outside of Unity and drop it into the Project pane. The second option is to select Assets on the Menu bar followed by the Import New Asset option. The third method for getting assets into Unity is actually outside of Unity itself, simply move the files into the Assets directory of your project's folder and the next time you launch Unity with that project, the new assets will be imported. Make sure to get the CH4–Knight.zip file found on the companion website for this book. This file contains an FBX version of the knight character with animations as well as two texture maps, which we will use and a text file documenting the animation list as seen in Table 4.4. Once the file has been downloaded, begin by unzipping the file, on Windows this can be accomplished by right-clicking on the file and selecting Extract Here on a Mac you can double-click the zip file and drag the contents out into a new location. You will be prompted with a dialogue where you want the file to be extracted; the default location is wherever you have the file stored currently,

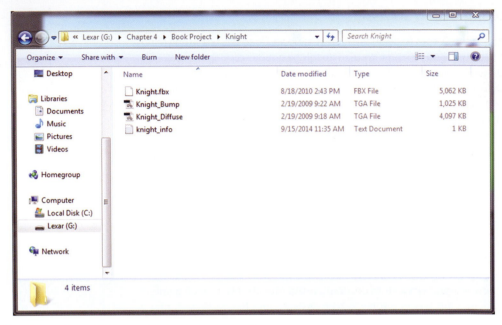

FIG 4.6 Folder view of the extracted contents from the "Knight.zip" archive file.

so that will work just fine. After waiting a few moments, the file should be extracted and we should have a directory structure similar to Figure 4.6. With the file extracted, we are ready to get the knight, Sancho Panza, into our game project, the steps are outline below.

1. Select the Assets folder within the Project pane.
2. Click the Create drop-down list and select Folder to create a new folder within the Assets folder of the project.
3. Change the name of the folder to Sancho.
4. Double-click the newly created Sancho folder so that the Project pane depicts the contents of that folder, as seen in Figure 4.7.
5. Now we will add all of the files from the uncompressed knight file into this folder, to complete this do any of the following:
   a. Select all four of the files from the "Knight.zip" file inside of your explorer window and drag them onto the open Sancho folder in the Project pane.
   b. Right-click in the open Sancho folder and select Import New Asset
      i. Browse to the location where the files are stored and select all of the files.
      ii. Click the Import button.
   c. Click Assets on the Menu bar and select Import New Asset from the drop-down list:
      i. Browse to the location where the files are stored and select all of the files.
      ii. Click the Import button.

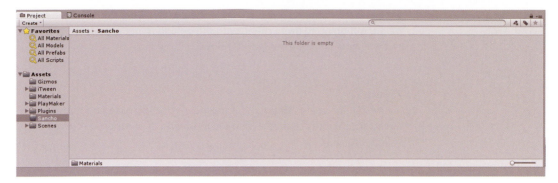

Note

Assets can also be imported into a project through the Asset store as was discussed in the previous chapter when importing the PlayMaker plugin originally. Remember, anything that is within a project is an asset.

The knight asset has now been imported into our Unity project, and the Sancho folder should now resemble the one depicted in Figure 4.8. Note that a new folder was created named Materials. Unity created a default material

FIG 4.8 New files have been created within the Sancho folder during the import process including children objects of the parent Knight object.

109

to be applied to our knight character and saved it within this Materials folder. We are not going to do anything with the default material that was created, as it will work fine for us, at least for now.

> **Note**
> When Unity creates Materials for meshes, it does so based upon the material that was created within the modeling application and saved within the FBX file.

> **Video**
> On the off chance that Unity incorrectly interprets the type of texture file that we are using when importing your assets, take a look at the "Fixing Textures" video on the companion website to correct this problem.

The other thing that we should notice is that the Knight object has a little triangle next to it. This is because the Knight object has several sub-objects or children that are attached to it and wherever it goes they go with it. We are going to go ahead and look at each of these children so that we understand what is within this particular asset. Different meshes, when imported, will contain different children depending on the construction of the actual object. If we click the triangle next to the Knight object, we can see that it will expand to reveal the contents depicted in Figure 4.8. The first two children, Knight and Pads, are the completed models for our character. The Knight model contains the bulk of the character, and the Pads contain the extra armor located at his elbows. If you select either one of these, you will see in the Inspector panel that this object contains the required Transform component as well as a Skinned Mesh Renderer and Material component. The Skinned Mesh Renderer component is used to assign a mesh, 3D object, to the Game Object, and the Material component will assign a Material.

The next two children of the Knight object are also called Knight and Pads. However, these two are the meshes themselves; these are the geometry that defines the shape of each of those objects. Clicking on either one of those will not reveal very much in the Inspector, because there is really nothing that we can do with these things other than assign them to Skinned Mesh Renderer components. Do notice, though, in the bottom of the Inspector pane, that we have a preview of these meshes as well as some information about them: vertex count, triangle count, and modifiers applied to the mesh (in this case, a UV modifier and a skin modifier).

Moving down to the last two children, the first one, C4D Animation Take, is the animation clip currently in the list of animations for this object. At the moment, this child contains all of the animation information that Sancho will need in order to animate within our game world. However, when we have finished with this section, all of the animation clips listed in

Table 4.4 will be displayed as children of the Knight object. The final child, KnightAvatar, is created by the Unity animation system and is something that we will be getting rid of shortly. The avatar objects that are created are used by the MechAnim animation system within Unity; we, however, will be using the Legacy animation system for this project. The MechAnim system is a wonderful tool for managing an object's animations within Unity, but not all objects are easily compatible with it and this Knight character is one such object.

> **Note**
> There will be many times during your indie and hobby game development projects that you will be using free or purchased assets from other sources. Those assets may or may not be compatible with Unity's MechAnim system.

4.7.3 Settings for Imported 3D Assets

Now that we have our character imported into Unity, we are ready to finalize some of the options and move on to bringing the character to life. Select the parent Knight object, the one with the triangle next to it, and we will begin with the Inspector properties for this object. There are three tabs: Model, Rig, and Animations. We will start with the easiest of these, the Rig tab. After selecting the Rig tab, we have a series of drop-down menus as depicted in Figure 4.9. If we click on the first drop down for Animation Type, we will be greeted with four different options. It is important that we be aware of these options as they define the type of animated object that Unity thinks this is. The first option is None that would be for any object that does not have any animations, such as a wall or maybe table. The next option is Legacy which we would use for any object that has animations with it but does not or cannot use the new MechAnim system of Unity. Our Sancho guy is going to be a Legacy Animation Type, so you can go ahead and select that. The last two options, Generic and Humanoid, are both for the MechAnim system which we will not be covering in this book, but those that are interested can find more information from the Unity manual on this topic at http://docs. unity3d.com/Manual/MecanimAnimationSystem.html. For now, however, select Legacy from the Animation Type drop down and click the apply button, the Knight character will re-import with those settings and notice that the KnightAvatar child object will be gone.

> **Note**
> Just because an object does not have any animations, does not mean that it cannot be moved around or interacted with within the game world by characters. In fact, we could build our own animations for objects directly within Unity using the Animation window.

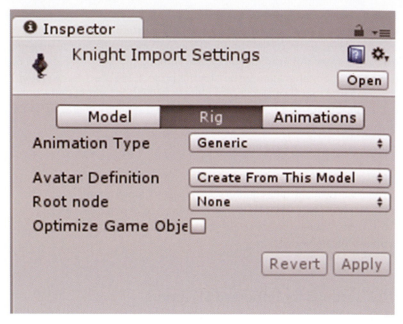

FIG 4.9 Rig options for a 3D asset imported to Unity.

For our next step of configuration, we are going to have to drop Sancho into the test world and get him sized up. Go ahead and place the Sancho character into the test scene and position him such that his feet are touching the ground object. In this particular scene, the only frame of reference that we have are the cubes that we had placed out in the world. We really do not know if Sancho is scaled to the correct size or not at this point in time. This is significant, because when dealing with an animated character or animated asset in general, we do not want to use the scaling tools to resize them as we did in the previous chapter. The scaling tool will work fine for any non-animated objects; however, if the object has built-in animations, then we run the risk of breaking the animations within them by scaling them up, or down for that matter. Therefore, to resize an animated object, we need to configure its Scale Factor within the Inspector pane. To access this feature, select the Knight parent object within the Project pane and switch the Inspector tab to the Model settings. Figure 4.10 displays some of the settings that are found within this tab. The first option is the Scale Factor for the model, we can modify this value to a different amount to alter how big or small it is within the scenes that it is involved in. By resizing through the scale factor, we resize all of the sub-components with it as opposed to scaling one part and not the others. Try experimenting with different scale factors by entering a new value and clicking the Apply button in the bottom right portion of the Inspector pane, it may be necessary to scroll down to see it.

While we can go ahead and scale Sancho to match the cubes in the scene or to match some other preconceived notion of how large or small the character should be, we will not really know if we have the right size or not. We have two approaches to solving this, either import some other meshes that we will be using for constructing the level later and set Sancho relative to them, or

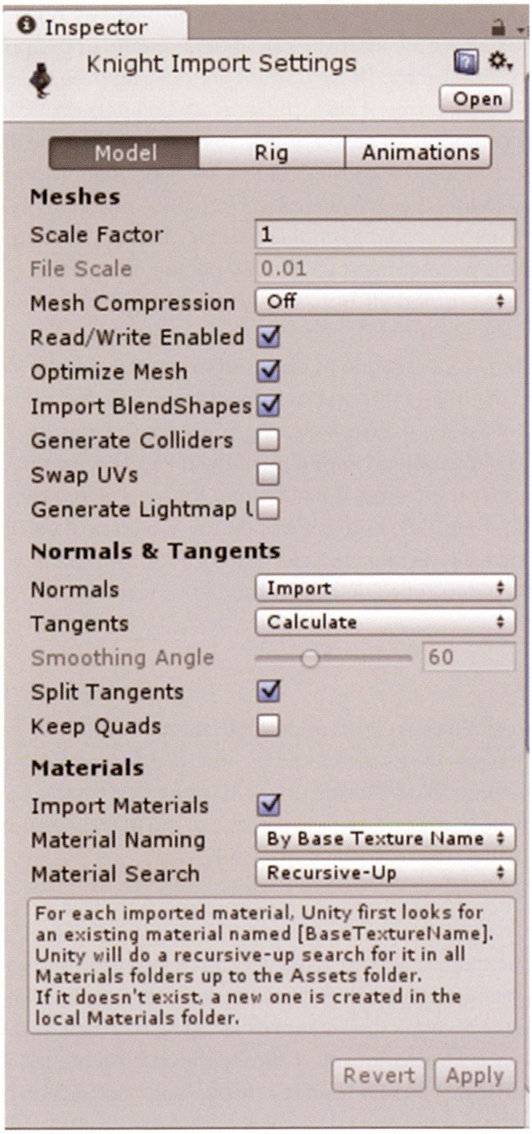

FIG 4.10 Settings available within the Model tab for a 3D imported asset.

we could, just leave Sancho alone for now and come back to scale him later once we have built a world for him to better interact with. At this time, we will take option number two and move on with the other features that we can adjust within the Model section.

Note
When using assets created by others, it is very rare that they will all scale together correctly, as we will encounter over the course of this project. This is OK as it can easily be adjusted through the Scale Factor of each object.

We have a fairly long list of options that are available to us; however, there are really only two that we are interested in understanding at this point in time, aside from the Scale Factor. These options are the Generate Colliders and Import Materials tick boxes. If we turn Generate Colliders on, Unity will apply a Mesh Collider component to the object. Remember from the discussion in the previous chapter that Mesh Colliders are expensive. Though they are quick and easy to use, they may cause performance problems as the project continues to grow and could definitely be a lazy habit for us to get formed early in our game development careers. By default, this option is turned off and we will keep it turned off. But, if we wanted to generate colliders for our meshes, we could turn this option on here. The primary advantage to doing that in the Model section as opposed to simply added a Mesh Collider component to the object through its Inspector Pane, is that we may have a large number of assets that we want to apply Mesh Colliders to. Therefore, we could select all of the objects within the Project Pane and within the Model tab for them turn on Generate Colliders, and they will all get Mesh Colliders constructed for them. One example use for this would be if we had a large number of concave type objects, cave entrances or overhangs, we could generate the colliders for all of them through this technique.

> **Note**
> While the Mesh Colliders are wonderful to use and can make some things much easier for us, we would be much better served, long term, to create custom colliders inside of our 3D application and apply them to the object instead, this way we could control the triangle count of these colliders, alas that is a topic for another day.

The other option that we want to take a very quick look at is the Import Materials option. As we mentioned earlier, Unity will import the materials that were created and applied to the object in the 3D application. Why, then, you may wonder, would anyone ever want to not automatically import the materials. There are a couple of reasons that you may want to turn this feature off, it is on by default. The first would be that the object did not actually have any Materials created for it in the other application; in which case, the material that will be created by Unity will be named Default and have a basic color applied to the diffuse channel, the albedo channel in the new physically based rendering system of Unity 5. The other is that the material created within the 3D application by whoever did it, was not named appropriately and when it gets imported we end up with a bunch of materials with random numbers in their names, something like Material #24. While we can go back and manually fix these material issues once they are brought in to Unity, if we are going to have to be doing a fair amount of tweaking to materials then it might be beneficial to us to just go ahead and not import them and create them manually within Unity.

The last section that we are going to look at and configure is the Animations tab for the Knight object. The full view of this tab can be seen in

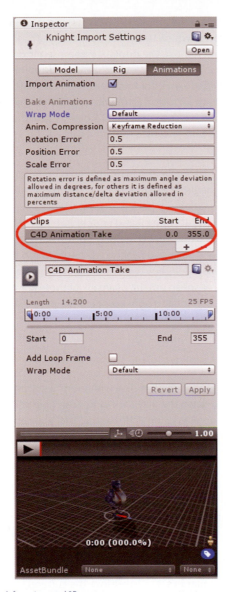

FIG 4.11 Animations tab for an imported 3D asset.

Figure 4.11. Before configuring our list of animations, take a moment to resize the Inspector pane a little bit, I would especially recommend resizing the animation preview pane that is at the bottom of the display so that you will be able to see Sancho moving better and detect any hiccups in the animations. All of the top default options in this section are fine to leave as they are, the Import Animation toggle would essentially turn this tabbed section on or off. We will come to the Wrap mode drop-down selection again in just a few moments when we start to break this animation into individual pieces. The other settings in the top portion deal with the compression for the animation. Compression is accomplished by removing redundant frames from the animation. This can be accomplished through Keyframe Reduction in which Unity will try to locate these frames that have very similar data and remove the duplicate frames, this default setting will work just fine for us. The error tolerance settings are values that we can adjust that Unity will use in order to determine if two keyframes are similar or not. For instance, the Position Error will look at two keyframes and if the difference in position is less than 0.5% (0.5 being the default value), Unity will consider those two keyframes to be the same as far as the compression system is concerned.

The portion that we are interested in modifying is in the clips section, which has been highlighted in Figure 4.11. By default, all of the animations that were in the animation clip have been imported as one sequence and we can see that it starts at Frame 0 and ends at frame 355. To preview this animation sequence, we can press the play button in the top left corner of the animation preview pane and Sancho will begin to run through all of these animations as though they were one clip, which essentially they are. We can slow down, or speed up, the playback of these animations by moving the time slider that is in the top right corner of the preview pane, the default setting is 1.00.

> **Note**
> When adjusting your animation clips within Unity, do not forget the option of slowing down the playback as this can help you to find hiccups and wrapping problems in the animation so that you can fix them by adjusting the start and/or ending frames for the sequence.

Before we begin setting up the animation sequences for Sancho Panza, we will look at the options that go with the process. Figure 4.12 provides a closer view of the Clips section that we are going to be working with. The clips section along the top, lists all of the clips that have been created and assigned to this particular object, currently there is one clip. To the bottom right of that section there is a "+" and "−" which will allow us to add a new clip to our animation set or to remove the currently selected clip from the animation list. Next down is the textbox that lists the name of the clip; by clicking within this textbox, we can enter a new name for the clip. The timeline that follows shows the length of the clip in seconds with two textboxes underneath it. The box to the left is the starting frame for the animation, and the ending frame is the box to the right. We can click within these boxes to enter whatever values we may want, but generally the values will come from an animation list like the one we looked at in Table 4.4. The Add Loop Frame toggle will have Unity create an extra frame at the end of the animation for looping purposes. This added keyframe would be the exact same as that at the start of the animation. The Wrap Mode drop down allows for the selection of the different types of looping that we can apply to the animation, a full discussion of these options is available in Table 4.5.

FIG 4.12 Clip creation and setting options.

Note

If you are unable to alter the start and end frame for an animation clip with an asset, there should be a button labeled "Clamp" directly underneath the timeline, click that button and you will now be able to alter those starting and ending frame numbers.

TABLE 4.5 Wrapping Modes Available to the Legacy Animation System

Wrap Mode	Purpose
Default	This setting will use the Wrap Mode that was set for the whole animation sequence at the top of the tab. It may be useful to set the default Wrap Mode to Loop if you know that most of your animations will need to loop.
Once	This will play the animation through one time and then stop, it is similar to Clamp Forever, however with Once, the animation has stopped playing.
Loop	When the last frame of the animation is reached, Unity will start back over at the first frame and keep playing the animation in a loop forever.
Ping-Pong	When the last frame of the animation is reached, Unity will play the animation backward back to the first frame of animation then turn around and play it forward again, continuing this process indefinitely.
Clamp Forever	When Unity reaches the last frame of the animation it will continue to play that last frame forever, in appearance this will look the same as Once, but Unity is playing an animation here, with Once it is not.

Now that we have an understanding of these options, we will go ahead and start chopping up the animation sequence into the clips that we need and get them ready to go for Sancho.

1. Review the animation listing found in Table 4.4.
2. Select the textbox that currently lists "C4D Animation Take" as the name of the animation.
3. Change the clips name to "idle" press the Enter key to set this new value.
4. Since this idle animation starts at Frame 0 we will leave the starting frame alone.
5. Select the textbox for the End Frame, currently it reads "355" change this value to "29."
6. Select the Wrap Mode drop-down list and use the Loop Wrap Mode so that while this animation is playing it will always loop it.
7. Click the "+" button to add a new clip to the animation list.
   a. Repeat from Step 2 using the names and values from the listing in Table 4.4.
8. Click the Apply button once all animations have been entered.

After following these steps, your Clips section should now match the depiction in Figure 4.13. As these animations were entered into the list, we needed to consider the Wrap Mode for each one. As it turns out, not all of the animations should Loop. Consider the animation name "die." We can imagine when this animation is going to be played; it will be when the character has been killed by something or someone. If we have this animation set to loop, then the character will fall over backward, dead, suddenly shoot back up to a standing position and fall over backward dead again. Rather, this animation should only play through with a Wrap Mode of Once or Clamp Forever. For our version, we have used once as the Wrap Mode for these, a full list of the Wrap Modes for each animation is found in Table 4.6.

Note

The wrap mode is one of the most overlooked animation settings. If your character's idle plays only once when the game starts, for instance, before debugging any scripts that you may have developed, take a look at the Wrap Mode setting for that clip and ensure that it is on Loop.

We now have all of the animation clips configured within our list of animations for Sancho Panza. In fact, if we select the Knight object from within the Hierarchy pane, the Knight that is in the scene, we will notice that he has an Animation component within the inspector and that if we click the triangle next to Animations, we will find the full list of animations that have been created and applied to this object (see Figure 4.14). This list of animations is an Array, an interesting method of storing information that we will return to later,

Clips	Start	End
idle	0.0	29.0
idle1	30.0	90.0
idle2	90.0	150.0
run-start	150.0	159.0
run	160.0	180.0
jump-all	185.0	231.0
jump-fly	190.0	210.0
jump-start-to-fly	185.0	210.0
bonk	235.0	264.0
boxing	265.0	285.0
solf hit	285.0	310.0
die	315.0	355.0

FIG 4.13 Clip list after the sequence has been cut based on the listing in Table 4.4.

TABLE 4.6 List of Wrap Modes for Each Animation

Animation Name	Wrap Mode
idle	Loop
idle1	Loop
idle2	Loop
run-start	Once
run	Loop
jump-all	Once
jump-fly	Once
jump-start-to-fly	Once
bonk	Once
boxing	Once
self-hit	Once
die	Once

that we can modify from here if we wanted to, though generally we do not want to alter it. The Play Automatically toggle means that the first animation in our list of animations will automatically play when this object is created in our game world, or not if we have the toggle turned off. For now, we will leave it turned on and start our game by pressing the Play button. We should see

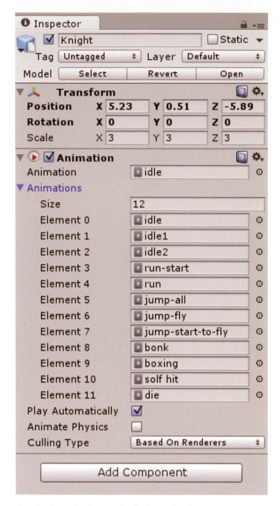

FIG 4.14 Inspector Pane for the Knight object within the Scene after the animation list has been created.

Sancho Panza standing in our game world with his shoulders rising and falling as he breathes the virtual air that surrounds him, idling his time away.

Note
While setting up your animation clips, take the time to watch looping animations play through their loops a couple of times before moving on. If the animation appears to jerk or sputter at the looping point, try adjusting the ending frame back or the starting frame up until you can get that transition to smooth out.

4.7.4 From 3D Assets to Player Controllable Assets

Sancho is out in our test world and appears to be quite happy with his new state of life. However, before he will be ready to become a controllable character, we need to add some things to the Game Object. The first of these components will be a Character Controller. This Unity component adds the functionality for us to be able to, well, control the character. We attach a Character Controller component, not script, to any Game Object that we want players to be able to control. It will provide some core elements for our character such as a collider; of course, we can still add more colliders to our character for other uses if we need to. The Character Controller is found in the Physics section of our components, so to add a Character Controller to Sancho: select the Add Component button followed by Physics and Character Controller. The new component has been added to our object as can be seen in Figure 4.15. The properties of this controller are going to give our character her base characteristics for movement, and Table 4.7 provides a breakdown of each of these properties. We will need to return to these settings and tweak them during testing as we progress, but for now adjust the height and radius of the controller such that Sancho fits nice and snugly within it.

During this process, it will also be necessary to move the Y value of the center property up some so that the center of the controller is not on the ground between Sancho's feet. For our version, we have set some initial values of: Center Y = 0.27, Radius = 0.2, Height = 0.55. It is nearly guaranteed that we will need to adjust these values later, but we need to start somewhere.

Our next change will be a very subtle one, but vital nonetheless. Currently, Sancho automatically plays an animation when the game starts; we need to turn that off so that the controller system that we build will be entirely in charge of any animations that are played, including the starting animation.

FIG 4.15 Character Controller component added to our Sancho character.

TABLE 4.7 Properties of the Character Controller Component

Property Name	Use of Property
Slope Limit	Character will only be able to move along sloped surfaces that have a slope angle less than this value.
Step Offset	When encountering stairs, character will only move up the stair if the height of the stair's step is less than this value.
Skin Width	Determine the thickness of the collider part of the controller. A low value could mean that the player can "see through" any walls that they collide with. Definitely a property to tweak if odd collision behavior occurs.
Minimum Move Distance	In order for the character to move within the scene, the player must be trying to move it further than this value.
Center	This is the center position of the collider part of the controller.
Radius	How wide the collider part of the controller is.
Height	How tall the collider part of the controller is.

In the Animation component, click the tick box for Play Automatically to turn that functionality off. While this was not entirely necessary, it will be encouraging for us as we implement our controller to see Sancho animate and know that he is doing so as a result of our state machine.

The final change we would like to make to our character is to go ahead and change the tag from "Untagged" to "Player." Player is one of the default tags that can be used and applied, and we can select it from the Tag drop-down menu directly beneath the name of the Game Object in the Inspector panel. Using tags is very important for processing and responding to any collision events between Game Objects. Sancho is now ready to become a playable character.

4.8 Character Control Systems with PlayMaker

Once the character asset has been imported into Unity and the animations have been configured the way that we want, we are ready to bring the character to life. We are going to split this section into three distinct parts that will be needed for this process. To provide life to a player controlled character, we will first need to determine exactly what we want the player to be able to do. By this we mean, what controls will the player have and how do we ultimately want the character to respond to these controls. It is possible to have a couple of ideas that we do not implement just yet, such as having the character die as other pieces will need to be in place in order for that to function correctly. But at this stage, we should definitely know the basic functionality that is going to be provided which we should be able to derive from our previous work in designing the character. Once we know what it is that we want to get from the player, for instance maybe the "W" key on the keyboard will move the character forward; then we just need to understand how to get that information from the player. Specifically, how will Unity know when the player has done such and such. Our final step, after grabbing the input from the player, will be to assign the actual functionality to the character, which we will do through some state machines created within PlayMaker.

Download

The final project package with the imported and configured *Sancho Panza* asset can be obtained from the companion website and found in the scene: "Chapter4_part2." Remember, this is a Unity package file to import and will require that PlayMaker is already imported into your project.

4.8.1 Designing the Character Response System

Since we are building a third-person, platformer-style, action–adventure game, we have an idea of the controls and functionality that we want to assign to our player character, Sancho Panza, based upon what is expected within this genre. Essentially, we want the character to be able to perform the following actions:

- Move forward and backward by walking and/or running
- Turn or rotate left and right
- Jump
- Attack bad things to defend itself
- Be hurt by bad things that might attack it
- Die after it has gotten hurt too much
- Pick up and collect items found within the game world

That is a good list for getting started and after having that basic functionality in place we can always add more later if we need to for some reason. Now that we have the basic actions figured out, we need to tie these character actions into some kind of event that occurs within the game world. Remember from our previous chapter that an event also means a transition within a state machine and that an action is something performed while in a specific state. Hopefully, you can already begin to picture how we are going to be able to construct an elemental state machine based on the events that we want associated with the actions that we want. We will now add some events to the list of actions that we have already formulated above, keep in mind that at this point we are still keeping our actions fairly generic; we will break them down into more detail in the next step. We also are not concerned with how to get the computer to do what we want; we are just trying to formulate what it is that we will want to happen. For now, we are going to follow typical control structures for third-person or first-person action-type games on the PC.

- Player presses the "W" key on the keyboard
  - Sancho will move forward
- Player presses the "S" key on the keyboard
  - Sancho will move backward
- Player moves the mouse to the right
  - Sancho will rotate or turn to the right
- Player moves the mouse to the left
  - Sancho will rotate or turn to the left
- Player presses the space bar
  - Sancho will jump
- Player presses the left mouse button
  - Sancho will do a primary attack
- Player presses right mouse button
  - Sancho will do a secondary attack
- Player does not avoid some bad thing in the game world
  - Sancho gets hurt
- Player lets Sancho's health get to 0
  - Sancho will die
- Player moves Sancho over a collectible item
  - Sancho will collect the item

Note
Any action that the player character is going to be able to perform should have some animation associated with it so that the player can see the character doing the action. There are exceptions to this, but this is a solid general rule to follow. This rule, taken to its conclusion, means that if we do not have a suitable animation, then the character should not do it.

While the list of activities that we want Sancho to be able to perform may not appear to be that much, it will be more than enough to keep us busy for the next few minutes or longer. Notice that some of these events really do not have anything to do with the player directly, specifically, when Sancho gets hurt, dies, or collects something. Sure, they are a consequence of the player's actions or inactions, but more importantly they are the direct result of events occurring within the game world specifically. For instance, in order to collect something, there has to be something in the game world to collect and Sancho has to run up to it. We are currently only working on the player controller mechanics of Sancho Panza, so some of what we have in our state machine list can be dropped for a later topic, such as after we add some objects into the game world. Another thing to consider on this is that until Sancho can move around, we do not need to worry about whether he can collect things or not.

Note

Always take things slowly and one step at a time. Build up any behaviors that are being created from the ground up, do not try to build everything in one go, add pieces to your state machines little by little and test them to make sure they work as expected. This approach breaks the problem down into smaller problems which are easier to solve and troubleshoot.

We have one more state machine list to build. This last list is going to dive into the details of what Sancho is doing with more specifics. By this we mean that we are going to break Sancho's generic actions down into individual and more specific actions. Do not worry about what the proper PlayMaker actions are or how to do this in Unity. Our first step is always to make sure that we understand what it is that we want to happen, make sure that we can explain what we want step by step in plain English before we ever try to convince the computer to do anything. If we do not fully understand what we want, then it is going to be very difficult to create a state machine that will work correctly. So, our next state machine list, will break these actions out a little bit and will also drop the actions that we are not worried about just yet, instead we will focus solely on the direct input events from the player and the responsive actions of Sancho.

- Player presses the "W" key on the keyboard
  - Sancho will move forward
  - Play a walk/run animation (run)
  - Have the camera follow the character
- Player presses the "S" key on the keyboard
  - Sancho will move backward
  - Play a backward walk/run animation (run)
  - Have the camera follow
- Player moves the mouse to the right
  - Sancho will rotate or turn to the right
  - Spin the camera to keep perspective
- Player moves the mouse to the left
  - Sancho will rotate or turn to the left
  - Spin the camera to keep proper view
- Player presses the space bar
  - Sancho will move vertically up in the air
  - If Sancho is moving forward/backward that motion will continue as well
  - Play an animation for jumping (jump-start-to-fly)
  - Camera follows Sancho
- Player presses the left mouse button
  - Sancho will continue whatever motion he is doing
  - Sancho will play primary attack animation (boxing)
- Player presses right mouse button
  - Sancho will continue his current motion
  - Sancho will play secondary attack animation (bonk)

4.8.2 Getting Input through Unity

There are two different methods for getting input from the player. The first is to put the specific key and button presses that we are looking for directly into the state machines that we create for the character controller. This seems like a reasonable approach, however, if we later decide that we want to change those keys and buttons to something else, we will have to come into our state machines and change all of them to the new buttons. Another thing to consider with this approach is that if we were to add secondary control mechanisms, for instance, the left thumb stick of a game controller for forward and backward motion, we will have to add those input sources into our state machines. Unity, however, provides a better mechanism by which we can grab the input from the user, this is called the Input Manager, and it is a wonderful tool for abstracting our state machines from the actual buttons and keys that the user presses.

To access the Input Manager, click Edit from the Menu Bar and scroll down to Project Settings then select Input from the pop-out choices. At first, it may appear as though nothing has happened; however, if we look at the Inspector pane, we will notice that it has changed to display the properties of the currently selected object, in this case the Input Manager. Click the triangle to the left of Axes to open up the default input configuration. Notice that the first item is Size and is set to a value of 18. The size indicates how many inputs we are allowing or using within our project. By entering a higher number, we can add more inputs to our project and the new ones added will be duplicates of the final item in the list, in this case Cancel. Lowering the value will remove current input axes from the list dropping the list down to the value specified. We are going to leave ours set at the default value of 18.

There are two major types of inputs that the Input Manager can track for us. The first is axis movement, such as that of the mouse or game controller thumb stick. Buttons and keys can also be assigned to the axis movement as we will be doing with the "W" and "S" keys for our forward and backward motion. The other type of input is a button press or click. The difference between these two is that the buttons can either be pressed or not pressed, those are the only values that we can get from a button. Axis movement, on the other hand, can have a range of values from not pressed to fully pressed in one direction. Consider an example of a typical first-person shooter on a console, your character will move faster or slower depending on the amount of pressure that you apply to the thumb stick governing the character's movement, Unity can measure this pressure through the axis input system. Within the Input Manager itself, there is no difference between these two types; the difference will be in how we grab the inputs within our state machines.

4.8.3 Building State Machines in PlayMaker

Notice that the process of getting our character control system did not begin with PlayMaker. As we stressed previously, it is vitally important to make sure that we have a clear understanding of what it is we want the computer to do way before we ever try to tell the computer to do it. When creating our initial state machine, do not worry about what the specific action or event will be for a specific state or transition. We can figure those out later, and as we will discover many times, the actual action is very similar to the plain English that we had used to describe it. In fact, after doing some work within Unity, you will find that your plain English state machines will begin to incorporate the actual actions to be used; the differences will be in the values of the properties for the actions, as we may not recall those off of the top of our head. Doing this, having a state machine with partially correct actions in it, is developing with pseudo code. That means, we are creating a state machine that is very similar to the one we will actually build within PlayMaker. It is close enough, actually, that we will not have to do too much work to it when we do get inside of PlayMaker, this will come with practice and time.

4.8.3.1 Moving Sancho

With our design work out of the way, we are ready to get our character doing what it should. It is at this point that one may wonder why we do not just use the built-in third-person character controller system that comes with Unity and that we noticed in the last chapter when we looked at the Standard Asset packages that are available. The reason that we will not be starting with that asset is twofold. The first being that the controller is controlled by C# scripts. In order for us to be able to make any changes or tweaks or additions to it, we would have to understand C# scripting which we currently do not. This leads us to the second issue. A common mistake made when learning game development is to go grab someone else's work under the idea that we can make modifications to it and through those modifications learn how to make a game. While in theory this sounds very reasonable, in practice the reality is that in order to make modifications to the work of others, we need to understand what it is that they did and built. If we do understand how they built their game, then we are not at the starting point of learning to make games, we are at a point of already knowing how to make games. This, essentially, is a situation of the chicken and the egg, in order to modify someone else's developed code we need to know how to write and read code in which case we could have written the code ourselves and are not as reliant on others developing code for us to modify. So, we will be creating a character controller system from the ground up and learn how to create our own stuff.

It is now time to open the PlayMaker editor window by selecting PlayMaker and PlayMaker Editor from the Toolbar. Before we add a state machine to anything, make sure that the knight object is selected within the Hierarchy panel and not the Project panel. Now we can go ahead and right-click within the PlayMaker Editor window to add a finite state machine (FSM) to our knight Game Object. Select the FSM tab along the top of the Properties pane of this FSM and provide a description for it as well as changing the name to something more meaningful. This may seem like a silly thing to do, but getting into the habit early of naming things descriptively and then providing comments explaining what they are will pay huge dividends for us later. We will name this particular FSM "Movement" as seen in Figure 4.16.

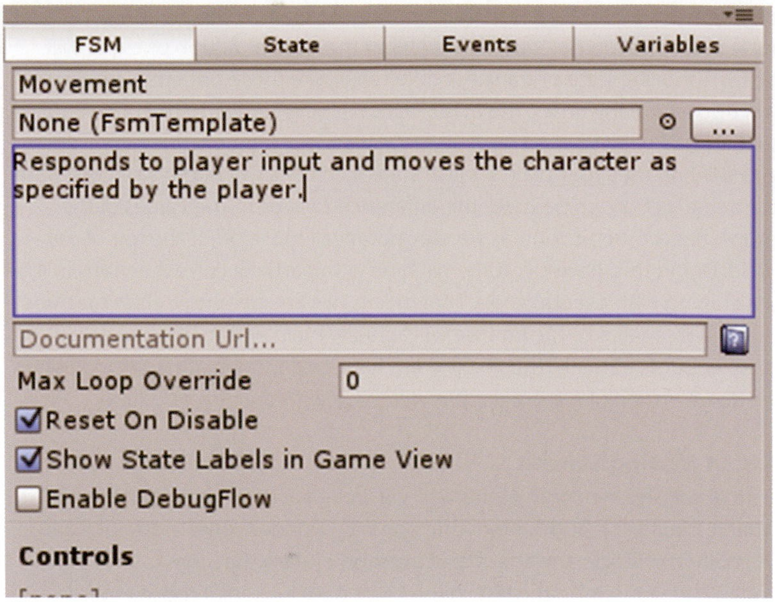

FIG 4.16 A renamed and described state machine.

We now return to the State tab to rename any states we add to this machine and to add actions to them as well. Returning to our descriptive state machine we developed earlier, we can see that as far as movement is considered, our character can move forward and backward. Turning is not really movement in that same sense. Just as we broke our steps down to be able to create a well-defined list of actions, we also need to look at our state machine list and decide if we have more than one state machine or not. As it turns out, we actually have several within this controller that we are constructing. We will need state machines that will govern: movement, turning, actions (left and right mouse buttons), and probably something else to handle him getting hurt and dying eventually. Try to make your state machines responsible for certain things, not necessarily responsible for everything. With that said, if we were building a controller for *Pac-Man*, we would not want different machines for the vertical and horizontal movement. All of the movement can be put into one machine. As we start making state machines, it will be difficult to immediately recognize when we should move to a new machine or not, however, as you work on your projects, if you reach a point where your transitions are becoming a tangled mass of spaghetti because all of the states can go to all of the other states, you may want to consider finding a logical separation and moving some stuff to another state machine.

Back to movement. So, our character can do two things in this machine, he can move forward and he can move backward. But there is also a third thing that we did not even consider when we built our state machine list earlier. This third thing is that Sancho cannot move at all; he can actually just stand there and idle away his time in the world. We now have three states for this machine. We are going to go ahead and build our first state, which will be the idle state. Inside of this state, Sancho will not move, but he will play one of his idle animations; in fact, we will allow him to randomly select one of them to do then he will just stand there and do it. Begin by changing the state name to Idle then add the "Play Random Animation" action to this state. A couple of new properties here with this state which we have described in Table 4.8. Go ahead and configure this action as depicted in Figure 4.17. In order to select which animation we want to play, just use the arrow icon button to the right of the text box for the animation name.

TABLE 4.8 Properties for the Play Random Animation Action

Property Name	Use of Property
Animations	List of animations that can be selected. This value should be set to the total number of animations that are available. Once that is done, specify each animation by name, from the drop-down list, and also provide a relative weight for how often it will be selected.
Play Mode	Once we start playing an animation, what should we do with any others that were playing, generally we will want to stop all other animations that were playing.
Blend Time	How long will the system spend blending the old animation with the new animation during the transition between the two.
Finish Event	What event should be fired when we finish playing an animation.
Loop Event	What event should be fired when we begin looping an animation.
Stop On Exit	When we do exit this state, should we stop playing our animations.

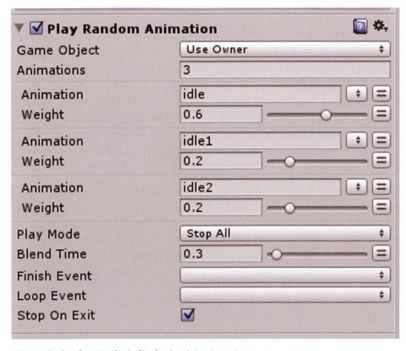

FIG 4.17 Final configuration for the Play Random Animation action.

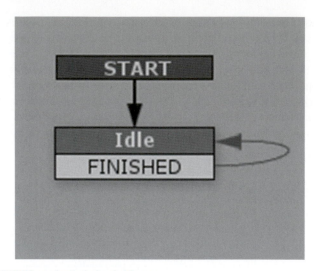

FIG 4.18 FINISHED event looping back to the Idle state.

At this point, we could go ahead and test this, but before we do, let's go ahead and get these idle animations to toggle back and forth from time to time. Currently, this animation system will randomly pick one of those three animations to play when we enter this state. But once we are within this state, it will keep playing whatever animation it was that it had randomly selected. So, what we need to do is to exit this state whenever the animations end or loop and restart the state. We can do this by adding a default FINISHED event to the Idle state. Right-click on the Idle state within the Editor view port. From the pop-out menu, select Transition Event and FINISHED. Finally, left-click on this newly added FINISHED event and drag it up to Idle, such that the arrow loops back on its own state as depicted in Figure 4.18. With our looping structure in place, go ahead and add the FINISHED event from the drop down for both the Finish Event and Loop Event properties. A quick play test of this reveals that Sancho stands there and every now and then plays a different idle animation. We could get fancy at some point and have the hand wave play when he turns to look at the camera (the player) and waves at them, but that is not a first run through on this controller system. We will save that for some tweaking later.

Sancho is now ready to actually run around and respond to the input from the player. The first step is to create some custom events. From the Events tab, we will enter the names of our new events in the Add Event text box (Figure 4.19). Currently, we are going to add two events, Forward and Backward. With the events created go ahead and add these new transitions to the Idle state. Once we add these new transitions, there will be a red exclamation point on the state. This lets us know that the state contains transition Events that do not actually transition anywhere. It will go away as we build the rest of the state machine.

We will now add a new state to our machine and name this new state Move Forward. Connect the Forward transition event from the Idle state to the

FIG 4.19 The Add Event textbox.

newly created Move Forward state. Go ahead and repeat this for the Move Backward state as well so that we no longer have any errors in our state machine. What we need to do next is to add an action to our Idle state that will be listening for any input from the Player that Unity will send us from the Input Manager and properly respond to it.

1. Select the Idle state
   a. From the Action Browser find the Axis Event action and add it
   b. Remove the Horizontal axis name, our movement is only forward/ backward and we will use the Vertical axis for determining that. Horizontal axis will be used later for rotation.
   c. From the drop-down menu for Up Event select Forward
   d. From the drop-down menu for the Down Event select Backward

Our Idle state is now responding to the input that is being passed to it, but our Forward and Backward states are not actually doing anything. It turns out that both of these states are very similar, so, if we build one of them and get it working, we should be able to just copy the actions over to the other state and with a few minor fixes have it working as well. As a result, we will focus on our Move Forward state and get it working first. There are a few things that we are going to have to do within this state, as we mentioned in our State Machine list from earlier. Sancho is going to have to move forward, play an animation, have the camera follow him, and we now also realize that Sancho is going to have to recognize when the player no longer wants to move forward and return to the Idle state. We will run through these steps real quick and then come back and take a closer look at the new pieces that we are using. Figure 4.20 displays the final version of the Actions within the Move Forward state.

1. Create a new event called Stop
2. Add this new event to the Move Forward state
3. Connect the Stop transition event to the Idle state
4. In the variables tab add a new variable called moveDirection
   a. Select Vector3 for the Variable Type
5. Add another variable called moveSpeed
   a. Select Float for the Variable Type
6. In the State tab find the Get Axis Vector action and add it
   a. Delete the word Horizontal from the Horizontal Axis text box
   b. For the red Store Vector drop down select the newly created moveDirection
   c. For the Store Magnitude drop down select the newly created moveSpeed
7. Find the Controller Simple Move action and add it
   a. Make sure that it is listed below Get Axis Vector, move it down if needed
   b. For Move Vector select moveDirection
   c. For Speed select the box with two lines in it to the right
      i. Now select moveSpeed from the drop down
   d. Change Space from World to Self (this will be important later)
8. Add an Axis Event action
   a. Delete the Horizontal axis
   b. For No Direction select the Stop event from the drop-down list
9. Add a Play Animation action
   a. Select run from the drop-down list of available animations

Go ahead and save everything and move Sancho away from the boxes. Play the game and see what happens, Sancho may be off the screen, in which case reposition your camera so that you can see Sancho and try pressing the Up button. The default Up axis in the Input Manager is "W" or the Up arrow key. It will also work with Up on the left thumb stick of a game controller if you have one connected. This should be very encouraging at this point, so let's see if we can get the back movement working also then take a look at what it is that we did for all of this. Go ahead and stop the game for now. Left-click on the first action in the

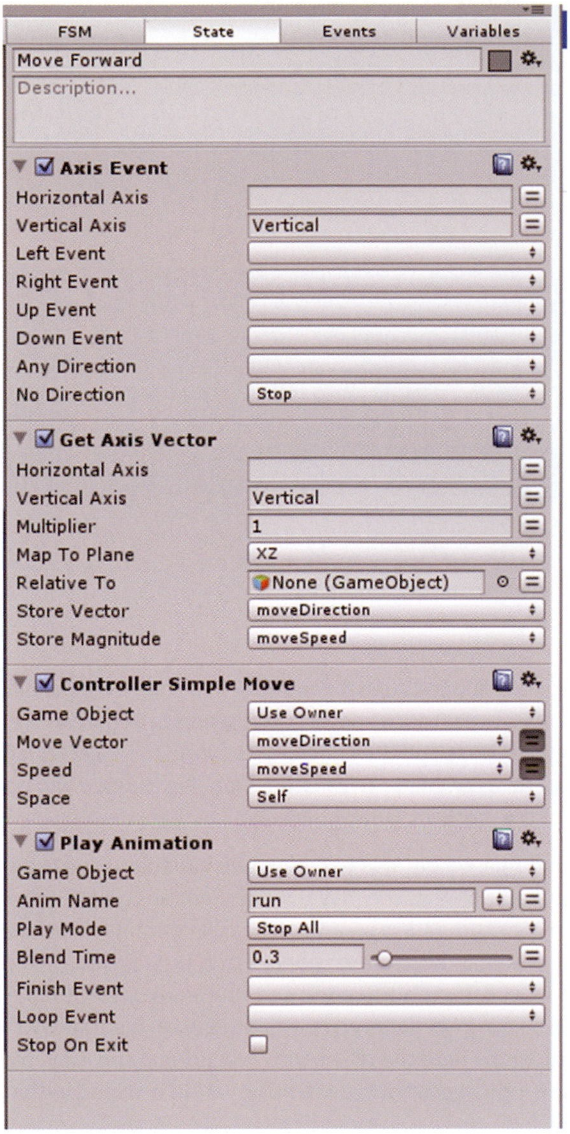

FIG 4.20 FINISHED Move Forward state.

Move Forward state and while holding down the Shift key, individually click all of the other actions as well. To copy the selected actions, click the gear icon by any of the actions or in the top right of the state itself (see Figure 4.21). After clicking on one of the gears, choose Copy Selected Actions. Now select the Move Backward state, press the gear inside of it and select Paste Actions. To finish up the Move Backward state, we will need to add the Stop Event and connect it to the Idle state. Now for some more testing, but before we do that, rotate Sancho in your scene slightly so that you can see him better from the camera angle that we currently have.

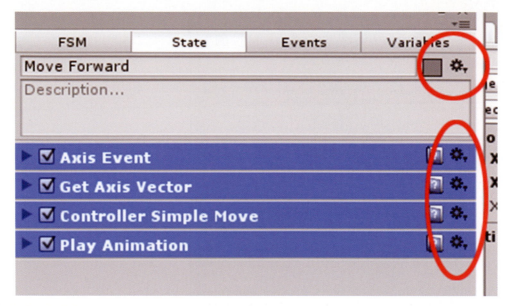

FIG 4.21 Gear selection icon.

With Sancho repositioned so that you can see him better, go ahead and test your scene. Make sure that he moves forward and backward as we would expect him to, if you fall off the edge of your world then just restart the scene. Except for a few minor tweaks, he is moving forward and backward very nicely at the moment. Now, what was all of that stuff that we just did?

The first thing that we did was to create two variables. One is being used to store the direction that the player wants Sancho to go. This type of information is considered to be a Vector3 as it contains three pieces of information within a three-dimensional world (x, y, z). Table 4.9 contains a list of the most commonly needed and therefore used variable types, these are also known as data types. The other variable that we created was a float to store how hard the player was pressing on the movement key, and the table indicates what type of information is stored within this data type as well.

The next thing that we did was to add a Get Axis Vector action. What this action does is to grab the value of a specific axis and assign it to a variable of your choice. What we are doing here is to use this to determine which direction the player wants to go. When the player presses the Up key, the axis vector value for that input is (0, 0, 1). The first two 0's are for the X and Y values, they are 0 because the player is not pressing any of those keys. However, the Z is 1 because the player is pressing the Up key, which is on that axis. If, however, the player were to press the Down key, the corresponding vector would be (0, 0, −1). More importantly for us, though, is that we don't actually have to know what those values are, all we need to know is that the player pressed Up or Down and that there is a direction associated with that. Let the computer take care of the number side of things. We are storing

TABLE 4.9 Commonly Used Data Types in Unity

Data Type	Use
Int	An integer value, a whole number. 0, 1, 2, 3, 4, etc.
Float	A decimal value, a real number. 0.0, 0.1, 0.2, 0.3, 0.4, etc.
Bool	Stores only two values, true or false.
String	Any collection of letters and numbers, or any collection of numbers that would never be used for math, such as a phone number.
Game Object	One of those things that is out in our game world, everything in the game world is a Game Object.
Vector3	Anything that is comprised of three components. Must be float components. Examples would include position or scale.
Object	Capable of storing any of the object types that exist within Unity, such as colliders, controllers, scripts, etc.

the directional vector in our variable we created for that purpose and also the magnitude of how hard the player is pressing in the direction. On the keyboard this will generally be 0 or 1, it does have two brief stops in between but they are not all that important to us. On a game controller though, this value will represent how much pressure is being applied in that direction on the thumb stick, therefore allowing us to have the character sneak if that is what the player is wanting to do and we are prepared for that.

After grabbing the input from the user, we used those values within a Controller Simple Move action to get our character going. Most of these are self-explanatory, except for the one that we changed and said it would be important later. The Space property defines which orientation the action will use to move along. Consider the image in Figure 4.22, the knight in this case is oriented differently than is the orange cube, check out the movement gizmos. So, by selecting Self we are making sure that Forward, means Forward as far as Sancho is concerned, not necessarily how the rest of the world views it. To see this better, switch the value from Self to World and test it, see how the behavior is different? This will be vitally important once we get Sancho rotating.

The last two actions that we added can be glossed over as they are the same ones that we used in the Idle state, Play Animation and Axis Event. Granted, in the Idle state, we used Play Random Animation, but as can be seen the only difference between the two is the list of animations. Instead of looking at them in more detail, we will go ahead and tweak our controller a little bit. Hopefully you noticed that while Sancho was running backward it looked really weird. That is because the animation that we are playing is actually for a forward movement not a backward movement. To fix this, we are going to get our run animation to play backward instead of forward. Inside of the Move Backward state add a Set Animation Speed action and position it right before the Play Animation action. We will now change the Anim Name to run

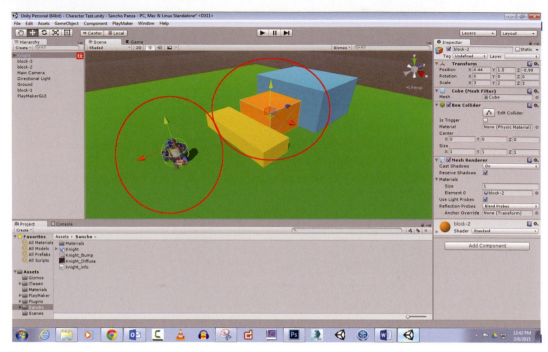

FIG 4.22 Two objects selected in the Scene—notice how their local axes are not the same.

and the Speed to be −1. Now test out the forward and backward movement and see what you think of that. Well that was fine, but if you keep testing, you will notice that if you go from backward to forward, the run continues to play backward, to fix this just repeat what we did inside of the Move Forward state except use a value of 1 for the Speed. Now, that is very nice.

We will do one more tweak to our movement and then go on to rotating Sancho around. He seems to move just a little too slowly for the animation. What we are going to do is create a variable that we can modify within the Inspector so we can change his movement speed, while the game is running and test out a nice feeling value.

> 1. In the Variables tab create a new variable called runSpeed.
>   a. Give it a variable type of Float.
>   b. Select the tick box for Inspector so that this will be visible in the Inspector. This is also known as a Public variable.
>   c. Give this a default value of 1 in Float Value.
> 2. In the state tab, use runSpeed for the Speed value of the Controller Simple Move.
> 3. Change the Speed value of the Controller Simple Move in the Move Backward state as well.

With these changes made, when we return to the scene notice that the runSpeed variable is now visible inside the Inspector panel for the knight object (Figure 4.23). Now, we can enter a new value right here in the

FIG 4.23 Newly created public variable runSpeed.

Inspector instead of going back into the state machine, in fact we can enter a new value, while the game is running to find a speed that looks and feels right. After some testing, we settled on a runSpeed value of 2. Notice, however, that what we have done is to also ignore the amount of pressure that the player is applying to the movement. Once again, in the case of the keyboard input, this makes no difference; however, in the case of a game controller or other input device, it will make a difference and we have essentially removed the player's ability to sneak around. For this particular project, we are not worried about the player sneaking around the game world as that is not a primary game feature or mechanic.

4.8.3.2 Rotating Sancho

It is now time to get Sancho rotating around so that he can see his world better. Now, it is at this point that we can consider the fact that he should be able to rotate from any of the states that he is currently in within the Movement state machine. However, how would we know which state to return to? It turns out that we could store the state we came from and do it that way, but it would be a whole lot easier if we just created a separate state machine for his rotation. This is a pretty key idea here, we can have multiple state machines within a Game Object and all of these state machines will work together. To create a new state machine for our knight character, select the drop-down menu where it lists Movement and instead choose Add FSM to Knight (Figure 4.24). We have gone ahead and created this new machine named Rotate and added the essential structure to it as depicted in Figure 4.25. As can be seen, we added two new states, created three new events, and connected all of them in what seemed a reasonable fashion. We are utilizing the exact same principles as we did with the movement, however, instead of moving forward or backward we are now rotating left or right.

Note
Each Game Object can have more than one state machine attached to it.

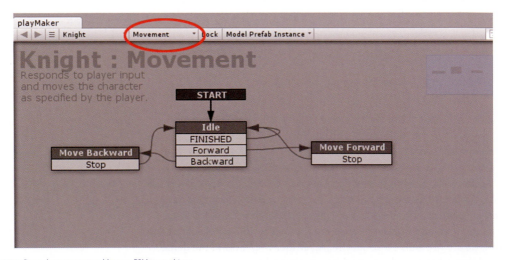

FIG 4.24 Drop-down menu to add a new FSM to an object.

138

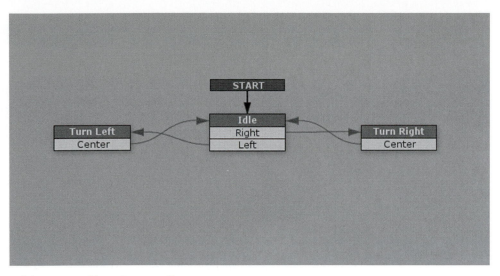

FIG 4.25 Skeleton structure of the rotation state machine.

Using what we just learned with the movement machine that we constructed this rotation should not be too terribly difficult. We have a couple of things to recognize about it. First, this machine does not play any animations; hence, it will not interfere with any animations that the Movement machine may be playing. Next is that Sancho will not actually be moving anywhere this time just turning, once again also not interfering with the actions of the Movement machine. We will begin by constructing our transitions, which will be based upon the Axis Event actions that we have already used. Inside of Idle, the axis event will respond to Horizontal with Left Event going to Left and Right Event going to Right. Inside of both turning states we will respond to the Horizontal axis with a Center transition event returning us to center. It is important to make sure that in both of our turn states, we are only responding to when the Horizontal axis has no direction, make sure to remove the Vertical axis from the list. Now, we just need to add an action to turn Sancho, this action is called Rotate (see Figure 4.26).

The first thing that we need to figure out is which axis we want Sancho to rotate around. In order to manually enter a value for the Angle around an axis, click the darkened icon with the double lines in it and the drop-down selection box will become a text box we can enter a value into. We want Sancho to rotate around the Y axis in his Self-Space. We also want to make sure that he does this rotation Every Frame. What we are saying here is that each frame, each time the screen is refreshed, if the player is holding down a rotation key, then go ahead and rotate Sancho a certain angle, we are using an angle of 2 for the initial test. Duplicate the Rotate action in the Turn Left state and see if Sancho can now turn and move. In your test, did Sancho turn the same direction regardless of which key you were pressing? Any ideas why this may have been so? This behavior was caused by our rotation command, they are both rotating by the same angle, change one of them to a negative 2 to turn in the other direction. We will leave it to you to find out which one should be positive and which should be negative. Remember, you can also

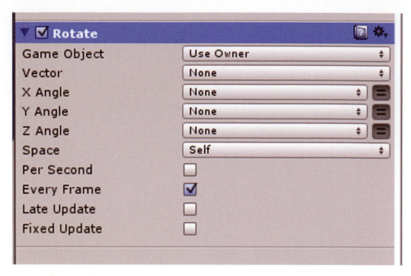

FIG 4.26 Rotate action.

try something and test it to see if it works the way you want it to or not, this iterative development with unit testing is very important and beneficial to us as developers.

4.8.3.3 Jumping Sancho

Download

To get the character motor script referenced in the next section, find the "CharacterMotor" Javascript file in the Chapter Resources section of the companion website and import the script into your project.

Our list of required things from our State Machine List is getting smaller and smaller, and Sancho is getter ever closer to being an interesting and fun little character to move around. We are down to the jumping capability of Sancho, leaving the attacking actions as an exercise at the end of this chapter. As of the writing of this book, the default controller systems within Unity have changed to such an extent that in order to get a character to jump we are going to have to utilize a script from the old version of the character controller system (Unity 4). We have provided a copy of this script for you to download from the companion website. The generic approach to getting Sancho to jump is going to utilize the following sequence of steps:

- Player presses the Space bar to start jump.
  - Sancho will play his jump start animation.
  - Sancho will play his jump fly animation and start moving.
  - Sancho will stop at the last frame of his jump fly animation and keep moving until hitting the ground.

> **Note**
> The character motor script that we are using is needed in order to have the character jump with PlayMaker. PlayMaker is a very powerful visual script editing and developing tool; however, it does have limitations and as of the writing of this book, there is no other way to get a character to jump in Unity 5 with PlayMaker other than to utilize this older script. Incidentally, this is the way that we made characters jump with PlayMaker prior to the release of Unity 5.

This seems fairly straightforward to implement, we will have an On Ground state that will be waiting for the Spacebar to be pressed. When the Spacebar is pressed, there will be a transition event to another state that will play the jump start animation. Once that has finished, we will transition to another state that will play the jump fly animation while getting Sancho to actually start moving. Once that has finished, we will transition to our final state that will keep Sancho moving and exit back to the Idle state when Sancho has hit the ground again. This basic flow of this structure can be seen in the completed FSM in Figure 4.27. Notice how we were able to construct this basic diagram out of the plain English state machine list that we developed fairly easily.

1. Create a new FSM and name it Jump.
   a. In the Variables tab create a new variable of type Bool named isGrounded.
   b. Within the Events tab create two new events one named "landed" and the other "start."
   c. Create a new state named On Ground.
      i. Add the transition event "start."
   d. Create a new state named Start Animation.
      i. Add the FINISHED transition event.
   e. Create a new state named Fly.
      i. Add the "landed" transition event.
   f. Create a new state named Reset.
      i. Add the FINISHED transition event.
   g. Connect the transitions and states as shown in Figure 4.27.
   h. Select the On Ground state.
      i. Add a Get Button Down action to this state.
         A. Button Name should be Jump.
         B. Send Event should be start.

Before we go too much further, let's pause for a moment and make sure we are clear with what has happened thus far. We have created a Boolean variable that we are going to use later to know if Sancho is on the ground

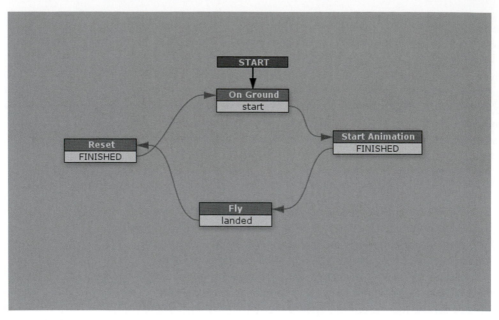

FIG 4.27 A completed FSM to control Sancho jumping.

or not, we will get this information from the characterMotor script that we just imported into our project. The two events that we created will be utilized by the states as we have connected them. The Get Button Down action is similar to the Get Axis action except that there is no positive and negative values, there is simply a Boolean whether the button has been pressed or not and if so then the specified event is fired by the action. For our next step, we are going to need to pull the characterMotor script into our FSM. This can be a bit confusing so make sure you take your time on this one.

We will start by adding the characterMotor script to our Sancho character. Locate the characterMotor script within your Project pane, it will need to be imported to the project before becoming visible in this pane, and drag it into the Inspector pane for the Sancho character. After releasing the mouse button, you will notice that the characterMotor script has now been added to the Sancho character as a new component. We can drag an object or an object's component into the actions panel within the PlayMaker editor and when we do so we will have the option of creating a Set Property or a Get Property action (Figure 4.28). These two actions allow us to reach into the object (or component) that we have just dragged into the panel and get information from inside of that object. When it comes to making a character jump, there is a lot of stuff going on; we have the character moving up and slowing down because of gravity and also checking for collisions with the ground. It is not a simple process, which is why we need this script to handle that for us. But we need information from the script. The two things we need from the script are to know if Sancho has landed on the ground

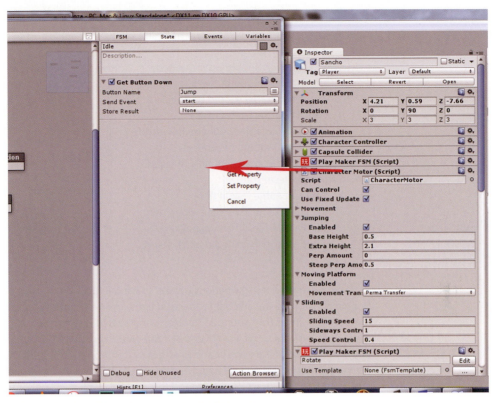

FIG 4.28 Dragging the characterMotor script component into the Action panel.

and also to force the script to either start or stop the jumping process. With that explanation out of the way, time to get at it.

1. Drag the Character Motor (Script) component into the action Panel for the On Ground state.
   a. Select Set Property.
      i. Property should be inputJump.
      ii. Set Value should be unchecked.
      iii. Every Frame should be unchecked.
2. Select the Start Animation state.
   a. Add a Play Animation action.
      i. Anim name should be jump-fly.
      ii. Finish Event should be FINISHED.
   b. Drag the Character Motor script component over again and select Set Property.
      i. Property should be inputJump.
      ii. Set Value should be checked.
      iii. Every Frame should be unchecked.

3. Select the Fly state.
    a. Drag the Character Motor script component over again and select Get Property.
        i. Property should be grounded.
        ii. Store Bool should be isGrounded.
        iii. Every Frame should be checked.
    b. Add a Bool Test action.
        i. Bool Variable should be isGrounded.
        ii. Is True should be landed.
        iii. Every Frame should be checked.
4. Select the Reset state.
    a. Add an Enable FSM action.
        i. FSM Name should be Movement.
        ii. Enable should be unchecked.
        iii. Reset on Exit should be checked.

We have seen most of these actions before, so we will focus on the new ones. Beginning with the Get and Set Property actions. The Get Property action that we are using is the grounded Boolean variable that is stored within the characterMotor script, variables are properties of objects. A property is anything that defines an object and provides customization to an object. As we mentioned, that script will handle testing for being back on the ground and when Sancho is back on the ground this particular value will be set to True. Therefore, if we can grab that value from the script and store it in our own variable inside of the FSM, then we can know when Sancho is back down and go ahead and transition to another state. The Set Property actions that we are using are the ones that will actually have the characterMotor script begin the jumping stuff that it does which would include all of the calculations for moving the character through the air. Since we have constructed our own controller scheme, we are essentially hijacking the input for our own purposes and through this Set Property action we can go back to the characterMotor and let it know that it is now time to begin jumping or not as the case may be.

The other new actions that we used are the Enable FSM actions, which we saw in the Rotate FSM. What we are doing here is to Force Unity to reset the animations within the Movement FSM when the character has landed. To see the issue, take the landed event from the Fly state and connect it directly to the On Ground state and now test it by jumping while your character is running. Notice that when the character lands again, Sancho does not transition back into the running animation. The reason for this is that he was in the running animation but then when he jumped, we started playing the jump-fly animation, granted we have landed again, but we have not told the system to start playing a different animation yet. So, a way to get around this is what we are doing with the Reset state. By turning the Movement FSM off and back on again, we are forcing that state machine to reset itself and to get Sancho to go back into his running animation, while he is moving. There will be many times that it will be necessary for us to turn state machines on and off.

One last thing on the jumping of Sancho before leaving this section. We may want to fine tune and tweak how high Sancho jumps. To tweak these settings, we can access the Character Motor script component within Sancho and inside of the jumping section are two values to play with: Base Height and Extra Height. The Base Height value is how far the character will go if the player were to press the jump button and release it almost immediately after pressing. The Extra Height is an additional height that will be added to the base height if the jump button is held down. This is not to say that the Extra Height is a double jump kind of mechanic, but rather this is similar to a sneaking kind of system except for jumping. You can have a little hop with a quick press or a solid jump with a longer press. Play around with these values some to get Sancho behaving in a way that you like.

4.8.3.4 The Camera Follows Sancho
Our final step in this chapter will be to get the camera to follow our player around and keep the player centered in the screen as a good third-person

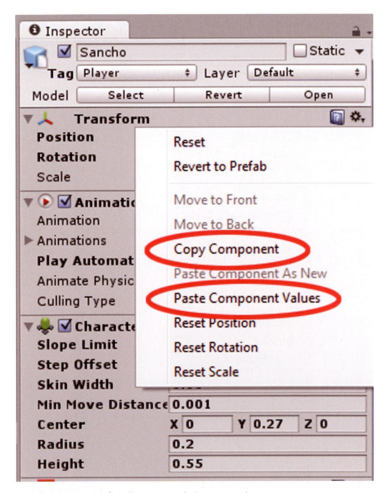

FIG 4.29 Component options from the gear icon in the Inspector panel.

camera system should. We can approach this either through a programming system or through a parent 1/n child hierarchy. As we have been doing some programming, we are going to advance our knowledge of Unity by looking into the parent–child technique for having the camera follow the player character. To begin, it will be easiest if we get our camera to be oriented in the same way that the character is and then tweak the camera from there. Select the knight character in the scene and in the Inspector panel click the gear in the top right corner of the Transform section. We will be looking for the Copy Component option from the drop-down menu as depicted in Figure 4.29. This will store all of the values of that component in the clipboard memory. Now, select the Main Camera in the scene and click the gear for its Transform component. This time select Paste Component Values from the drop-down menu of Figure 4.29 to paste the Transform values of the knight character into those of the Main Camera. Now, the Main Camera is positioned and oriented as the player's character is.

We can move the camera using the movement gizmo and also rotate the camera to get a view of the player character that we are happy with. To finish up the following aspect of the camera, grab the Main Camera in the hierarchy view and drag it down onto the Sancho game object, as shown in Figure 4.30. This has created a relationship such that the camera is a child of the Sancho object. Wherever the player's character goes, the camera will follow and will maintain the same perspective as that which we have established for it.

FIG 4.30 Main Camera as a child of the Sancho game object.

There will be many times that we will need to set up relationships such as this for other game objects throughout a project.

> **Note**
> While a camera is selected in the scene, the bottom right corner of the Scene Editor will show a preview of the scene as viewed through the camera, this helps us to set out cameras up the way we want them.

4.9 Summary

In this chapter, we explored the history of characters. We tend to think of characters as being unique to each story, however, as we discovered in this chapter there tends to be a pattern that characters fall into as far as their purpose within the story. By understanding these character archetypes, we can create characters to fulfill specific roles within stories and our games. However, not all games need to have characters and even if we incorporate characters into our games, it may not be necessary for us to utilize every archetype that is available. Even with these character archetypes, however, games do have some specific needs that will require characters to fulfill these very specific roles, roles that have no equivalent in traditional stories or movies. When we import assets into Unity, we need to take the time to configure them, especially any animations that may be coming into the game project with the asset. Through the power of state machines and PlayMaker, we can create functional state machines fairly quickly that will allow us to add controllable aspects of the characters that we do put into our games. These state machines are easily managed and expanded upon as our game project grows, and we need more functionality from the components. As we wrap up this chapter, we now have the basics of a moveable game character in our testing level, in our next chapter, we will construct the essential infrastructure for a couple of non-player characters and get them tested out and working in a test scene as well.

Vocabulary

The Writer's Journey
The Hero with a Thousand Faces
Joseph Campbell
Christopher Vogler
Protagonist
Antagonist
Hero
Shadow
Mentor
Herald
Trickster

Threshold Guardian
Ally
Shapeshifter
Quest Giver
Merchant
Informational character
Asset
Concept art
Texture maps
3D Mesh
Animations
UV Unwrap
FBX file
Character controller
MechAnim
Scale factor
Keyframe reduction
Loop
Ping-Pong
Once
Wrap mode
Character controller
Variable
Vector3
Float
Int
String
Bool
Input manager

Review Quiz

1. Who wrote *The Writer's Journey*?
2. Who is famous for his comparative studies of the world's legends and myths?
3. Consider the classic movie *Star Wars: A New Hope*, develop a list of the characters from the movie and match them to the character archetypes that we have studied.
4. Where is the Input Manager located inside of Unity?
5. When importing 3D assets with animations into Unity which rig system should be used if you do not want to utilize Unity's MechAnim system?
6. Which component would we have to add to any Game Object if we wanted the player to eventually be able to control it?
7. Which PlayMaker action can be used to get the status of one of the axes from the Input Manager?
8. What is the variable type that we should use to store a value like 3.14?

9. Which PlayMaker action should be used to play an animation on a Game Object?
10. When moving a character with PlayMaker, why do we store the vector of the movement axis from the Input Manager?

Exercises

1. Modify the Fire1 and Fire2 inputs to be used with *Sancho Panza* as his boxing and bonk actions.
2. Add a new FSM to Sancho's control system called actions and get his animations playing for the bonk and boxing animations. Now, Sancho should be able to punch and belly bonk. (HINT: While there are different ways of doing this, one approach would be to create a new FSM called something like Actions and do everything in here for the bonk and the boxing like we did for the moving. You may notice some odd behavior with this approach; take a look at the Enable FSM action that we used within the Rotation FSM).
3. Import the following free assets from the asset store as potential characters for the *Sancho Panza* project and configure them with animations for the next chapter:
   a. Free Fantasy Spider by Kalamona
   b. Skeleton Pack by bshGame
   c. While you are getting those assets take a look around at the other free characters available, maybe you can find some things that spark your creativity for characters in your own project.
4. Import the following assets developed by Arteria3D and found in the Chapter Resources section of the companion website in the "Arteria3D-Characters" file:
   a. The donkey colt
   b. Fluffy sheep
   c. Pig
   d. Shetland Pony
   e. Teresa Female Merc
   f. Sanson Knight with Spear
5. Create a brand new Unity project named "Breakout" that could be used for creating a clone of the classic *Breakout*. Within this new project add a 3D Cube Game Object that could serve as the player's paddle and construct a player control system using PlayMaker for this system.

Design Document

We are going to update our *Sancho Panza* design document with information about our primary character, *Sancho Panza*. We are going to develop a basic character background for him as well as include the artwork that has been created for him. We will also include the control scheme that will be associated with our lead character and incorporate information for our lead antagonist, shadow, in the game and any of his henchmen/henchcreatures (which may not be a word, but should be, and these guys would also be known as threshold guardians and possibly even tricksters/shapeshifters). In both cases, we are going to only use freely available resources within the asset store of Unity.

Download

Updated version of the *Sancho Panza* design document can be downloaded from the companion website: "DesignDocument_chapter4.docx."

Consider your design document that you have been working on thus far and add the following to it:

1. Hero/shadow characters.
   a. Include: backgrounds, descriptions, essential art, control schemes or behaviors.
2. Threshold guardians and/or tricksters.
   a. Include: backgrounds, descriptions, essential art, behaviors.
3. If you think you may need more characters, implement them as well, although you may also want to table this portion until after we have looked at stories.

CHAPTER 5

Non-Player Characters

In the last chapter, we explored the various character archetypes that exist and looked at how we can use those to help generate characters to populate our game worlds. Our focus, at the time, was primarily on the player character, or the hero. In this chapter, we will expand our programming knowledge by bringing in behavior state machines for a couple of non-player characters. Responding to player input is a fairly straightforward process as we develop the states and the actions that will provide the given functionality for specified inputs from the player. However, when it comes to building behavior systems for characters, we need to have the system gather its own information and respond to it. We will take a brief look at the world of artificial intelligence (AI) and implement a rudimentary system for our Sancho Panza game. We will also consider the complexity of the behavior and response system that is required based upon the character archetype that is being implemented.

- What Is Artificial Intelligence?
- Different Types of Artificial Intelligence
- Determine the Needed Behavior of a Threshold Guardian
- Implementing the Behaviors for the Threshold Guardian

5.1 What Is Artificial Intelligence?

We tend to have these Hollywood ideas of what AI is and as a result define it through these grand conceptualizations. For instance, we may define AI as the character Data from the television series *Star Trek: The Next Generation*. Or, we may define AI as HAL 9000 from the movie *2001: A Space Odyssey*. While both of these are wonderful examples of what AI could someday become, neither actually provides a definition of what artificial intelligence *is*. At its core, AI is most easily defined as a computer or other device making a decision on its own based upon inputs provided to it. We could expand this definition to include learning by saying that AI is a computer or other device becoming better at a certain activity based upon engaging in or observing that activity and learning about it. But, to keep the waters clear, we will stick with the first definition. Any time that a computer makes a decision, it is utilizing artificial intelligence.

The decision-making process must involve a situational question and a choice to be made. For instance, asking a computer what the value of 2 + 2 is and getting back the answer of 4 is not indicative of AI within the confines of our current definition for it. We are going to exclude performing numerical calculations from our conceptualization of AI. However, making a decision based upon that calculation will be considered a form of AI. For instance, our merchant character may decide that if the player has more than 20 of a certain item, then the merchant will only offer half the value when buying them from the player, this particular merchant is a shrewd one, or greedy depending on how you look at it. These calculations and comparisons are vital for the system to determine that an event has occurred, but it is the response to the event that we consider to be AI within this book. We will leave more esoteric and academic discussions of this topic to others.

5.2 Some Different Types of Artificial Intelligence

There are many different areas of AI being studied, pursued, and even implemented. In this section, we are going to briefly touch on a few of them, specifically the ones that are most relevant to game development. After reading this section, you may start to find some answers to some of your questions about why game characters or entities behave in a certain fashion. Table 5.1 provides a brief summary of these types of AI.

5.2.1 Scripted Behavior

Scripted behaviors are some of the most commonly implemented character behavior systems within video games. Scripted behavior systems use a state machine to implement the AI and for the character to determine which behavior it should do at any given point in time. The essential idea here is

TABLE 5.1 Summary of the Different Types of Artificial Intelligence Presented

AI Type	Pros	Cons	Good Fits
Scripted behavior	Get the exact behavior you want Know what it should be doing	Extremely predictable	Action games
Random behavior	Is not predictable	Can be difficult to debug	Game with no strategy component or strategy games aimed at children
Expert systems	Decision process mimics an expert	Need solid understanding of system Can be predictable	Classic strategy games such as chess
Mathematical modeling	A much less predictable scripted behavior system	Must construct the mathematical models	Action games
Evolutionary systems	Closely mimics our decision-making process	Difficult to debug	Life simulators

that we as the developers figure out exactly what we want a character to be able to do and what would cause it to do any one of the things that it can do as well as what would make it stop doing a specified thing. Essentially, what we want it to do would be the actions within various states and the things that cause it to stop performing those actions would be the transition events leading to another state. Consider the example of a scripted behavior for a security guard in an action style game. We want this guard to be able to do just a few things, namely

- Patrol her assigned guard area
- Attack any intruder (the player) that may enter the area
- Issue an alarm if possible
- Chase the intruder (the player) if they try to run away

That is all that we want that particular character to do, granted it is a simplistic behavior system, but then again how many games have we played with just that layout or something extremely similar to it and had fun? Always remember that as a game developer your job is to entertain your players and help them have fun first and foremost. Consider the state diagram depicted in Figure 5.1 for a graphical representation of the basic behaviors for this character. As you can see, this style is tailor made for a visual scripting environment such as PlayMaker.

This type of system is a good choice for most action types of games, as we know what each type of character should be doing within the game and we will have very tight control over these behaviors while the game is running. This type of system is also fairly easy to debug as the boundary conditions that cause transitions to occur should be straightforward to set up and therefore test. We, as the developers, know what the agent should be

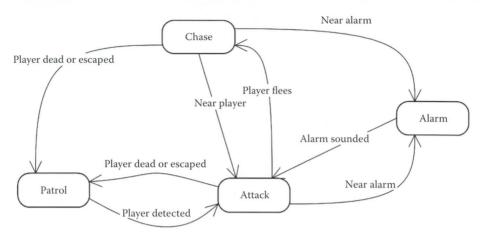

FIG 5.1 State machine for a scripted behavior mechanism.

doing in a given situation and as such can quickly determine whether the system is working correctly. However, these types of systems tend to be very predictable as they follow patterns and humans are very good at detecting the occurrence of patterns even if we may not consciously know that we are doing so. Due to the predictable nature of these situations it can be fairly straightforward to find and exploit weaknesses, which as game players we have all done. For instance, these well-defined patterns would cause problems if we were to implement this type of AI within a strategy game, as the computer opponent would always respond the same way to a given situation and the human player would know this after playing a couple of times.

5.2.2 Random Behavior

Random behavior is an odd choice for an AI mechanism, but remember our definition for AI at the beginning of the chapter. For our purposes, AI is defined as any time that the computer makes a decision, whether the decision is a good or bad one is entirely irrelevant within the confines of this definition. This approach frees us to consider such things as random behavior as a form of AI. With random behavior, the system is free to choose any activity that it is capable of performing, for any reason it wants. Essentially, whenever a decision needs to be made, the agent will randomly pick from among the activities that it can do and execute that random selection. We could make this a little more interesting by providing different weights to the options, such that they are not evenly distributed but each has a different likelihood of being selected during a decision moment. For instance, consider the random idle animation of Sancho from the previous chapter. While that decision in and of itself is far from an AI system, we can get a glimpse of how random decision making could be used.

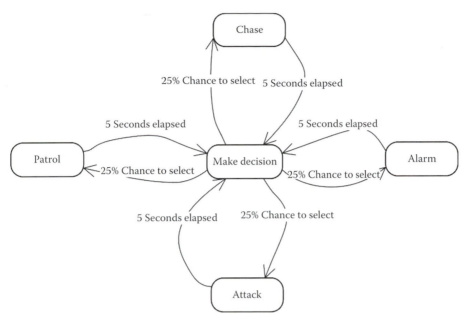

FIG 5.2 A completely random version of the guard agent.

Consider our sentry guard from the previous section. A random behavior system would be one that every few seconds the agent would reach a moment of decision making and randomly select one of the actions to perform as depicted in Figure 5.2. This means that the agent may go off and sound the alarm when the player first spawns into the level simply because that was randomly selected. Completely random behavior like this would not be good for our game for two reasons. The first is that the player would not find the computer characters to be very engaging, and it would be somewhat like existing within an insane asylum. Now, if the setting of our game *were* an insane asylum and at least some of the characters *were* insane, well then that would be different. But for a supposedly rational character, random behavior would just not be acceptable. The other flaw with this approach is testing, due to the random nature of the behaviors, it becomes difficult to test and make sure that all behaviors are working correctly as we have no idea when a given action will be selected by the agent.

As a solo decision-making mechanism, random selection works best with board style games that do not involve strategy or with children's games. For instance, a random selection engine would work very well for an implementation of a *Tic-Tac-Toe* mobile app being targeted for children. For young children, the strategy of this game is often very elusive and the random nature of the agent would be such that the child could as likely win and as they could lose. A scripted behavior would too easily defeat the child every time and frustrate the child. In fact, a random implementation of a *Tic-Tac-Toe* game was built for my kids when they were young and they spent hours playing it and trying to develop strategies to defeat it as they could never quite nail down the best approach to beating it.

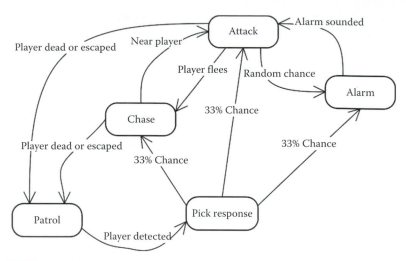

FIG 5.3 Scripted behavior enhanced with a random twist.

However, if we were to add a random system to a scripted behavior, we will be getting to a slightly more interesting mechanic. Consider Figure 5.3 in which now the agent may attack or sound the alarm at any point during an encounter with the player, making it slightly more challenging for the player to determine how quickly or how long to engage with the enemy agent. Getting these system balanced out to more closely model a human decision-making process will come in when we look at mathematical modeling. Also notice that the state machine is becoming more complex as we add more possible transitions from the various states. Of course, with the machine as diagrammed, the agent may try to sound the alarm more than once, possibly an undesirable effect or then again an interesting side effect that would give the illusion of a panicked guard.

5.2.3 Expert Systems

Consider the possibility of creating a set of answers to common questions where the answers were all provided by experts in the field. Something similar to the teacher's manual for a book. Essentially that is what an expert system is. These systems are constructed by compiling a collection of information from experts in the field, whatever that may be, and finding out what they would do in a given situation. Expert systems are commonly used in real-world situations as assistants with help desk operations as they can potentially guide those with technical problems to the most likely solutions given provided problems and symptoms. As far as an approach for AI within a video game, these could potentially work very well with some types of strategy games, such as *Chess*, or even as management components within sports games. By polling football coaches, we could develop a set of solutions, play calls, for given problems, game situations. This would provide a more engaging and challenging opponent for the player to deal with.

Expert systems are implemented in the same way as the previous techniques that we looked at, at least as far as core implementation is concerned. If we consider the solutions provided within the set of solutions as potential states for the agent to transition to, then we could see that the event that causes the transition to a specific state in the expert system is going to be the specific situation that led to the expert suggesting such a solution. The complexity of our agent's behavior will then be limited by two factors. The first limiting factor is the number of solutions that we obtain from those that we consider to be experts. The second factor is the number of initial situations or conditions that we can imagine in order for the experts to provide a solution. For instance, our expert system would have to have a default solution or action to do if it is facing a situation not specifically defined for it.

At first glance, an expert system seems like a wonderful idea; however, if we consider the possible actions that a player can actually perform in a game we will quickly recognize that there are not that many different situations to encounter. In which case our carefully crafted expert system has become nothing but a scripted behavior in which the behaviors and actions were decided by experts as opposed to the game designer. We have thrown this word "expert" around quite a bit, but who exactly would qualify as an expert? Ultimately, this would depend on the game that is being created; however, some possibilities might include grand chess masters, sports coaches or analysts, politicians, historians, and psychologists. It all depends on the game that we are creating, but an expert system would not fit all games. For instance, an expert system would not make *Donkey Kong* any more believable of a game character than he already is. Although an expert system could make the manager of your rival baseball team a whole lot more believable and therefore more fun to play against.

5.2.4 Mathematical Behavior Modeling

A mathematical model of a behavior system is somewhat like combining our previous three systems into one system. The approach here is to build a model of the decision process including percentages for each decision such that the agent's decision process more closely mimics that of a human player. Consider your experience playing a shooter style of game. When do you reload your weapons, when do you hide behind cover, at what point do you disengage so that your shields may recharge, when do you charge in guns blazing and when do you hold back. There are many other questions that we could ask as well, but most likely your answers to the above questions were something along the lines of "it depends." Your answer showcased an interesting aspect of how we play these games; specifically, we do not necessarily follow a set pattern. But the computer agents in these games do follow strict patterns through their scripted behaviors; however, with a mathematical model we can instead have the character make decisions in a less structured and more believable fashion.

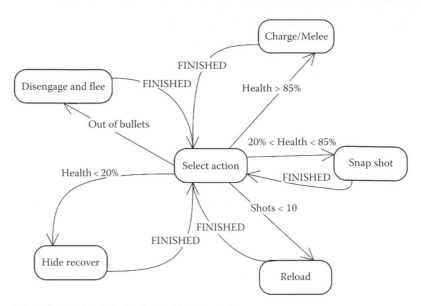

FIG 5.4 State machine for the Attack state of the sentry guard.

We will break this down into a more understandable form through an example. Returning to our sentry guard that we have been discussing and building upon we will expand one of the states that we have created, specifically the Attack state. As it turns out, there are many things going on in the attack state as can be seen in Figure 5.4. The character has multiple things that it can do and this is a fairly nice scripted behavior for it. However, it is also a very rigid system as it will always reload when the ammunition gets below ten shots. Likewise, it will also always hide when the health gets below 20% and re-engage when the health is back up to 75%. Players will quickly pick up on this behavior and start to exploit it as it has some very glaring weaknesses.

We can breathe some fresh air into this decision-making process by building a mathematical model to better mimic when certain decisions should be made. Consider the changes made in Table 5.2 comparing the events that cause the transitions to occur. Now, certain decisions become more likely as conditions increase; however, there is the possibility of those decisions being made earlier. For instance, the decision to re-engage after hiding may now be made at any point from 30% to 75% health with the likelihood gradually increasing until we reach 75% health and the agent must re-engage. Now this is just a quick sketch of a possible system for this sentry agent. While this may serve as a solid starting point, it will have to be tweaked through much play testing. This is an interesting concept to mention at this point. So often, the AI of a game is left until later in the development of the game leaving not enough time to fully design, implement, and test interesting behavior mechanics. If we are wanting a more complex system, such as this model for the sentry guard, we will have to be developing and testing this in conjunction with other work. For instance, there can be a separate scene created in our project for testing the sentry guard and our AI developers

TABLE 5.2 Comparison of Traditional Scripted Events to Modeled Events

Action	Scripted Event	Modeled/Weighted Event
Charge melee	Health above 85%	100%—Health at 80% 0%—Health below 84%
Snap shot	Health between 20% and 85%	95%—Health at 84% 5%—Health at 1%
Reload	Less than 10 shots in gun	0%—Gun fully loaded 100%—Gun is empty
Hide and recover	Health below 20%	5%—Health at 84% 95%—Health at 1%
Disengage and flee	No more bullets to reload	0%—All bullets 100%—No bullets

and game testers can be working on this scene and tweaking at *the same time* that other scenes are being developed. A solid mathematical model of behavior is an excellent choice for a shooter style game or other action-based game with the computer playing the role of an adversary. While such an approach could be used for an ally of the player, keep in mind that the players will get frustrated if the ally opts to re-engage before they are really healthy enough to do so.

Granted this is still a simple example, but we can begin to see how the behavior of the agent is becoming less rigidly scripted and more fluid. Through this approach, the agent becomes *more likely* to do something in response to the player's actions, but there is still no guarantee until a certain threshold is reached. As a result, it is possible that the guard runs away very early in the conflict or that the guard just continues to shoot at the player right up until the moment that the guard is killed. As mentioned, this is just a preliminary run through with some exaggerated values to help us to better visualize how a system might work, there would be much tweaking ahead of us to get this model balanced correctly.

5.2.5 Evolutionary Systems

Evolutionary systems most closely mimic the decision-making process that we actually go through. Given all of the possible actions that we could select to do, our thought process will provide some sort of benefit analysis to each one and compare these benefits against each other. Sometimes, we will have actions that will mutate somewhat as we consider all of the possibilities and eventually settle on one that we consider to have the most benefit to us. If we were to consider a game such as *The Sims* as a quick example, we may be able to clarify this somewhat (see Figure 5.5). When a computer-controlled Sim character reaches a time to make a decision, it could (emphasis on *could* because this is not how it was actually implemented within the games) create a solution set of available actions by randomly selecting a bunch of things that it could do at that moment in time. From the solution set of actions, the agent then would evaluate each one based on some comparative model

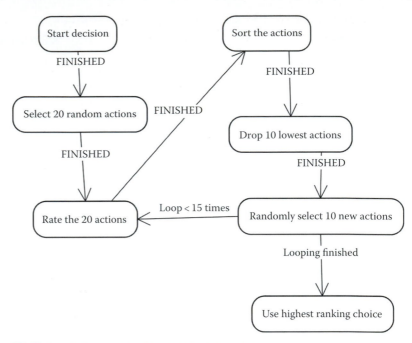

FIG 5.5 A graphical representation of the potential evolutionary decision process.

to determine the usefulness of making such a decision. For instance, if the character had just returned from work, then it would not be very useful for the character to head off to work. Thus, that action would be valued very low. Through this evaluation process, the actions available can be ranked from a "best" to a "worst" and the "best" one selected. After ranking these, the agent could keep the top ten or so and add a few more random ones to this. Repeat the ranking system and repeat the random additions. Through this approach, the agent would evaluate many if not most of the available actions and end up selecting the one that scored the highest on the final rankings. At least that would be a potential implementation in a nutshell with a few details left to be worked out.

With these evolutionary techniques, of which genetic algorithms are a very strong contender for use in video games, the agent will not always make the same decision when faced with the same situation. At first glance, the behavior may appear to be random, but it will not be long before the players will pick up that the behavior is not random, that the behavior is actually benefiting the agent in some way. The interesting thing about these approaches within a video game character is that we ultimately do not know exactly what the agent will do in a given situation, we can make guesses based on governing factors, but it would only be a guess and could be wrong quite often.

Generally speaking, evolutionary techniques are very valuable in the academic setting as they allow researchers to have computers develop a wide range of unknown solutions to a given problem, ultimately picking the most optimal solution available for the problem. However, within a video game setting, these approaches do not immediately lend themselves to the behaviors of most computer-controlled characters. For instance, if we allowed a fully evolutionary approach to decision making for a merchant character, that character may decide that it is more cost-effective to gather stuff outside of town on her own rather than waiting for a player to show up and sell the materials to them. As a result of that decision, the store in town may be closed because the merchant is out gathering supplies and never reopens because the merchant was killed in the process. Granted, we could prevent the decision-making system from pursuing such possibilities for the agent, but if we restrict the evolutionary system too heavily then it will essentially become a mathematical model of human behavior. This type of system would really only be applicable to a game in which there are a wide range of actions that can be performed at any given moment in time, such as *The Sims* mentioned earlier.

5.3 Selecting an Artificial Intelligence System

The first decision that must be made when developing your behavior functionality is to determine which of the AI approaches you wish to implement. The type of system selected should be based on several factors:

- What type of game are we making?
  - Action games do not necessarily require the same level of AI complexity as a strategy game.
- Who is our target audience and what do they expect?
  - There is a big difference between targeting children or casual players versus targeting hard-core simulation gamers.
- How much time do we have for creating the AI?
  - If our game is on a quick development cycle, then the AI is on a quick cycle as well.
- Do we have people that work on the AI while the rest of the project is developed?
  - Keep in mind the tweak and test and repeat cycle for the more complex AI systems, we cannot have our game in a perpetual stall while we tweak and tweak the AI.
- What is our programming level?
  - If we are just starting out programming, then maybe the scripted approach will work best for us and not be too frustrating to implement.

Note
The fun factor of the game is the final deciding factor when working with computer-controlled characters. If their behavior detracts from the fun then change it, even if that means going with a simpler type of AI.

Based on these questions and our answers, we are going to employ a scripted behavior system for our threshold guardian. We may return to it later and add some flavoring with a random element or two, but for our first game and our first shot at this, if we can manage to get a threshold guardian to respond to the actions of the player that would be a major accomplishment for us and a very solid step in the right direction. Do not try to learn everything in one project, set goals for yourself with each game project that you take on and always improve your skill set, but do not overreach. We will learn far more by completing games than by starting the process and quitting mid way to start another project because we got stuck in the first project.

5.4 Designing a Threshold Guardian

When approaching a character or entity that is intended to challenge the player in some way, we should recognize that such a character falls into the category of a threshold guardian archetype from the previous chapter. Now, it is not necessary that this threshold guardian have a fully fleshed-out character background with goals and a reason for being, though there will be cases when the game would definitely benefit from that level of detail. Consider our spider that we added to the project in the exercises from the last chapter. We could turn this into a spider similar to Shelob from *The Lord of the Rings*, but as noted in the design document, this is more of an overgrown and common spider that has taken over the area that Sancho is currently in. Also, there are many of these spiders. They are here for the sole purpose of challenging the player, though once we get to a story we may enlarge their roles some and revisit their characters. Remember, game development is an iterative process and many of these pieces work with and off of each other as the game is being designed.

The spider is here to provide a classic action game challenge to the player. The player will need to get past these spiders to get to other areas of the scene and to find things that they may need for completing the current game level. It is important that we know what we need from the characters before we start designing an AI system for them. It is also important that we know what we can make the characters do as well. For instance, we do not have an animation sequence of this spider spinning a web to capture Sancho, so as cool as it may sound to do that while we design the AI we cannot actually make the character do that, at least not yet.

Table 5.3 lists the animations that are available within the spider object as well as some ideas of what we may use them for. When using assets that others have created, do not limit your creativity to the names of the animations, watch each animation a few times and see if there is anything else that you could use the animation for. For that matter, you could even consider what it might look like if played backward using the trick we used in the previous chapter to help Sancho walking backward look correct.

TABLE 5.3 Animation List Available in the Free Spider Object

Animation Name	Possible Uses
refpose	This is the default pose for the object, maybe as a frozen spider.
walk	Standard patrol or injured escape.
run	Player is spotted and spider is charging to attack.
attack1	Good base attack for the spider.
attack2	Can use as a secondary attack.
idle	Spider is wounded and trying to recover or is trying to decide where to go next.
taunt	Spider has spotted the player and is preparing to charge or as a defensive block.
hit1	Can be used when the spider gets hit, or when it lands after jumping/falling or if we were to allow it to spin a web.
hit2	Definitely a just got hit although could also be used if the spider was on a slippery surface.
jump	Jumping can also be used when the spider initially spots the player and is ready to charge them.
death1	Death, nothing else really comes to mind.
death2	Another death, or badly injured, or sleeping.
allanims	This plays all of the animations, not useful to us at the moment.

In Figure 5.6, we have provided the rudimentary skeleton of what we will construct for the behavior of this agent. Notice that constructing AI systems, even if we do a small AI, is more complex than creating a response system to the player. For our spider object, it is going to have to be able to make the decisions for what to do at the appropriate time which adds some complexity to what we need to do. For now, we are just looking at an overview of what we would like to have and will break each piece down in more detail in the following sections.

The essential concept here is that we want the spider to wander around the world or at least a part of the world doing spidery things and just being

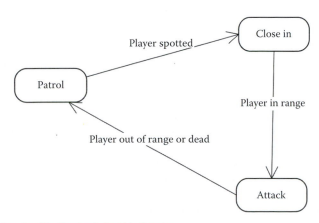

FIG 5.6 Overview of the AI system for the spider character.

a spider. But, whenever the player (which could be expanded later to include other characters as well, for instance an ally character if we had one) gets close enough to the spider, the spider should close in to attack or defend its territory depending on your perspective. Once the spider gets close enough to kick or bite the player we want the spider to launch into some nasty attacks and just start beating up the poor player. If the player is able to escape from the spider and be too far for it too attack, then the spider will return to its daily patrol. An interesting thing should happen at that point in time, if the player is still in range for the spider to see the player, then the spider will close in again, essentially chase the player around. The spider will continue this process of attacking until either the player has escaped or been killed.

This is a good overview of the primary controller system for our spider. However, that is not enough design work for us to begin an implementation just yet. We still need to take a look at exactly how the spider should go about patrolling and closing in and attacking. Figure 5.7 depicts a potential design layout for the patrol system. This one is fairly straightforward. We want the spider to figure out where it is going to go, Get Location, and then move until it gets there. Once it has arrived, we want it to find another location and get to moving again. However, before we just gloss over that too quickly, we are also going to want it to play some kind of walking animation, while it is moving over to the new location as well.

The process of pursuing the player should be more straightforward. By having a Controller state machine that is responsible for actually knowing when to chase and when to stop chasing all our Pursue state machine is going to have to be responsible for is actually moving the spider toward the thing that it is chasing. Since there are no logical decisions that it needs to make, those are made by the Controller itself, the Pursue state machine will only need one state, the one that moves the spider. But, we still need to consider what we want the spider to do as we design this. Figure 5.8 provides an overview of how we would like this Pursue FSM to function. Essentially, it is going to look at what it is chasing, move toward what it is chasing, and play some type of animation to make it look like it is walking or running or hopping.

The process of attacking is more complex from an implementation perspective than we would initially expect. But if we take our time through designing it first and at least attempting to consider the various factors and anticipate issues then our implementation process will go much smoother. An attack, either by the spider, the player, or some other object in the game, must

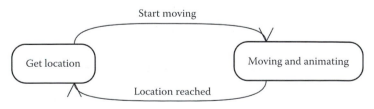

FIG 5.7 Basic layout of the potential Patrolling FSM.

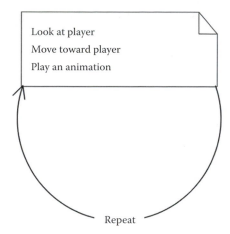

FIG 5.8 Design layout for the Pursue FSM.

FIG 5.9 Layout design for the Attacking FSM.

run through three distinct stages and these stages are not necessarily always going to be within the same state machine or even within the same game object for that matter. The first stage is to perform the actual attack, which we can see in Figure 5.9. The spider will attack its target object, by playing some type of attack animation and then go into a rest between attacks. We really do not want the spider to just constantly be attacking, but rather to make some type of lunge then to pause a moment or two before striking out again.

The design of Figure 5.9 would get our spider *looking* like it is attacking something. This is important and this is the first stage of the three that we must complete. The second stage is to have the spider or weapon know that it has hit the player. In order to know that the player has actually been hit as a result of the attack, we will need to construct some collision detection. As it turns out, Unity will handle all of the collision detection for us once we have the collider components added and positioned as we would like. So, this means that all we would need to do is to *respond* to these collisions when they occur. Figure 5.10 displays a design view of our collision response system for the spider. As you can see the idea here is that whenever a specific collision occurs with the player, the spider is going to hurt it. Fairly straightforward, but the key here is to consider where such a state machine should be placed.

The final stage we need to take on, which is in some ways a continuation or sub-stage of the collision detection, is to actually hurt the object that we have hit. This has been separated into its own stage here, because in our project at hand, we plan to implement a health system for the things that

FIG 5.10 Collision response system for an attack.

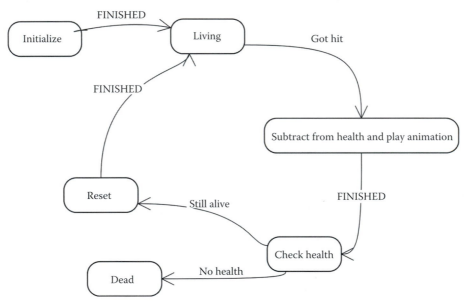

FIG 5.11 Design layout for the Health state machine for the Sancho character.

populate the world, this will allow for power-ups and other things to be added as we move along. Figure 5.11 displays the design of a health system for our Sancho character. This same system could be copied in to other objects that we want to provide a health system for. The logical flow here is to begin by initializing all of our internal health components; at first glance, it may seem unnecessary, but if we were to add in the capability of a character to respawn, then we would have to reinitialize everything at that point. Once everything has been set up, the system will go into a Living state where it will just wait until it is hit by something that can hurt it.

Several things must happen in fairly quick succession once the player does get hit by something painful. We begin by playing an animation and subtracting some points from the character's health, whatever that may be. After completing those, it is necessary to figure out if the character is still alive or not, basically did the damage that was just caused kill the character. If so, then we will play some kind of animation showing the player that the character is dead and then make sure that the character knows that it is dead as well. If the damage did not kill the character, then it is necessary to begin winding back toward our Living, or Idle if you will, state. On our way, there we will need to reset everything to wait for the next hit.

Now that we have all of the systems that we will be using designed and thought through, we are ready to begin the implementation process and bring this threshold guardian to life. As we go through these next few sections, we will find that many of the ideas that were represented within the design work will fall straight into the state machines that will be built for the objects. We will also discover that there are some things that were not included in this design that will need to be added to the actual implementation. These will be minor things that will be specific to how we need to get the system to behave the way we have described here in the design work.

5.5 Implementing the Threshold Guardian

In this section, we are going to construct (implement) the various state machines that we have just finished designing. During the process, it may be necessary to rework some of our design ideas, though hopefully not too drastically. While doing the design work in the previous sections, there was no way for us to test what we were thinking. The focus was entirely on thinking about the spider from a logical perspective to make sure that our minds were wrapped around what we were going to build. Now that we are actually going to build it, we will do this in a series of consecutive steps slowly building up toward the final version of our spider. This will force us back into the iterative development process that we have discussed previously. Following a design → implement → test → tweak → repeat form of development cycle will make our lives so much easier as we get to more and more complex systems to create. Though, as we said, we are hoping to not have to fall back onto the design component too much, we would prefer the process to be more of implement → test → tweak → repeat. For this character AI, which once it is finished could be applied to any other character in the game with very minor changes and tweaks; we are going to construct it in the following order:

- *Controller*: Responsible for managing all of the major states and transitions for the AI.
- *Patrolling*: Responsible for having the spider patrol a specified area within the game world.
- *Spotting the Player*: Handles chasing after the player once the player has been spotted by the spider.
- *Attacking the Player*: Once the spider gets close enough to bite or kick at Sancho it will.
- *Hurting the Player*: Responsible for being aware of the health of the character, in this case it will be Sancho as we saw in the design stage, and knowing if Sancho has died.
- *Connecting Attack and Health*: With the attack system and health management system constructed, it is now time to connect these and get the functionality going that we have been driving at.
- *Final Tweak*: With all of the systems in place, it is time for some play testing, bug hunting, and tweaking.

Note
We have quite a few things that we need to do to get this all working. We are going to be stretching ourselves with more complex state machines within PlayMaker; however, if we take our time through these next sections, we should all come out of this with a functioning AI for the spider.

5.5.1 The Controller

This is essentially the brain of the spider deciding what it should be doing and when. We are going to go ahead and construct this brain and get it in place than add the sub-components one by one. To begin, select the spider object in the scene and add an FSM to it. We will call this FSM Controller. Next create the events and variables that are listed in Table 5.4. For the detectionRange variable, be sure to click the Inspector check box to make the variable visible within the Inspector panel as this will make it much easier for us to tweak the spider's sensitivity later. As far as the Spider being killed, we will handle that through a different mechanism, an independent health system inside of the spider that will also be duplicated and modified for use with Sancho. The essential rationale here is that while the spider cannot detect the player, it will follow its patrol path; however, as soon as it does detect the player it will close in on them and attack. If the player manages to escape, the spider will return to patrolling. It will also be necessary for us to go ahead and create four other FSMs for the spider, and we will populate them later: Patrolling, Pursue, Attacking, and Health. In fact, as a result of our previous design work, we even already have an idea of the layout of these other state machines, everything is starting to fall together for us now. Figure 5.12 shows the skeleton of the controller FSM built within PlayMaker. While we do not have

TABLE 5.4 Events and Variables Needed for the Spider Controller FSM

Events	Variables and Types
In Range	detectionRange → Float → Inspector
Player Lost	playerDistance → Float
Player Spotted	attackRange → Float
	enemy → GameObject
	targetAlive → Bool

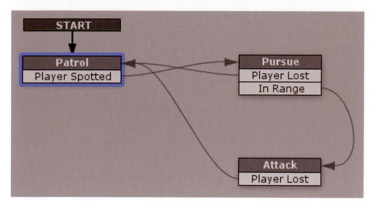

FIG 5.12 Skeleton of a controller state machine inside of PlayMaker.

any actions associated with any states yet, being able to throw this out there is a positive and confident step forward.

> **Note**
> Remember that variables only exist within the FSM that they were created in (unless we have specified them as Global, which we have not). This means that other FSMs cannot interact with these variables, at least not directly.

1. Select the Patrol state
    a. Add a Player Spotted transition event
    b. Add an Enable FSM action
        i. Enable the Patrol FSM
        ii. Reset on Exit should be checked
    c. Add a Find Closest action
        i. With tag should be equal to Player
        ii. Store object in enemy variable
        iii. Store distance in playerDistance
        iv. Every frame should be checked
    d. Add a Float Compare action
        i. Use playerDistance for Float 1
        ii. Use detectionRange for Float 2
        iii. Set Less Than to the Player Spotted event

We just threw some pretty cool stuff into this state and before rushing off, we will take a look at these actions and how they work together. To begin, we have the Enable FSM action which was the solution to one of the exercises from the previous chapter, or at least one of the solutions. In order to get Sancho to animate correctly when the player boxed or bonked, it was best to disable the Movement FSM and turn it back on after Sancho had finished his action. So, in a sense, there is nothing new there, just using the same thing. Now, consider this for a moment, the purpose of this controller is to turn the other state machines on or off depending on what the spider should be doing, so enabling each FSM within the appropriate state is going to abstract our actions.

> **Note**
> One of the interesting things about programming is that we can oftentimes create very complex behaviors or systems using seemingly simple code structures. Always remember that there is not a single action that will do everything that we need, we must put the actions together in sequences to get what we want and those sequences are built from simpler actions.

Abstraction is a key concept when it comes to programming. The idea here is similar to that of a black box. With a black box, we give it something and it then gives us something in return. How the black box goes about doing this we may not have any idea and we do not need to know how the black box functions in order to use it. For example, it is not necessary to understand how an internal combustion engine works in order to drive a car. To bring this back to programming, we have a state in this controller called Patrol. When this state is activated, the first thing it does is to fire up another state machine that is responsible for that actual work of getting the spider to go from one location to another. Our Patrol state in the Controller FSM has no idea how that Patrolling FSM is actually doing the patrolling and it does not need to know how it works. All the controller needs to know is that the Patrolling FSM is there and that it will handle getting the spider to patrol.

The next two actions in this state are responsible for figuring out when we should leave this state and go do something else, specifically attack the player. As a result, both of these actions must be performed every frame, that is to say they must be constantly updating. We begin with the Find Closest action. What this one does is to find the closest object within the scene that has a specific tag. Back in the last chapter, we looked at tags and how they can be applied to a Game Object in the scene. Our Sancho character is currently tagged as a Player object, and it is this tag that we have the Find Closest action looking for. This action will find the closest object that matches this tag and allows us to keep a reference to that object in a variable. It will also calculate the distance between the source; in this case, the spider, and that closest object that it could find. This distance can also be stored within a variable for us to use throughout this machine. This distance is determined through vector mathematics (as the position of each object is stored internally as a Vector3 data type) and results in a floating point value, a number with decimals. We will store this value in our variable named playerDistance.

Now that we know how far away the player is from the spider, we just need to see if the player is close enough to the spider to trigger an attack impulse from the spider. It is somewhat like finding a snake on a path and wondering how close it will let you get before it strikes, which by the way is not a course of action we are recommending here. This comparison is done through the Float Compare action. PlayMaker includes comparison actions for int, string, and objects as well. A comparison can provide us with one of three answers: greater than, less than, or equal to. From these three possibilities, we could potentially branch out in three different directions. In our case, all we care about is whether the player's distance is less than the detection range that we have provided. Currently, the detection range is 0 which is perfectly fine for now although it essentially means that the spider will not detect the player until they are right on top of each other, their distance is 0. However, pretty soon we will return to this value and start changing it to find a good aggression for our spider.

> **Note**
> When comparing two values that are exactly the same, for instance 4 and 4, the only possible response is equal to, 4 is neither less than nor greater than 4 it is exactly equal to 4.

The other variables that we created during this step, namely the attackRange and targetAlive variables are going to be used later. For the moment, we will simply define how they will be used and plug them in later. The attackRange variable will be used in the same way as the detectionRange variable was except it is to determine a transition from the Pursue state to the Attack state. We cannot use the same detectionRange variable as the range that will be allowed to trigger actual attacking of the player will be much closer than the detectionRange. The targetAlive Bool variable will be utilized in the Attack state as there are ultimately two reasons that could cause the spider to stop attacking, either the player has gotten away or the player died. We will see all of these come together as we get to these states.

5.5.2 Patrolling

There are two primary approaches that we can use to get our spider to patrol around the game world. The first, and the one we will utilize for now, is to drop empty game objects into our world and create an actual path that we want the spider to follow. This means that for each spider we will have to create and position these waypoints and assign them to the spider. The second approach is to have the spider itself pick a random direction to go and to just take off. The best version to use is really going to depend on what you want the spider to be doing and what you need out of the game that you are developing. For example, if we want the spider to guard a specific building or cave, then it cannot just go wander off in some random direction, it will have to follow a specified path. Then again, if we just want a wandering spider on the level doing its own thing, then it will definitely need to have the ability to randomly pick where to go.

We will begin with the scripted patrol mechanism for our spider. For our first take at this, we will get our spider to patrol the edges of our test scene. Create four Empty Game Objects (GameObjects → Create Empty) and place

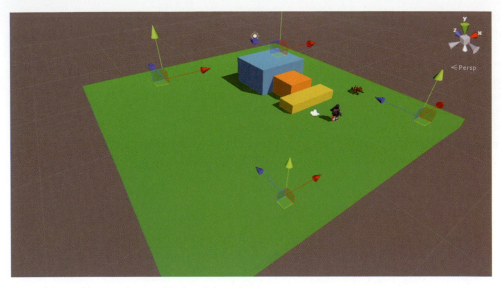

FIG 5.13 A sample layout of the empty objects used for the spider's patrol pattern.

them roughly in the corners of the test level. Empty Game Objects do not contain any components, hence the name empty; however, they do still have a transform component as all objects that exist within a scene must contain that component. Since they are empty and do not contain a Mesh Renderer component it will not be possible for us to see them within our scene, however we will still be able to select them within the Hierarchy panel. This is when forming the habit of following good naming practices begins to pay some dividends as we may end up with many various objects scattered about our level that we cannot see and can only identify from the names that we have given them. Figure 5.13 depicts a basic layout for these dummy objects, you can see the four game objects because of the four visible movement widgets in the scene. We have also gone ahead and named the empty objects as spider_waypoint_01 through spider_waypoint_04. Now, it is not necessary that you follow that naming scheme per se, but definitely utilize some naming scheme that helps you to not only know what these objects are for but also which one is which. We could construct this waypoint system by using Cubes (or other 3D shapes) instead of an empty object. Once we have them in place, just disable the Mesh Renderer component to make them invisible. By converting the default colliders on these objects to triggers, we could use trigger events to know when the spider has reached its target location. There is usually more than one way to get a task accomplished when creating your behavior scripts.

Note
Figure 5.13 is a composited image. Unity's standard behavior when you select multiple objects is to place the gizmo in the center of all the selected objects, not to provide individual gizmos as visualized within that specific image.

TABLE 5.5 Variables and Single Event Needed for the Patrolling FSM

Events	Variables and Types
Out of Bounds	index → Int
	finishRange → Float → Inspector
	moveSpeed → Float → Inspector
	nextTarget → Game Object
	waypoints → Array → Game Object → Inspector

It is now time to build the Patrol FSM that we designed earlier. Select the Patrolling FSM from the drop-down list of available state machines on the spider object. Within this state machine, we will need five variables and one custom event as depicted in Table 5.5. Two of these variables are going to be used for controlling the spider's movement from the Inspector, remember this is a great way to test, tweak, and finalize our settings. The moveSpeed variable will be used for how fast the spider actually moves, we will want this as a variable so that we can tweak it, while the game is running until we get a speed that not only matches how fast we would like the creature to go, but also looks good with the animation of the creature. The finishRange variable is going to be used to determine how close we have to be to the waypoint in order for the system to have considered us to have arrived at that location. Generally speaking, we need some wiggle room within a game system to get things to work and flow smoothly. Since both of these are going to be used within the Inspector, be sure to turn on the Inspector check box when these variables are created. The other three variables are all used for our waypoints.

The reason we will need multiple variables for those waypoints is that we are going to be using them as a list of locations for the system to select from when it is time to select a new location to move to. The most common approach to handling a list of things within a programming environment is to use something called an *array*, which leads to all of these variables that we are going to need.

The nextTarget variable is going to be the next waypoint that the spider is traveling toward, or from the design it is going to be the location that the spider is moving to. The waypoints variable will store a list of all of the waypoints that we want the spider to visit, in the order that we want the spider to patrol them. The index variable will be used to specify which one of the waypoints within our array of waypoints we are currently considering using, more on this shortly.

Arrays are an interesting and extremely valuable variable type (actually a data structure which is a method of organizing and storing our data within a computer) as they allow us to store a list of things. The things that we store in an array can be any of the standard variable types such as float or string. The array can also store a list of objects, such as Empty Game Objects that have been placed in a specific scene. Since arrays are lists of things, that means we can navigate through our list in order. For instance, when you have a to-do list or a shopping list you can scan through it from top to bottom until you find the item or thing that you are specifically looking for. We can also know where we are within our list, for instance someone could ask "how far along are you on that to-do list?" and you could glance at it and immediately tell them that you are on the fourth thing or fifth thing or whatever. This location of where we are within the array is referred to as the array's index value, hence our index variable that we have created.

Arrays also know how big they are which is equivalent to knowing how many things are in them, or at least should be in them. After creating the waypoints variable, change its Array Type to Game Object and make sure to select the check box for the Inspector, we are going to make this a variable that is visible within the Inspector Pane so that we can tweak it from there. Before leaving this variable, notice the text box labeled Size. This array property is how large the array is, or how many things we can put into it. In our case, this will equate to how many waypoints this particular spider will have within her patrolling pattern. If we want to add or remove waypoints, we would change this Size property to whatever value we would like, we could also adjust this value from the Inspector if the array is set to be an Inspector visible variable as ours is. Do not worry about Element 0 through 4 just yet, we will get to these as soon as we finalize the patrolling FSM. Figure 5.14 depicts the skeleton of the Patrolling FSM with all of the states connected through the appropriate transition events. Later, we will return to this state machine to add another state for the spider to find the nearest waypoint and continue patrolling, but we will work with that once we have a basic patrol system up and going.

Note
The Tooltip textbox for variable properties allows us to enter some text that will display next to the mouse cursor when a user hovers the mouse over the variable within the Inspector. When working with other developers, it is a good idea to provide a description of what the variable will allow the developer to change when modifying it. The Tooltip will have no impact on a variable that does not have the Inspector box checked.

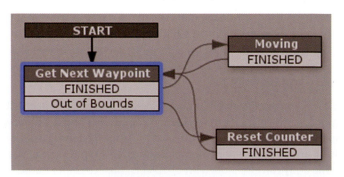

FIG 5.14 Basic skeleton of the Patrolling FSM.

During the design phase for this particular state machine, we laid out the essential logic of what we want it to do, but now that we know we are going to have to use something called an array to store all of our various waypoints, we are going to have to take a moment to look at how arrays function. The approach to using an array is to pull the current value out of the array and store it in another variable, we called this nextTarget. That index variable is keeping track of where we are located within the array of waypoints. Now, here is the tricky part about this: each time that we grab a waypoint from our array (we are not removing it, it is still there we are just copying it) we need to increase that index variable so that the next time we take something out of the array we will know to get the following item. Another way to look at this is when we write a long list of numbers from one page to another; many times we will keep our finger on the number that we are writing down. Then, when we finish writing that number, or copying it, we move our finger down that list and copy the next number. In this example, our finger is serving as the index variable, it is keeping track of where we are within the array and if we do not move our finger we will keep copying that same number over and over.

We need to be careful with that index variable that we are using to reference items within the array. The value of that index variable must fall within the valid range of our array. For instance, if we have an array of size 10, then the index variable could be anything from 0 to 9. Notice that was not 1–10. Numbering within computers begins at 0 that is the first number. For us, we begin counting at 1 because 0 means we do not have anything so we tend not to count that specific value, though when looking at numbering systems we actually do start at 0. Back to point, our index variable, for this specific spider, must be anything with the valid range of our array size, which is currently set to 4 that means our index can be anything from 0 to 3. If our index variable is out of that range, the computer will give us an "index out of bounds" or "index out of range" error message. Errors are bad, we do not like errors and would prefer to avoid them. So, in order to avoid that out of bounds error, we are going to have to be careful with what we do with the index variable.

With all of our variables and events created and the basic state machine structure in place, we will now put together the actual syntax of the actions that we are going to need for this. We will begin with the Get Next Waypoint state:

1. Add an Array Get action.
   a. Select waypoints from the drop-down list for the Array value.
   b. Switch to variable mode (the button with two lines) for Index and select the index variable.
   c. For Store Value select the nextTarget variable.
   d. Leave every frame turned off, as we only want to do this once each time we are in this state.
   e. For the Index Out Of Range event, select the Out of Bounds event transition that we have already connected to our state.

2. Add an Int Add action below the Array Get action.
   a. Select the index variable from the drop-down list for Int Variable.
   b. Enter a value of 1 in the Add text box.
   c. Leave Every Frame turned off.

This state is a deceptively simple looking sequence of actions, but there is a bunch of activity going on here and the power of the array is starting to come to the forefront in this. We begin with the Array Get action. With the way that PlayMaker handles arrays, the values within each individual index of the array can only be accessed through an Array Get or Array Set action. This is because the system is recognizing the array as a variable type, so the visual scripting interface only allows us to do stuff with the array as a whole entity if we were to drop the array in to a variable selection slot. This is very nice for us as it allows us to keep our array nice and safe and makes it more difficult for us to accidently alter the values that are stored within it. What we are doing in the Array Get is grabbing the actual Game Object (which happens to be a waypoint) from the index location within the array. So, if the value of index is 1, then we are grabbing the second waypoint in our list of waypoints (remember numbering started at 0, so 1 would be the second on the list). On the other hand, if index was 3 we would be getting the fourth waypoint from the list. At any rate, whichever waypoint we are getting we are letting our nextTarget variable equal that waypoint so that we can reference it through the nextTarget variable.

The Event that is associated with the Array Get action is an error or boundary condition event. Boundary conditions are the extreme values that can be associated with things, such as arrays, within the set of values that are valid. For instance, in our waypoints array, the boundary condition values would be 0 and 3, beyond those values we are outside of the valid range for this particular variable and have therefore exceeded its boundary. As a general rule, when programming, you want to test the boundary conditions heavily as that is the place that our programs are most likely to break and lead to errors. This specific event is fired whenever the value of index is outside of the valid range of values for our array. If we were to try to grab an array element outside of the valid range, it would not exist and odd behavior would be the result for our game. In this case, we can handle the situation of going out of bounds very cleanly through this Event condition included with the Array Get action. As a thought question, before we jump right into it, if the value of index were outside of the valid range what should we do, how should we handle that? For the solution, follow these steps:

1. Select the Reset Counter state.
   a. Add a Set Int Value action to the state.
      i. Select index for the Int Variable.
      ii. Enter a value of 0 in the Int Value textbox.
      iii. Leave the Every Frame turned off.

In the event that our index variable has exceeded the valid range of values for the array, we will utilize the Out of Bounds event which in turn will send us to Reset Counter. Once inside the Reset Counter state, we will use the Set Int Value action to specifically set that index variable back to a valid value for the waypoints array. Specifically, we will reset the index back to the first value within the array of waypoints.

Back to the Get Next Waypoint state for the final action, Int Add. The Int Add action will add a value to what is currently within an int variable. For instance, if our index variable is currently at 1 the Int Add action will add another 1 to it making the value stored within index equal to 2. We can add any values we want to the Int variable, as long as the value being added is another integer value. We can even add the value of another integer variable to our variable if we want to. Figure 5.15 provides a graphical representation of how these two actions are working together allowing us to navigate through our list of waypoints, one at a time.

The final state in this machine to construct is the Moving state which will be responsible for actually moving the spider to the next waypoint. This will be performed in three distinct steps: turn to look at the waypoint, move toward the waypoint, and play our walk animation while we are moving.

1. Select the Moving state.
    a. Add a Smooth Look At action.
        i. For Target Object, use the variable selection list and choose nextTarget.
        ii. Select the check box for Keep Vertical.
        iii. Select a value for Speed, we went with 5.
        iv. All other values can be left at default.
    b. Add a Play Animation event next.
        i. Select the walk animation from the drop-down list (or run).
        ii. Other values leave at default.
    c. Add a Move Toward action as the last event in the sequence.
        i. Use the variable selection list to assign nextTarget to the Target Object.
        ii. Turn Ignore Vertical on.
        iii. Set the speed to be our moveSpeed variable from the variable list.
        iv. Set the Finish Distance to be our finishRange from the variable list.
        v. Select FINISHED for the Finish Event.
        vi. Leave the others as default.

The Smooth Look At action is used to get an object within a scene to look at something else, to turn and face that something else. We can have it turn to face an object or a specific location somewhere within the scene. In our case, we are having our spider turn to face an object, the next waypoint that

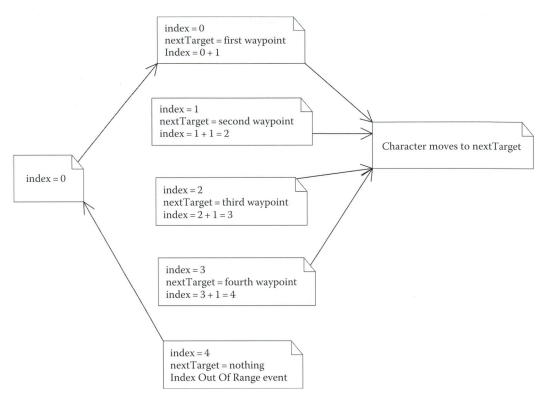

FIG 5.15 Logical flow through the array of waypoints.

it is going to go to. Even though nobody can actually see the waypoint, it does exist in the game world and does have a position. The Smooth Look At (or even the Look At action) will grab that position and do what needs to be done to get the object to turn to face it. This saves us a tremendous amount of work on our own as far as trying to figure out which way we need the spider to turn, we can let Unity figure that out for us. The Keep Vertical check box is just having the object ignore looking up or down to see the target, and there will be times that we want our object to use the vertical and others when we do not. This is one of those check boxes that it is easy to forget and end up with slightly odd behavior from our characters later.

> **Note**
> Remember that nearly all of the actions that we use within PlayMaker are actual methods within the Unity API. This means that if or when you decide to study C# scripting for yourself, you will be able to leverage much of your PlayMaker knowledge as you already know many of the things that you will need to do. As an example, the Move Toward action equates to the Vector3.MoveToward() method within the API. If you know how to use the action you basically know how to use the method, very nice.

We have used the Play Animation action before, so we will not discuss it again here. The Move Toward action is used to get one object to move toward either another object or a specific location within the scene. In our case, we want our spider to move toward the next waypoint from the array of waypoints. Just like with the Smooth Look At, the Ignore Vertical will have the system ignore any difference between the object and its target vertical position. This is good, because if they are not perfectly aligned vertically, then our spider might end up creeping into the air or slithering in to the ground as it attempts to move toward the next target leaving us with either a floating spider or a spider with only its head sticking out of the ground. Our Max Speed will determine how fast the spider moves and we will tweak this from the Inspector in a few minutes. Finally, the Finish Distance will be the error tolerance for how close the spider has to get before it moves to the next one, something like the neighborhood rule for getting the out at second base during a double play in baseball, for those that may be familiar with the sport.

With the state machine constructed for the spider, it is time to test and tweak it. Back in the Unity Scene Editor, make sure that you have the spider object selected so that we can see all of its properties within the Inspector Pane. The first thing we will do is populate that array with the empty Game Objects that we have already created. The easiest way to do this is to drag a waypoint from the Hierarchy Panel and drop it into the corresponding location in the array. For instance, spider_waypoint_01 should be added to Element 0 in the array. When doing this, do not release the mouse button once you have selected the waypoint from the Hierarchy, you want to grab it with the mouse and drag it over to the Element you would like to add it to. With the waypoints populated as seen if Figure 5.16, it is time to run our game and see what happens. Notice when we press the play button nothing seems to be happening, why? We can see the spider doing its animation, but it is not moving.

In order to get our spider moving, we will to have to give the moveSpeed variable a value in the Inspector. We are going to start with a value of 1 and the spider takes off moving. If you are having difficulty seeing the spider with your game view, switch back to the scene view so you can see the whole scene with the spider moving from that perspective instead. The scene view is very valuable when tweaking things. We have now run into our next little issue. The spider walks along until it just stops walking and kind of bounces back and forth. It is really close to the location of the next waypoint, but it is not there exactly. Currently, our error tolerance for this is set to 0; obviously, this is not going to work. Try increasing that finishRange value until your spider gets unstuck and goes on to the next waypoint. Make sure that your spider correctly navigates through the four waypoints, making any adjustments you need to these two variables. Our final settings for these were a moveSpeed of 0.8 and a finishRange of 1.5. Our spider now patrols, we are ready to move on, though play your game at this point to double-check and make sure it is working as expected.

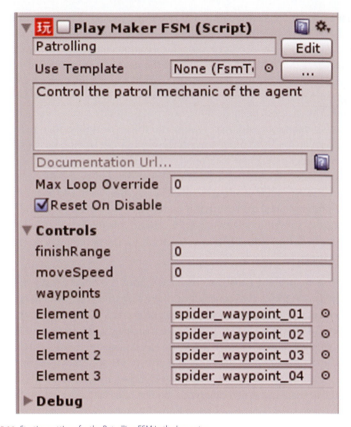

FIG 5.16 Starting settings for the Patrolling FSM in the Inspector.

Note
If your spider is stubbornly refusing to move, make sure that it has a Character Controller component attached to it within the Inspector.

Video
We can extend the patrolling behavior of our spider by either telling it to not patrol or telling it to pick its own random path to follow instead of using waypoints. These additions to our spider are demonstrated in the video "Advanced Spider Patrol" found in the videos section on the companion website.

5.5.3 Spotting the Player

Now that both our spider and player character can move around in the scene it is time to get them to respond to each other. Sancho will already respond to the spider, because the player will respond to the spider. By this, we mean to say that Sancho is already capable of charging into the fray to fight the spider that is handled by the player pressing the buttons to move Sancho closer to the spider. The spider, on the other hand, must make this decision on its own. In order to get this to work, we will need the spider to recognize when Sancho is nearby and then for the spider to actually close in and pursue the player until the spider can finally bite or kick at Sancho. If we pause for a moment here, we will recognize that not only do we already have a very strong idea of how to do this, but the essential components are already in place, they just need some tweaking.

The first step that we need to accomplish is for the spider to notice Sancho nearby; although if we think about it all the spider is actually noticing is a Game Object with the Player tag, this may prove useful later. For this, we will return to our Controller state machine that we built earlier. At the time that we built it, we left the detection range set to 0, this is found in the Patrol state of the controller. If we were to increase the value of that detectionRange variable that we have already created, then we should be able to find a nice threshold range for our spider's sensitivity to the presence of Sancho. At the moment, we just want to get a ballpark idea to make sure that our transition from Patrolling to Pursue is working. We will go ahead and run the test scene and keep increasing the detectionRange variable within the Inspector until the Controller transitions from the Patrol state to the Pursue state, as seen in Figure 5.17. As it turned out, with our current scene a value of 7 got the spider to transition to the Pursue state indicating that the spider now knows Sancho is there.

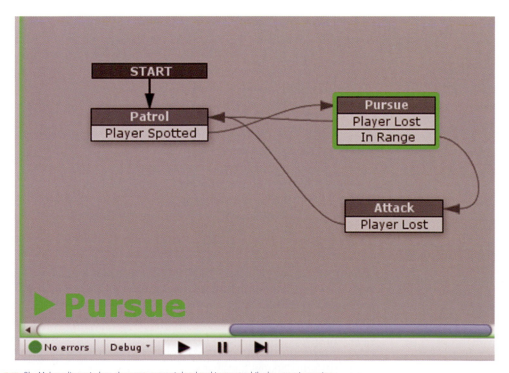

FIG 5.17 PlayMaker editor window, the current state is bordered in green while the game is running.

Our next step is to transition out of the Patrol state and into the Pursue state within the controller. Our Pursue state is going to be responsible for a couple of different things: It needs to switch the Pursue state machine on which will handle the actual chasing of the character around the scene, it needs to be able to go back to the Patrol state if the character happens to get away, and it needs to be able to transition on to the Attack state if the spider gets close enough to bite at the player. Before looking at the actual solution below, take a moment to consider how this could be done based upon what we already know and have done thus far, as we already have the information we need and have used the actions that we are going to use except for one action which will be new. Although, this state could be constructed without the new action and only using ones that we used to construct the Patrol state earlier.

1. Select the Pursue state in the Controller state machine.
   a. Add the Player Lost transition event.
      i. Connect the transition to the Patrol state.
   b. Add the In Range transition event.
      i. Connect the transition to the Attack state.
   c. Add an Enable FSM action.
      i. Select the Pursue FSM.
         A. Enable set to true.
         B. Reset on Exit set to true.
      ii. Add a Get Distance action.
         A. For Target use the variable selection option and select enemy.
         B. For Store Result store it in the playerDistance variable.
         C. Do this every frame.
      iii. Add a Float Compare action.
         A. Float 1 is playerDistance.
         B. Float 2 is detectionRange.
         C. Greater Than will use the Player Lost transition event.
         D. Do this every frame.
      iv. Add another Float Compare event.
         A. Float 1 is playerDistance.
         B. Float 2 is attackRange.
         C. Less Than will use the In Range transition event.
         D. Do this every frame.

The only new action in this list is the Get Distance action. We could have done the Find Closest that we did in the Patrol state, but we are going to have a single-minded kind of spider such that once he finds a target he stays with that one until it is dead or escaped. This Get Distance action, like the Find Closest action, allows us to determine the actual distance, as a float value, between our source object and the target object. Based upon this distance, we will perform different transitions.

Now that the spider can detect the player, it is time to get the spider to chase after Sancho. We actually already know how to do this too, we will do it the exact same way that we did the waypoint navigation, except instead of using an array of waypoints with the Move Toward action, we will just use the Sancho game object that is in the scene and the spider will then chase poor Sancho wherever he goes. You may have noticed this as a possibility while building the waypoints and testing the scene if you grabbed one of the waypoints and moved it around while the game was running, the spider did what needed to be done to try to catch that waypoint.

1. Select the Pursue state machine not the Pursue state within the Controller machine.
   a. Create a new variable of type float named chaseSpeed.
      i. Make sure that Inspector is turned on for it.
   b. Create another variable of type Game Object named target.
   c. Change the default State 1 to a different state name, we went with Chase for ours.
      i. Add a Get FSM Game Object action.
         A. Select Controller from the list for FSM Name.
         B. Select enemy from the list for Variable Name.
         C. Store Value should be target.
      ii. Add a Play Animation action.
         A. Select the run animation.
      iii. Add a Smooth Look At action.
         A. Use the variable selection for Target Object to choose target.
         B. Turn the check box for Keep Vertical on.
      iv. Add a Move Toward action.
         A. For the Target Object use the variable selection to choose target.
         B. Turn on the check box for Ignore Vertical.
         C. Set Max Speed to be the chaseSpeed variable.
         D. Leave the other default values as they are.

We have seen many of these steps before, there are only two things that we would like to discuss before moving on. The Get FSM Game Object action is a new one for us. We can access the variables that are within other state machines by using the Get FSM and Set FSM actions followed by the appropriate variable type that we are after. What we are doing here is grabbing the game object that was tagged with Player from the controller state machine and making sure that our Pursue state machine is chasing after the same object that originally got the spider's attention to begin with. The every frame really is not necessary, as the only time that the target object from the Controller would change would be if the spider had lost sight of the object and returned to the Patrolling state. If it were to return to the Patrolling state then the Pursue state machine that we are currently in would have been deactivated. So, you can either turn the Every Frame on or off, it should not impact the functionality of our system either way. Finally, the run animation was selected as we want it to appear as though the spider is being aggressive and move more quickly to attack something or defend its territory than when it was just trudging along doing its own thing.

The spider now chases Sancho all over the place and as we tweak the chaseSpeed variable we can get a smoother looking animation sequence as well as a more challenging speed. In this tweaking process, you may want to consider changing the animation speed, like we did to get Sancho to run backward, to get a better timing between the speed that the spider is moving at and the speed that the animation is playing at. Now that the spider is chasing Sancho as aggressively as he is, we are ready to implement some attacking. Play the game before moving on to make sure that this stage is working as expected, if the system gets stuck in the attack state then we are good.

5.5.4 Attacking the Player

In this step, we will work on getting the spider to do a basic attack and to detect when it has hit the player, we will actually leave hurting the player for the next step. It is a good idea to break your work down into small sub-problems or sub-projects that can be more easily tested. For instance, if we were to construct all of this in one go and it did not work correctly it would be far more difficult for us to track down exactly which part of the implementation is not working correctly. That may seem like a trivial thing to worry about, but it is an infuriating one when we run into it by getting over confident and implementing too many pieces at one time, which we are trying to avoid. We will begin by returning to our Controller state machine and filling in the Attack stage as depicted.

1. Select the Attack state in the Controller state machine.
   a. Add the Player Lost transition event and connect it to Patrol state.
   b. Add an Enable FSM action.
      i. FSM Name should be Attacking.
      ii. Reset on Exit should be on.
   c. Add a Get Distance action.
      i. Target is enemy.
      ii. Result should be stored in playerDistance.
      iii. Every Frame should be on.
   d. Add a Float Compare action.
      i. Float 1 should be playerDistance.
      ii. Float 2 is attackRange.
      iii. Greater Than will lead to the Player Lost event.
      iv. Do this Every Frame.

The core of the Attack state is now in place. There is one section that we have left out, but it has been left out intentionally at this point as it is part of causing damage to the other object that is being attacked. Since we do not plan on getting that up and running until the next section, there is no point in trying to get it working just yet, rather we will focus on the basic attack pieces and detecting that collision for right now. We have used all of the actions from above previously, so there is nothing new to discuss about them. Moving onto the Attacking state machine, we can construct the following:

1. Change the Start 1 state to Attack.
2. Add another state named Cool Down.
3. Add a FINISHED event to both states and connect them to each other.
   a. Attack connected to Cool Down.
   b. Cool Down connected to Attack.
4. Select the Attack state.
   a. Add a Play Random Animation action.
      i. Change the number of animations to 2.
      ii. Set animation 1 to attack1 with a weight of 0.6.
      iii. Set animation 2 to attack2 with a weight of 0.6.
      iv. Set the Finish Event to FINISHED.
5. Select the Cool Down state.
   a. Add a Play Animation action.
      i. Select idle as the Anim Name.
   b. Add a Random Wait action.
      i. Select 1.5 for Min.
      ii. Enter 3 for Max.
      iii. Finish Event should be set to FINISHED.
      iv. Real Time should be turned on.

Once again, we are familiar with all of these actions, except for one. By now, we are beginning to see that these actions are reused many times in different states and that with our current knowledge of the available actions we can already build some pretty interesting behaviors. But, back to the point, the new action is the Random Wait action. There are two varieties of this, the Random one, which we are using, or a non-random one that is just called Wait. In either case, they work by pausing in the current state, or specifically by not allowing the current state to end, until after the specified time has been reached. We can do this in either Real Time, which would be seconds through the use of a time scale applied internally, or in game time without utilizing any type of time scaling. At first glance, it may seem as though we could have done this all in one state, play our attack animation and then wait right there before starting the state again. The problem with that approach is that it would have had the spider be static, no animation, between the attacks. Going with the approach that we did use we can have the spider play its idle animation between attacks. At this point, we should go ahead and test our system thus far and make sure that the spider is playing an animation, waiting, and playing another one.

For the collision system, we will need to add some colliders to our spider object. But it is not quite as simple as just adding a collider component to

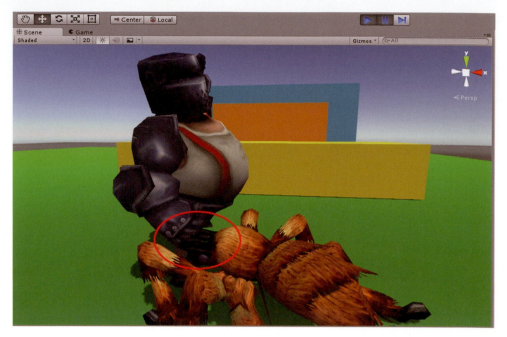

FIG 5.18 Spider caught as it bites Sancho, notice the teeth.

the spider itself. What we really need to do is add colliders to the parts of the spider that will actually be "attacking" the player, which will involve a little bit of research. What we are going to do is manipulate a view in the scene editor such that we can see the Sancho character and also the spider when it is close enough to attack. Once we have the view setup we can go ahead and run the game and click on the Scene tab to return to this scene view while the game is running. After waiting a few moments, our spider will come in to the view and we can pause as it starts to attack the character. Figure 5.18 provides a display of the game paused just as the spider is trying to bite Sancho. Now for the catch, figuring out exactly what that is, notice how that part of the spider has moved forward. This movement is being done within the animation and is not actually affecting the position of the spider itself at all. Even though those teeth have moved forward, the spider is still right where it was. This means that if we were to attach a collider component to the spider, that component would not have moved with the teeth, so we need to find those teeth.

> **Note**
> Pausing a running game to look around in the Scene editor or the Inspector pane to find something is very valuable. Even more valuable is the ability to advance the game one frame at a time by clicking the frame advance button to the right of the pause button. Through this tool, we can move the game forward one frame at a time and really see what is going on.

FIG 5.19 Child objects of the spider in the scene.

With the game still running, but paused, click the triangle next to the spider within the hierarchy view to open up all of the child objects of the spider as shown in Figure 5.19. In order to find those teeth, we are just going to start clicking on the children and the scene editor will show us where that child object currently is in the scene. To get a better feel of what we are looking at, once a child object is selected, go ahead and use the Next Frame button to move the game forward a couple of frames and see how that piece is moving, if it is moving. We selected the very first object, called Box01, which appears to be connected to the spiders head or something. Using the Next Frame button, we were able to play the game forward and see that this Box01 object moves with the animation. The other objects move with the animation as well, but Box01 was the first one we tried and it solved the problem at hand, the Spider01 child object would have been a good selection as well. Ultimately which one we select only matters based on one criterion; does it move with the animation. If it does then that child object will work just fine for what we want.

We can go ahead and stop the game running now that we know what part of the spider we are after; in our case, we will be using Box01 as the parent object for our next step. What we are going to do next is to create a new Game Object, like we did with the cubes and the ground a couple of chapters back, and attach this new object to the Box01 child of the spider. Once it is a child of Box01, we can then reposition the object so that it aligns with the mouth area of the spider. This will allow us to detect collisions with the mouth when it hits Sancho, as it turns out while the spider is kicking its mouth moves forward as well.

Note
There are two types of collisions: blocking collisions and trigger collisions. In a blocking collision, the objects cannot pass through each other. In a trigger collision, they can pass through each other.

1. Make sure that the game is not currently running.
2. Add a new capsule object to the scene (GameObject—3D Object—Capsule).
3. Make the capsule a child of Box01 by dragging it in the Hierarchy panel onto Box01.
4. Rotate, scale, and position the object so that it is aligned with the spider's mouth.
   a. You should now have something similar to Figure 5.20.
5. Turn off the Mesh Renderer component of the capsule object.
6. Click the check box for Is Trigger within the Capsule Collider component.
7. Rename the capsule object, if you want to, something like Jaws_ Collider is pretty cool.

The first step in responding to an attack collision is now in place after the construction of the capsule Game Object. The next step is to add some functionality to this object through a State Machine. In order to implement the design that we created previously for this character, we will need one variable and one custom event in our new state machine. The new event is

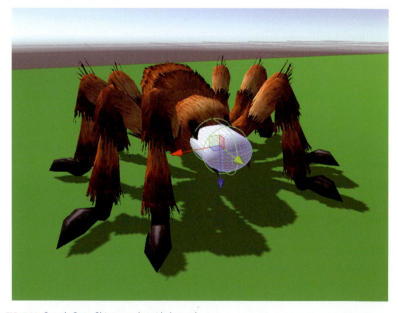

FIG 5.20 Capsule Game Object over the spider's mouth.

for when the capsule hits the player, as such we will call this event Hit Player. The variable is used to track what it is that the spider is supposed to be attacking and therefore what it should be colliding with. For this example, we have created this variable as a Game Object type and named it target. We are not going to be able to complete this state machine until after we have completed the health system within Sancho. But we will drop in the basic pieces here.

1. Change the name of State 1 to Idle.
   a. Add the Hit Player transition event.
   b. Add a Trigger Event.
      i. Trigger is On Trigger Enter.
      ii. Collide Tag is Player.
      iii. Send Event is Hit Player.
      iv. Store Collider is target.
2. Create a new state name Hit.
   a. Connect the Hit Player from Idle to this state.
   b. Add a FINISHED transition event and connect to Idle.

The actions that we will need within the Hit state cannot be added until after we have the health system constructed within Sancho. The Trigger Event action is a new one and one that it is worth a few minutes of looking at as we need to know how to get collisions out of Unity and respond to them for many different game-play systems. To begin, this action requires a Collider component that is of a Trigger type. We took care of this when we constructed the Capsule Game Object and turned on the check box for the Is Trigger within the collider component. There are three distinct types of events that can occur with triggers, as depicted in Table 5.6. It is important to keep these in mind as there are many different things that we could use triggers for. For instance, by using the On Trigger Stay we can have the system perform some action, or sequence of actions, as long as an object is within a certain area of the scene that is defined by a trigger that we have put out there (Game Object with a Collider component set to Is Trigger and the Mesh Renderer turned off).

TABLE 5.6 Three Different Trigger Events That Can Occur within Unity

Trigger Function	Purpose
On Trigger Enter	Event occurs on the frame that the object collides with or enters into the area defined by the trigger collider.
On Trigger Stay	Event is called every frame that the object is still within the boundary that is defined by the trigger collider.
On Trigger Exit	Event is used on the frame that the object leaves the region defined by the trigger collider and is no longer in contact with it.

The next three pieces of the Trigger Event action define what object we are colliding with and what to do. We begin with the Collide Tag. Any object can collide with any other object within a scene provided they both have colliders. However, we usually only care about specific collisions and we can use the tag system within Unity to be able to find and group the objects that we care about. In this case, the only collision that we care about with the spider's mouth is when it happens to hit some other object that is tagged as a Player, any other collisions will be ignored by this action. If we have had a collision with the object tag that we are interested in, the action will proceed with the next two steps. The first step is what transition event it should do as a result of this collision and the second step is to keep the thing that we hit in a variable in case we want to do something with that object, such as cause damage to it.

Except for a couple of actions to finish of the functionality of the system, our spider attack is ready and functional, we will move on to the health system for Sancho and then return to finalize the missing actions within this state machine.

5.5.5 Hurting the Player

We now have the pieces in place for the spider to attack and if we were to test our game so far, the spider appears to attack. It spots Sancho, runs up to Sancho, and then proceeds to begin attacking him with two different attack animations. It also appears as though the collider that we constructed is intersecting with Sancho. It is now time to get the other piece of this puzzle in place. This health system may have many states within it, but as we saw in the design stage, it is not as complex as it may appear. It just has many small pieces that we need to take our time and construct as we go along. Table 5.7 lists all of the events and transitions that we will need within this state machine and Figure 5.21 displays the skeleton of it constructed within PlayMaker.

The damage variable is used to indicate how much damage is caused to Sancho by the attack. We are going to allow the object that collides with Sancho to specify this damage value that is going to make it possible for different things within the scene to cause different amounts of damage. And if the damage variable of the attacking object is set as an Inspector variable, then we could adjust that damage amount from the Inspector panel rather than having to come back in to the PlayMaker state machines to adjust the values. The health variable will store the total amount of health that Sancho currently has while the maxHealth is the maximum amount that he could have. The maxHealth

TABLE 5.7 Events and Variables Needed for the Health State Machine of Sancho Panza

Events	Variables and Types
Died	damage → Int
Hit	gotHit → Bool
Keep Going	health → Int
	isAlive → Bool
	maxHealth → Int → Inspector

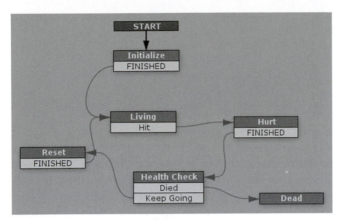

FIG 5.21 All of the states and transitions in place for Sancho's health state machine.

will be utilized when initializing the health of the character and by making it an Inspector variable we can enter any value we like directly within the Inspector panel for this object. For immediate testing we will give this maxHealth a value of 20 knowing that we will change it in the Inspector to 100 later.

The two Boolean variables are used for the state machine to know if Sancho has been hit by something as well as if Sancho is still alive or not. It will be important for other objects to know if Sancho is still alive as well, consider the Attack state from the spider previously, it will keep attacking until Sancho has escaped or is no longer alive. The gotHit variable is really just going to be used as a test to determine whether we have been hit, the same thing could have been accomplished through the use of a Global Event within PlayMaker, but that is something that we will look into later. Now we will populate these states with the needed actions, we will begin with the Initialize, Living, and Hurt states.

1. Select the Initialize state.
   a. Add a Set Int Value action.
      i. Int Variable should be health.
      ii. Int Value should be the maxHealth variable.
      iii. Do not do Every Frame.
   b. Add a Set Bool Value action.
      i. Bool Variable is isAlive.
      ii. Bool Value is checked.
      iii. Do not do Every Frame.
   c. Add a Set Tag action.
      i. Tag is Player.
2. Select the Living state.
   a. Add a Bool Test action.
      i. Bool Variable is gotHit.
      ii. Is True is the Hit event.
      iii. Every Frame is checked.

3. Select the Hurt state.
   a. Add an Int Add action.
      i. Int Variable is health.
      ii. Add is damage.
      iii. Every Frame is not checked.
   b. Add a Play Animation action.
      i. Anim Name is self-hit.

We will pause here and take a quick look at these actions and states that we have constructed thus far. Beginning with the Initialize state, we see that we are setting the health and isAlive status variables for Sancho. The only new action in this state is the Set Tag action. This action serves two purposes. The first is a safety net just in case we forgot to set the tag of the object in the Inspector. The second purpose, is to change the tags later to help the spider behave and quit attacking the dead Sancho. If you recall, we utilized a Find Closest action in the spider and it looked for the closest object with a specified tag, in this case it was Player. Once the target that the spider is attacking is dead, we will switch this tag on the target to something other than Player and the spider will then ignore it. This is going to prevent the spider from looping through those states that it has and instead short circuit that whole process by making the thing it just attacked no longer a Player tagged object and therefore not anything that it cares about.

The living state is simply checking the status of that gotHit Boolean variable every frame. This variable will be turned to true by something when it hits it, for instance when the spider collider triggers the collision with Sancho we will reach in to this state machine and set this value to be true causing Sancho's health logic to proceed to the next step. We could have also used something called a Global Event within PlayMaker for this same effect. A Global Event is one that can be triggered by anything anywhere. So the spider trigger collision could, instead of setting this Boolean variable to true, trigger that Global Event. The use of the variable instead of the Global Event is a purely personal choice in this particular situation, there is no definitive advantage one way or the other.

The final state that we have populated thus far is the Hurt state. This one is fairly self-explanatory as we have seen all of these actions in other states before. When the character gets hit, it will subtract a certain amount from its current health and play some type of animation to indicate to the player that the character has been hit. This is important as we need to provide feedback to the player so that they are aware of what is happening within the game world. When we get to the GUI elements later we may return to this and add some numbers that rise from Sancho and fade away indicating how much damage he has received, which could work nicely with the health bar that will be adding at that point in time. Now, we will finish this health management system for our character.

1. Select the Health Check state.
   a. Add an Int Compare action.
      i. Integer 1 is health.
      ii. Integer 2 is 0.
      iii. Equal goes to the Died event.
      iv. Less Than goes to the Died event.
      v. Greater Than goes with the Keep Going event.
      vi. Do not do this Every Frame.
2. Select the Dead state.
   a. Add a Set Tag action.
      i. Tag is Dead (will need to create a new tag for this).
   b. Add a Play Animation action.
      i. Anim Name is die.
   c. Add a Set Bool Value action.
      i. Bool Variable is isAlive.
      ii. Bool Value is not checked.
      iii. Every Frame is not checked.
   d. Add an Enable FSM action.
      i. FSM name is Actions.
      ii. Enable is not checked.
      iii. Reset on Exit is not checked.
      iv. Repeat this for the Movement and Rotate FSMs as well.
3. Select the Reset state.
   a. Add a Set Bool Value action.
      i. Bool Variable is gotHit.
      ii. Bool Value and Every Frame are not checked.

Beginning with the Health Check state, we have used an Int Compare action, which is the same thing as the Float Compare we have used before except for integer values, to make a decision based upon the current health value of the character. If this health value is at or below 0 we can go ahead and transition on to the Dead state; otherwise, we will begin resetting everything to return to the Living state and await another damaging hit from something.

The Dead state has some interesting pieces within, we have seen all of these actions but it is the reasoning and logic behind their use that makes this one interesting, as the logic for behaviors begins to really take form for us. First, we will change the character's tag to Dead, which will require creating a new tag for that, so that the spider will ignore this character when looking for the closest thing to attack. Next, we will turn off all of the other state machines within Sancho so that the player cannot keep running around and doing stuff after they have died. If we were to allow a respawning system (which we will later), we would need to link it in here, but that is a topic for a later time. The reset state is simply resetting the Bool gotHit variable back to its initial value of false and handing control back to the Living state to await another hit.

5.5.6 Connecting the Attack and Health States

Sancho is now ready to be hurt by things in the world and the spider is ready to hurt Sancho, all we need to do is to connect these two sections together for our final piece of functionality on all of this. Sancho's health management system is correctly constructed and the work that we need to do resides in the spider and in the spider collider object that we attached to Box01 earlier, for ease of reference we named our spider collider object Jaws_Collider. We will begin with the final connections for the spider object.

1. Select the Attack state in the Controller state machine of the spider.
   a. Add a Get FSM Bool action.
      i. Game Object is Specify Game Object.
      ii. For the object itself select the variable option and select enemy.
      iii. FSM Name is Health, this will not be available in the drop-down menu and you will have to type it, make sure spelling and capitalization match the name of the FSM from Sancho.
      iv. Variable Name is isAlive, once again will have to manually type it, make sure capitalization and spelling match.
      v. Store Value is targetAlive.
      vi. Every Frame is checked.
   b. Add a Bool Test action.
      i. Bool Variable is targetAlive.
      ii. Is False is the Player Lost event.
      iii. Every Frame is checked.

When we built the Attack state earlier, we allowed the spider to leave this state if the player object was escaping so that the spider would begin chasing again. Now, we are adding the ability of the spider to leave this state whenever the player object is dead. In order to do this we will have to utilize one of the Get FSM Value actions that we have already used, this time to get the FSM value from another object rather than from our own object. Our enemy variable has been used to identify which object it is that the spider is attacking so; therefore, we will use that to reference the FSM of the object that we are attacking as well. By using a variable for the object, we are not able to select anything for the FSM or the variable name. This is because at the moment of development, the system does not know what object the enemy variable is referring to, but once the game is running that variable will refer to an object. The trick here is that any other objects we allow the spider to attack, by giving them the tag of Player, we need to make sure that they also have a Health FSM and an isAlive variable so that this will work for all of them. This is essentially allowing all objects to share the same framework of a health management system. When typing in the FSM name and variable names, make sure that the capitalization and spelling matches that which is in the object. This is a common place for errors to occur and they can be deceptively difficult to find. Finally, we add a Bool test on the value that we have gotten from the health management system and can kick the spider controller out of attacking and back to patrolling.

Next, we need to move on to the Jaws_Collider object and the state machine that we constructed for it. What we need to add to this one is within the Hit state. Once the system has detected a collision with a Player tagged object we want to cause damage to that object by reaching in to its health management system and setting both the gotHit variable to true and the damage amount to whatever damage we are going to allow to be caused. For instance, we can set the damage caused by the spider to be 10 and the damage caused by the shadow character to be 30 or whatever.

1. Select the Hit state.
    a. Add a Set FSM Bool action.
        i. Game Object is Specify Game Object.
            A. Specified as the target variable.
        ii. FSM Name is Health, be careful of the spelling and capitalization.
        iii. Variable Name is gotHit, be careful of the spelling and capitalization.
        iv. Set Value is checked and Every Frame is not.
    b. Add a Set FSM Int action.
        i. Game Object is Specify Game Object.
            A. Specified as the target variable.
        ii. FSM Name is Health, be careful of the spelling and capitalization.
        iii. Variable Name is damage, be careful of the spelling and capitalization.
        iv. Set Value is −10, or whatever value you would like to use.
        v. Every Frame is not checked.

Now, when the Jaws_Collider object hits Sancho during an attack by the spider, Sancho's health system will process through all of its states. The process through the states of the health system begins by setting the gotHit Boolean variable to true so that the systems know it has been hit. We are specifying how much damage is being caused by the biting spider during its attack, in this case 10 points of damage. Sancho's health system will determine if he is still alive or not leaving our spider to determine what it must do next as well. We have now completed the essential construction of our AI system for the spider threshold guardian character within our game project.

5.5.7 Final Tweaks

Our spider is now completed and connected with the Sancho health system it is time to do some play testing. Some key things to look for as we test this system are:

- Does Sancho respond properly to getting hit? (plays his self hit animation)
- Does the spider close in and attack Sancho? (should have been tested earlier, but double-check)
- Does Sancho die when he should? (if he has a starting health value of 20 and the spider causes 10 points of damage, then Sancho should fall over dead after two hits)
- Does Sancho stay dead when he gets killed?
- Can Sancho run away from the spider?
- Can Sancho run away after the spider has attacked him once?

Hopefully, your system passed all of our current play test metrics that we were looking at. If not, look back and double-check your state machines paying special attention to variables used and the order that the actions are placed within the states. PlayMaker executes the actions in order from top to bottom, so if there is an action giving the state the option of firing a transition event before another action that never seems to be running it may be caused by PlayMaker exiting that state, switch the order of those actions and see if the problem is resolved.

During the play testing, you may have noticed a couple of other bugs that cropped up. We essentially have two different types of bugs that occur. The first type is when the system does not behave as we wanted it to which is always caused by a mistake on our part, either giving the system a command that does not do what we think it does or using the wrong variable or something. The other type of bug that can happen is when the system does not do something that it probably should because we simply did not even think about that while we were designing and implementing everything. We currently have one of the latter types of bugs, but did you notice it? The spider cannot attack Sancho while he is moving. So, how could we fix this? Through some more play testing and fiddling with the attackRange variable we can find a value that will allow the spider's attack to be triggered while Sancho is still moving with the potential of causing damage, though as a rule it will not cause damage since Sancho is moving when the attack is started and odds are when the Jaws_Collider gets to where it is going Sancho will be gone. We could increase this range some more, but as we do so, we should also consider sliding that Jaws_Collider object out away from the mouth region to make sure that we can still trigger a collision event with Sancho.

In play testing, our way through this one, a new bug popped up because we had not considered it either. If the spider goes in to its Attack state while Sancho is moving and Sancho stays within attackRange of the spider, it is possible for the spider to be facing the opposite direction of Sancho and every now and then making a random lunge into blank space. Not something that we want, this can be adjusted by adding a Smooth Look At enemy object within the Attack state of the controller state machine.

The final tweak that we are going to concern ourselves with, and there are some others but we will leave those for you to play around with and tweak as you see fit, is going to be the process of returning to its patrolling. Currently, the spider will return to patrolling by going to the next waypoint in its list of waypoints. But it is possible that in our mad attempt to escape the crazed spider we have led it on a wild goose chase all over the map until we ultimately lost, since we cannot fight back there was a definite advantage for the spider. In order to do this we need to utilize a global event transition, which was discussed earlier, and do some searching in our array.

1. Select the Patrolling state machine within the spider.
   a. Add a new event called Finished Attacking.
      i. After creating the event click the check box to the left of the event name to make it a Global Event, see Figure 5.22.
   b. Create a new state and name it Find Closest Waypoint.
      i. Add a Global Transition to this state and select the Finished Attacking event.
      ii. Add a FINISHED event and connect it to the Moving state, your modified state machine should resemble Figure 5.23.
      iii. Add a Find Closest action.
         A. With Tag is Spider Waypoint (will need to create this tag and put all of the spider waypoints within it).
         B. Store Object is nextTarget.
      iv. Add an Array Contains action.
         A. Array is waypoints.
         B. Value is nextTarget.
         C. Index is index.
      v. Add an Int Add action.
         A. Int Variable is index.
         B. Add 1.
2. Select the Controller state machine.
   a. Select the Patrol state.
      i. Immediately after the Enable FSM action add a Send Event action.
         A. Event Target is Game Object FSM.
         B. FSM Name is Patrolling.
         C. Send Event is Finished Attacking.

We begin this process by creating that global transition event, which only required clicking a check box to go from a regular transition to a global one. In the new state that we added to the Patrolling state machine, we have the system searching to find the nearest Spider Waypoint tagged item just

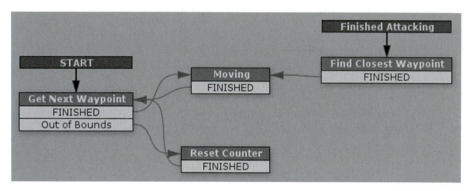

FIG 5.22 Global event check box for events in PlayMaker.

FIG 5.23 Modified version of the Patrolling state for the spider.

as we had the Controller searching to find the nearest Player tagged item. Now you can begin to see the power of organizing the objects that we have in our scenes and tagging them as it abstracts out what we need the actions to accomplish. Keep in mind that while we can hard code things, in the end it is much better to use variables or other tools such that the values are determined at runtime rather than at development time because things may change. Hard coding refers to providing exact numbers and values for things rather than variables, such as using a number of 2.5 (for instance) as the maximum speed of the spider rather than the moveSpeed variable. Hard-coded values are also more difficult to modify as we need to find and replace all the locations in which the hard-coded values were used. Always try to avoid these hard-coded values whenever possible.

After searching for and finding the closest Spider Waypoint type of object, we are going to store that object within the nextTarget variable that the Patrolling state machine uses to determine where it is going. The next action is an interesting one, what we are doing here is figuring out which one of the waypoints in our array of waypoints is the closest one that has been selected as our next target. This is very important, because we need to know where we are at within our array and therefore which waypoint will be the one that we will be targeting after the spider has arrived at this closest one. The Array Contains action is used to accomplish this task, specifically to find a specified thing within the array, in this case the nextTarget Game Object. Remember, arrays can store other variable types than just Game Objects, we just happen to be using this one to store a Game Object. Once the action has found that particular thing within the array it will store the index of that thing that it found, the location of that thing within the array, in the specified variable, in this case the index variable. We end this state by adding one to that index variable so that the index is pointing to the *next* waypoint in our array. If it happens that the index is now out of bounds because of that addition that is fine because once the Moving state has completed and control goes back to the Get Next Waypoint state it will pick up the Index Out of Bounds error and kick control down to the Reset Counter state.

The last thing that is needed to get the system to utilize that new global transition event we just added is to put a Send Event action into the Patrol state of the Controller state machine. Make sure that this action occurs *after* the Patrolling FSM is enabled; otherwise, the event we are trying to trigger will be inside of a disabled FSM, which means that the triggered event will not do anything. When sending events with this action, we need to specify where we are sending the event to, the Event Target, as well as what type of Event Target we are sending it to, in this case the FSM Name. By specifying Game Object FSM as our Event Target, we are telling PlayMaker that we will be sending an event to an FSM somewhere. In the GameObject section we could have specified another object, such as say the enemy variable that we have. The FSM Name component then specifies which FSM within the GameObject target we are sending our event to and finally which event we want to send, the Send Event piece.

Playtest our final AI system for the spider and make sure that it is working correctly, specifically get the spider to chase you to a far corner of your scene and make sure that when you get away, or die if you prefer, that the spider will return to patrolling by starting with the nearest waypoint instead of the one it was heading toward when it got sidetracked by spotting Sancho.

5.6 Prefabs

Now that we have completed the basic construction of our Sancho Panza character as well as some NPCs for him to interact with, we will create prefabs from these assets. The ability to create prefabs is a very powerful feature within Unity. A prefab is a Game Object that is essentially a holder for other game objects and components. That is to say that we can create a prefab of our Sancho character asset (or any of the others) that is currently in our scene and all of the pieces that comprise and define this asset will be stored within the prefab, including any settings and tweaks that we may have made to Inspector level variables. By creating these prefabs, we can add our completed characters back into another scene without having to reconstruct them as we did in this chapter. Any changes that we may make to the characters later can be updated into the prefab as well so that the changes will appear across all scenes using the character or we can keep the changes to only the current scene.

To create a prefab for Sancho, find the Prefabs folder in the Project pane. When we open this folder, notice that there are already four prefabs in here, these were created when we imported the Skeleton asset in the last chapter. Grab the Sancho object in the Hierarchy panel and drag it down into the Prefabs folder of the project pane. This has now created a Prefab object in the Project folder that can be added to any other scene we like and when we add him we will get all of the FSMs and settings that we have constructed thus far. Be sure to create prefabs of other complex assets that we create. If we forget to create a prefab of an asset, we can always reload the scene and create a prefab by dragging the asset from the Hierarchy panel and into the Project panel.

5.7 Summary

In this chapter, we explored the basics of AI systems so that we are now familiar with the broad concepts within this field. While as game developers, we all have the goal of making more believable and engaging computer characters to populate our virtual worlds, it is not quite as simple as toggling some setting in our game engine from low intelligence to high. There is a wealth of programming complexity to create rich behavior systems for our characters and if we have that as a goal, then the AI system must be developed early in the game cycle not late. We will need more time and more testing the more complex our AI system becomes and as such we cannot wait until all the rest of the game is completed then throw in a strong AI. If we were to opt to wait until later in the development of the game, then we will have to recognize that the decision-making systems we will have to use will not be able to be as rich and deep as we may have envisioned in the beginning. Another key factor to keep in mind is that elusive fun factor, if a more complex intelligence system makes our games less fun to play then the complex intelligence system has to go. We can create some very nice characters for our games by combining our character knowledge from the previous chapter with the information from this chapter and sculpt non-player characters with the illusion of depth and complexity, even if their behaviors lack it. We have hit on some pretty heavy programming and logic concepts in this chapter with the arrays and the global events, be sure to practice with these some to make sure you are comfortable before moving on.

> **Download**
> You can find the finished scene for this chapter in the complete project package on the companion website, the scene name is: "Chapter5_part2."

Vocabulary

Artificial intelligence
Expert systems
Evolutionary systems
Random behavior

Scripted behavior
Mathematical behavior modeling
Abstraction
Comparison
Array
Data structure
Boundary condition
Hard coded

Review Quiz

1. Why would a game developer opt for a scripted behavior AI system?
2. What is one of the strengths of a mathematical model for an AI system?
3. Why are evolutionary AI systems not used in too many games?
4. What should the final factor be when selecting an AI system for your game project?
5. How can other state machines access an internal variable of a specified state machine?
6. When using a Find Closest action what is the purpose of the object's tag?
7. When comparing two integer values, what would be the result of the comparison is 15 less than 15?
8. What can we do to make a Game Object invisible within a scene?
9. What is the difference between a collider and a trigger?
10. What does the index of an array do?
11. What can be stored with array variable types?
12. If a character is starting to float into the air when using a Move Toward action, what might the problem be?

Exercises

1. Implement an attack system for the Sancho character.
   a. This will require constructing a health system for the spider
   b. The first stage of the attack system is already in place. For the other two stages you will need to:
      i. Add appropriate colliders to Sancho and give them Collision Detection state machines.
      ii. Construct the health system for the spider so that it can be damaged and killed.
         A. HINT: When it is killed it should not be able to patrol or pursue or attack.
2. Implement an Ally character archetype with the Arteria3D donkey that we imported in an exercise from the previous chapter.
   a. In designing the Ally behavior consider the following:
      i. It should follow Sancho around the scene.
      ii. It should not stand on top of Sancho, so when it is close it should do something else, consider the animation list of things that it can do.

3. Using the extra animals we added to our project in the last chapter (the ones from the Medieval Farm Pack developed by Arteria3D), add one of these to your scene and construct an AI system for it (though do not use the fluffy sheep as we will do something specific with that one in a future chapter). Consider the following:
    a. What role should the animal serve in this project?
        i. This will be easier to answer after our next chapter on story, but all of these pieces are intertwined and it never hurts us to think ahead.
    b. What all can it do?
    c. Should it be attackable by the spider?
    d. Should it be attackable by Sancho?
4. Construct a rudimentary AI system for the shadow character, the Sanson character from Arteria3D imported in the last chapter.
    a. This will be very similar to the spider, in fact for the moment it will be the same as the spider. There will be other states added once we know more about the story in the next chapter.

Design Document

In this addition to the *Sancho Panza* design document, we have added the logic for the threshold guardian as described in this chapter. We have also added the essential logic for the shadow character as well.

> **Download**
> Updated version of the *Sancho Panza* design document can be downloaded from the companion website: "DesignDocument_chapter5.docx."

Consider your design document that you have been working on thus far and add the following to it:

1. Essential logic for the behavior of a threshold guardian, shadow, and ally.
2. You may also want to begin considering the behavioral logic for other characters that were added in the previous version of the design document as this behavior may serve as a spring board for some story and quest ideas coming up next.

CHAPTER 6

Story

Characters are a great place to start developing our game ideas. After creating the characters, or even while creating them, we will often begin developing some ideas for game mechanics. Game mechanics are what the player can do, which we will be looking at in the chapter on game mechanics, Chapter 8. For this chapter, however, we are not going to look at what the player *can* do, but *why* the player is doing it or anything for that matter. Story is the reason why things are happening within a game. Our stories may be grand and epic sweeping tales spanning galaxies or they may be straightforward tales. In either case, many of the core elements of the story will be extremely similar. Our story can provide guidance for the rest of the development of the game; that guidance will include game mechanics as well as the design of the levels and environments for the game. By the end of this chapter, we will have laid a solid foundation for our Sancho Panza project by adding a story providing a reason for the characters to be where they are, doing whatever it is that they will be doing, as well as the essentials of what will occur during game play. This foundation is ultimately what we will build our game on.

- What Is a Story?
- The Core Components of Stories
- The Greek Drama and Theater
- Monomyth and the Hero's Journey
- Story as a Game and Level
- Backstory as Narration and Dialogue

6.1 What Is a Story?

When we hear the term "story" we bring in many of our own preconceptions as to what a story is and what it is not. For our purposes we will go ahead and define a story as a relating of factual or imaginary events and characters. We are going to leave our definition very streamlined, which will allow it to be more flexible. For instance, we are going to exclude any ideas or interpretations of entertainment. Many would define a story as something told or presented to an audience for the sole purpose of entertainment, for example, a news announcement would not be considered to be a story. While there is nothing wrong with that we want to keep our definition very simple. Just because something is not necessarily entertaining, in whatever way that may be defined, should not automatically preclude it from being a story. While many stories may be entertaining, they can be used for other purposes than to simply pass the time.

Humans have historically used stories for many purposes throughout our history. We have stories to explain how we got here and why we are here. We have stories to teach our children right and wrong. We have stories to challenge our thinking of how society is and whether it should be the way that it is. Stories can be related to an audience in many different ways as well. We can use the written word in books, relate a story orally as a storyteller, or act out a story in a movie or play or through a video game character. The story, for our purposes, will serve to provide the reason why the events in the game have happened or are happening. However, a story does not necessarily have to be the central component of a game.

6.2 Does My Game Need a Story?

The short answer to this, just as with characters, is "no, your game may not need a story at all." There are many games that do not need a story in anyway whatsoever. Puzzle games, card games, casino games, even some strategy games can be wonderful gaming experiences without any explicit story content at all. The purpose of a story within a game is not to describe the action of the game. Stories also do not describe the core mechanics of a game. As an example, we can have an action-based game that focuses on the core mechanics of jumping over rolling barrels or jumping over alligator-infested pits, and the game can be tremendously fun without having a story to the game. What the story provides, however, is the reason why the character is trying to jump over those barrels to begin with, to save his girlfriend at the top of the building from the monkey that kidnapped her. We can simply place the goal at the top, in this case the girlfriend, and simply tell the player your goal is to get the girl at the top. However, it will not be long before players will want to know how she got up there. While it is not necessary for us to develop and provide this story for the players, it does not hurt us to do so either. In fact, through the development of a story for a game we may, as was previously mentioned, uncover some new game mechanic ideas that we can incorporate into the game.

> **Note**
> Even though we do not need stories within our games, people have a tendency to desire stories, a tendency to want to know why something is occurring. If we do not provide stories for our players, they will create their own stories anyway.

6.3 How to Tell a Story

When telling a story it is generally a good idea to start at the beginning, so to speak. A generic rule of thumb for structuring the retelling of a story is the Hollywood 3-Act structure. Figure 6.1 provides a graphical representation of this approach to storytelling. Within this approach to storytelling, the story begins with Act I in which the characters are introduced and the primary conflict or problem that occurs within the story is introduced as well. Following the introductions, the story progresses to Act II in which the hero character faces a series of challenges with various degrees of success. The challenges are intended to be leading the hero toward a final conflict with the antagonist of the story. Along with the challenges within Act II, the hero will also meet the ally characters that will help throughout the story as well as several of the guardians and other characters. Finally, the story concludes with Act III in which the climactic conflict occurs with the hero beating this final challenge and being able to finish the story.

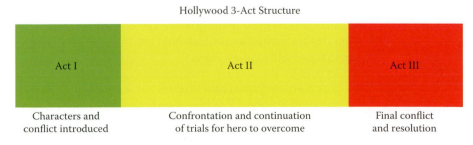

Hollywood 3-Act Structure

Act I	Act II	Act III
Characters and conflict introduced	Confrontation and continuation of trials for hero to overcome	Final conflict and resolution

FIG 6.1 The Hollywood 3-Act story structure.

6.4 The Building Blocks of a Story

Creating stories is an artistic process. There is a tremendous amount of creativity and flexibility inherent in the process of creating stories. Despite this, though, each story is going to contain the same six core components that it was built from. As discuss these building blocks and provide examples, we need to keep in mind that becoming good at creating stories takes practice. There is no magic formula that can be followed to guarantee a successful and intriguing story. To be precise, despite the definitions of building blocks and the theories discovered and presented by both Aristotle and Joseph Campbell there is still no guarantee that a story we create will be a good story (however that may be defined by other people or critics). But, following these techniques may help to keep us on track as it is very easy to get sidetracked while working on stories. With that introduction out of the way, the six building blocks of a story are characters, setting, problem, plot, solution, and theme.

6.4.1 Characters

The characters are the beings that inhabit the world of the story. More than that, the characters are central to the story, essentially the story is about things that happen to these characters. As we saw in the previous chapter, there are several different types of characters that fulfill very distinct needs within a story. At its core, a story really only needs to have one character, the main character. We can have a story with just this one character in which they are struggling to overcome something within the world or their environment, such as the movie *All Is Lost* starring Robert Redford. However, as a general rule, we tend to prefer stories with more than one character, we like to have bad guys to dislike and look forward to their eventual downfall at the end of the story. It is important that these characters be interesting and engaging and that we take the time to develop them as thoroughly as we can, especially the primary characters within the story.

6.4.2 Setting

The setting is the world in which the story takes place. In the context of game development, the setting is the game world, or the virtual environments that we allow the players to play the game within. As with characters, the more detailed the setting is the more engaging the audience will find the story to be (although there are some very obvious exceptions within the games that we play). We have two things to consider when it comes to the setting of our story:

1. Does the setting adequately describe the world that the action will take place within? For instance, if we were to say that we are making a space game and that the player gets to have a spaceship that he can walk around inside of and do stuff, what does the spaceship look like? Furthermore, where can the player take the spaceship and what can they do there?

2. Does the setting match the characters and the story? The creation of fantasy worlds is wonderfully fun; however, when doing so we must maintain a consistency throughout the world and develop what this world is and why it is the way that it is. An irony for us, as game developers, as that it is very common that much of our work in story and setting (as was also the case with characters) may not make it into the final version of the game that we develop, but that does not mean that we should not figure some of these things out anyway.

We will be exploring setting in more depth and detail in our next chapter, so we will hold off on further discussion of constructing a setting for a game until then, though we should consider that the setting and backstory of our game world are very closely related partners. The backstory defines the background of our world, how it got to the point that it is currently at. The setting becomes the current representation of this backstory, for instance, if our backstory involves a nuclear exchange between global superpowers, then it would logically extend that our setting would incorporate nuclear fallout zones and regions, the two are very closely related.

6.4.3 The Problem

Every story must have a problem or a challenge that is being faced by the main character. A story where the character does not face any type of challenge not only is boring but is also technically not even a story (based upon the fact that a story should have these six core components). What the conflict is within a story can range from self-serving, such as to save girlfriend from the top of a building, to explorations of social issues such as the challenge presented to Scout's father to defend an innocent man in a deeply racist community. However, in either case that was just presented, the challenge in and of itself is still simple and straightforward. We have a tendency to try to overcomplicate challenges within stories that we create, this is really not necessary. Keep the problem faced by the character simple. We can introduce complexity within the plot, but the core problem faced should be definable within a single sentence maybe two, if it takes more than two sentences to define the problem faced by the main character then that is an indication that we still need to work on some details because we may not be too clear about it ourselves just yet.

Another aspect of the primary conflict within the story is that we can have either internal or external conflict within traditional stories. Internal conflict revolves around a hero character suffering through some inner emotional or mental turmoil and must overcome whatever this internal barrier is in order to be successful in resolving the primary conflict of the story. The external conflict occurs when the problem encountered by the hero character is outside of the hero themselves, for instance, Darth Vader provides an external source of conflict for Luke Skywalker within *Star Wars*. It is possible to mix these and provide both inner and external challenges to the hero over the course of the story. For instance, Sauron presents an

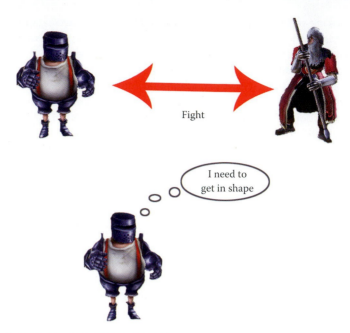

Fight

I need to get in shape

FIG 6.2 Internal versus external conflict within a story.

external conflict to Frodo during *The Lord of the Rings* as Sauron attempts to take the one ring from Frodo. However, throughout the story Frodo also struggles with an internal conflict as the ring continually tempts him with power (Figure 6.2).

One of the simplest conflict structures that can be created for use in a story is a love triangle, as shown in Figure 6.3. While the traditional version of a love triangle does involve a love interest, for example, two suitors pursuing the same potential mate, however, this structure can be extended beyond this traditional perspective to involve any one goal being pursued by two different characters. In order for the love triangle system to work, the goal must be mutually exclusive, meaning that only one of the characters can possess the goal (this is also referred to as a zero-sum game within game theory). Using this as a framework, we could create a conflict within a story in which both the hero and the shadow want to have control and authority over an island with a small village in it. Since they both want to control the island, it follows that only one of them can actually possess this goal, hence the primary conflict that drives the story between the two characters (we will use this as the primary conflict within our Sancho Panza story).

Note
A zero-sum game is any game or competition in which there can be only one winner, whether a team or individual. Within a zero-sum game, there must be a defined loser and a defined winner. Chess is an example of a zero-sum game (except in the case of a stalemate).

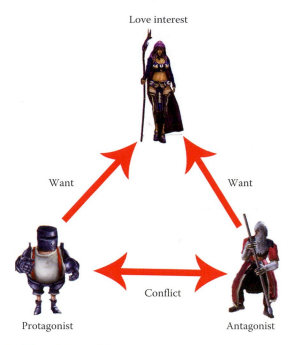

FIG 6.3 Love triangle form of a story conflict.

6.4.4 The Plot

The plot is where all of the action within a story takes place. Plot is not what the story is about; rather, the plot is the retelling of the events that transpire during the story. Another way to look at plot is attempts by the characters to learn about the problem and to solve the problem that is central to the story. As you can see, if there were no problem for the characters to work on, then there would also be no plot or events taking place within the story. Plot is where things get very interesting for us as game developers and we really walk away from the academic realm of story and story development.

Within books and movies, the story writers have strict control over the flow of the action that is occurring within the story. However, within video games it is the player that has control over the flow of the action. That is to say that the story is advanced through the actions of the player and in order to help the player along, we as game developers may need to make sure that the player does what we need them to do in order for the plot to be consistent. We will discuss this more when we get to implementing our story within a game.

6.4.5 The Solution

All good stories must eventually come to an end and that is the solution. This ending of a story is the solution to the problem that was presented within the story. It is possible that the solution leads to a new problem, a sequel, but the solution must be complete and resolve the currently presented problem. With the solution to the problem now presented, the world should return to some level of balance or order that it had at the start of the story. Although, it would be preferable for the world to actually have a new order or better order than what it had at the beginning of the story. It is also important, as we will discover when we look at Aristotle, that the solution to the problem, the resolution of the challenge, provide the audience with a sense of fulfillment. As storytellers, we want our audience leaving the story with a feeling of completeness, a feeling that all ended just as it should. This, however, may be trickier than it sounds.

6.4.6 The Theme

The theme of the story is what the story is about. All stories are ultimately about *something* whether it be good versus evil, social injustice, or what it means to be alive, the story is about something and is exploring that something through the characters, challenges, events, and solution of the story. Table 6.1 presents some common themes for stories, we as story writers are definitely not limited to just these few themes, but there is something very subtle and very important here. All stories throughout time have been about these themes, our story may be a new story with unique characters involved in different events, but at its core, our story will still, most likely, be about one of these common themes. And that is OK. New story writers get too caught up with making sure that their story is new, that the story they are telling has never been heard before. That is an admirable goal, but take a critical look

TABLE 6.1 Some of the Common Themes of Stories

Theme	Description	Example Stories	Example Games
Man versus nature	Man's attempt to survive within a world that he or she cannot directly control.	*2012* *Jurassic Park*	*Half-Life*
All things change	Throughout life and experience, things change, not necessarily better or worse; they just change.	*Where the Wild Things Are* *Bridge to Terabithia*	*Sims*
Revenge	The main character has been wronged in some way and is out to get revenge, sometimes even justice, though the two can be mutually exclusive.	*Carrie* *The Lone Ranger*	*God of War*
Man versus society	Similar to the struggle against nature, but this time the struggle is against the flow of a social structure surrounding the main character.	*The Lord of the Flies* *Schindler's List*	*Deus Ex*
Overcoming adversity	The main character must overcome many obstacles just to have their life return to some level of normalcy.	*Slumdog Millionaire* *Gone with the Wind*	*Heart of China*
The power of love	Despite everything that is happening, in the end, love will conquer all things.	*Snow White* *Pretty Woman*	*Leisure Suit Larry*
Good versus evil	There are just bad people in the world that want to do bad things and we must overcome them.	*Star Wars* *The Lord of the Rings*	*Oblivion*

at the books we read and the movies we watch. Take an objective look at the games that we play. What are all of these *about*? Creating a new theme for your story is not nearly as important as telling your story well. In fact, we would argue that some of the greatest stories revolve around these classic and simple themes, but they are great not because of what the story is about per se, but because of *how* the story is told. They are great because of the timeless characters, the wonderful plot, and the nearly perfect solutions.

6.5 Aristotle and the Greeks

As game developers, we can easily gloss over the theory and principles of theater and drama. However, as game developers we are actually creating the next incarnation of theater and drama and as such we could do well to be at least summarily familiar with the theories and principles of these fields. While it is true that not all games need stories or characters, if we are developing a game that does involve characters and stories then it is all the more relevant and important for us to consider some of what we now know about drama and what we currently know about drama is largely drawn upon the work of Aristotle and other Greeks.

Drama was to the Greek society what television and movies are to our society in many ways. The Greeks produced many plays and of those many were great and many were not so great. Just as we have many critics of our TV shows and movies, the Greeks began developing a critical eye toward their own writing and performances. The greatest of these critical evaluations was a work called *Poetics* by Aristotle written sometime near the middle of the fourth century BCE. Aristotle looked at several aspects of theater within this work including characters. Aristotle focused on tragedy within this particular work, his writings on comedy have been lost to time, for our purposes we will define tragedy as a story in which the hero falls or fails to accomplish a great task set before them. We will add to this that a tragedy is also a serious story and one dealing with some themes of moral right and wrong. With these basic definitions in place we can begin to see the potential relevance of Aristotle's ideas being applied to the games that we may develop today. Aristotle has developed a list of core components needed within a tragedy, which have been highlighted in Table 6.2, and continues by ranking the

TABLE 6.2 Aristotle's Six Parts of Tragedy

Principle	Description
Plot	The arrangement of incidents and events within a story.
Character	Agents that cause the events of the plot to occur and advance the story.
Thought	The reasoning and rationale behind the words and ideas.
Diction	The expressing of words and ideas.
Melody	Music performed by the chorus.
Spectacle	Visual representation of stage and characters.

parts of a tragedy in order of significance as plot, character, thought, diction, melody, and spectacle. We will be taking a look at each of these in turn and attempting to find an application to modern game development and design.

6.5.1 Plot

Aristotle considered the plot to be the single most important aspect of the tragedy. As we saw earlier, the plot is the events that occur within a story or tragedy. For Aristotle, however, he was mostly concerned with the Unity of the plot, that is to say that one event necessarily follows from a previous event. Plots should have a beginning, a middle, and finally an ending, which is also the same principle as the Hollywood 3-Act story structure that we saw earlier. The events that occur within the plot should follow each other in a reasonable, probable, and even necessary flow of events. This is Aristotle's Unity of plot.

It is also important that the plot of a story be complete in and of itself. This implies that the audience can enjoy the story without knowing anything about the story beforehand. Consider an audience watching the final *Lord of the Rings* movie without having any knowledge of the first two movies, *The Lord of the Rings* is complete, but the individual components of it are not complete in and of themselves. Our games should be complete when the player gets to the end of the game. We can always make a sequel building on the characters and events of the game, but we should not require our players to play the second game in order to know how the story will end that we have presented within the first game.

The concept of Unity within the plot also involves the idea that all actions occurred as a result of elements within the plot. This is to say that any event that occurs must be a result of some previous event that also occurred within the plot. We should not have plot events in which there was no background or reasoning behind the occurrence. While it is possible to have random and disconnected events as components within a story, they should not be the driving force of the story, rather the driving plot events should all be connected within the current plot structure.

The beginning of the plot is simply the starting point of the story. It is not necessary that the beginning is the result of any previous events primarily because if those events are relevant to how the plot got to the point that it is at, then those events are also relevant to the story at hand. However, the beginning should still be a reasonable extension of the understood world. Basically, the beginning of our stories should logically reside within the story world that we have created, although the full and detailed description of how the story world got to the point of the start of our story is not necessary to be related to the audience. Even though we do not need to relate this information to the audience, it is good information for us to have on hand as it helps us to understand the world of our story and also provide material that we can draw upon for story elements. This backstory of the world that we have created can be dropped into our story at various places to not only give the audience (player) tidbits of information, but also to give the story a deeper sense of being real, of being lived within. The beginning of the plot must be a chain of events in a cause-and-effect manner that gets the ball of the plot rolling. For instance, when Luke's uncle purchases the droids from the Jawas at the start of *A New Hope*, the ball has begun rolling in a cause-and-effect fashion of the plot leading to the next set of events that necessarily follow; namely, Luke cleaning the droids and discovering the recorded message. One thing leads to another in a fashion that is necessary and consistent within the story, this is the first act within the Hollywood 3-Act structure.

Following the beginning of the plot, the story would enter into the middle stage. This stage is caused by the events from the beginning and it is in this stage that the character is faced with challenges that culminate in a climactic challenge to the character of the story. This stage of the tragedy is the longest component of a story and is the second of the Hollywood 3-Act structure. The plot events occurring during this stage should be escalating in a logical and consistent fashion toward the climactic event of the story, building tension within the story and the audience. This tension and emotional investment of the audience is an important concept for Aristotle as he felt that the tragedy must bring a well of emotions to the audience and that we as storytellers must make the audience *feel* something.

This brings us to the final act, the resolution or end. It is here that the conflict originally presented by the plot and the driving force behind the climax is resolved, one way or the other. Within the resolution, it is also our responsibility to provide the audience with a catharsis, or a release of the emotions and tensions that we have built within them. This is seeing the good guy beat the bad guy at the end of the story. As an audience we have gotten to where we really do not like the bad guy and we need to see and experience the good guy winning in the end so that we can have a release of these emotions. Figure 6.4 depicts this Aristotelian structure in a Freytag Triangle.

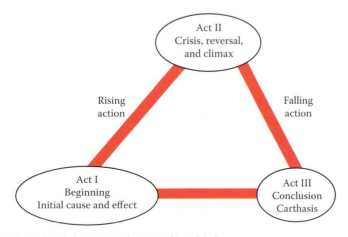

FIG 6.4 Freytag Triangle demonstrating the pattern of Aristotle's plot.

Within the confines of the plot, Aristotle considered there to be a need for plot twists or redirections of the expected action. Aristotle presented two types of potential plot twists: change or reversal of fortune and recognition. All plots have a change or reversal of fortune, in the simplest of plots this change of fortune is when the bad guy loses in the end despite their expectation to win. Specifically a reversal of fortune occurs when the events of the plot switch such that the result of the event leads to the reverse of what the character causing the event expected to happen. A simple example would be a character pulling a trigger of an unloaded gun only to have it not shoot any bullets. If the character had been relying on the gun's ability to fire bullets when the trigger was pulled, then the character has now suffered a reversal of fortune. More complex plots have a change of fortune and recognition, or a change from innocence. This occurs when a character goes from not knowing something to having knowledge. Depending on the knowledge that is learned, the character will either have a very positive or negative emotional response, either great love and happiness or great sorrow and despair. This knowledge discovery should go hand in hand with reversal of fortune.

Bringing this knowledge into the development of a game can be accomplished through revealing information to the player at the same time that the character finds the information. This is a challenging task to accomplish, as we will see in Sections 6.7 and 6.8 when we design and implement some of our own story elements; however, we must remember that the player is not only the audience of our story but also the lead character, the hero. As a result we need the player to experience the story as the hero, to experience the story through the eyes of the hero so that the player's thoughts may align with those of the hero. We need the player to discover knowledge at the same time, or close to it, as the hero of the story does. The player must experience the themes of the story through the eyes and emotional construction of our hero character.

6.5.2 Characters

It is interesting to note that Aristotle placed plot as more significant than characters to the quality of a tragedy. We may be tempted to reverse that and put the characters as the most important components; however, if we consider, as Aristotle did, that the only role of the characters is to provide an agent of action or a mechanism for advancing the plot then it would stand to reason that the characters would have a secondary role in comparison to the plot. The motivations and desires of the individual characters should in some way be linked with the events of the plot but should not supersede the plot and the flow of the event within the plot.

Aristotle also believed that it was necessary for the hero character to have some fatal flaw within their personality that would ultimately lead to their downfall over the course of the tragedy. Whether characters in story-driven games need fatal flaws or not is highly debatable, but the characters within our games should be intricately linked with the plot events of the game. After all, if the character serves no purpose within the game, then why should we spend the time and resources developing the character for the game? It is at this point that the intricate relationship between character and story comes back to the forefront of our design process. If our game is not a story intensive game, such as Sancho Panza, then we are able to shortcut some of these ideas. However, if it is our goal to develop a deep and engaging story for the players to participate in and explore, then the characters within that story world will have to be the driving force behind the plot, specifically the player's character will have to be pushing the plot forward.

6.5.3 Thought

Thought refers to things that are affected as a result of the use of language. Essentially, Aristotle is arguing that all the words spoken by a character within a tragedy are the result of a thought process by the character. Characters within dramas are not merely repeating written lines, they should be living entities that are experiencing the story from their perspective and as a result are having thought processes about everything that is occurring, at least everything that they are aware of. As a storytelling tool, this becomes a valuable mechanism to be used to help the audience know what a character thinks or feels about certain events within the story. As a result of knowing how those events have impacted the character, the character's following actions would flow more necessarily from the events that have preceded. It is within this area that we can bring the theme of the story back into play by revealing how the characters in the world feel and think about the theme at hand. As the story progresses, character's thoughts about the theme may change and this we generally consider to be character growth.

6.5.4 Diction

Diction is the process of words being expressed within a tragedy. Keep in mind that with Aristotle's work he was looking at tragedy and also at epic poems, so the significance of words and how those words are expressed would understandably be fairly important. Is the expression appropriate to the plot and events that are occurring? Does the expression match with the character? Aristotle's focus here is how the words are used and making sure that the idea is clearly expressed to the audience. Aristotle considered the metaphor to be one of the more powerful mechanisms that could be employed because complex ideas could be spoken in a manner that the audience would understand on an intuitive level. It is a little difficult to create a clear and direct relation with Aristotle's work and with game development on this particular topic. But, we could consider the language that is used within our games and recognize that if the words do not match with the plot it can be a jarring experience for the audience or player. We can also recognize, from Aristotle on this point, that the words we do utilize within the game, whether spoken in dialogue or read by the player, should be consistent with the whole game experience and should be precise at expressing the ideas that we are trying to get across. Whether this component of tragedy is more important than the remaining ones, especially within game development, is doubtful but it is still an important component that we should consider during design and development.

6.5.5 Melody

Like spectacle, as follows, Aristotle did not spend much time specifically defining melody within tragedy. But it would stand to reason that he was referring to the musical component of the tragedy. In Greek tragedy, it was common for there to be a chorus, or what we would almost consider to be a narrator, that provided comments and thoughts about the action taking place on the stage, generally during some type of interlude between scenes. Considering the role that the chorus played in providing narration to the audience, even prepping the audience for an upcoming scene with some question to consider, we can see the relationship to music and audio as it is used in movies and games today. A dramatic musical score can prep the audience for an event that is about to occur on stage. The same thing within a video game, as the player nears a final battle with the level boss, the music may step up a pace or two as a device to inform our players of something about to occur. As a device used in this fashion, we can see how melody is very important to engaging the audience with the events of the plot by keeping the audience engaged and aware of those events. Likewise, we should give serious consideration to the audio that we utilize within our games, as we will see in a later chapter.

6.5.6 The Spectacle

In Aristotle's thinking, the spectacle referred to visual appearance of the stage and the actors. Aristotle does not specifically define spectacle but we could think of this as referring to the costumes and the props on the stage, though Greek tragedy generally did not rely too heavily on these visual components to begin with, which may be a reason that Aristotle ranked this as last. However, as we shall shortly see, perhaps his ranking is more universal and consistent than we may first think. For us, as game developers, we can think of the spectacle as referring to the graphics that we have created and are using within our game. Common thought has the graphics as the most important component of a game. However, if we use Aristotle as a guide for developing story and character-driven games, we will recognize that the graphics are not as important as those other components are to the experience of the story. Regardless of how amazing our graphics and visual effects are, if we do not have the other components, then it is possible for our game to fall short, especially if we have set out to develop a story-based game experience which many modern games do. Consider the last few games that you have played, what do you remember most? The amazing graphics or the story? It is interesting to note how much time we, as gamers, spend complaining about the story within a game. We may complain about graphical glitches, but we rarely complain about the overall graphics of a game, we rarely complain about the spectacle of the drama that we have participated in. If anything, we will be upset about an ending that did not seem right to us, but will let the graphics slide. Perhaps Aristotle was right in that the spectacle of the drama is not as important as the rest of it and perhaps we as game developers should seriously consider this as we work on our own projects.

6.6 The Return of Joseph Campbell

Joseph Campbell, as we learned in the previous chapter, spent his life researching myths and legends around the world in order to determine if there were any connecting threads between them. He had a Jungian approach to the psychological aspect of his research drawing on Carl Jung's work with dreams and with the representation of characters within those dreams. During this research, Joseph Campbell discovered a trend that kept occurring among heroic legends and tales throughout the stories that we tell regardless of our ethnic or cultural background. This similarity existed regardless of time period of the stories as well. It appeared to be a universal component of the stories that we tell. Joseph Campbell wrote of this in *The Hero with a Thousand Faces* and referred to it as the "Journey of the Hero" or sometimes called the "Cycle of the Hero." Christopher Vogler also wrote of this phenomenon and modified it for use in screen writing, in which we will find more immediately relevant to our work at hand as story writers for video games, within *The Writer's Journey*, in which we drew upon in previous chapters for essential character archetypes. Figure 6.5 provides a quick overview of the cycle of the hero in the form that Christopher Vogler modified from the work of Joseph Campbell. While Joseph Campbell's work is foundational to the theory of hero mythology, Christopher Vogler's work will be more immediately applicable to us as the process of creating stories for games and writing screenplays for movies have a lot of similarities.

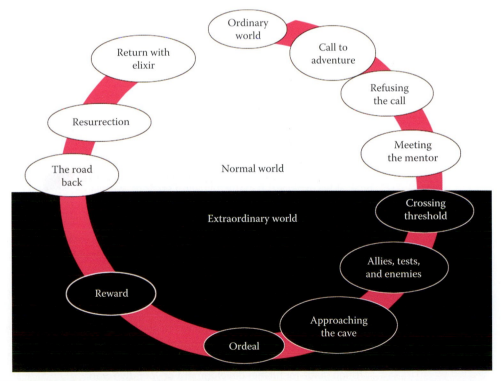

FIG 6.5 The journey of the hero as modified by Christopher Vogler.

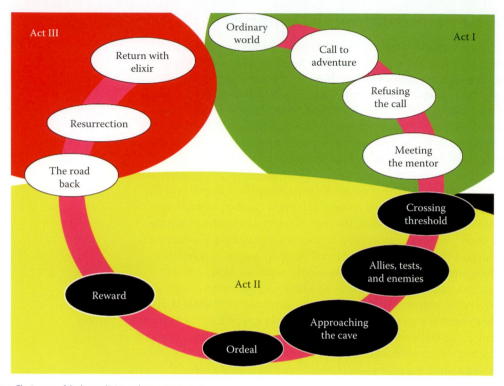

FIG 6.6 The journey of the hero split into a three-part structure.

Before we break into discussions of each of the components of the hero's journey, we should recognize that this hero's journey can easily be split into a three-part structure, as shown in Figure 6.6, thereby falling into the structure proposed by Aristotle and also the Hollywood 3-Act structure that we have mentioned earlier. While it is not necessary to follow this as absolute rules, they can provide us with a blueprint from which to direct our work and a generic outline of how we may wish to proceed. This blueprint is not intended to replace Aristotle or any of the building blocks of a story, rather, the journey of the hero indicates which plot points occur at which point in time, as we explore this in the following sections, we will see how each of these plot events naturally occurs from the previous ones just as Aristotle would have wanted and that there is Unity within the plot. It is not necessary that these parts of the hero's journey be followed in exact order, as some of them can be reversed or even occur simultaneously, however some must naturally flow from predecessors.

> **Note**
> The journey of the hero is not a guaranteed blueprint to success, it is not necessary to have all of the components or to even follow its structure at all; however, for new story writers, it may serve as a starting point and rough guide for further development of your own work.

6.6.1 The Ordinary World

The journey of the hero begins with the hero living their normal unassuming life in the normal world. It is in this stage that the hero is introduced to the audience, there may even be hints of the conflict of the story, though the focus at this point is the hero and their everyday life. Consider the Shire that Frodo is living in as *The Lord of the Rings* opens. There is a birthday party going on and life is continuing as it always has and, it is assumed by the hero, as it always will. We can also consider the world at the beginning of *The Legend of Zelda: The Wind Waker* in which our hero character is living his normal life doing normal things unaware of the adventure that he is about to begin. It is in this ordinary world that the story begins to attract the audience by providing a hero and world in which the audience can appreciate, associate with, and perhaps even long for.

This ordinary world also serves as a counterpart for the world encountered throughout the rest of the journey. This can serve as a constant reminder of what the hero is fighting for and why they continue to struggle onward. Many heroic journeys will lead the hero into an unknown world that will be quite different, if not completely opposite, from the world in which they began the story. This is also the world that the hero hopes to one day return to after the quest has been completed.

6.6.2 Call to Adventure

Life in the ordinary world cannot continue forever, otherwise there would not be much of a story to tell, at least not one with any action to speak of. At some point the everyday life of the hero will be interrupted by a call to adventure. This may come in many forms, it may be a message in the mail, the discovery of something within the attic, or even the villain themselves may make an appearance of sorts marauding through the ordinary world and upsetting all that the hero values. Many times this call to adventure is delivered by the herald character as in Princess Leia's call for help that Luke had stumbled upon. This is the point in the story that everything gets going and the tension begins building toward the inevitable final conflict.

6.6.3 Refusal of the Call

The hero, out of humility or fear, will refuse the call to action. They will provide excuses such as not being skilled enough, or being too small, or having responsibilities that they cannot abandon. It is generally stressed by the hero that they would go off on this grand adventure, but for reasons that they consider to be obvious they simply cannot and someone else should go instead. This serves as an important point within the story as it is a notification to the audience that the actual adventure is about to begin, that the ordinary world is about to be left behind as the hero enters into the extraordinary. If the hero continues to refuse the call, something tragic will happen that will force them to respond.

6.6.4 Meeting the Mentor

The mentor character type, as mentioned in the last chapter, is here to instruct the hero in all things heroic and get the hero going in the proper direction. As a result, there must come a point in time when the hero meets the mentor prior to the adventure getting fully underway. This meeting may occur as part of the call to adventure or part of the hero's refusal to answer the call, but it must occur before the hero has crossed the threshold into the unknown world. As the hero meets the mentor they will be given what they need to get their adventure fully and truly started, but will still have to discover and learn along the way. The character of Morpheus from the movie *The Matrix* served as the mentor to Neo. Neo originally refused the call to action by stepping back into the building rather than climbing the scaffolding outside, however later Neo would meet with Morpheus again and at that point Morpheus gives a rough explanation and offers Neo the choice between the blue and red pills after which Neo has crossed over into the extraordinary world and the adventure is fully underway.

6.6.5 Crossing the Threshold

Once the hero has heard and responded to the call to adventure they must make final preparations and cross this first threshold completely leaving behind the ordinary world and entering into the unknown on the quest that has been laid out before them. This is Neo awakening in the "real" world, or Luke boarding the Millennium Falcon to depart from Tatooine, or Frodo crossing the river and leaving behind the Shire and all that he has known.

> **Note**
> Notice the recurring mention of certain movies and stories in this discussion. This is pointed out as these are considered to be great stories by many people and yet these great stories so closely follow the model of the hero's journey, whether intentional or not. Consider the possibility that stories structured along this blueprint, when well executed, may touch a deep and unconscious nerve within the audience that resonates within them and leaves a lasting impression.

6.6.6 Tests, Allies, and Enemies

The hero is fully engaged in their quest and adventure. During the course of the adventure, the hero will face many tests and trials. The hero will be successful at some of these and the hero will stumble and fail at others. Generally speaking, the tests and trials become increasingly difficult the further the hero travels into the unknown world; we could even think of this as levels becoming progressively more difficult as the player advances through the game toward the final boss. During this journey, the hero will encounter enemies that will stand in the hero's way of completing tests and trials along the way. The hero must overcome these guardians in order to continue their adventure. As well as the guardians, the hero will also encounter the allies and tricksters during this stage of the story. This is the time that Luke and Han spend on the Death Star during *A New Hope*, with trials and tests gradually becoming more challenging to get through. Some of the tests involved direct conflict with guardians, whereas others involve some puzzle to be solved such as the famous riddle of the Sphinx.

6.6.7 Approaching the Cave

This stage occurs after the hero has settled into this new world that they now inhabit. The hero has grown accustomed to the trials and challenges of this new world and is now ready to enter into the strongest point of the extraordinary world. As the story approaches this central conflict keep in mind that we are not approaching the climax of the story itself just yet. Rather, we are approaching a major tipping point in the life of the hero character as the hero faces their most daunting task to date and may even appear to die in the process. Many times this approach will be guarded by entirely new guardians with completely different challenges that must be overcome by the hero, but by this point in time they are well prepared for this moment even if very frightened to continue. The journey into the Mines of Moria is the approach to this innermost cave for Frodo's journey within *The Fellowship of the Ring*. He has been well prepared and has come to an understanding of exactly how dangerous this new world is in comparison with the Shire. Although, there will be new guardians, a cave troll and a balrog for instance, and much more difficult tests to come, Frodo is ready to enter into the cave and face this ordeal.

6.6.8 The Ordeal

Once the hero has entered into the cave, the central ordeal can begin. It is during this test that the hero may appear to die or may actually die. Allies may be lost during this conflict. This is a very strong conflict but it is not the climax of the story. Rather, this conflict serves as the tipping point of the hero's journey to give them the final resolve needed to face the climactic conflict. The hero will grow during this stage, moving beyond an egocentric world view to one that is more altruistic in nature as the hero becomes more concerned with the safety of the world than with their own safety.

6.6.9 The Reward

With the ordeal out of the way, the hero receives some award from this extraordinary world, perhaps it is Princes Leia herself as Luke Skywalker is able to escape from the Death Star with her following the ordeal in the trash compactor in which he appeared to have died. The hero is also enjoying the fact that they did not actually die during the ordeal and though everyone knows that the ultimate evil of the story is still out there somewhere, for the moment the hero is allowed to pause and rest. Take a moment to savor the victory at hand.

6.6.10 The Road Back

Upon successfully completing the ordeal and obtaining the reward, the hero is given some type of option as far as staying in the world that they are in, the extraordinary world, or returning back to the ordinary world, or at least some close resemblance to it. This is the moment when Luke watches Obi-Wan die at the hands of Darth Vader, Luke could stay in the extraordinary world and fight bravely, but Obi-Wan's voice from the beyond urges Luke to run and ultimately begin his journey back to the ordinary world. The hero is still deep within the extraordinary world and as a result the journey back may not be an easy one, though it should be easier than was the approach to the cave earlier. Here the story is transitioning from the second act to the final act. The story is picking up speed as it begins to rush the hero and their allies toward the climactic conflict of the story that we as an audience have been waiting for.

6.6.11 Resurrection

This is the climactic conflict within the story. This is where the hero will face their most daunting task and one more challenge with death in order to save the world. This is the moment of Luke hurtling along the trenches of the Death Star, alone and the last chance for the rebels to destroy the space station before the rebels themselves will be destroyed. It is in this final conflict that the hero must die to themselves in some way, they must be resurrected into a new hero whether this is through the brave awareness that Frodo must continue his journey alone to save others from the temptation of the ring or Luke's realization that he must use the Force and not rely on his physical senses. As storytellers, we need for the audience to be aware of this change in the hero, not because we have told them that it happened, but because they see it happen within the character.

6.6.12 Return with Elixir

The hero has survived the ordeal and the resurrection; they are now ready to return home with the ultimate reward. Perhaps this reward is a galaxy free of planet-destroying space stations or it may be an individual with the ability to be a savior for the mindless masses that are trapped within a computer simulation of the twentieth century. At any rate, the hero now has something of value to share with others within this ordinary world.

6.7 Story Design

With the building blocks and principles of story creation in place, we are ready to step through the construction of a basic story for Sancho Panza to explore. We will break this apart into chunks as we work through this process. For new story creators, the process can seem a little daunting, which is why we have selected to create a checklist of sorts, at least for starting out. Keep in mind that this style of approach is not for the creative process of the story but for the building blocks of the story. Once we have all of the building blocks in place we can then relax and let the story go where it will as long as it stays within the artificial confines that we have built for it. This is an extremely formulaic approach to story creation, after having created a few, this kind of approach can be modified or dropped to better fit your creative style. Remember, this is an introduction to these topics and you are encouraged to expand your references and knowledge as you see fit.

> **Note**
> Creating stories is an art form and like all other art forms it takes practice to get better at it. The more stories that you create and write, the better your story creation skills will become. This means that our first story creation probably should not be the generation-spanning epic that we have a couple of ideas for. Put that great idea on the shelf and practice with some smaller ideas and return to the epic later. With completion comes confidence to create and complete many stories.

6.7.1 The Theme

What is this story about? This question is not the traditional question of who is in the story and what happens to the characters of the story. This is the purpose of the story, the theme of the story, the grand thing that we are trying to say within our story. This is a stumbling block for many as we want our story to be about something so much larger than we are; we want our stories to be epic and eternal. That is all fine and good, but we are making video games, and at the end of the day, the video game must be fun to play; the video game does not *have* to have a memorable and thought-provoking theme to explore within the story.

While considering the theme of the story, we also want to consider the game itself, at this point we are essentially asking "so, what is my game about?" We should already have an idea of what our game is about as many times with game development the whole process begins with "wouldn't it be cool if…" and it is that if that the game is about. Now the question is whether we can turn what the game is about into what the story is about, or perhaps vice versa if this all began with a story idea that we want to build a game around. In our case we are making a straightforward platformer style of game with some adventure elements to it. We would like to have some enemies for our hero to fight and then conclude with a boss battle. This example leaves us with a question that we may not have considered before because it is relevant to the story but not necessarily relevant to the game, why is the player fighting the boss? This leads us to the primary conflict of the story, but within the conflict we can also find what the story is about. Considering the sampling of themes that was proposed in Table 6.1, we have opted for the classic good vs. evil for this story.

223

This particular theme will not require much work on our part as far as translating from the story to the game. Through a backstory revelation at the start of the game, either with a voice-over narration or by means of some scrolling text, we can let the player know that the bad guy is the bad guy and that Sancho is the good guy as they battle each other for the little island that they are on. The bad guy having evil plans for the island and its inhabitants, while Sancho wants only good for his new subjects. Many story themes can be established in this same style by telling the player up front what the primary conflict of the game is about. While the journey of the hero provides wonderful material for the creation of compelling stories, for many games we will not need stories of that level of complexity. Although, if you are planning on developing a sweeping role-playing game or adventure style game, the journey of the hero will provide you with plenty of guidance for further development of the game's story.

6.7.2 Characters

Whether we begin this process with the story and then create the characters or work in reverse is entirely arbitrary and dependent on your workflow or the sequence in which ideas occur to you. Inspiration is an elusive creature to catch, so when it passes your way make sure to jot down whatever fascinating thoughts occurred to you before they are forgotten. In our case, we wanted to explore a game idea based on the character of Sancho Panza from the classic of Spanish literature *The Ingenious Gentleman Don Quixote of La Mancha*. This character was chosen as the hero primarily because he is in many ways an antihero and could provide with some comical or at least light-hearted game-play moments. For us, we wanted to steer away from a game that takes itself seriously and thought that the characters would be a good place to start with that approach. Another contributing factor was the knight asset itself, when it was first discovered by us in *Unity Creative Magazine*, it just looked like it wanted to be Sancho Panza someday.

The characters that we create need to match the story or the story needs to match the characters that we have already created. For instance, based on our work from the previous chapter, we already have a grouping of essential characters, so now the story should be molded such that it fits with these characters we have in hand. To do this, we need to consider the abilities and backgrounds of the characters that we created and recognize that certain stories or settings just would not work very well. Dropping Sancho Panza into World War II, as an example, would be an extremely forced setting and just would not feel right. Having already created our characters, we can move on to the next section.

6.7.3 Setting and Backstory

Where and when the story takes place is going to be absolutely vital when we get to our next chapter on creating the virtual world for our game. As was just mentioned, the setting should match with the characters. More than that, we need to start considering some game-play-specific elements when we consider the setting of the story. In the case of Sancho Panza's setting, we were able to draw from the original work by Cervantes for much inspiration.

It is at this point that we should mention Copyright law. Generally speaking, you cannot use characters and stories created by other people within your own work. The original creators own a copyright on the material that is also known as intellectual property. This means that we could not create a game with a mustached plumber named Mario as our lead character without expecting Nintendo to contact us with some pretty nasty legal letters and suits. Nintendo is not protecting their intellectual property because they are jerks that cannot play well with others, they are doing it because the Mario character was created by them and can only be used by them or those that they license to use it. We would do the same with characters that we create. Therefore, when creating your characters and stories make sure that you are not using copyright material within your project as this will cause your project to be put in storage at some point in time and will also damage your reputation as a game developer. There are some legal defenses for using copyright material such as noncommercial usage or satire.

Another aspect of copyright law is an area referred to as public domain. This includes all material for which there is no copyright holder and included within this category is all work that was published prior to 1923. What this means for us as game developers is that all of those wonderful classics of literature that were written prior to 1923 can be taken off the shelf and dropped straight into a game, provided that our version of the work is actually based on the original publication and not some movie remake of it that we recently watched at the theaters. However, it is not our intention to provide an in-depth coverage of intellectual protection law and precedent; we would encourage you to do some further research into these topics before you decide to do any commercial work of your own.

Returning to the setting at hand. Throughout the story of the knight Don Quixote, Sancho is promised an island of his own to rule once Don Quixote has completed his tasks of knight errantry. At the completion of such tasks it is customary, or so Don Quixote has read, for the knight to be awarded with vast tracts of land and other worldly goods. Being a noble knight, or a close approximation thereof, Don Quixote has promised to pass on to his faithful squire Sancho an island to rule when the adventures are over. Of course, this does not actually occur within the story, although the Duke and Duchess characters within the story do put on a farce of making Sancho governor of a nonexistent island that they have named Barataria and that is where we come in. Using this as a basis for our creation we are going to drop Sancho onto some island with a medieval town for him to be the fair and just governor of. Unfortunately for him, there will also be some competition for this post of responsibility over the fair village of the island. As mentioned, the village will be medieval with wood buildings and various animals roaming the area. We will have the village abandoned of its inhabitants, chased away by the villain of the story, though there will still be some farm animals that have been left behind. As a side note on this, by having an empty village, it will also cut down on character models and animations that we will need to either find or create to add to the project; this will in turn simplify some of our game development tasks. Our basic setting is now in place as we all have various images of what such an environment might look like and in the next chapter we will set about creating this environment through the use of assets provided by Arteria3D.

For the backstory of this setting and plot, we have the content from the book of *Don Quixote* to draw from as far as events that have led the world to being in the condition that they are currently in. However, that information is not necessary to be known in order to play our game and enjoy the story that we have laid out. This backstory provides us with much that we can draw upon as well as give us ideas that we can incorporate into our own product if we want to. For instance, we could have a cameo appearance of the Duke and Duchess, though not of Don Quixote himself as he is actually dead by this point in time, unfortunately.

One final point before moving on, and we will cover this in more detail in the next chapter, the setting must be one that is conducive for a video game and also restraining for the player. By this, we mean that to create a setting of an infinite universe such as the galaxy of *Star Wars* is going to require a lot of asset creation and also will need to allow the flexibility for the player to literally go wherever they want to, though we could use the plot to steer the player in the direction that we need them to go. In our case, we have selected an island not only because it came from the original book, but also because it creates an enclosed and complete environment for the game to take place in with a natural boundary of water preventing the player from traveling away from where the action is.

6.7.4 The Problem

We have already hinted at this fairly extensively in looking at the theme of the story. The theme and the central conflict tend to have a fair amount of relationship with each other. In our specific situation, we have already stated that the theme of the story is good vs. evil so the central conflict of the story is one between the hero, Sancho, and the villain, Sanson (introduced in our design document from the end of the previous chapter), both desiring the same thing. This is the basic lover's triangle that we discussed earlier and modified for our needs as seen in Figure 6.7. Both characters are fighting for control of the island named Barataria and only one of them can actually control the island and its inhabitants, which are just a bunch of farm animals that have been left behind. Ultimately the central conflict of a story should be one that we can express in one or two sentences; if it is more complex than that, then we are incorporating many different conflicts and events and

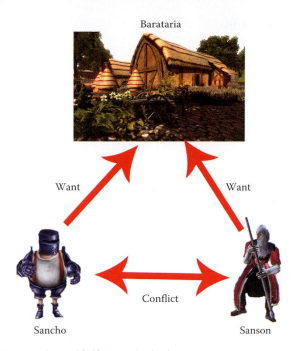

Barataria

Want

Want

Conflict

Sancho

Sanson

FIG 6.7 The lover's triangle as modified for our need within this story.

getting them all confused. The central conflict is only the one thing that the hero and shadow are ultimately at odds about, all of the other challenges throughout the story are building to the final conflict, but are not actually part of the conflict itself, just events that naturally lead to that final conflict. Remember Aristotle, all events should naturally follow from each other and our plot should include all of the necessary events of the story.

6.7.5 The Plot

The plot of a story within a game is going to vary based upon the type of game that is being developed. A story-centric game will have an engaging plot with plot twists throughout the experience for the player, such as encountered in many of the older point and click adventure games such as *King's Quest* or even within the *Myst* series of games. For action style games such as *Super Mario World* or our Sancho Panza project, we are not engaging in a complex story line, for us the plot will be straightforward, what Aristotle would have referred to as a simple plot as we will not even use any plot twist devices during this story, there is simply no need for them. This is reinforcing the idea that we have stressed throughout this chapter, deep engaging story lines within a game are wonderful, however always keep the needs of the game, both fun and playability, at the forefront of your design. Creating revolutionary game-play systems to implement stories in different ways than has previously been done is a noble goal and one to definitely pursue, however probably not as your first game project in an introductory book.

6.7.6 The Solution

With video games, it is very difficult for us to get the cathartic experience that Aristotle deemed so important for the solution of the conflict. Although, we do end up with a cathartic experience as game players having overcome the final challenge of the game. We can allow these to be one in the same for our purposes, which means that the solution to our conflict must present the player with a suitable challenge such that they have an emotionally releasing experience from finally beating it and winning the game. This is not to say that we should abandon all hope of having a cathartic experience from the story itself, but always remember that the playability of the game trumps all other issues, unless we are going out of our way to explore different ideals of game experiences as some games are beginning to do now. For our case, we will rely on a sufficiently challenging final battle with Sanson, once the player has gotten through the challenges and trials that will lead to that conflict. It will be an action game sequence similar to the boss battles at the end of games such as *Sonic the Hedgehog*. The full design of this battle will fall into Chapter 8 coming up shortly, for now it is sufficient for us to know that the resolution of the conflict will come from a direct confrontation between the hero and the villain and that the hero will win, though in the case of the game it may take the player a few tries to get the hero through this final conflict.

6.7.7 Dialogue

This is a special category of story design that only needs to be considered when creating video games. During the development of a play, novel, or movie, we have complete control over the dialogue and it is exactly as we have written it; this means that we would essentially write the dialogue the same way that we would any other parts of the story. However, within video game development, dialogue is oftentimes something that the player gets to participate in providing the player with the illusion that they are in some way altering the progression of the story. Generally speaking, they are not really changing the story, it is more like the old *Choose Your Own Adventure* book series; the player is only picking one of the prewritten story lines to follow.

When designing the dialogue for our game, we need to consider the following needs:

- The dialogue should be relevant in some way to the story.
- The dialogue needs to provide information to the player.
- The player should have options to select their response during the dialogue.
- The dialogue must be designed such that the player will get needed information.

Making the dialogue relevant to the story means that the player does not engage in random small talk with various non-player characters (NPC) over the course of the game. As game players, we immediately think that this would be a wonderfully cool thing to do as it would make the world more immersive and more real and just generally better. While it does have that potential, consider the possibility of the player of an adventure game in which they need to talk to a specific NPC in order to learn the combination for a locker somewhere. But, in this game we have made it so that the player can actually talk to all of the NPCs and have irrelevant conversations about things that have nothing to do with the story or the quest at hand. This in turn makes it very difficult for the player to find the key character that they need to talk too and as a result the player gets stuck not knowing what to do next. We could alleviate this by placing a special icon over the one character that needs to be talked to, but in so doing we have just lost that sense of immersion that we were after because now the player can just look at their map and go straight to the key conversation bypassing all of the others that are there. As a result, it will be easier for us as designers and easier for our players if we just focus on creating dialogues relevant to the game and any of the irrelevant small talk type things we just relegate to one-off comments rather than lengthy dialogues. Besides, how much fun would it be to talk to the 30th NPC about the weather and the taxes in the town?

Note
Everything that is placed in a game requires art assets, programming, design, and work. Always focus on the required key components of a game to make sure it is playable.

We can create our dialogues as complete scripted events that the player can watch and listen to as they unfold; we usually refer to these as cut scenes. While these are very useful, they are not interactive; the player is watching a movie unfold and has no impact on what happens. To alleviate this, many dialogues within games will allow the player to respond to what the other characters have said. We can present the player with a couple of different options in this response system. The first is to display to the player exactly what their character would say and let the player select the option that they prefer. The other option is to present the player with a mood response and let the player select how their character will respond but not exactly what words they will say. There are advantages and disadvantages with both of these. In the first case, the player will know exactly what their character will say, but this may lead to a wall of text options that the player has to read before making a selection. The second case will present the player with less to read when making a selection, but oftentimes the player's idea of an angry response and the developer's idea of an angry response may not exactly match leading the player to wish they had selected something else because that was not what they wanted to say.

When we create dialogue trees, we need to make sure that there are no dead branches in the tree. By this, we mean that if the player needs to get a

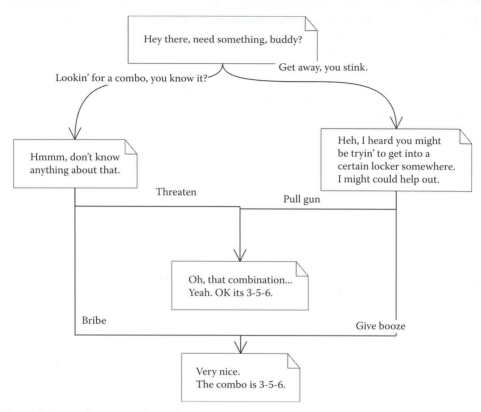

FIG 6.8 Example dialogue tree for getting a combination from a character.

combination from the character in this conversation, then regardless of how they navigate through the dialogue, they end up with the combination. It is tempting to punish the player for being mean or whatever, however, if the player cannot get the information that they need, then they are stuck in the game and cannot continue. This was a problem that plagued many of the early text and point and click style adventure games in which a player might have to completely restart because they missed something along the way. That can be a very frustrating game-play experience, though we as designers should be willing to push the envelope by introducing consequences for player action. These are all things to consider and to practice as we continue to sharpen our game development skills. Figure 6.8 depicts a small dialogue tree for this simple combination example that we have been discussing. In this example, we are going to provide the player with both complete sentence responses and action responses to select from. This particular example will involve an interaction between the player character and a hobo-type character in a subway somewhere. We have kept this example intentionally short.

As can be seen in the example dialogue tree, we have made sure that the player is going to get the information regardless of how they navigate through the conversation. We do not want the player to get stuck in our game because they are opting to play it differently than we think that they should. The key to this, though, is to try to maintain some sense of continuity throughout the conversation. For example, while the player can get the conversation by being angry with the NPC, the NPC gives the information reluctantly and if we were to introduce a relationship monitor system to the game, the player may have their relationship with this specific NPC negatively impacted by this exchange.

There are several tools that can be used for designing and testing your dialogues. While Microsoft Office (or other office compatible application) can be used, it can be difficult to scroll through various screen and pages to track your dialogue. Because of this, we recommend using Chat Mapper, which is a free-to-use application that is excellent for developing and testing your dialogue trees.

6.8 Putting the Story into the Game

Download
You can find the starting scene for this chapter in the complete project package on the companion website, the scene name is: "Chapter6_part1."

We have already discussed that many of the story elements will be put into the game as we continue working on developing the project. For instance, the setting will be put in as we construct the virtual world and the levels. The solution will be put in place with the final boss battle. The plot events will be put in place through levels or challenges that we present the player with, perhaps rescue a chicken from a marauding spider, for instance. But there are other pieces such as the backstory of the conflict and even plot events to an extent that do not naturally lend themselves to a section of a video game. For these, we are going to have to be deliberate about how we approach these and in so doing we will encounter some aspects of video games that we have already experienced.

The primary consideration that we have to make is how are we going to get information to the player. Story information is given to the audience in other media through action on the stage or through words written in the book. The audience is directly given the information, and we will adopt this same approach and make sure that our players know the answers to the key questions of who, what, why, where, when, and how by telling them what they will need to know during the course of the game, which brings us to how we will tell them. We essentially have three techniques that we can leverage: voice-over narration, written text on the screen, or dialogue with other characters. We will look at each of these in turn and develop a brief example for each.

> **Note**
> The following sections are not intended to replace the chapters covering audio and the user interface (UI). As a result, we will not be going into great detail about the features of the audio system or the new UI system within Unity, saving such discussion for the relevant chapters. Here, we will get to the nuts and bolts of what we need to know in order to get our immediate task accomplished. After learning about the UI system and audio system, these topics will be revisited and the initial implementation presented here will be expanded and corrected.

Before going into our examples, however, we will create a new scene so that we are only testing out these new features and not worried about all of the characters that we constructed in the previous chapters. Select File → Save As to save our current scene as a different scene, in our case we have named this new scene "Chapter 6 Testing" and saved it within the Scenes folder of our project. Next, we will go ahead and remove all of the things that we really do not need for our current purposes. Specifically, we will remove all the characters except for Sancho and his wife Teresa, the waypoints used by the Spider, and the blocks that we had originally placed in this scene. Now, we are ready to try out some new things within this scene.

6.8.1 Voice-Over Narration

For our opening of the first level of the game, we are going to use a voice-over narration in order to set the stage with the relevant backstory information. We are not going to tell the player everything at once, just the basic pieces that they need to get the game going. In order to do this, we will have to consider our backstory and determine what the player needs to know to begin the game. There are two different directions that we can go with this, option one is that the player does not *need* to know anything they can just play and option two is going to be to provide them with some background.

> **Note**
> It is important to not tell the player everything in one go as this can be information overload and lead to the player not remembering everything. Instead, give the player the information that they absolutely must have, with a little flavor on the side, and add more story details and information as the game progresses.

With option one, this really depends on the game that you are designing. For instance as a platformer and action–adventure style game, it is quite plausible for the player to just start the game and begin playing. Many platformer games do not actually have much of a story or at least not one that extends to a huge backstory. Our game is on the light-hearted side of the action–adventure genre, meaning that we are leaning more toward platformer with just a little bit of the other thrown in. As a result, we could easily get away without providing any backstory information to the player; however, we are opting to not run the game quite that lean, but would rather throw in some of the action–adventure genre by providing our platformer with a bit of a backstory to get the player up and going and also to help set the stage and theme for the player, which brings us to option two.

For the voice-over narration, we are going to add an audio file to the project and then get it to play within the game. For a full discussion of the options and features of the audio system for our basic game take a look at Chapter 9. At the moment, all we need to know is that in order to *play* an audio file we will need an audio source component added to an object and in order to *hear* the audio that is being played within the game we will need an audio listener component added to some object. Generally speaking, the audio listener is added to the main camera or player character as it is where the player hears the audio from, so it would make sense for our player's ears to be located where the player is. The audio source, on the other hand, can be added to whatever we want playing the audio (more on the relationship between listeners and sources later).

We have already laid out our basic backstory earlier, so all we need to do is to voice act that backstory and record it. For the audio recordings that we will need to create, we are going to utilize the free program Audacity (a more detailed discussion of it is found in Chapter 9). There are other tools out there that can be used, however Audacity is free, easy to use, and very powerful. The audio file that we are going to use can be found on the companion website.

Download
You can download the required backstory audio file from this chapter's section of the resources on the companion website: "intro_narration_backstory.mp3."

1. Create a new folder within the Project panel to store audio files; we will call this folder Audio.
2. Import the mp3 audio file by dragging it into this newly created folder.
3. Create a new empty GameObject.
   a. Change its name to Narrator or something along those lines.
   b. Make the Narrator object a child of the player (Sancho).
   c. Change the position of the Narrator to 0, 0, 0.
4. Add an Audio Source component to the Narrator.
   a. Figure 6.9 depicts the default properties of the audio source component; notice the Play On Awake feature; this means that the audio source will automatically play something when it is created (when it wakes up).
   b. Add the intro_narration_backstory audio file to the AudioClip property within the Audio Source component, check Figure 6.10.

We now have an object that will serve to play any narration audio files that we may use during the game. It was not necessary to create a separate object as we

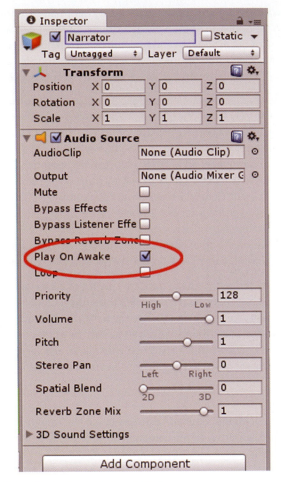

FIG 6.9 The default settings for the Audio Source component.

did, but you can see how this is abstracting out the uses of the objects such that this particular object we will use only for narration. By adding the object to Sancho, it will follow him around wherever he goes and whenever we have something that needs to trigger a narration, we can simply utilize this Narrator object and tell it what audio file to play. We will specify the audio file inside of PlayMaker at a later time once we have moved out of our testing scene and have more game pieces in place. For the moment, however, this will do as a testing run and we will tweak this when we start putting more of the game together, specifically once we get some interesting things and areas within our game world setup.

Note
We can assign audio files to our audio components by either dragging them to the AudioClip property of the Audio Component or we can assign it at runtime within PlayMaker. At the moment assigning in the Audio Component does what we need to do.

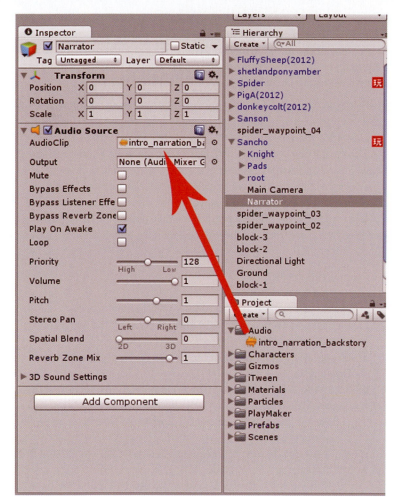

FIG 6.10 Adding the correct AudioClip to the Audio Source Component.

6.8.2 Written Text

Written text can serve several purposes that we need to consider during the design component of our game projects in which we will look at in more detail in Chapter 10. As we design our games, we need to consider the user interface and how we will provide information to the player, written text is one of those options. During the design stage, however, we are not going to think of everything, but as the game is developed and play testing begins to occur we will discover issues within the game that we had not considered. A potential solution for some of these issues is the use of written text or even voice-over narration. An example of a common problem that will pop up during testing is the player not knowing what to do next, as developers we are so close to the project that we forget what we have told the player and what we have not. We know so many things about the game that the player does not and tend to assume that the player has the same knowledge that we do, they usually do not though. So, when we start getting complaints about not knowing where to go or what to do, a quick fix is to throw in some written text somewhere and that problem is now solved. Knowing that this is a potential problem we will go ahead and solve it now by giving the player their first "quest" of our game (though it will not be complete, yet, we will finish it up later).

The GUI (Graphical User Interface) system of Unity has been completely reworked in version 4.6 and this new system has continued into version 5 of Unity. The basic idea of the interface is that all UI elements are drawn onto a Canvas object. So, in order to get any UI elements into our testing scene we will need to add a Canvas to it and add the basic elements that we will use. For the moment, what we are going to build is a starter notification that will tell the player that they must go find Sancho's donkey, Dapple. We are not adding any testing to see if they have completed the quest or not, just a simple notification to get them off and going. If the player clicks on the message then the message will disappear.

1. Create a cube object.
   a. Name it Sample Text.
   b. Place it somewhere in front of Sancho in our test scene.
2. Create a Canvas Game Object and make it a child of the Sample Text object we just made, Game Object → UI → Canvas.
   a. Change the Render Mode of the Canvas to "World Space" (check Figure 6.11).
   b. Adjust the Width and Height in the Rect Transform section of the Canvas (Figure 6.11).
      i. We are going to use values of 5 and 2, more on these values in a later chapter.
   c. Move the Canvas next to the Sample Text object; notice that it is still quite large.
      i. Now we will scale this canvas and reposition it until we have something that we like (Figure 6.12).
         A. For positioning we have used the different angles to get the Canvas positioned roughly above the empty object.
   d. With the Canvas in place, we will now add a button to it. Right-click on the Canvas and select UI → Button.
      i. For this example, we are going to leave the Panel with its default settings.
      ii. There is a Text object that is a child of the button, select that object.
         A. Enter our text message as shown in Figure 6.13.
      iii. At the bottom of the Inspector for the Button is a section for specifying what to do when the button is clicked (Figure 6.14).
         A. Drag the Sample Text object to the field currently labeled None.
         B. Select No Function and switch that to GameObject → SetActive.
         C. Make sure the check box is left off.

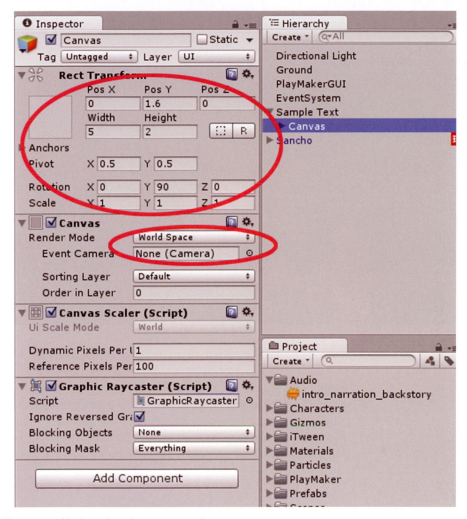

FIG 6.11 The properties of the Canvas object, the rotation may not be necessary on yours.

After playing our adjusted level, we can see that we have a nice little text message displaying in the game world for the player to see. Yes, we have done some new things in this step; however, we want to keep this chapter focused on story concepts and save the detailed discussion of these UI components and how they work for Chapter 10. This is now providing the player with valuable information that they may need for playing the game; more specifically, the information is filling in some story components for the player. In this case, we are telling the player what they need to accomplish, which is to say that we are telling the player what the next plot point is within the story. Until that plot point has been accomplished the story will not move forward to the next stage. This is giving the player the illusion of controlling the flow of the story, but in actuality this is a very linear approach.

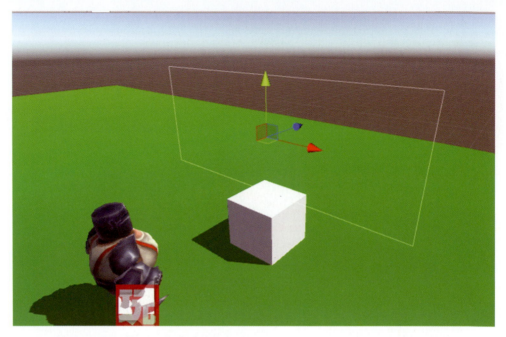

FIG 6.12 Position of the Canvas object above the cube that was added to the scene.

Note

Creating nonlinear story lines for games is not quite as trivial as making a design decision that our game will not be linear. There is a movement within the industry to create more content that gives the player more creativity and flexibility within the story structure that has been created.

We may have a couple of very minor issues at this point: does the player know that they have a donkey? If we included the information in our backstory narration, which we did, then the player should know that their donkey is named Dapple. However, it may be that the player skipped over the starting narration or did not listen to it (which brings us back to the possibility of adding in subtitles). We will address the possibility that the player does not know who Dapple is in our next section.

6.8.3 Character Dialogue

Earlier in this chapter, we discussed the difficulties that must be considered when creating a dialogue for the game project. For our Sancho project, we are going to create and implement a starter conversation to be placed at the beginning of the game between Sancho and his wife Teresa. It is not necessary for us to construct a huge dialogue tree in order to demonstrate the principles at work here, so we will keep our tree relatively short as can be seen in Figure 6.15. The first thing we need to determine is what information

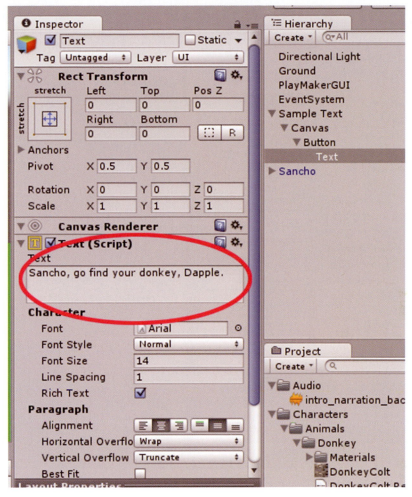

FIG 6.13 The properties of the Text object child of the Button.

we are trying to get to the player. In this case, we want to tie the backstory narration into the game so that this first conversation is going to serve the purpose of letting the player know what they need to do and why they need to do it. We can view this conversation as bridging a gap between the backstory narration and the little written text box that we created in our previous example. We will use a combination of complete responses and actions as we did in the combination locker example earlier.

Now that we have the basic outline of the dialogue in place, we can go ahead and implement this within our game. Looking at the dialogue tree that is presented, we can see the PlayMaker state machine emerging from the diagram and ready to be dropped into the project. This will be a fairly straightforward process building upon the written text example that we just completed and the previous work that we have done with finite state machines (FSM) within PlayMaker. A basic guideline is that we are going to present the user with a written text screen as we did previously then the buttons displayed will be

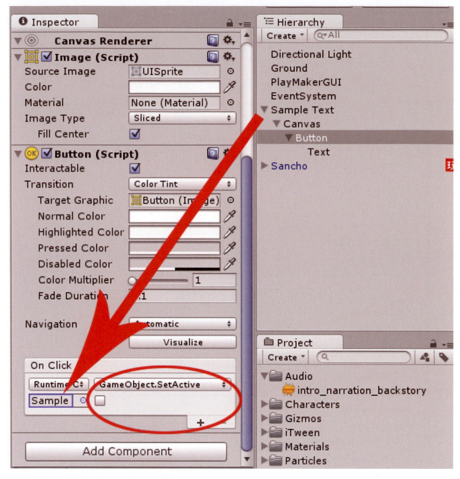

FIG 6.14 The On Click() properties for the button on the Canvas.

the options that the player can select from to continue the dialogue. Before we implement the full dialogue for this encounter, however, we will ned to implement the system so that it will recognize when the dialogue should start and get it ready to fire up; Figure 6.16 depicts an overview of this state machine.

1. Select the Teresa character so we can get her configured to trigger our conversation.
   a. Add a box collider to Teresa.
   b. Adjust the settings of the collider so that the box is nicely around her, not too tight because we will need them to be triggers that respond to Sancho getting close to her; our settings can be seen in Figure 6.17.
   c. Add an FSM to Teresa called Starting Dialogue (we will construct this later).
      i. Disable this FSM in the Inspector for Teresa.

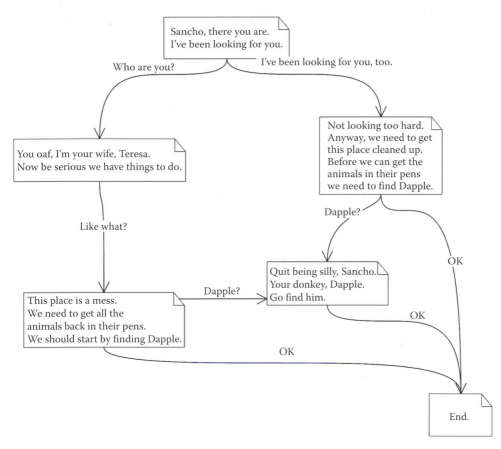

FIG 6.15 Dialogue between Sancho and Teresa.

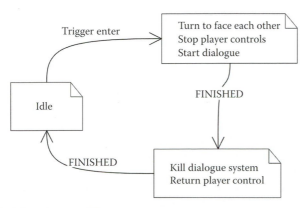

FIG 6.16 The dialogue detection and firing system.

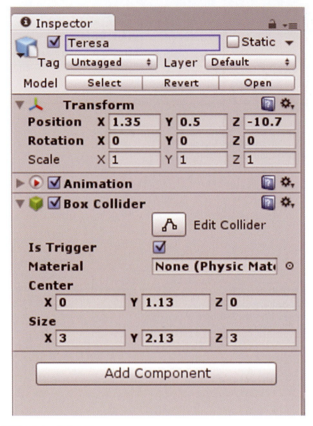

FIG 6.17 Collider settings for Teresa.

d. Add another FSM to Teresa (this will start the conversation system, call this FSM Dialogue Detection this FSM should match Figure 6.18).

    i. Add a state named Idle.

        A. Create a new event named Start.

        B. Add Start event and connect to Begin.

        C. Add a Trigger Event action.

            I. On Trigger Enter.

            II. Collider Tag = Player.

            III. Send Event = Start.

    ii. Add a state named Begin.

        A. Add a FINISHED event and connect to Close state.

        B. Create two Game Object variables that are visible in the Inspector, one for Sancho and the other for Teresa. In the Inspector, drag the appropriate Game Object into those variables. See Figure 6.19.

        C. Create a Bool variable named isOver with a default value of false.

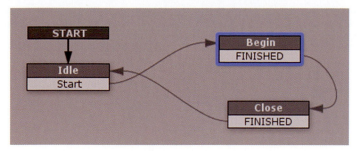

FIG 6.18 The basic structure of the dialogue detection FSM.

D. Add two Smooth Look At actions.
    I. The first one has Teresa look at Sancho.
    II. The second one has Sancho look at Teresa.
    III. Figure 6.20 depicts these settings and use Inspector variables to store the Sancho and Teresa objects as needed.
E. Add Enable FSM actions to disable all of Sancho's controller FSMs as seen in Figure 6.21.
F. Add a Play Animation action.
    I. Use Specify Game Object and set that to the Sancho variable.
    II. Select the Idle animation from the drop-down list.
G. Add a Bool Test action.
    I. Test every frame for True and if it is True do the FINISHED event.
H. Add an enable FSM action to turn on the Starting Dialogue FSM.
    I. Leave the Reset on Exit box checked to turn this off when we leave here.

iii. Add a state name Close.
    A. Add a FINISHED event and connect to Idle state.
    B. Add Bool Flip action and set the variable to isOver, this will flip the value of the variable.

We now have the basic detection system in place to determine if Sancho has entered into the area to start the conversation and if so to go ahead and get everything ready for the conversation to take place. In order to test this, we will need to set our isOver Bool to be an Inspector variable so that we can change its value while the game is running. Go ahead and run the game. Try moving Sancho toward Teresa and notice how Sancho stops moving, and Teresa turns to face him. In fact, Sancho also turns to face her. Sancho also quit running and goes into his Idle animation. Now click Teresa in the Hierarchy so that we can see her properties in the Inspector and go ahead and switch that Bool variable to True (see Figure 6.22). Now Sancho can run away from the conversation; also notice that the variable immediately went back to False, which is the Close state doing its thing. We can now run away from Teresa and if we come back to her

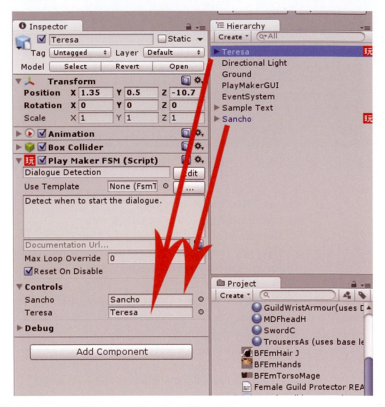

FIG 6.19 Assignment of the Sancho and Teresa Game Object variables.

it will all start back up again. With the detection system in place we are now ready to construct the dialogue system itself.

We will begin the construction of the Starting Dialogue FSM by first building the written text box that we will utilize for the dialogue text and Sancho's responses. This time we will add some new details to the text system that we previously created such that it will roughly match the diagram depicted in Figure 6.23. In order to do this, we will need a Canvas object that we will attach to Teresa. And attached to the Canvas we will need two Button objects for when Sancho has two options to select from, a Text object for Teresa's words, and a Text object along the top for her name.

1. Create a Canvas object and attach it to Teresa and adjust its size and position as we did earlier.
   a. Add a Text object and attach it to the Canvas.
      i. Change the name of this object to be Speaker.
      ii. Rather than changing the Height and Width of the Speaker object, use the Scale tool (Figure 6.24) to resize the text box to be visible and fit within the Canvas.
      iii. For the Text, change it to Teresa and change the color as well; we have gone with a reddish type of color.

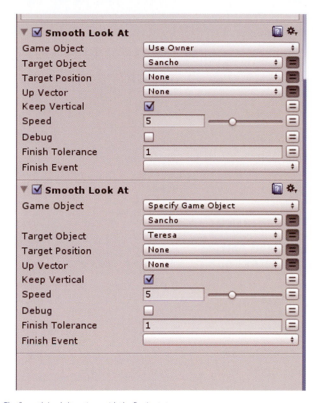

FIG 6.20 The Smooth Look At actions with the Begin state.

b. Add another Text object and attach it to the Canvas.
  i. Name this one Dialogue.
  ii. Position it such that it fits into the remainder of the Canvas area; for testing purposes, we entered the longest text that Teresa will speak from Figure 6.15 to make sure that things line up. It may be necessary to rework the Canvas and the Speaking text as well, and remember to save room for two possible options for Sancho. Figure 6.25 shows our final version including the buttons.
  iii. While this can be a tricky process, we can use the Horizontal Overflow and Vertical Overflow options set to Wrap and Overflow to have text wrap vertically and horizontally better (see Figure 6.26).
c. Add a Button object to the Canvas.
  i. Rename to Option_1.
  ii. Position and scale as needed using Sancho's line of "I've been looking for you, too." for testing.
d. Add a final Button object to the Canvas.
  i. Rename to Option_2.
  ii. Position and scale as needed using Sancho's line of "Who are you?" for testing.

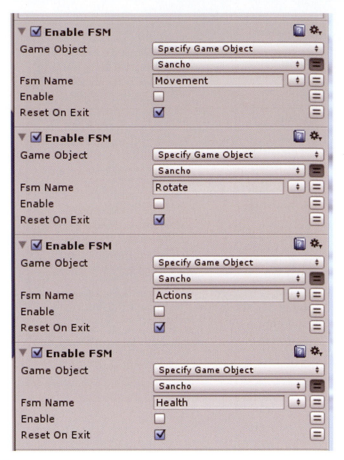

FIG 6.21 Disabling all of Sancho's player controller FSMs.

With the basic dialogue box in place, it is now time to construct the Starting Dialogue FSM such that it can display the correct words for Teresa with the current response options for Sancho. Along with the display, our Starting Dialogue FSM must also properly respond to the button clicks from the player and update the dialogue to match that which has been designed and diagrammed earlier in this section. However, as of the writing of this book, the uGUI (Unity GUI system we have been using) action support is not included as a part of the standard PlayMaker package. This means that we will need to add some new actions to our default PlayMaker action set by utilizing the Ecosystem package browser we installed back in Chapter 3 when we were looking at both Unity and PlayMaker.

> **Note**
> Before installing new actions, always check to see if the needed action is already in your PlayMaker install. You can do this by typing the name (or part of the name) of the action that you are looking for in the search bar of the Action Browser in PlayMaker. In this case try searching for uGUI to see if any of the actions are included before assuming that they are not.

FIG 6.22 The isOver variable that needs to be switched during testing.

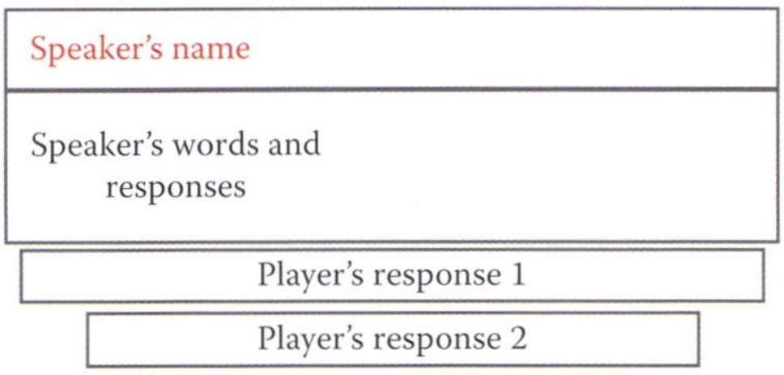

| Speaker's name |
| Speaker's words and responses |

| Player's response 1 |
| Player's response 2 |

FIG 6.23 Basic outline of the elements and components within the text system.

FIG 6.24 The Scale tool is the currently selected box in the image.

FIG 6.25 Final version of the Canvas with the Text and Buttons in place.

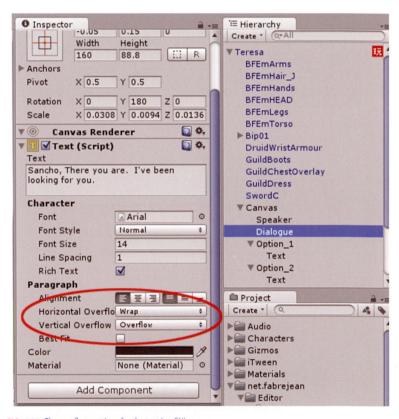

FIG 6.26 The overflow settings for the text in uGUI.

1. Get back into the Ecosystem browser.
   a. PlayMaker (top of the Unity toolbar) → Addons → Ecosystem.
   b. Select "Use the ecosystem!" (if necessary).
2. Search for the uGUI button actions we need by entering "uGUI button" in the search box and clicking Search button (See Figure 6.27).
   a. There should only be one result "uGUI button on click."
   b. Select that result and click Get.
   c. After it has downloaded and added the action to your Unity package, you will have an orange label at the bottom letting you know that the PlayMaker system is being recompiled to incorporate this new action (also depicted in Figure 6.27).
3. Close Ecosystem.

The action that we just added is going to allow PlayMaker FSMs to respond to button clicks being generated by buttons within the new UI system. In our earlier example with the written text, we kept things out of PlayMaker and handled responses directly within Unity; however, in our conversation version, we will have to utilize PlayMaker to update the text that is being

FIG 6.27 The Ecosystem browser with uGUI button search results and Unity compiling.

displayed in both the text areas and the buttons; this will require the FSM being able to respond to button clicks through this newly added action. This ability to expand PlayMaker with custom actions allows the system to be continually growing and evolving as Unity does so as well.

We are now, finally, ready to implement within the Starting Dialogue FSM all of our needed transitions and states as we have already defined in the design of this conversation. Table 6.3 presents the variables that we are going to need for this as well as the custom events that we will create. With those variables and events in place we are ready to put this FSM together using actions that we already know as well as the new action that we just added. Figure 6.28 depicts all of these variables and the values that have been assigned to them. To make sure that the system works as we want it to, we are going to go ahead and turn off the Canvas and the Starting Dialogue FSM so that they both get turned back on and are functional by the FSM within PlayMaker. To do this click the check box next to Play Maker FSM (Script) Starting Dialogue. For the Canvas, however, we do not want to disable the Game Object itself, but the Canvas component that is within the Canvas object (see Figure 6.29).

TABLE 6.3 Custom Events and Variables for the Starting Dialogue FSM

Name	Settings
button_1	GameObject variable with inspector checked. Drag the Option_1 button into this variable in the Inspector.
button_1_text	Object → Unity Engine → UI → Text variable. Check the Inspector box. Drag the Text object from Option_1 into this variable in the Inspector.
button_2	GameObject variable with inspector checked. Drag the Option_2 button into this variable in the Inspector.
button_2_text	Object → Unity Engine → UI → Text variable. Check the Inspector box. Drag the Text object from Option_2 into this variable in the Inspector.
dialogue_text	Object → Unity Engine → UI → Text variable. Check the Inspector box. Drag the Dialogue Object from the Canvas into this variable in the Inspector.
Journal	Object → Canvas variable. Check the Inspector box. Drag the Canvas object from Teresa into this variable in the Inspector.
speaker_name	Object → Unity Engine → UI → Text variable. Check the Inspector box. Drag the Speaker Object from the Canvas into the variable in the Inspector.
onClick_1	Event. Used for when the player clicks button_1.
onClick_2	Event. Used for when the player clicks button_2.

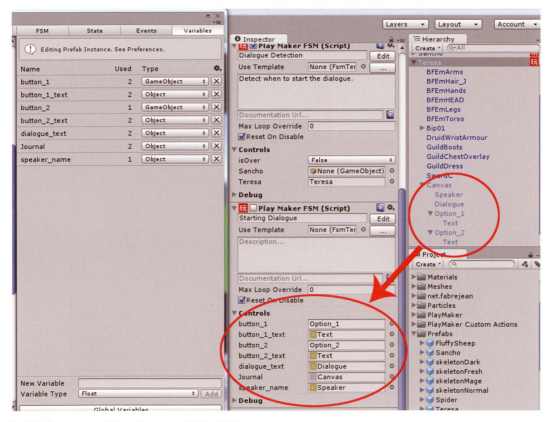

FIG 6.28 The Inspector variables and assignments for Teresa's dialogue system.

Video

We have provided a video detailing the initial configuration and setup for this state machine. There are a bunch of variables that need to be created and this video may help to clarify any issues with the process. The video "Starting Dialogue Variables" may be found in this chapter's section of the videos on the companion website.

1. Begin by laying out the states and transitions to roughly match that from the design sketch of the conversation. We have named each state with the first couple of words Teresa will say to help identify the states; Figure 6.30 shows this final layout.
2. Select the Start state.
   a. Add a "U Gui Button On Click Event" action to this state.
      i. Set Game Object to use the button_1 variable that we just created by selecting Specify Game Object and then switching to variable.
      ii. Send Event should be onClick_1.

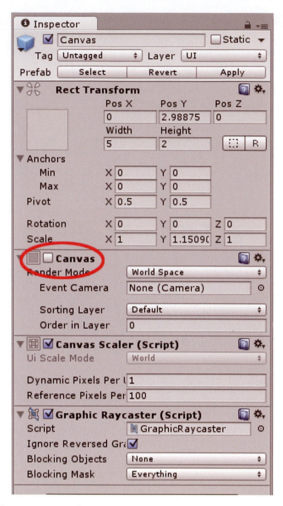

FIG 6.29 The Canvas component to deactivate.

b. Repeat for the second button.
c. Add a Set Property action.
   i. Target Object is Journal.
   ii. Property is enabled.
   iii. Set Value is checked.
d. Add a Set Property action.
   i. Target Object is speaker_name.
   ii. Property is text → string.
   iii. Set Value is "Teresa."
e. Add a Set Property action.
   i. Target Object is dialogue_text.
   ii. Property is Text → string.
   iii. Set Value is "Sancho, there you are. I've been looking for you."

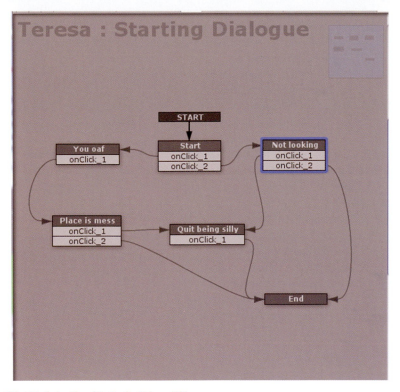

FIG 6.30 Final outline of the Starting Dialogue FSM.

f. Add a Set Property action.
   i. Target Object is button_1_text.
   ii. Property is text → string.
   iii. Set Value is "Who are you?"
g. Add a Set Property action.
   i. Target Object is button_2_text.
   ii. Property is text → string.
   iii. Set Value is "I've been looking for you too."
3. Select the "You oaf" state.
   a. Add a Set Property action.
      i. Target Object is dialogue_text.
      ii. Property is text → string.
      iii. Set Value is "You oaf. I'm your wife, Teresa. Now be serious we have things to do."
   b. Add a Set Property action.
      i. Target Object is button_1_text.
      ii. Property is text → string.
      iii. Set Value is "Like what?"

c. Add an Activate Game Object action.
    i. Game Object is Specify Game Object and select button_2 from the variable list.
    ii. Activate should be unchecked.
    iii. Reset on Exit should be checked.
d. Add a "U Gui Button On Click Event" action to this state.
    i. Set Game Object to use the button_1 variable.
    ii. Send Event should be onClick_1.

4. Repeat this process for the other states of the conversation changing text and setting active as needed (this is an exercise at the end of the chapter).

5. Select the "End" state.
    a. Add a Set FSM Bool action.
        i. Set FSM Name to be Dialogue Detection.
        ii. Set Variable name to be isOver.
        iii. Set Value should be checked.
    b. Add a Set Property action.
        i. Target Object should be Journal.
        ii. Property should be enabled.
        iii. Set Value should not be checked.

Video

The steps for this interactive conversation may have been somewhat confusing in the text version; take a look at those same steps in our video available at the companion website: "Starting Dialogue."

We now have a fully functional conversation system in which it begins when the player gets close enough to trigger it and then responds to the player's choice of words for Sancho. There are still some things that we would like to correct within it, specifically some of the visual layout of the text, but for a quick dive into the uGUI system we have learned a tremendous amount. We will return to this dialogue system in Chapter 10 when we learn more about the GUI system and at that point will pretty it up. It would also be nice to add some voice acting to the characters so that Teresa's words could be voiced by someone and Sancho's words could be voiced in return, this is something that we could easily add in once we know how to get audio playing with PlayMaker. We are going to make one final tweak before leaving this chapter, though, and that will be to convert our written text example from earlier into a journal instead.

Notice that in this state machine we have made extensive use of variables. While we could have done direct property setting by dragging the Game Object from the Hierarchy and releasing it into our PlayMaker Action panel, that approach would have created a headache when moving this Teresa object to another scene as a Prefab. Any value setting that we had done through this approach would have been lost in the transition to another scene, however, but using variables as we are doing all we will need to do in our game world scene will be to reassign what those variables are through the Inspector panel, which will be pretty easy to do and then the state machine we have constructed for this dialogue will work just fine with the new dialogue system we create later.

We have also introduced a new action in the Activate Game Object action. The Set Property action that we used for all of the values we changed during the course of the dialogue can only be used on variables of type Object; this means that we cannot use that action to enable or disable a Game Object itself, only a part of a Game Object. We already have a Game Object variable for our two buttons to use with the U GUI On Button Click Event action so it makes more sense for us to utilize those variable references to the Game Objects to turn buttons on or off as we may need. For instance, if Sancho only has one available response in a conversation moment, he does not need to have both buttons on the screen at that time. The Set Property action is a very powerful action as we can use it to reach into any object and set values for that object.

6.8.4 Journal Systems

Journal systems really are nothing more than glorified written text systems. Their primary purpose is to remind the player of the tasks that they need to complete and quite possibly why the task needs to be completed. For our basic example project we will only remind the player of the task at hand, specifically "Find Dapple."

1. Attach the Journal to Sancho.
2. Turn off the Box Collider and Mesh Renderer components for the Journal.
3. Using the Game View move the Journal so that the text is behind and below Sancho (or some place that you find pleasing).
4. Disable the Journal object within the Inspector so that it is not visible anymore.
5. Select the Teresa object.
   a. Enter the Starting Dialogue FSM.
      i. Select the End state.
         A. Add a Set Property action.
            I. Target Object is Journal.
            II. Property is enabled.
            III. Set Value is checked.

Now we have a journal that updates with the appropriate information after the conversation has ended. We can do some testing of things, such as not allowing a conversation to occur if the player currently has a quest or at least not allowing the conversation to complete, but that kind of stuff we will hold off on implementing at the moment. Once again, we can pretty things up as we learn more about the uGUI system within Unity and the tools that we have available to us.

6.9 Summary

In this chapter, we looked at the principles and theories behind story creation to provide us with a foundational set of building blocks that we can utilize when constructing stories of our own. While it is not necessary that we follow any of these rules, it is necessary for us to know what the rules are before we start breaking any of them. Too often we try to blaze our own trail and while this is a very good thing for us to do, we need to make sure that we have an understanding of the current trails, where they go, and why they are there before launching off into our own. We have also looked into a quick example of using those building blocks to construct the core components of the story for our Sancho Panza project. While we can still add some pieces and flavor to the basic story here and there, the essential story is now in place for our game and we are beginning to develop a good understanding of who is in the game, why they are in the game, what will happen during the game, and what the game will be about. These are important questions for us to get nailed down before we start making a game. We need to know where the game is going as that will guide us and provide a stabilizing force during the rest of the game development process when we will sometimes feel overwhelmed and completely lost. Adding more of the story elements and components to our game will be much easier as we learn more about both Unity and PlayMaker, but our journey is well underway at the moment and we are now ready to construct a world for our story to take place within.

> **Download**
> You can find the finished scene for this chapter in the complete project package on the companion website, the scene name is: "Chapter6_part2."

Vocabulary

Story
Hollywood 3-Act structure
Poetics
Setting
Problem or primary conflict
Internal conflict
External conflict
Love triangle
Zero-sum game
Plot
Solution
Theme
Thought (Aristotle on tragedy)
Diction (Aristotle on tragedy)

Melody (Aristotle on tragedy)
Spectacle (Aristotle on tragedy)
Journey of the hero
Ordinary world
Call to adventure
Refusal of the call
Meeting the mentor
Crossing the threshold
Test, allies, and enemies
Approaching the cave
Ordeal
Reward
Road back
Resurrection
Return with the elixir
Audio source
Audio listener

Review Quiz

1. What are the individual components of the Hollywood 3-Act structure, and how are they derived from Aristotle's work in *Poetics*?
2. How does the journey of the hero fit into the Hollywood 3-Act structure?
3. What is an example of an application that could be used to design dialogues for video games?
4. What is an example of an application that could be used to create and edit audio files?
5. Which Unity component must be added to a game object in order for that object to play audio files?
6. Which Unity component must be added to a game object in order for the player to hear audio files?

Exercises

1. Consider a favorite movie or book of yours and apply the hero's journey to it. Does it have all of the components of the journey?
2. Complete the conversation between Sancho and Teresa from the chapter example.

Design Document

In this addition to the *Sancho Panza* design document, we have added the essential components of the story for the game, including a back story. We have also developed some basic plot lines to follow that can be incorporated into the levels of the game or may be utilized as small side quests.

Consider your design document that you have been working on thus far and add the following to it:

1. For essential story components, consider the following points:
   a. What is the theme of your story? Remember it does not have to be an epic story or even a complex one.
   b. Will you incorporate plot twists into your work?
   c. What is the backstory of your world and characters?
      i. How much of this will the player need to be aware of?
      ii. How will this be communicated to the player?
2. What quests or level challenges will you incorporate to work with your story and to advance it?
   a. How will this information be given to the player?
      i. If using voice-over, what will be said?
      ii. If using character dialogues, what will be said?

CHAPTER 7

Environment

The creation of virtual environments and game worlds is a topic that by itself could easily fill a book. Our goal in this chapter is not for the reader to emerge on the other side knowing every detail about this fascinating subject. Rather, our aim is for the reader to have a solid foundation of the tools and techniques used within Unity to create game worlds. With this solid foundation in place, we will be prepared to expand our knowledge into more intricate environments, especially through a more detailed exploration of lighting. When creating a game world, it is important to keep in mind the needs of the story and the needs of the game; the two must merge in this area even more so than in the previous topics. The game world becomes the visual representation of the story's environment and setting as well as the location in which the player experiences the game that has been created for them.

- Environments for Stories
- Environments for Games
- Unity's Terrain Tool

- Unity Trees and Water
- Placing Imported Assets
- Lighting with Unity

7.1 Environments for Stories

In the last chapter, we saw that stories have settings, the locations, and times that stories take place within. We can alter this vocabulary from setting to environment without changing the meaning or usage of either word. Therefore, the use of environments for stories is that they fulfill the role of the setting for the story. These settings are important, as we saw in the last chapter, but before we write this section off as a summary of the last chapter, we need to reiterate a key concept. If we do not know the setting of the story, then we do not know the environment of the story and therefore we do not know the environment of the game that we are about to develop. While many games do not need stories or characters, many games do and if you are developing a game that does utilize characters then you will need a story of some type no matter how rudimentary or complex it is. It is important that we take our time when developing the components of our story, while we should leave some flexibility within for growth and exploration in certain areas that we discover during the development process, we need to have these basic building blocks pretty solidly nailed down and understood. When we start talking to an environment artist to build some virtual worlds or concepts for our story we need to know a little more than "it is on some medieval type island." For instance, with our Sancho story our environment is a little more fleshed out with some room for interpretation as can be seen in the design document from the end of the last chapter.

Stories need environments that will allow the characters to do whatever it is that the story will require of them while also allowing for interesting interactions and challenges to appear within the plot. The environment of a story should also provide access to the primary conflict that drives the plot of the story. The readers and viewers of a story will experience many nuances of the story through the environments that are selected as a part of the story. An example is the starting planet of Tatooine in *A New Hope*. This desolate starting location helps the viewer to, like Luke, want to travel to some other places; it also helps to define the characters that we were introduced to within the spaceport where Luke met Han Solo. Imagine the same scene taking place in an upscale 5-star resort on a vacation planet with tropical breezes blowing through the open windows and little umbrellas in everyone's drink. The image (the environment) does not match that of the characters and the events occurring which creates a jarring experience. Therefore, when working on the environments of the stories, we need to objectively look at the events that will occur, the primary conflict, and the characters that will be involved. Most stories have many different environments for different scenes or chapters within the story.

> **Note**
> It is very possible to create jarring environments that do not match characters and events for the purpose of comedy or some social statement that is trying to be made within the story. Be careful of always following the blueprints of story creation, this is a creative process and while these guidelines are a good start be willing to break the rules, but only after you know the rules.

7.2 Environments for Games

With the environment created for the story such that we can easily (within reason) tell the story with our desired plot events, we are ready to move on to converting that environment for a video game. Video games are similar to movies in many ways, specifically they are both visual and tell stories to an audience through a limited screen perspective. By this we mean that the audience of a movie (or game) can only see what the camera allows them to see whereas the reader of the book does not have a visual representation of the setting, but a mental and imaginary view of it. Games, however, differ from movies in that the player is oftentimes allowed to manipulate the view of the world by moving the avatar and therefore the camera. Unlike movies, where the audience is stationary and we take the audience where we want them to be and show them what we want them to see, in video games, the audience (the player) take themselves where *they* want to be and see what *they* want to see. As we saw in the previous section, the environment gives the audience a lot of hints as to the events and characters within a current scene. The environment also sets the mood to heighten any emotional content that we might be trying to deliver to the audience. Therefore when designing environments for video games we need to keep the following concepts in mind:

* What can the player do?
* What should the player not do?
* What does the player need to know?
* What does the player already know?
* What challenges (plot events) are being presented within this level (scene or chapter)?

7.2.1 Controlling the Player

Addressing the first two questions of our list essentially comes down to controlling the player. The first aspect of controlling the player is allowing them to do whatever it is that they should be able to do. For instance, in the construction of our Sancho Panza control system we have given the player the ability to make Sancho jump; therefore, our environment may have platforms at different heights to allow the player to do these things that they can do. On the other hand, just because a character (or player) *can* do something does not mean that we have to make it a relevant part of the game. For instance, we can create the environment of Barataria without any raised platforms, so that even though Sancho can jump, it is not a relevant aspect of the game-play experience, it is just a little extra something that the player can do. To further illustrate this, consider the first-person shooter games where it is possible to draw and holster your weapon. This specific action is not necessarily relevant to game play because pressing the fire button automatically draws the weapon and fires it; it is just an action that the player can do and an action that many of us do select many times as we run around the worlds during the game because we think it looks cool or is fun.

We can now see that the actions that the player's character is capable of performing must play a rule in the design of our game environments: running, jumping, crawling, crouching, hiding, and so on. At first glance this may seem an obvious statement to make, specifically in regards to running or walking, but consider the difference in views between walking and crouching. These differences we will have to take into account as we design the level because we will need to make sure that the art assets will work at both levels; we will also need to make sure that our collisions will work at both levels. We have all played games with "map holes," spaces in the game world where we can slip through to a different spot or drop down to a different level than the rest of the game. These types of things are going to happen with development (we would all *like* to ship a game with no bugs at all, but some always seem to creep in); however, we can try to limit these mistakes as much as possible. A further example would be if the character can swing a sword, if so we need to make sure that our environments and rooms will be large enough to allow this action to occur without the sword seeming to rip through walls and mountains.

Beyond the needs of the character's interaction with the world, we need to consider the plot needs of the current level that the player is playing within. By this we mean that the story may require that the hero character find all of the sheep that have wandered off and return them to their pen before continuing on. Our level design must allow for this to happen in such a way that is fun and engaging (very elusive ideas to begin with). We need to create an environment that presents challenges to the player but also allows the player to do what they need to do. In allowing the player to find the sheep, it may be necessary to close off other parts of the environment to make sure that the player does not wander too far away or get off on some sidetrack and be unable to complete the task at hand. The sheep that they are after should be accessible, that means that there should not be anything the player can do or go to that will prevent them from being able to complete the current challenge. Another way that we see this story need controlling the environment is within boss battles. Generally speaking, once the player triggers the boss battle portion of the level they cannot run away or skip past it, they must fight the boss and win in order for the story to progress.

There are many ways that we control where the player can and cannot go within an environment. We can use hidden barriers or walls, those are the times when you are running around in a world and suddenly you just cannot go any further. There is no obvious reason why you cannot go any further except that the level designers do not want you too. This is a very useful technique, though we could enhance it some by making those areas hazy or fuzzy so that the player might understand that they will be going there later, just not yet. These are artificial boundaries and some of our games will require such devices to keep the player where we want them to be.

Natural boundaries, on the other hand, are geographic aspects of the natural environment that prevent a player from going in a certain direction. These can include mountains, oceans, rivers, lakes, canyons, and so on. These are very powerful approaches to keeping the player where we want them to be; however, there are two catches with using this technique. The first is that we will have to build that type of content or we will have to make sure that our story supports such content. For instance, the isle of Barataria very nicely supports the idea of using an ocean to keep the player from leaving the area that we want them to be. The second consideration with this technique is to make sure that the geography is very heavily play tested. Many players will consider a mountain range to be a challenge and will do everything they can to get past it somehow. This may lead to very unexpected and unfortunate results if we have not programmed in a possible method of cleaning things up in case the player does find a way to the top of the mountains and jumps off of our game world.

The final technique that we can use to control the player's location and actions is essentially a combination of the two. We can have doors, gates, fences, and other props within the game world that will become unlocked or open once the player has completed the task in the given area; for instance, after the player finds all of the lost sheep, a door will become unlocked that will allow them to leave the town pasture and continue to the next challenge. Keep in mind that the point of levels is to present the player with challenges. It is tempting for us as designers to consider ourselves to be in competition with the player as it is our job to kill the player as many times as we possibly can. But the reality is that we need to consider ourselves as partners with the player. We are working together to tell a story. As developers we have laid down the framework of the story, but the details and nail biting action will be written by the players themselves. Does the hero beat the boss with just a sliver of health left barely surviving the challenge or does the hero come in and absolutely dominate the villain beating them into submission?

7.2.2 Informing the Player

Now that we understand that we will have to control where the player goes and what they can do, we need to recognize that we will have to in some way get this information to the player. For instance, if the player is looking for sheep and trying to return them, we need that information relayed to the player through the environment. Now, there are many ways that we can let the player know what challenges they face, some of which we looked at in the last chapter. We can also utilize a mini-map with icons for quest objects or superimpose arrows on the screen to tell the player which way they should go, both of which would truly fall into the category of user interface design rather than environment design. However, our environments can still provide the player with clues; for instance, there could be footsteps indicating which way the sheep have gone. There could also be an empty pen with its gate open and a sign with a sheep on it to indicate that there should be sheep inside of this pen but for some reason they are not there.

Aside from utilizing the level to help the player with quest-type items, we can also use lighting, simple particle systems, audio, and basic animation to draw the player's attention to components within a level. For instance, we could have a small glittering particle system floating above some gate to indicate that the player could interact with the gate in some way. With an interior environment, we can utilize the lighting to help steer the player in a specific direction, making areas of the environment that are not important darker to keep the player from wasting time in those sections, even though many players will anyway.

Another classic example is having an item that can be picked up or collected rotating to draw the player's attention to it and help the player to differentiate it from other objects that cannot be interacted with. In our game worlds, we will essentially have two types of objects that we have placed. The first are objects that are there to decorate the world, to give it a real feeling, to give it a sense of lived in. The second are objects that the player can interact with. As designers we should help the player to differentiate between the two objects, otherwise knowing which one of the 100 rocks that can be picked up and used becomes an experience of frustration rather than fun.

The last thing that we do with our environments as far as giving information to the player is continuing the backstory, story, and theme of the experience we are wanting for the player. We can provide posters of villains on various walls throughout a town to keep reminding the player of who the bad guy is and why they are so bad. Or we can put books and parchments around various houses that the player can find and read to learn more about the history and backstory prior to the start of the game. We should also consider the color scheme that we use throughout our environments as darker colors give a more oppressed feeling, which may be an emotion we are wanting to convey to the player.

7.2.3 Challenging the Player

We have alluded to this component already in that the environment is where the plot events occur. However, while the specific plot event may be to find the lost sheep and return them to the pen, it is up to the environment design to provide the actual challenge for doing this. If we were to have an empty pen and put five sheep directly outside of it that would not be much of

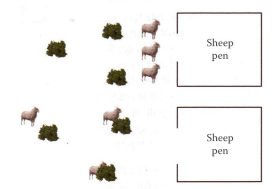

FIG 7.1 Two approaches to the lost sheep plot event.

a challenge. We could, instead, present the player with an open pen and then place the five lost sheep somewhere that requires the player to go find them, thereby presenting the player with a challenge, see Figure 7.1. The difficulty of the challenge that we present to the player will be governed by the type of game that we are creating and the type of game experience that we would like for the player to have. Therefore, as we design the environment, we need to take into account the things that the player can do; for instance, if the player can jump four units horizontally, then we could make a ledge that is 3.8 horizontal units away thereby presenting the player with a challenge to get across that gap in the world. Knowing what the player can and cannot do plays an important role in how we design our environments for the games.

7.2.4 The Final Design

With a solid understanding of what we can do in our environments and why we should do it, we will now put all of these to practice and design our island of Barataria for Sancho and Sanson to fight over. As we begin our design, we need to consider the points that we have previously discussed and make sure that we provide challenges for the player while still allowing the player to complete the given task in an environment that is consistent with the style and theme of our game project. We already have a natural boundary for our game as it will take place on an island surrounded by water, thereby preventing the player from leaving the island. However, something that we will have to consider in regards to this is that even though there is water, the game does not actually know that the player cannot go that way. So, while we will be on an island surrounded by water, we will still need some artificial boundaries in place to keep the player from walking out into the water and eventually falling off of our map. Perhaps, some boundaries a little ways from the shore and when the player collides with them we can display a message to the player saying "I don't know how to swim" or something along those lines so that the artificial boundary blends into the natural one in a way that is intuitive and logical. Figure 7.2 provides a rough sketch of what we could do as the isle of Barataria. Creating sketches of our environment is going to be very important as it will serve as

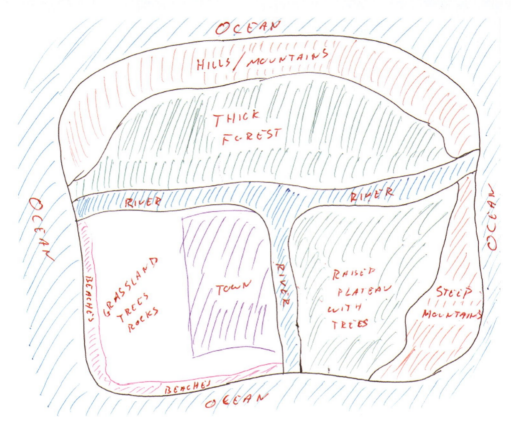

FIG 7.2 Rough sketch of the isle of Barataria with its boundaries.

a guideline for the actual construction even though we may end up varying from it somewhat while we build the environment.

With the basic island in place, we can now begin to consider the story needs of the island. As already mentioned, there is going to be a small abandoned town on the island. As Sancho and Teresa arrive at their new kingdom, they will have to clean things up before the residents will want to return to this island. Cleaning things up will include getting the animals back where they should be, eliminating the spiders that have taken over some parts of the island, eliminating the skeletons that Sanson has called upon to be his enforcers, and then finally eliminating Sanson himself so that the island is safe for the peaceful inhabitants to return to their houses. Figure 7.3 depicts another sketch of Barataria, this time with some story elements added to it so that we can begin to see how to break this environment apart into different "levels" as the story progresses. It is not necessary that your game world be broken down to so closely mimic the Hollywood 3-Act structure; we opted to do so as an example of the potential link between the story work and the game environment itself. At this point, we may want to consider adding some more boundaries of sorts to keep the player from wandering into another part of the story that we do not want them to be interacting with until they have completed the current task at hand.

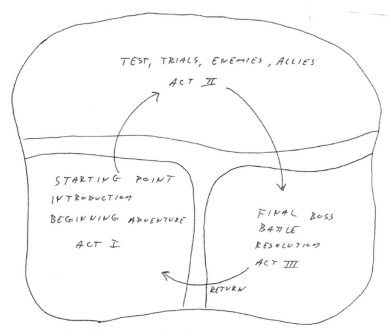

FIG 7.3 Rough sketch of Barataria broken up for level progression.

Now that we have our basic sketches in place, we will zero in and start getting a little more detail regarding the first component of our story, finding Dapple and then getting the sheep back into their pen. Figure 7.4 provides a rough detail sketch of this so that we can begin to imagine how this portion of the environment might look. It is very possible that as we actually construct this we will make some alterations to it to better fit the game not to mention add details to it that will help it fill it in better. However, while we may make adjustments, those changes must still stay consistent with the overall theme and design of both the game and story. If we stray too far, then the game we end up making is not the game that we had designed. With these rough sketches in place, we now have an idea of what types of assets and things we will need to have available within Unity in order to construct the environments as designed. This may be one of the most important aspects to design prior to implementation. By developing a list of assets that we need, we know what we need to go find or to create from scratch. It is important to know what we will need and to get all of these things gathered together, or to use some kind of place holders, while constructing our worlds (Table 7.1).

> **Note**
> Always remember that the actual game play is more important than the theoretical designs we create on paper. Use the designs as guides, but be willing to make changes if the design does not work quite as well as intended.

FIG 7.4 The town on the isle of Barataria.

TABLE 7.1 A Brief List of Assets That Will Be Needed on Barataria

Bridges	Barrels	Boxes	Gates
Trees	Stumps	Tools	Chairs
Rocks	Hay	Tables	Plows
Grass	Blacksmith stuff	Benches	Well
House	Wagons	Walls	Troughs
Barn	Fence	Bushes	
Stable	Walls	Carts	

7.3 Creating the Terrain in Unity

We will begin the construction of the terrain by creating a new scene within the project folder; we will name this scene "Barataria." We will begin the construction of our terrain by adding a basic terrain game object to our current scene. Do this by selecting GameObject → 3D Object → Terrain (see Figure 7.5). Once the new terrain has been added to the scene it will appear in the Hierarchy panel as well as be represented in the scene view as a very large white plane. This is our starting terrain which can now be edited and sculpted into whatever it is that we would like. It is also possible to import height maps to use for the construction of a terrain and to even grab data out of Google Earth and pull it into Unity to create a terrain based on real-world GPS data. However, both of those techniques are beyond the scope of this book; our goal is to get our minds and hands around the essential tools that we have available to us here within Unity.

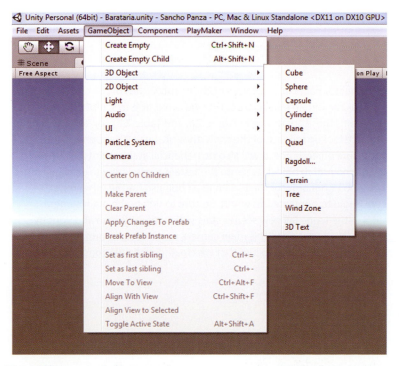

FIG 7.5 Adding a new terrain object to a scene.

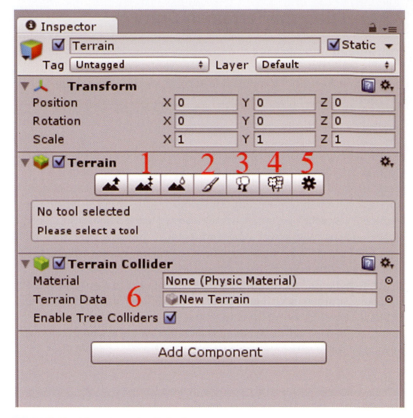

FIG 7.6 The Terrain Inspector panel and tool options.

The Inspector panel now displays both the properties of the current terrain as well as the terrain editing tools that we can utilize to sculpt and decorate our terrain. These are shown in Figure 7.6, and Table 7.2 provides a quick reference lookup for each of the tools, though we will be spending only a little time on each one. It will also be beneficial at this point if we throw our Sancho prefab object out onto the terrain somewhere to serve as a scale point not only for the terrain itself but also for the other objects as we begin to populate this world. Be sure to delete the main camera that is in the scene (all new scenes start with a main camera and light by default). We do not need this main camera as our Sancho prefab asset will have a camera attached to him that we created when we constructed the character controller system.

Note
Full documentation of the Unity terrain system and tools can be found in the Unity manual and documentation at: http://docs.unity3d.com/Manual/script-Terrain.html.

TABLE 7.2 Quick Reference of the Tools within the Terrain Editor

#	Name	Use
1	Height tools	Perform sculpting of the terrain by raising, lowering, and eroding the terrain.
2	Texture painting	Allows textures to be painted onto the terrain to give the surface the look and feel that is desired.
3	Tree painting	Allows the painting and placement of trees onto the environment.
4	Grass and details	Allows the painting of grass, rocks, and other details onto the surface of the terrain.
5	Terrain settings	All of the settings and configurations for the terrain can be altered from this location.
6	Terrain collider	Controls and configures the collision surface that is created by Unity to work with the created terrain.

7.3.1 Settings

We will begin with the tool all the way to the right in the toolbar for the terrain editor, the Settings tool. Most of these settings we are not going to get into here, but we do want to take a look at the terrain resolution properties as depicted in Figure 7.7. We are looking at these settings first as any modifications made to them can clear out any other work that we may have done to the terrain, so we will try to get it to the appropriate sizing first.

> **Note**
> Full documentation for the various terrain settings can be found in the Unity manual located at: http://docs.unity3d.com/Manual/terrain-OtherSettings.html.

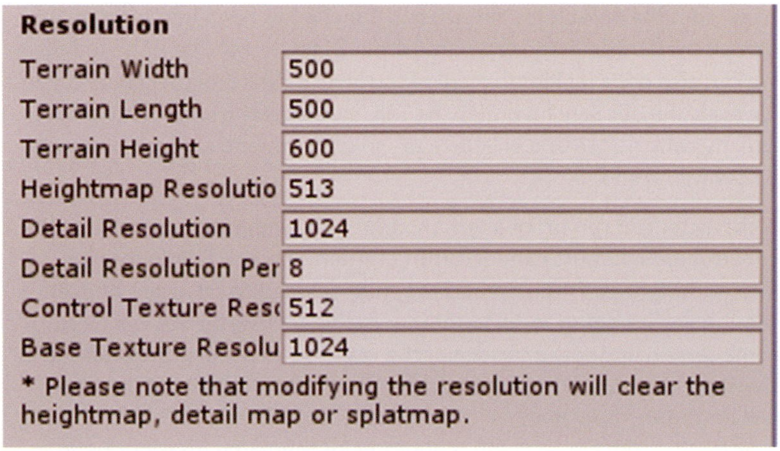

FIG 7.7 The default terrain resolution settings.

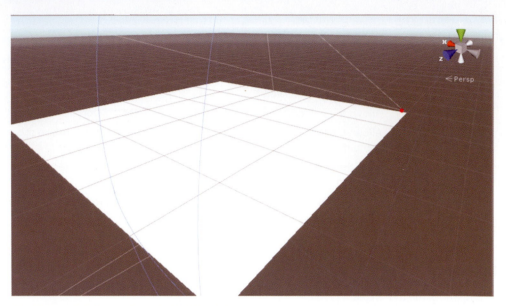

FIG 7.8 The default terrain size in comparison to the default Sancho character.

The first settings that we want to look at are the terrain width, length, and height. These are defining the size of the terrain in three-dimensional space. The sizes of these dimensions are in world units, so if we know the world unit size of other assets we can construct a reasonable terrain based off of those values with a little bit of math (e.g., Sancho is roughly 1.5 Unity world units tall as we have constructed him thus far). Also, on the issue of Unity world units, a unit in Unity is equal to 1 meter, although, realistically speaking it can be whatever we want it to be, but as far as the physics engine is concerned 1 unit is 1 meter. Or, we can look at the size of the Sancho asset that we have added to the scene and construct the terrain size visually. Figure 7.8 gives a rough idea of these scales as the terrain pictured is the default terrain size and Sancho has been imported at his default prefab size in the top right corner of the terrain, he is the red mark. We can also get a feel for the size of the level by starting the game, since we are using our Sancho prefab, he will have all of the stuff that we have already constructed and will be ready to start running around this newly discovered scene.

A character can run off of a terrain, depending on how they were constructed and ours can run off the terrain, thereby falling forever into nothingness. This is something that we need to be aware of even though we are going to surround our island with water, we will need some terrain under the surface of the water so that the player can run through shallow water without falling into oblivion. The height value will determine how high we can construct the terrain. Our environment is not going to have any high mountains so this value does not need to be anywhere near as high as it is so we will go ahead and lower the terrain height to a value of 75 or so and set the width and length to be

250 although you can experiment with these values by running Sancho around to find an island size that feels best to you. These values can be changed later and with the flat terrain it is difficult to really get a feel for these sizes. When raising terrain it will become a flat surface once the terrain has been raised to the maximum value specified here. The other settings are fine at their default values.

> **Note**
> There are two pitfalls to watch out for when making terrains. The first is making the terrain too large, thinking that we want an epic landscape to explore; keep in mind that we need to decorate this epic landscape and this takes time. The second, is making the terrain too small for the things that we want on it. Rule of thumb, make it just a little bigger than you think it should be and always remember you can change the width and height if need be later.

7.3.2 Terrain Collider

As we mentioned earlier, the Terrain Collider is responsible for the collision object that will be attached to the terrain to keep other objects from falling through it, hopefully. The terrain collider will create a collision object that matches the surface of the terrain, much like a mesh collider can be used to exactly match the surface of a mesh that has been imported into the game. The three properties of the Terrain Collider, as pictured in Figure 7.9 provide the only configurations available for the collider object on the terrain. The material references the Physics Material to be applied to the collider object. We are not utilizing Physics Materials within this project, but we could consider this to be a material that would provide presets for the friction and bounce effects when an object collided with the surface. We could create a terrain of Jell-O by using a Physic Material with a soft, rubbery bounce back on it, for instance. The Terrain Data property refers to which Terrain object the collider is referencing when creating its collision surface. Notice that in the Project pane, there is a terrain object for the terrain that we created in our new scene. Finally the Enable Tree Colliders property will either turn the colliders on trees painted onto the terrain on or off depending on the setting of the property. Keep in mind that trees painted onto the terrain are not the

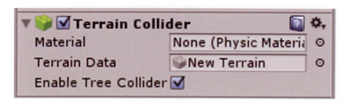

FIG 7.9 The Terrain Collider properties.

same as trees added as individual objects into the game world, but we will have more on this later.

7.3.3 Height Tools

Now that we have specified a maximum height for our terrain to keep from constructing the Himalayas we will turn our attention to the terrain height tools themselves. The first of our terrain height tools is the raise/lower tool, number 1 in Figure 7.10. This tool allows us to raise or lower the terrain by sculpting these details through the brush settings that we specify. The brushes section of the Terrain tool component allows us to select the type of brush that we want to use for doing our sculpting. Currently, it is not possible to import or create custom brushes, though the brushes available provide a tremendous amount of flexibility and creativity already.

The first four brushes to select from are standard round brushes with various falloff amounts. This falloff is an important concept to grasp if it has not been encountered before. Figure 7.11 provides a graphical representation of the difference between the first brush and the fourth brush when painting with a solid black color. As can be seen, with the first brush, the center point has 100% of the black color and as we move along the radius of the brush size to the perimeter of it that amount drops until it eventually reaches 0% of the black color at the perimeter. On the other hand, the brush with no falloff, the fourth brush, has 100% of the black color throughout the area of

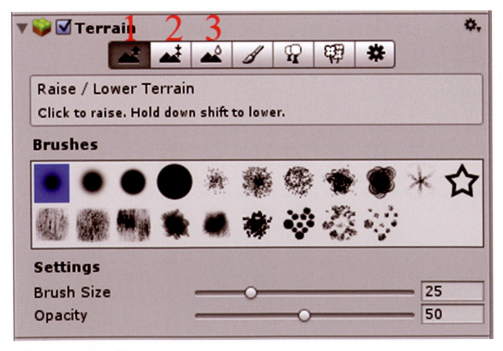

FIG 7.10 The three terrain height tool buttons.

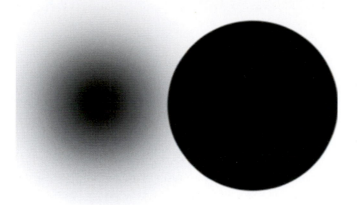

FIG 7.11 Brush falloff on the left versus no falloff on the right, both brushes are the same size.

the brush with no decrease in this percentage. This is going to translate into the sculpting by having 100% of the sculpting power in the center of the brush and decreasing until we get to the perimeter. If using one of the oddly shaped brushes, then the 100% points will be the darkest portions of the brush with the falloff going through shades of gray until reaching 0%.

The next aspect of the brushes will be the Brush Size and the Opacity settings. The Brush Size is going to determine how large the brush is. It is generally best to start off with a very large brush for broad strokes and then decrease the brush size when doing detail work. The Opacity is going to be the strength of the brush or how hard we are raising/lowering at the 100% point within the brush falloff. These values take some practice and playing around with to get a solid understanding of and the reader is encouraged to play around with a few different terrains and different brush settings to see how things work. With this tool holding down the left mouse button will raise the terrain while left-clicking with the SHIFT key pressed down will lower the terrain.

The next tool, Paint Height (number 2 in Figure 7.10), is essentially the same as the first tool except rather than sculpting the height directly, we can set a target height and the tool will then raise or lower the region appropriately in order to hit that target height. Setting the target height can be done holding down the SHIFT key and left-clicking a region on the terrain or by entering a specific value with the Height slider beneath the Opacity setting. The Flatten button (to the right of the Height slider) will flatten the whole terrain to the height level that is selected. This is an interesting tool that can be very useful for resetting or even raising terrain to a default level. With this tool it can be easier to create paths, roads, plateaus, or other flat surfaces within a terrain assuming that the flat surface is all at the same height. One final note on this tool, terrains cannot be lowered below the level of 0 (which is the default level that terrains are on), so if we are going to want valleys or rivers or what not,

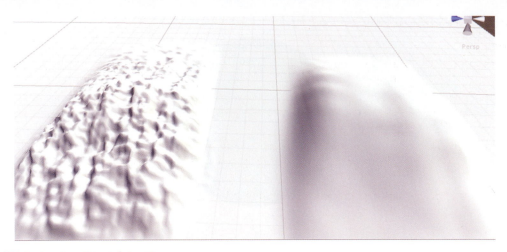

FIG 7.12 A noisy and smooth terrain feature set.

the terrain will need to be raised before it can be lowered, which we can do very quickly with this tool.

The final tool is the Smooth Height tool (number 3 in Figure 7.10). Unlike the previous tools, this one is not intended to raise or lower the terrain but rather to get the terrain to be smoother in its transition between heights. When using the other tools, the terrain that is raised or lowered can end up with some rough and jagged edges. The Smooth Height tool can be used to get these to transition better. Jagged height transitions will become difficult to navigate sections of the game world in which the player is more likely to get stuck when traveling the environment, which is something that we would prefer to avoid whenever possible. The settings for this tool work the same as the settings for the Raise/Lower Terrain tool. Figure 7.12 depicts the difference between a noisy terrain and a smooth terrain. Both of the terrain patterns were generated with one of the noisier of the Raise/Lower Terrain brushes. However, the pattern on the right of the image was then smoothed with the Smooth Height tool to create a more eroded kind of surface and a surface that would be easier to navigate for the player. The different controls for creating terrain are summarized in Table 7.3.

Now that we know what tools are available to us and how to use them it is time to create the isle of Barataria, or at least version 1.0 of this environment. Using the sketch that we created earlier, we will create an environment in which the outer portions are lowered (below sea level) to serve as our beach areas. We are also going to create the rivers that are being used to divide the island into the different chapters of the story. We will need to keep in mind the size of Sancho to avoid making terrain details that are overly exaggerated within the game world. Another thing for us to consider is that the houses and buildings that we add to the environment later will need to have flat surfaces that they are put onto, perhaps a place for the Paint Height tool or just something

TABLE 7.3 Summary of the Controls with the Terrain Height Tools

Use	Controls	Tool
Raise terrain	Left-click or hold down left mouse button while moving mouse.	Raise/lower terrain
Lower terrain	Hold down the SHIFT key while left-clicking or hold down left mouse button while moving mouse, with SHIFT key pressed.	Raise/lower terrain
Raise/lower terrain	Left-click or hold down left mouse button while moving mouse. Will raise or lower to the level specified by the target height.	Paint terrain
Smooth terrain	Left-click or hold down left mouse button while moving mouse.	Smooth height

to keep in mind as we construct our game world. Also, as we have mentioned, pay attention to scaling, try some different dimensions for your terrain with the intended player object to get a feel for how big or small the area is before spending a lot of time on the construction of the terrain.

1. Make sure that Sancho is at 0 on the Y-axis, at a height of 0.
2. Use the Paint Height tool to raise the terrain to a good level above sea level. The idea here is to use Sancho as a visual base for how deep the water will be he can run in. We have set the Height property to 1 and used the Flatten button to raise the terrain to this level, see Figure 7.13.
3. Use the Raise/Lower Terrain tool to lower the boundary of the terrain to be beneath sea level and leave the rest of the island raised.
   a. We have used a Brush Size of 60 and an Opacity of 50.
   b. We used the second of the Brush types.
   c. Remember, hold the SHIFT key with the left mouse button pressed in order to lower terrain.
4. Carve out the rivers with the Raise/Lower Terrain tool.
   a. Change to the first of the Brush presets, that falloff will be more appropriate for a riverbed.
   b. Drop the brush size to the mid-20s.
5. Add some hills to portions of the island with the Raise/Lower Terrain tool.
   a. A higher opacity will make the hills steeper, experiment.

With the basic terrain in place, we will add some hills and other details after we get some other assets placed on it, we are ready to test it and see how it feels. However, without some textures and other assets on it, it is fairly difficult to get a good grasp of the terrain as we have created it thus far. Figure 7.14 depicts the roughed in island as it currently stands.

FIG 7.13 The terrain adjusted to its deepest water point with Sancho as a guide.

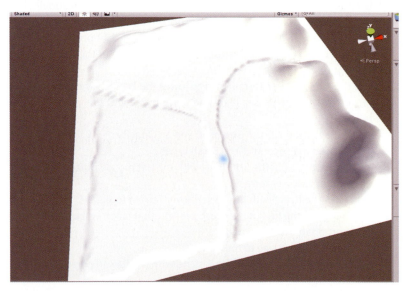

FIG 7.14 The roughly sculpted island of Barataria.

The very small black speck in the lower left-hand corner is Sancho, so this island is quite large, perhaps too large, but we can block portions of it off and leave them for later development. Therefore, we need to go ahead and get some basic textures and water thrown onto this terrain and start getting our pieces to come together.

> **Note**
> If while testing, your character runs through the terrain or under the terrain or just generally does not seem to stay on the terrain the way that it should, save your scene and try again. With the early versions of Unity 5, saving the scene eliminates this slightly odd behavior.

7.4 Dressing a Terrain with Standard Content

Terrain content is slightly different from other assets that we import into a project. Assets that we use on a terrain are assets that are added to the terrain through one of the terrain tools that we have mentioned in the introduction to the Unity terrain system. Trees, bushes, grass, dirt textures, grass textures, and other similar assets are all added to the terrain through the tools provided by Unity and as a result are treated slightly differently than other assets. Trees that are painted onto the terrain are not individual trees that we can click on and reposition if we like. We could add the trees as individual assets; however, this would prove to be a very tedious and frustrating process. Likewise, we could add bushes and other small details to the terrain as individual assets; however, it will be much quicker to use these tools. Perhaps one of the most important will be the Paint Texture tool as we will use this to paint the various textures onto the surface of the terrain to give it the look and feel that we want.

Our project currently does not contain any assets that we can use with the terrain tools. We could go find some on the Asset Store or even through other free or purchased sources on the Internet. However, we are going to utilize the standard environmental assets that come with Unity 5. To add these to our project select Assets → Import Package → Environment as shown in Figure 7.15. Once the package as finished decompressing, we do not need everything that is included within the Environment package, we can deselect the unchecked items shown in Figure 7.16 as it will not be necessary for us to worry about CrossPlatformInput and the scripts available in the Utility folder during the construction of our island terrain. Therefore, we click the check box to deselect the following folders: Editor, Utility, and CrossPlatformInput (inside of the Standard Assets folder). This will leave us with a new folder in our project named Standard Assets and within it will be some assets that we can use to decorate our new island, specifically we will have trees, ground textures, grass textures, and some water.

7.4.1 Painting Textures

The first thing we would like to do is get some basic textures onto our terrain to have an idea of what areas are what type of surface. We can use textures that we find through the Asset Store or free ones that we may find online (there are several free texture sites online) or even textures that we have

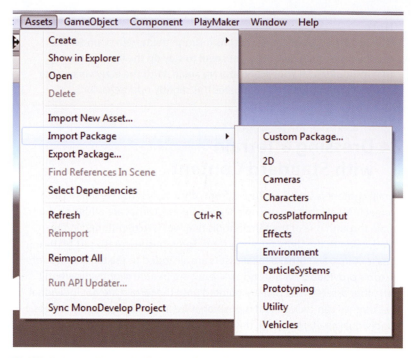

FIG 7.15 The location of the standard Environment Asset package.

purchased as part of a texture library or we could make our own from scratch using a 2D graphics program such as Photoshop. For our purposes, we will use the terrain textures that are provided by Unity as part of the Standard Assets package that we just added to the project. In the project pane, browse to Standard Assets → Environment → TerrainAssets → Surface Textures. Your Project pane should now match that of Figure 7.17. We can see that we have the essential textures for a terrain, specifically: cliff, grass, rocky grass, rocky mud, and sand. We are going to apply these textures to various areas of our terrain; Table 7.4 provides an overview of where we would like to apply these textures. Before painting textures onto a terrain it is important to consider what we want the terrain to look like at various areas.

Note

When using other textures as sources for your terrains, be sure that the textures are tileable, which means that they can be repeated over a large area without an obvious seam. Figure 7.18 depicts the difference between a tileable and nontileable texture; notice the obvious seam horizontally and vertically on the nontiled texture versus the tiled texture. Both textures in the example were created by tiling four copies of the same image into the texture, but the one on the left tiles without the obvious seams of the nontileable texture.

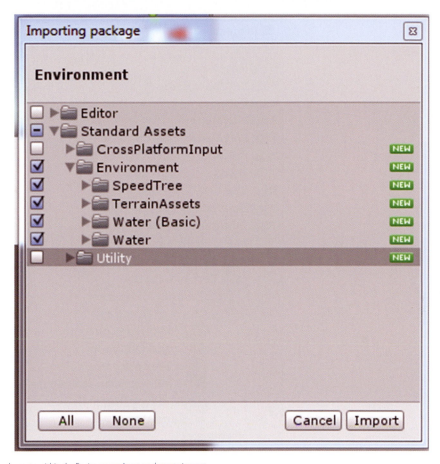

Unity's texture painting tools will allow us to layer textures with opacity as well, so we are not limited to only one texture per section of terrain. Figure 7.19 depicts the properties that are available to the Paint Texture tool. The Opacity and the Target Strength work together to allow the blending of one texture with another. The Target Strength setting specifies the maximum opacity that we can get when we keep painting the same texture over an area. Just as the Raise/Lower Terrain tool would raise or lower more when we applied it to the same area, the texture we are painting will be painted thicker when we keep applying it to the same area. It will have the opacity specified by the Opacity setting, but we can make the texture more opaque (less transparent) by continuing to paint it over the same area until we have reached the Target Strength. With a Target Strength of 1 that means that if we keep applying the texture to the same area we will eventually not be able to see any textures that may have been beneath that area. Before we can paint any textures onto our

FIG 7.17 Location of the default terrain textures within the Project pane.

TABLE 7.4 A List of the Terrains and Textures to Paint

Texture	Locations
Cliff	The sides of any steep mountains that we may have carved (or we CAN use the smooth tool to get rid of the steep cliffs if we would rather).
Grassy hill	All areas that we want grass on.
Rocky grass	Any areas that we want grass showing through rocks, CAN also do this through blending the textures.
Rocky mud	The riverbeds.
Sand	The beaches and also used within the town area where the grass has been killed.

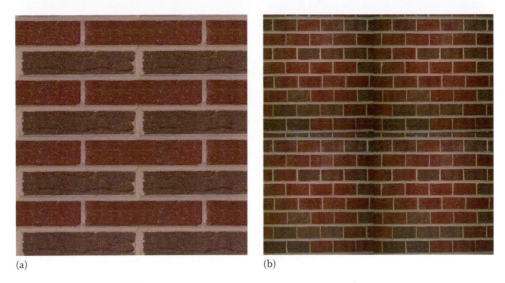

(a)   (b)

FIG 7.18 A tileable (a) versus nontileable (b) texture.

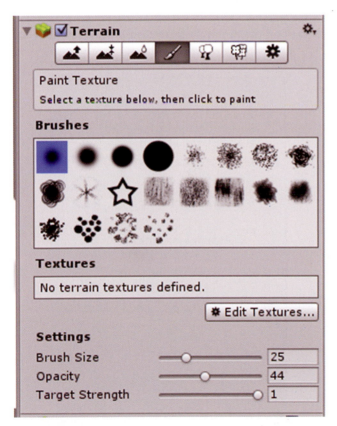

FIG 7.19 The Paint Texture settings.

terrain, we will need to add some terrain textures to the list of Textures applied to the terrain.

1. Select the Paint Terrain texture tool (number 2 from Figure 7.6).
   a. Click the Edit Textures in the Paint Texture settings.
      i. Select Add Texture from the pop-out menu, the Add Terrain Texture box will appear (Figure 7.20).
         A. Drag the SandAlbedo texture from the project pane onto the Albedo slot in the dialogue box (see Figure 7.21).
      ii. Click the Add button to close the Add Terrain dialogue.

When we closed the Add Terrain Texture dialogue box notice that Unity automatically applied that texture to the whole surface of our terrain. This is the default texture on the terrain, or we can think of it as the base layer and the rest will be added above it. We can already picture that if we adjust the Opacity settings when painting a grass texture onto this base layer we will be able to have some grass growing within the sand, or some sand emerging from our grass however it is we want to look at it. If we keep painting the grass over the same areas we can develop a nice thick grass field or paint sparingly and having a dying grass field. The Size and Offset options we have left alone until we can take a closer look at how the texture looks on the surface of our terrain.

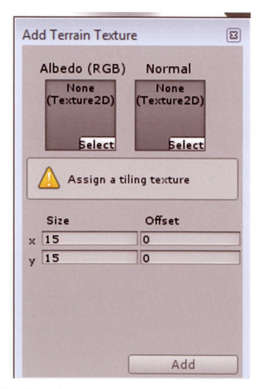

FIG 7.20 The Add Terrain Texture dialogue box.

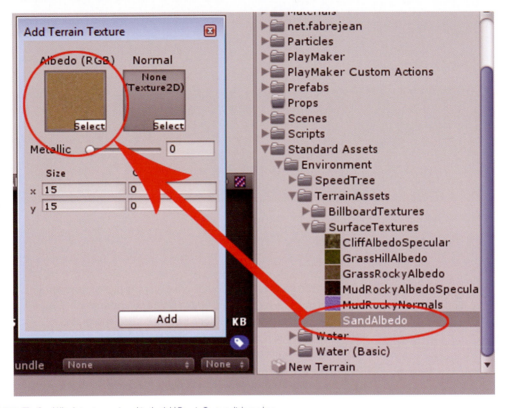

FIG 7.21 The SandAlbedo texture assigned in the Add Terrain Texture dialogue box.

To do this, switch to the Game View and we can now see Sancho standing on the sandy terrain, although the sand does not seem quite right. Now we will adjust the size of the terrain texture to see if we can find something that feels a little better with Sancho. Select the Edit Textures button again and this time click Edit Texture from the pop-out menu which will bring us back to the Add Terrain Texture dialogue (except now it is labeled as the Edit Terrain Texture dialogue). Adjust the size values until you find one that feels about right. It is best to keep them at the same number since the original texture is a square we want to scale it (change the size) uniformly in both directions to maintain the original ratio. We have gone with a value of 3.5, though you are free to select any value that you prefer, select the Apply button after making changes. Figure 7.22 depicts the difference in the sizing of the terrain texture. Now that the base layer is in place, we will add the grass texture above it.

1. Select the Edit Textures button.
   a. Select Add Texture from the pop-out menu.
      i. Add the GrassHillAlbedo texture to the Albedo portion.
         A. Adjust the sizing to match the sizing that was used on the sand, we can adjust it again later if it turns out not too match.
         B. Click the Add button.

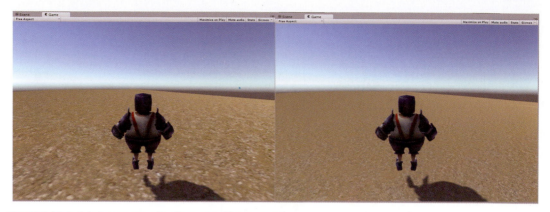

FIG 7.22 Left is the default texture size, right is the new size of the terrain texture.

2. Select the grass texture from the Textures applied to the terrain, should now be highlighted with a blue line underneath (Figure 7.23).
   a. We will paint the transitions between sand and grass.
      i. Use the first of the Brush presets.
      ii. Change Brush size to 25.
      iii. Change Opacity to 3.
      iv. Use left mouse button to paint the edges of the beach around the island, see Figure 7.24.
   b. Fill in the rest of the grass.
      i. Select the third or fourth brush preset.
      ii. Change the Brush Size to 75.
      iii. Change the Opacity to 50.
      iv. Paint in the rest of the grass areas.
         A. To get thicker or darker grass keep painting the same area.
         B. For lighter or patchy grass lower the Opacity.
         C. Leave an area for the buildings, will apply more textures there later.

Note
Many times it is easier to paint terrain textures with single clicks of the mouse rather than holding down the mouse button, as this gives more precise control over the flow of the texture.

We have now painted in the sand and the grass areas of our terrain; Figure 7.25 shows the terrain as it currently stands. Painting in other textures will be left as an exercise at the end of the chapter, but we can already begin to think ahead toward the muddy rocks in the riverbeds and some rocky grass areas around the mountains or maybe even in the fields to break them up some.

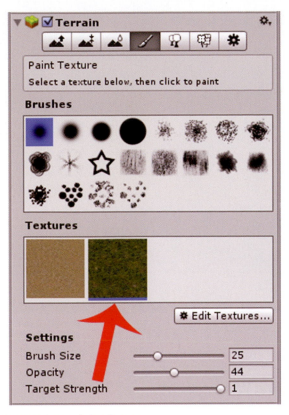

FIG 7.23 Blue highlight at bottom of selected texture.

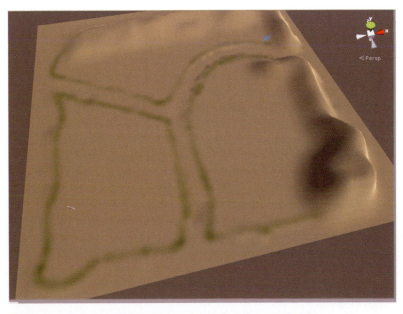

FIG 7.24 The grass borders painted in with a low opacity so the sand can creep through.

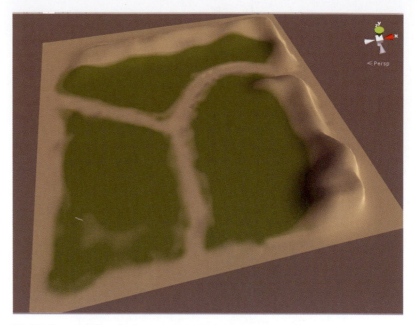

FIG 7.25 Terrain with the sand and grass textures painted.

7.4.2 Adding Water

With the essential terrain textures painted onto the terrain, we are going to add some water for both the ocean and the river through the island. Unity 5 includes several different water assets that we can utilize within our games, depending on the level of detail that we want from the water. These water objects can be found within the Standard Assets → Environment folder of our project. There are two folders for water, one is labeled Water and the other is Water (Basic). The essential difference here is that the Water folder contains all of the assets needed for the water objects that were included with the licensed Pro version of Unity 4 whereas the Water (Basic) folder contains the assets that were included with the original free version of Unity 4. With the release of Unity 5, all of the Professional features (well nearly all of them) are included with the Personal Edition of Unity. So, even as free users of the game engine, we have access to the Professional water asset if we want that level of detail for our projects. The Professional water assets include very nice reflection and refraction features to define how the light behaves as it comes in contact with the water. The basic version of the water, however, is going to work very well with this particular project and will blend in with the rest of the assets that we are using. Both sets also include prefab objects for daytime or nighttime lighting conditions and environments. The water assets ARE circular planes, except for the Water4 object which is a rectangular plane.

Note
Now that we are starting to put our game together more, we need to be aware of the quality level between assets. Our game should have a consistent look and feel throughout and our assets should all be of similar quality level so as to not stand out in sharp contrast with each other. This is the driving reason behind our selection of water for the scene.

1. Find the WaterBasicDaytime Prefab within: Standard Assets → Environment → Water (Basic) → Prefabs.
2. Drag the WaterBasicDaytime prefab into our game scene.
   a. Use the Top view (click the green arrow on the movement gizmo in top right of Editor) to position the Water asset roughly in the middle of the terrain.
   b. Change the X and Z scale value of the Water asset to get the circle around our terrain (200 worked well enough as it should be large enough to fade into the horizon in game play).
   c. Use the Raise/Lower Terrain tool to make any further adjustments to the terrain.
      i. For instance, raise the terrain around the river or use the Smooth Terrain tool to smooth out the transition to the beach.

Now the water has been added to the scene and we have made some more changes to our terrain to get a better feel for the environment. It is starting to come together quite nicely and is beginning to look like a good world. If the scale of the water asset is too small then the player will see the edge of the world rather than the illusion of the water going on to the horizon; Figure 7.26 depicts our work thus far and while it does not have flowing tropical beaches of white sand begging for tourists, that was not exactly one of our goals. Although, as we move on to adding some trees and other decorative items to this terrain, we may return to the Terrain Tools for some more tweaking.

7.4.3 Adding Trees

Trees are an interesting asset within Unity and must be treated differently from other assets, at least if we want to be able to utilize the Place Trees tool within the Terrain Editor (number 3 of Figure 7.6). The Place Trees tool allows us to paint trees onto the surface of the terrain just as we have done with the textures. This makes for a very quick approach to putting trees onto our game world. However, when we are painting trees, we are painting only one type of tree and so we need to be very aware that having a thick forest of the same tree is a rather odd looking experience for the gamer when playing our levels. Unity provides us with three different trees that we can put onto our terrains (though we can create our own trees with tools such as SpeedTree or traditional modeling packages such as 3ds Max or Maya LT). As our focus is not on the process of creating the assets but how to use assets in a game, we are not going to look into the process of creating our

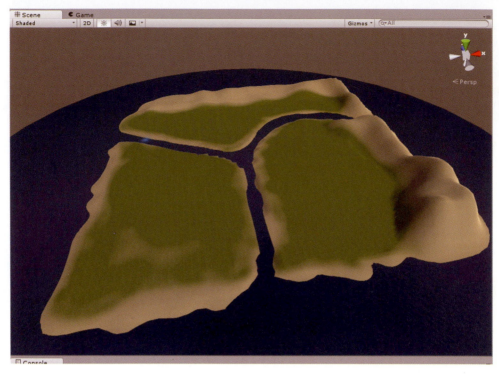

FIG 7.26 The isle of Barataria after the water has been added and the terrain tweaked some.

own custom trees; we will content ourselves with the three supplied trees. There is a broadleaf tree, a conifer tree, and a palm tree as can be seen in Figure 7.27. We can search through the Asset Store for more trees, but these three will take care of our needs for the project at hand.

For our island layout, we are going to put some palm trees near the beach area. The broad leafs we will use through the pasture region, though somewhat sparingly as we want it to be more pasture than forest. We will have a denser forest area in one of the other sections. Finally, we will use the conifers for our mountainous regions of the island. But, first we will take a look at the Place Trees tool in more detail before trying to use it. Figure 7.28 depicts the properties that we have available with this tool.

The Brush Size and Tree Density settings are similar to the Size and Opacity settings of the previous tools that we have looked at. A higher tree density will place more of the trees within the area defined by the brush. Notice that with this tool there are no brush presets, only a circular brush with no falloff range. This means that trees will be randomly distributed within the area of the brush and that the number of trees placed by Unity will be defined by the Tree Density value. The Random Height setting allows us to randomize the height of the trees which will allow for some variety among the trees and help them to not all look exactly alike. The Lock Width to Height setting allows the width of the tree to scale uniformly to whatever random height the tree is at. With that option turned off, we can select a random width for the

FIG 7.27 The standard trees: broadleaf, conifer, and palm.

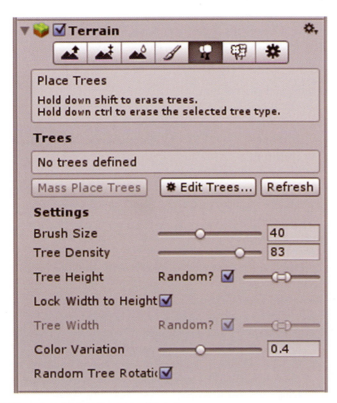

FIG 7.28 The settings of the Paint Tree terrain editing tool.

tree or we can opt to have the tree be the width that is defined by the prefab object that we are using. The Color Variation and Random Tree Rotation are vital settings for the illusion of different trees within the forest. Both of those settings will provide subtle changes to either the color or the Y-axis rotation of the tree such that at first glance the trees will seem different. Of course given serious scrutiny players will notice that the trees are the same, have you taken a close look at the trees in the games that you are playing recently?

Before we begin to place trees onto our terrain we need to take a quick look at the two different methods that we have available within the terrain editor toolset. The first approach is to paint the trees utilizing the settings that we have just explained. When doing so, trees will not be painted on top of other trees, so we can create forests of different types of trees by decreasing our density and painting multiple types of trees in the region. We select which tree we want to paint in the same way that we selected which texture we wanted to paint in the last section. The other method is to use the Mass Place Trees button. When we use this button to place trees, we are given the opportunity to select the total number of trees to be placed, almost like a density for the paint tool, and the Place Trees tool will then place that total amount of trees randomly throughout the whole terrain. This approach is very beneficial if we have a uniform terrain that will contain the same type of trees throughout the whole environment. The random settings will be utilized with this tool as well. The primary drawback to this tool is that it will randomly place trees throughout the terrain, which in our case would include the portions of the terrain that are currently underwater. Any erroneously placed trees can be removed by holding the SHIFT key while left-clicking with the brush.

1. Select the Edit Trees button.
   a. Select the Add Tree option from the pop-out menu.
      i. Drag the Palm_Desktop tree from Standard Assets → Environment → Palm to the Tree Prefab slot in the Add Tree Dialogue.
      ii. Click the Add button.
   b. Decrease the brush size such that we can limit the painting of the trees to the shoreline area of the island. We have used a setting of 5 in our example.
   c. Leave Random Tree Height selected.
   d. Leave Lock Width to Height selected.
   e. Change Color Variation to 1 to maximize the variation of color within the trees.
   f. Leave Random Tree Rotation checked.
   g. Paint palm trees along the beach areas of the island.
      i. CTRL-Z will undo any painting.
      ii. SHIFT-Left-clicking will erase painting.
      iii. Experiment with different density settings to find the tree density that you like best for your terrain, in our example we have used a setting of 45.

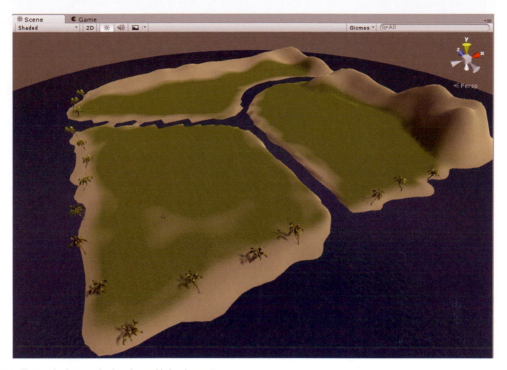

FIG 7.29 The initial palm trees that have been added to the terrain.

We have now painted some palm trees onto the beach head regions of our island as seen in Figure 7.29. We can look at them through the Editor and make sure that we like the general placement of the trees; however, to get a better idea of how the trees are working with our environment, we need to go ahead and play test the game and see how they feel with Sancho running around. There are several questions that we want to answer to as we do these play tests:

- Does the graphical quality of the trees blend well enough with Sancho?
- Are the trees too tall in comparison to the lead character? Too short?
- Are the trees too wide in comparison to the main character? Too skinny?
- Are there too many trees in our environment? Too Few?

With these questions as a guide we can explore the beach head with Sancho and see what we think. The too many or too few question is a more relevant one than we may first think. If we have too many trees in an environment not only might we need to start thinking about performance issues, but we are also hiding our environment. Basically, the player cannot see the game world as well as we may like, then again maybe we are trying to hide things from the player. The needs of the story and the needs of the game tie into how many trees we place and how the environment feels with those trees once we are playing the game. There is no rule of thumb that can be applied here; each game and environment is unique in its needs and in its intended result. We are going for a light platformer action–adventure kind of thing, a game that does not take itself too seriously, yet is still consistent within its own story world. With that goal in mind, the amount of palm trees seems reasonable at the moment.

With the palm trees in place, we will go ahead and add some of the Broadleaf trees. These trees would make for excellent forest trees which is how we will approach the Northern portion of the island. But, they will also make for nice shade trees within a pasture which will be our approach to the Southwestern portion of the island, the starting area. Use the same steps previously outlined to paint in the Broadleaf trees, you will find them in Standard Assets → Environment → Broadleaf → Broadleaf_Desktop. Utilize the questions from previously as well to get the environment that you want. Figure 7.30 depicts our current terrain with the Broadleafs added in the way that we have described.

> **Note**
> When painting trees onto a terrain, it is a good idea to paint a small number near the main character and follow through with the questions on height and graphical quality before spending a great deal of time painting throughout the terrain. This allows us to get the height adjusted however it feels best for the environment, then we paint trees throughout the terrain.

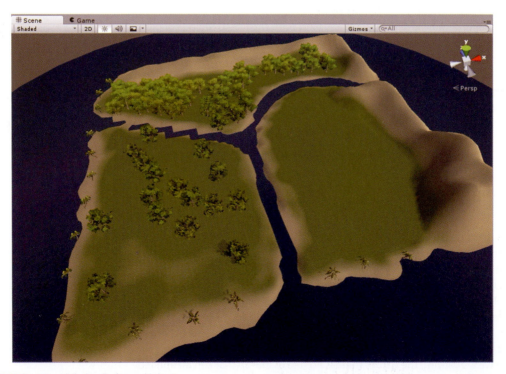

FIG 7.30 Barataria with the Broadleaf trees added to it.

FIG 7.31 Left is the default tree size, right is the tree size set at 0.7.

Realistically speaking, we have already tested the graphical quality of the trees with Figure 7.27 when Sancho was standing next to them, for the most part it looks as though the tree should do fine, though those Broadleaves and conifers sure feel tall, but in game play it is easy to picture Sancho climbing one of those Broadleaf trees. However, if we want to adjust the size of the trees, as shown in Figure 7.31, we can turn off the Random Tree Height check box and adjust the value in the slider box to be whatever we want. An interesting thing at this point, since we will be playing the game from ground level, the player will not actually see the height of the trees so having all of the trees as the exact same height will not actually impact the appearance of the game while playing.

One last comment before moving on, the Refresh button next to the Edit Trees button does not allow you to make brush setting changes and then have them applied to the trees that are on the terrain. This is why it is strongly encouraged that you do test paints with your trees to see how they look and feel before painting the whole terrain. Rather, the refresh button is used to update the trees whenever you have made changes to the actual mesh of the tree inside of the Project pane. If we were to load the palm tree into SpeedTree and modify it so that it looked different, perhaps straighter, for example, we would then re-import that asset into our project. However, in order to get the palm trees already on our terrain to reflect the changes made to the original mesh we would have to select the Palm_Desktop tree from the Trees selection in the Place Trees tool and click the Refresh button. Now we are ready to move on to grass leaving the conifer tree placement as an exercise. Perhaps it would be nice to raise that whole Southeastern side of the island to a higher elevation and populate it with conifer trees.

7.4.4 Adding Grass

The last tidbit of terrain detail that we can add is going to be some grass, weeds, shrubs, or other small greenery. These are created through the use of Billboards. Billboards are actually 2D textures that turn to face the player so that the player is always looking at them from a perpendicular or straight-on direction. This is going to take less computing power when running than having actual 3D shrubs in our game world, yet will provide just enough extra detail to give the environment a believable feeling, which ultimately is our goal.

> **Note**
>
> As we continue adding content into our game world we need to always keep performance issues in mind. With every polygon or texture that is added, there is memory and processor time involved. The more we add, the more resources we need and the slower the game will run, especially on lower end systems. While it may seem like a great idea to throw every bell and whistle into our game that we can find, always remember that if our players cannot play the game then it really does not matter how cool it looks. One of the biggest culprits of performance is real-time shadows, they look great but they slow things way down, more trees equals more shadows.

To add grass and other details to our terrain, we use the Paint Details tool (Number 4 from Figure 7.6). As can be seen with Figure 7.32, the Paint Details tool does not provide us with any properties that we have not already utilized with the other tools. In fact, it looks identical to the Paint Texture tool and the settings work the same as that tool did as well. The Refresh button will work the same as it did with the Place Trees tool. However, the Edit Details button is going to have some different options, we can either Add Grass Texture or Add Detail Mesh. The grass texture is going to be a 2D billboard as we mentioned and is not limited to "grass" specifically, but can be any type of small plant that we want to place on the surface of the terrain. The Detail Mesh will allow us to add rocks (though not really large rocks such as boulders as we will see shortly) or other modeled details. This will let us paint these details onto the terrain rather than having to individually place them throughout the terrain which would be extremely time consuming.

We will begin with the Add Grass Texture properties, as shown in Figure 7.33. The first setting is the texture itself that we will be using. As has been mentioned, textures are 2D images, so you cannot add a mesh to this slot, but only a 2D image. Min Width and Max Width provide the minimum and maximum width of the texture when placing them; this in turn creates a nice randomization especially when combined with the Min and Max Height properties. We will need to experiment some to find the best values for these settings before painting a lot of grass onto our terrain. When grass is painted onto the terrain, it can be painted in patches and the Noise Spread property allows us to better randomize the patchiness of these sections of grass.

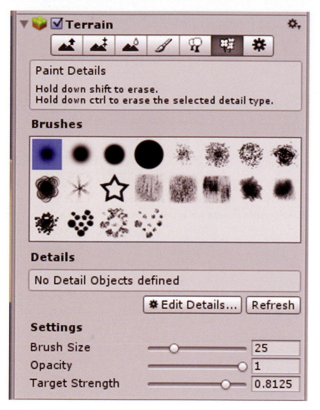

FIG 7.32 The Paint Details properties.

The higher the value of the Noise Spread the more randomness that we will have within the patches of grass that are placed on the terrain. The Healthy and Dry color provides a color range for the system to select from to give even more variety to the appearance of the grass. Once again, testing will need to be done to find the best colors here as these colors are essentially color overlays onto the texture. Therefore, if we set the Healthy Color to be white then we will see the texture exactly as it appears with its true coloration; however, by providing a green hue, we are overlying that green hue onto the texture which may or may not provide the look that we want. Finally, the Billboard check box allows us to turn on or off the billboard features that were discussed earlier. As a general rule it is best to leave this checked so that the grass will always be facing the player.

1. Select the Edit Details button.
    a. Select Add Grass Texture from the pop-out menu.
    b. Add the GrassFrond01AlbedoAlpha texture (Standard Assets → Environment → TerrainAssets → BillboardTextures) to the Detail Texture slot.
    c. Leave the other settings at default for a test.
    d. Click the Add button.

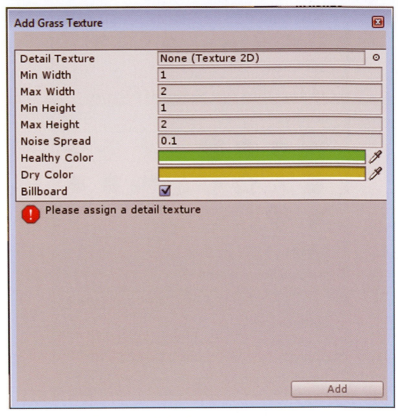

FIG 7.33 The Add Grass Texture property dialogue box.

2. Paint some grass around Sancho.
   a. Notice how quickly the details are painted.
      i. Adjust opacity and Target Strength as needed. We have placed ours at 0.05 and 0.06. Grass can be laid on thicker by painting over areas as needed.
   b. Play the game to view the grass and answer the questions concerning it that we asked about trees earlier.
      i. We found the default grass to be too high, nearly up to Sancho's shoulder. So will lower the height for the next test.
3. Use CTRL-Z to undo any painting.
4. Make adjustments to the grass texture by selecting the Edit Details button and Edit from the pop-out menu.
5. Once the settings are set, paint the pasture area with grass.
   a. We found the Healthy Color to be a little too green and toned it back toward white some while darkening it as well (RGB = 110, 97, 198).
   b. We set our heights to range from 0.2 to 0.7.
   c. Finally, we raised the Opacity of the brush up to 0.35 for our final painting of the thick grass in the pasture.

With the grass painted throughout the Southwestern portion of the island, we can do some cleanup. By decreasing the brush size and using the SHIFT key when painting we can get the brush size down to remove any grass that might have been placed on the beach itself, or even within the water which tends to be a fairly common occurrence. We will return to deleting grass and touching things up after we place the buildings into the environment and when we create any paths through the area as well. While play testing the scene, you may have noticed that the grass is swaying like water with waves passing over it. This is to simulate wind; however, the trees themselves are not moving which creates a disjointed appearance. To fix this, return to the Terrain Settings and in the Wind Settings section, adjust the values while the game is running so you can see the change, until you get the grass to settle down. In our Wind Settings we adjusted the Bending to be 0.05, there is still some movement in the grass but not very much. The same could have been done through adjusting the Speed setting as well.

The Add Detail Mesh properties are much the same as the Add Grass Texture properties as shown in Figure 7.34. Rather than using a 2D texture, this option utilizes a prefab object that contains a mesh. The Width, Height, and Noise Spread options work the same as they did with the Grass Texture tool. The Healthy and Dry color is a bit odd, especially if we are using this in conjunction with objects such as small rocks. Otherwise, the color settings work just as they did with the textures. The final setting is the Render Mode. A Render Mode of Grass treats the detail meshes as though they were 2D billboards like the grass that we painted. The other option is Vertex Lit which will render the meshes as 3D objects within our environment which will be what we want in many situations when using complex mesh shapes. The Detail Mesh tool is best used for painting shrubs or other objects that provide details to the terrain, but that the player can walk through because collisions are not supported with Detail Meshes, hence a reason to not paint large boulders with this tool. Also, be aware that meshes with materials that have transparencies on them do not always show up correctly when using the Paint Details tool. We have found the Paint Details tool best used for grasses, weeds, and other ground clinging details, for all others we use the Place Trees tool, which we will show a couple of examples of next.

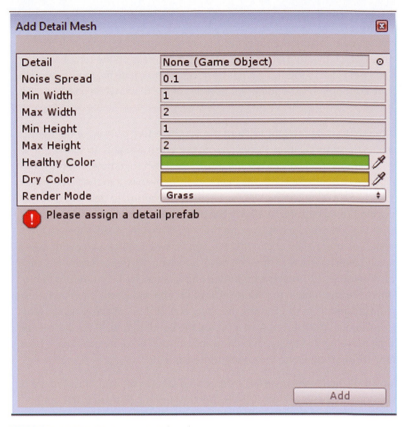

FIG 7.34 The Add Detail Mesh properties dialogue box.

1. Open the Asset Store (Window → Asset Store).
2. Search for "bush free."
   a. Several options appear, but we are going to utilize the pack created by Nobiax/Yughues (Yughues Free Bushes), select that link.
      i. Select the Download button.
      ii. After the package is downloaded and uncompressed, select OK to import all of its contents into our Project.
3. We now have a new Folder (Meshes) within our Project pane and this folder includes the bushes that we just added.
4. Add Bush 04 prefab to our scene to test (Meshes → Bushes → Bush 04).
   a. Notice that the bush is really big, too big for our environment.
   b. Find the Bush 04 mesh file (Meshes → Bushes → Bush 04 → Meshes).
      i. In the Inspector panel change to the Model tab and adjust the Scale Factor to 0.02.
      ii. Click Apply.

5. In the Inspector panel for Bush 04 remove the Mesh Collider component, we are going to allow the player to walk through the bushes.
6. Select the Apply button near the top right corner of the Inspector panel to update the Prefab object with our changes (no collider).
7. Remove the Bush 04 prefab from the scene.
8. In the Place Trees tool of the Terrain inspector, select Add Tree from the Edit trees pop-out.
9. Click the Add button, there will be a warning in the console window about changing the material, for our purposes, we can ignore this warning.
10. Change Brush Size and Tree Density as needed. We are using a size of 20 and a density of 15.
11. Paint some bushes onto our terrain.

We now have some bushes within our scene. If we don't want the player to be able to pass through the bushes, then we just need to add a Box Collider component to the Bush 04 prefab asset and use the Refresh button within the Place Tree tool, give this a go and see how it works for you. We can continue to add trees, grass, and rocks to our scene (in fact Nobiax/Yughues has a very nice free rock pack available in the Asset Store) until we have the environment looking as we would like it to using the same techniques that we have outlined within this section. However, always remember that the more trees you add the more shadows must be calculated. Also, the more grass you add the more the system must consider the sway of the grass, try making a very thick area of grass and a sparse area and see if your system has any performance issues between them. With our basic terrain in place, we are now ready to bring the buildings onto Barataria.

7.5 Adding Imported Assets

Download
Get the Arteria3D Medieval Farm Pack from the companion website in this chapter's section of the resources. The file name is: "Arteria3DMedFarm_generic.zip."

Before we add our imported assets into our new scene, we need to get the assets imported into our project. After downloading the zip file from the companion website, unzip it into a directory of your choice and we will begin the process of bringing these assets into our project and then into the new environment that we are creating. This process is very similar to the one that we followed for importing our character assets a couple of chapters back, though this time we will also do some work on importing the textures and putting the materials together for the assets as they come in. Before

TABLE 7.5 Folder Structure of the Arteria3dMedFarm__generic.zip file

Folder	Contents
Model formats	All of the meshes that we will be importing.
Normal maps	Normal map textures, these are used to provide the illusion of depth and bumpiness on meshes.
Terrain textures	Some extra terrain textures that could be imported and utilized within the terrain texture painting if desired.
Textures	Diffuse texture maps for the meshes, these provide the default appearance of the object under regular lighting.

beginning, make sure to download the file and to get it unzipped on your computer. After unzipping it you will find four folders within as noted in Table 7.5.

1. In the Project pane create a new folder for storing these assets. We have selected "Arteria Farm" as our folder name.
2. In the Model Formats folder select the MedievalFarmLayout(2010). fbx file and drag it into the Arteria Farm folder in the project to import it.
3. Select the MedievalFarmLayout(2010) mesh in the Arteria Farm folder and place it into the scene.
   a. Rotate it and move it as necessary to get it to fit onto the Southwestern portion of the island somewhere (see Figure 7.35). Do not worry about tress or what not, they can be removed later if needed.
   b. Move Sancho closer to the town.

We have now placed a major asset into our game world. Steve Finney at Arteria3D has provided a one mesh asset that contains a small farm town for us to use. This will save time from having to manually place assets and will also help with getting the scaling right and consistent. There are two distinct approaches to constructing environments for a game. The first is a modular approach in which the modelers construct little sections of buildings that can then be put together in any fashion that we want. This is very useful for many different types of game projects in that it will essentially limit the number of assets that need to be created. Consider, rather than creating nine distinct houses, we could create three wall sections, three door sections, and three window sections, these could now be combined to create far more than just the original nine unique houses that had been made. The other approach is to create the town or environment entirely within the 3D modeling application and to import it as one chunk for the game. This is easier for the level designers as we then just drop these

FIG 7.35 Initial placement of the town asset from Arteria3D.

complete chunks into our worlds; however, this does have other drawbacks, such as difficulty with camera culling if we need to do such things. For our project at hand, we will do just fine with the main town already created and then manually placing a few details here and there.

With the town in place we will take Sancho and run into the town to take a look at how this looks and feels, specifically in relation to sizing. Figure 7.36 depicts Sancho as he has come up to a nice wagon that would serve good for sizing purposes. Based on this, it looks as though Sancho and the town are sized very well with respect to each other. All we need to do is to finish putting the town together, take a look at some of those trees and grass popping up inside of there and maybe Barataria will be ready to come to life.

1. Create a new folder inside of the Arteria Farm folder named Textures.
2. In the Textures folder from the zip file select all of the files and drag them into the newly created Textures folder in our project to import them.
3. Repeat for the contents of the NormalMaps folder.
4. In the Textures folder of the Arteria Farm folder (in the Project pane), select all of the textures that end with _NRM (these are the normal maps and we need to adjust something on them).

FIG 7.36 Sizing test of Sancho inside of the town.

a. In the Inspector panel change the Texture Type from Texture to Normal Map.
b. Uncheck the Create from Grayscale check box.
c. Click Apply.
5. Open the Materials folder inside of Arteria Farm.
6. Select the MFVThatchedA material.
a. Change the Shader from Standard to Legacy Shaders → Bumped—Diffuse.
b. Drag the MFVThatchedA texture from the Textures folder into the Base (RGB) Texture slot and the MFVThatchedA_NRM texture to the Normalmap slot, see Figure 7.37.
c. Notice that the name of the material matched the name of the texture we needed.
7. Repeat for the rest of the materials.

We intentionally selected one of the off the wall materials as our example to make sure that it contained both a normal and diffuse map, not all of the materials will have a normal map texture for it in which case just leave the normal map slot blank or select Legacy Shaders → Diffuse. The Standard shader that we switched from is the new physically based rendering system in Unity 5. While it is possible for us to have used these textures within that shader system, the textures were not specifically designed for physically based rendering. There is a slight difference in how the diffuse texture and the albedo textures are created. Rather than risk getting odd shader behavior out of our materials we just switched the materials to the

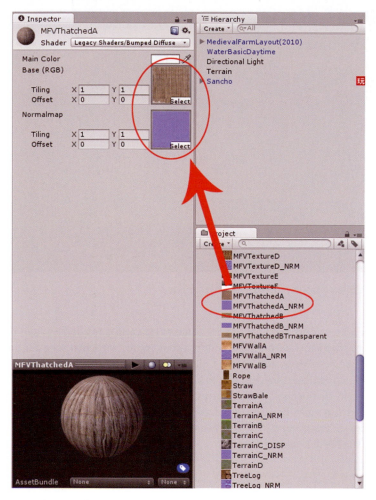

FIG 7.37 Applying the diffuse and normal maps to the proper material channels.

legacy material system which will work very well for our project at hand as we are not trying to create overly realistic surfaces and materials. We have opted not to focus on the creation of materials here as that process relies on knowledge of texture creation as well, but for those interested, there is a more detailed discussion of the new Standard Shader in Unity's documentation found at: http://docs.unity3d.com/Manual/shader-StandardShader.html.

The other change of note is with the MFVThatchedBTrnsparent material set the Shader to be Legacy Shaders → Transparent → Bumped – Diffuse. After correcting all of the materials, we should be able to take Sancho back by the same wagon from the sizing test and have something similar to Figure 7.38 which will enable us to really get a feel for the graphical continuity and make sure quality levels are consistent. This is starting to

FIG 7.38 Sancho back in the town with the textures applied.

look pretty good. The final thing that we need to do is to add a collider to this to stop Sancho from running through it. In this particular case our best bet is going to be to add a Mesh Collider component to the asset (actually it will be our quickest bet, not the best one), though the mesh collider should generally be the choice of last resort. We cannot add the Mesh Collider to the main asset, however, as it has no mesh in it. We need to open the MedievalFarmLayout(2010) object and select all of the objects within it and add the Mesh Collider to them.

> **Note**
> Rather than using a Mesh Collider as we did, a better option would be to add Cube Game Objects to the scene and position them around the various building structures within the game world. Once we have positioned around the wagon, for instance, we would make it a child object of the town and also turn of the Mesh Renderer component so that it is not visible. This would be the best approach to creating the colliders for this town. For a video demonstration of this take a look at the video found on the companion website: "Town Colliders."

To add any other assets into our scene, follow the same steps that we took in getting the main village in place. Arteria3D have provided some nice assets that we can bring in and throw around our scene in various places for some nice set decorations. Although, it looks like we may need some bridges at some point in order to get across those rivers, but we will cross that when we come to it. Actually, you will cross it in the exercises.

7.6 Lighting the Environment

Lighting an outdoor environment is much easier than lighting an interior one. Usually an external environment is lit by one prominent light source, the sun. Although if we were to construct a night scene then we would be faced with some different challenges. Lighting is an art form and something that you have to be willing to be patient with to get just right. We will provide an overview of the lighting system provided by Unity in this section, by looking at the four different light objects that are provided.

The four light types are defined as follows: direction, point, spot, and area lights. The properties that they each have are listed in Table 7.6. An area light is a rectangular plane that defines where the light is coming from and the light is cast only from within that rectangular area. The light is cast perpendicular to the plane in the direction specified. Spot lights are similar to flashlights or search lights in that they represent a cone of light starting at one source and being cast out into the world. Point lights are like a light bulb. The light provides the source of illumination and all light is cast in a complete sphere around the source and emanating outward. Directional lights are intended to mimic light sources such as the sun. They provide an infinite plane that the light is cast from and the light travels in the direction specified by the angle of the source (Figure 7.39).

With the fixed camera setting that we are employing and the selection of a daytime environment there is not much to add as far as lighting goes for our current world. Although, as a simple experiment, compare the feeling of the world as it currently is to one with the following changes made to the properties of the directional light, Figure 7.39 depicts the default property values for this object:

- Set the color to a cool blue (RGB: 103, 184, 251)
- Drop the intensity to 0.55
- Drop the bounce intensity to 0.4

Our world has now become not a night world per se, because of the white glow along the horizon, but it definitely has become a dusky world. A world in which the sun has just recently set and the fireflies should be just beginning to emerge.

7.7 Boundaries

With our environment nearly complete, we are just left with the addition of any boundaries to our world to make sure that the player stays exactly where we want them too. For this, we are going to create some Game Objects and

TABLE 7.6 Common Properties of Light Objects within Unity

Property	Use	Which Lights
Type	Which of the four types of light it is, can change here rather than adding a new light and deleting.	All
Width	Width of rectangular area defining the light source.	Area
Height	Height of rectangular area defining the source of the light.	Area
Baking	Select between baking the light to a lightmap (very fast game performance) or using entirely real-time lighting (slow) or a combination of the two.	Directional, Point, Spot
Range	Maximum distance the light will cast.	Spot, Point
Spot Angle	How wide of an angle the spot light covers.	Spot
Color	What color the light is. This gives the light a hue, think of cool blues for nighttime or warm oranges for a lazy afternoon.	All
Intensity	The brightness of the light.	All
Bounce Intensity	The real world is lit by light bouncing off of various objects; this property defines how bright the light will be when bouncing. Above 1 and the light bounces brighter than when it hit, less than 1 and it will be dimmer.	All
Shadow Type	Determines which type of shadows will be used. Hard and soft shadows are differentiated by whether the edge of the shadow is sharply defined (hard) or is fuzzy (soft).	All
Strength	Will specify how dark the shadows will be.	All
Resolution	Sets the resolution of the shadow map, higher resolution will be higher-quality shadows.	All
Bias	Adds a distance to the shadow map so that parts that are on the shadow border will get the proper lighting.	All
Normal Bias	Same as bias but for insetting shadows along a normal map.	All
Cookie	A texture that defines a shadowed region within the cast light, very useful for creating the illusion of a light being cast from within a lantern, for instance.	Directional, Point, Spot
Draw Halo	Can draw a halo around the light source, can be a very nice effect.	All
Flare	A flare that can be rendered at the location of the light, like a lens flare.	All
Render Mode	How important this light is to be rendered, the default option will work for most lights.	All
Culling Mask	Use this to select objects that will not be impacted by this particular light.	All

FIG 7.39 The properties of a Directional light.

place them at the edge of our terrain to keep the player from being able to run off the terrain and fall into the nether land beyond.

1. Hide the Water object so that we can more clearly see the terrain.
2. Add a new Cube Game Object to the world.
3. Position the new Cube toward one of the sides of the terrain.
4. Rescale the Cube so that it is big enough to be a wall on one side of the terrain, something like 1, 50, 260. See Figure 7.40 as an example.
5. Make sure the wall is even or slightly overlapping with the edge of the terrain.
6. Disable the Mesh Renderer component of the cube.
7. Copy the Cube to the other side and the top and bottom of the terrain.
8. Create an Empty Game Object and name it Boundary or something.
9. Make the four cubes child objects of this new Boundary object.

What we now have is such that the player cannot escape from our terrain. In the next chapter, we will want to add some more details to this system but for the moment, all we need to do is to make sure that we are able to control where the player can and sometimes more importantly cannot go.

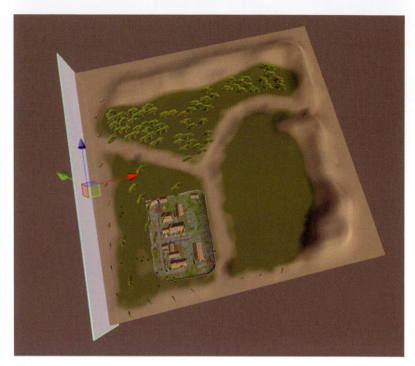

FIG 7.40 A retaining wall on one side of the terrain.

7.8 Summary

Throughout this chapter we have constructed an outdoor environment for our game characters to perform within. Outdoor environments involve more work as far as a terrain is concerned than do indoor environments. However, getting the lighting just right with an indoor environment can be a very challenging process, not to mention getting all of the assets placed inside of the building or dungeon or whatever. When building games, there will be times that you will need both interior and exterior environments for your story. The skills that we have learned in constructing the isle of Barataria can be applied to the construction of a cave system going into the mountains of the island if we were to include such a level within our game, though we would require models and textures for the cave object much like the town itself. Interior scenes will require that all of the assets be constructed externally of Unity, whereas we can use the terrain tools directly within the engine to construct much of the level when building an outdoor world. Before rushing off to bring custom content into the terrain tools within Unity, take the time to get a good feel for the tools with the default assets that have been provided. Environments are vital to the games that we make and play; these are portions of the project that take some practice and time to get just right. Sancho can now run around the island that has been given to him and explore it; our game project is now ready to have some mechanics and game-play elements added to it and really start coming together.

Vocabulary

Terrain
Unity unit
Terrain collider
Normal map
Diffuse map
Standard shader
Physically based shader
Legacy shader
Tileable texture
Opacity
Mass place trees
Place trees tool
Raise/lower terrain tool
Smooth height tool
Paint height tool
Paint terrain tool
Paint details tool
Billboard
Directional light
Point light
Spot light
Area light

Review Quiz

1. What is the difference between a natural and artificial boundary within a game level?
2. How can trees be removed from a terrain after they have been painted on?
3. How can a terrain be lowered after it has been raised?
4. Why is the Paint Details tool not a good choice when adding large rocks to the scene?
5. What is the use of the Refresh button within the Place Trees tool?
6. Why is it important to place a few things near a character before detailing the whole environment?
7. What are some of the factors that can impact the running performance of a game?

Exercises

1. Clean up the interior of the town by removing any trees or bushes that are coming through buildings or in other ways causing problems.
2. Import the other models provided by Arteria3D and place them within the environment.
3. In the Asset Store find the Simple Wooden Bridge by VR and add it to the environment so that Sancho can get across those rivers.
4. Raise the terrain on the Southeastern portion of the island and place Conifer trees with some bushes and other details to set that region apart from the rest of the island.

Design Document

In this addition to the Sancho Panza design document, we have incorporated our design elements for the environment of the isle of Barataria. These details have included rough reference sketches of the environment to create as well as a list of assets or items that we would like to include within the environment. Finally, we have also added a breakdown of the environment and how it should pertain to the story that has been developed previously.

Download
Updated version of the *Sancho Panza* design document can be downloaded from the companion website: "DesignDocument_chapter7."

Consider your design document that you have been working on thus far, and add the following to it:

1. Consider the primary environment needed for your story:
   a. What does the story need from this environment?
   b. What will the game need from the environment?
   c. How will you be able to give the player what they need and control the player at the same time?
   d. Develop a sketch of this environment.
   e. Develop detail sketches of key areas of the environment.
   f. Break the environment up into regions that can be used as levels.
   g. Develop a list of assets that will be needed for this environment.

CHAPTER 8

Mechanics

The mechanics are the engine of the games that we play. The mechanics are formed by the rules and the expectations of the games and govern how we play as well as what we can do within a game. Without game-play mechanics, we really do not have a game. Even something as simple as moving a character around an environment is a mechanic as there are rules governing how the character can move and what the player must do to make the character move. In this chapter, we will look at what these mechanics are and how we can figure out which mechanics our game might need. After getting a basic understanding of these game mechanics and where they come from, we will look into designing and implementing a couple of them for our ongoing Sancho Panza project.

- What Are Game Mechanics?
- How Do We Know What Mechanics We Want?
- Designing a Life System
- Designing a Collection System
- Implementing the Life System
- Implementing the Collection System

8.1 What Are Game Mechanics?

Game mechanics are where the game play truly comes from. These are the rules that govern how things inside of the game work. More than this, they also govern what the player can and cannot do as well as what the game can and cannot do to the player. We will break these mechanics down into four different categories as we look at what they are and provide examples of each. There is much debate within game development circles as to how we should classify game mechanics and what should or should not be considered to be a game mechanic. We are going to take the approach that any rule that is within a game is a game mechanic and will divide these into categories so that we are able to recognize which mechanics are absolutely vital to the game and which ones are only needed for this version of the game. Or to put it in another way, there are rules that if we did not use in the game, then the game would not be the same game. And then there are rules that we could modify or even remove altogether and still have essentially the same game. The mechanics that we will look fall into one of the following categories:

- Core Mechanics
- Victory and Loss Conditions
- Balance Mechanics
- Story Mechanics
- System Mechanics

8.1.1 The Core Mechanics

Every game has a set of internal rules that define how the game must be played and these are the core mechanics of the game. These core mechanics form the fundamental rules that a player must know and understand in order to be able to play the game. For instance, in a game of hide and seek, the mechanics are such that one person is "it" and they have the task of trying to find and tag the other players that will be hiding somewhere within a defined game area. We can further enhance this rule set by saying that the person who is "it" must close their eyes and count to 100 prior to beginning the search for the hidden players. These, in a nutshell, form the core mechanics of that particular game system. Another example of core mechanics can be seen within the work that we have already done on our Sancho Panza project. Sancho can move around within the game world that has been created and he can fight with spiders when he encounters them. Those form the rules governing how Sancho can interact with the world that is around him, or what he can and cannot do with the game thus far. Generally speaking, core mechanics are not complex or difficult to explain, the fuzziness of the rules of various games comes from the other categories of game mechanics, and Table 8.1 lists some examples of core mechanics.

TABLE 8.1 Examples of Core Mechanics

Mechanic	Use	Example
Shoot or be shot	The player must shoot and destroy the bad guys while trying not to be shot and destroyed by the bad guys.	Any first-person shooter game
Matching	Player must find matches, usually in a group either horizontally, vertically, or diagonally, of similar shapes and/or colors.	*Bejeweled*
PvP	Player competes against other human players directly in a zero-sum game.	Capture the flag or death matches
Co-Op	Multiple players work together to complete a task that cannot be completed by a single player on their own.	Raids in MMOs and many Facebook games
Exploration	The player must explore the game world they are presented with in order to discover items.	*Shape of the World*
Combos	The player can achieve higher scores and more powerful actions through the combination of actions in specific sequences.	*Smash Bros.*
Time limits	Each stage of the game must be completed within a certain time span otherwise the player will have to start over or at least restart from a specified point.	*Sonic the Hedgehog*
Achievements	Player must complete actions or collections in order to accomplish goals and victory conditions within a game.	*Animal Crossing*
Building	The player spends the game constructing various buildings or objects within the game.	*Minecraft*

8.1.2 Victory and Loss Conditions

Most games must have a winner and a loser; however, that may actually be defined. Regardless of how many players are involved in a game, the game ends with a definitive winner and loser. There are exceptions to this concept, however, as not all games have an endgame to them, they can be played for as long as the player wants to play them; *The Sims* franchise is an example of a game series with no definitive end to it. Although, one could argue that there are individual victory conditions scattered throughout the game such as getting promotions and that the player creates their own victory conditions while playing the game such as buying the big mansion house. So, even though the game may not explicitly create the victory conditions, there are victory conditions nonetheless as the players will create them. We can have a victory condition in which only one player wins and all of the others lose, this is referred to as a zero-sum game, or we can have victory conditions in which there are varying levels of winning and losing, a non-zero-sum game and the work of John Nash within economic theory. In either case, there are rules that define when a player has or has not won the game. These rules are the mechanics of the victory and loss conditions. In the case of Sancho, the loss condition is when the player has died and has no more Sancho lives left, and the victory condition is encountered when the player has removed Sanson from the isle of Barataria. Victory conditions within games can be categorized as presented in Table 8.2.

TABLE 8.2 Different Types of Victory Conditions

Mechanic	Use	Example
Points	During game play, players are able to earn points for various actions, and at the end of game play, the player with the most points wins.	Sports games
Acquisition	Gathering resources or territory is the point of the game and at the end of the game the one with the most wins.	*Risk*
Race	Players compete to see who can get to a certain location within the game first. The first one at the location is the winner.	*Mario Kart*
Conquest	The point of the game is to eliminate all of the other player's playing pieces, thereby being the only player with any pieces left in the game.	*Checkers*
Riddles	Players must try to solve a riddle or puzzle in order to determine the solution to the game, and once the solution has been found they have won the game.	*Mastermind*

8.1.3 Balance Mechanics

Games that are unbalanced are not fun to play. Therefore, as we design our games, we need to consider mechanics and mechanisms to keep the game play balanced and fun for everyone that is playing it, especially if we are looking at a multiplayer game. But, even in a single player game, if the game is too easy to play then it is not quite as much fun as it could be. The type of balance mechanic needed, if any, will depend entirely upon the game itself, but a classic example of a balancing mechanic is the blue shell from the *Mario Kart* series. The whole purpose of that one item is to slow down the player that is in the lead and allows the other players a chance to catch up; it maintains the level of challenge for all players and keeps the game interesting. This is generally referred to as a catch-up mechanic as it allows other players to catch up within the game. Balance mechanics are the fuzziest of the game mechanics as players do not initially understand why these rules are in place, and designers do not always realize the need for them until playtesting the game down the road. At first glance, the rules seem arbitrary and aimed at punishing certain types of game play, but after playing the game many players begin to realize the significance of these balancing mechanics, first as new players that need the extra help within the game and then later as expert players that need a little more challenge to the game.

8.1.4 Story Mechanics

We have already mentioned that not all games have or even need a story as a component of the game. But for those that do contain a story, there are rules and mechanics that we add to the game that are directly derived from the needs of the story. An example of a story mechanic would be the rules that govern dialogue trees within the game. Remember, everything that occurs within a game is a result of scripted behavior and therefore the result of a rule set. In this case, the rule is that when the player gets close enough to character X a conversation begins and the player can select from a given set of responses depending on previous responses. While at first glance this may seem to be a very weak mechanic within a game, there have been many games developed in which the process of talking to other characters was vital to advancing the game and eventually winning the game; *L.A. Noir* is an example of one such game. Any emotional relationships and the rules that govern how those work and impact game play are also mechanics based upon the needs of the story and the story within the game. Other examples of mechanics derived from the story of the game include the victory condition itself, which is a direct result of the resolution to the primary conflict of the story; the game is about how the player goes about getting to that point and winning.

8.1.5 System Mechanics

System mechanics govern how the player interacts with the system and how the system interacts with the player. This may not seem to be very important at first glance, but designing a control system for a keyboard is different than one for a game controller which in turn is different than one for the Kinect device. For instance, if the Sancho game were played with a controller plugged into the computer, we would be able to sneak Sancho around by lightly pressing on the thumb stick. However, there is no way to lightly press a key on the keyboard; therefore, if we wanted the player to be able to sneak while using the keyboard, we would have to introduce another key that was used specifically for sneaking around. These mechanics must be considered as we design the interface systems for the game. The way the screen looks on a traditional monitor is very different from the way the screen looks within the Oculus Rift Virtual Reality (VR) headset. In fact, the difference is such that it is important to limit the amount of text used with VR headsets as it is more difficult to read the text (with the current technology). These mechanics need to be considered when developing a game; in fact this was mentioned much earlier when we discussed target platforms during our initial exploration of the design document for a game.

8.2 Where Do Mechanics Come From?

The ideas for the mechanics of our games come from several places. The first, and probably the most common, is from the game genre itself. For instance, in the case of the Sancho Panza project, it was decided early on that the game would be a platformer game with some action–adventure elements. As a result of that genre decision, there are certain things that the game *has* to have in order to fit into that genre; there are specific game-play components that we must allow for. These components, as we looked at earlier in this book, would consist of the ability of the player to control a character, how that character moves within the game world is a set of rules. It would also be necessary for us to allow the player to solve challenges either through finding and collecting items or through combat, both of which are further defined by rules that comprise the mechanics of those systems. As can be seen, we have already constructed some game mechanics for our game when we created the character controller systems and the rudimentary combat system.

We also get ideas for mechanics from playing other games. As we play other games, we like the way that a game does something, or perhaps dislike a certain game's approach, and as a result of this experience we try to incorporate similar systems into our own designs. Copyright law is a somewhat behind the times as far as digital media and video games are concerned, but as a general rule it is not possible to copyright a game mechanic. This basically says that I could not copyright the game mechanic of allowing my player character to destroy monsters in the game by jumping onto them. What I can copyright and therefore protect is the character itself: what it looks like, how it sounds, and to an extent how it moves. But the rule of being able to jump on your opponents to kill them cannot be copyright protected. After all if it could, then we would not have the many different types of first-person shooters or even the matching games that we play online. As you play other games, pay attention to the things that you like and do not like. But, it is important to be able to qualify *why* a certain mechanic was enjoyed or not. Perhaps you can get some good ideas from being aware of what it is that you do and do not like in the games that you play.

Another method of developing mechanics for our games is through playtesting and trying to get the game balanced to be an enjoyable experience. This is where we get our balancing mechanics from as a general rule as these are things added into the game after we discover that the game does not work quite the way that we thought it should, or that players do not play the game exactly the way we wanted them too. The best way to demonstrate this will be through a quick story. During the summers, we provide a 2-day game development camp for middle school students. In this camp, the kids are taught how to create a 2D arcade space shooter kind of game with a flying spaceship and some asteroids and aliens to challenge the player. The kids all want to make the spaceship shoot lasers. Once this is done, the kids thoroughly enjoy creating a glowing wall of laser death, that is to say holding down the space bar and constantly shooting lasers to form a complete wall (see Figure 8.1). However, they become very bored with this game because there is zero challenge to them as players. This is game balance, an unbalanced game seems like it would be wonderfully fun to play at first, but we quickly realize that what truly makes a game fun is the challenge of beating it and knowing that we beat that challenge where other players have failed.

8.3 Designing Our Mechanics

We are going to create a couple of example mechanics for our Sancho game including a checkpoint system which will comprise of the ability to respawn the player when they die, killing off the player when they get into water, and finally allowing the player to collect objects within the game world to fulfill specified quests. We have already implemented some game mechanics within our project as well; for instance, Sancho has a health system that we

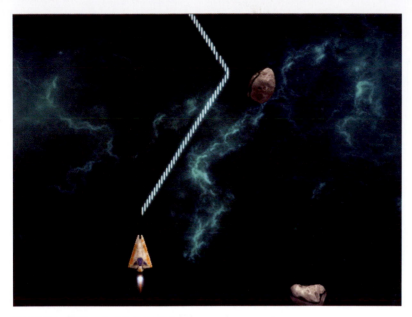

FIG 8.1 The wall of laser death in an arcade shooter.

added with the artificial intelligence (AI) NPCs, Sancho can run and move around the world based on the player's input, and Sancho can talk to his wife Teresa, although we will be returning to that one and tweaking it quite heavily as soon as we get to the UI system inside of Unity. The key to creating mechanics, as with everything else we have done thus far, is in the design phase. Through designing the rule system that we are going to implement, we are forced to understand the mechanic. Without this deep understanding of how and when it should work, it is extremely difficult to actually implement the mechanic into our game.

8.3.1 The Checkpoint System

This is a game mechanic that is derived directly from the genre of game that we are creating. As players play through action–adventure games or even platformers, they expect to have their progress automatically saved so that if they die they can return to that save point rather than all the way to the beginning of the level. These are referred to as checkpoints. We are going to create two checkpoints in our example. The first checkpoint, we will position within the town near Sancho's initial conversation with Teresa. The second checkpoint, we will position on the bridge leading over into the Act II region of the game environment. This way if the player dies while exploring the thick forest over there, they will respawn on the bridge as opposed to all the way back in the town itself. We have all played games with checkpoint systems and have an idea of how they work, but just to make sure, we are going to step through this

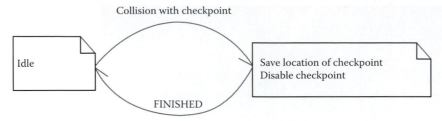

FIG 8.2 The state machine layout for the checkpoint system.

design process to guarantee that we know what to do and also that we have what we will need.

> - When the player comes in contact with a checkpoint:
>   - Save the checkpoint so the game knows.
>   - Get rid of the checkpoint so it cannot be activated again.

This seems to be a fairly straightforward approach to our checkpoint system. The state machine for it, as seen in Figure 8.2, will sit and wait for the collision to occur as specified in our list given previously. Once this collision occurs, we will save the location of the checkpoint that we collided with and then destroy it. Getting rid of the checkpoint is a subtle but important point. We do not want the player to have activated the third checkpoint, for instance, and then while running around to accidently reactivate the first checkpoint. This would cause the player to respawn back at the initial starting point rather than at the final checkpoint that they had gotten to.

8.3.2 Respawning Sancho

Similar to the previous example, respawning the player's character is an expected mechanic within the action–adventure genre. Players expect to not have to run through the whole game with only one life. It is expected that the player will die at least once during the playing of the game and that after the character dies, the player should have their character respawned so that they can continue playing. Ideally, the respawning of the character would occur at the most recently discovered checkpoint as was mentioned in the last section. We will skip the state machine list this time, instead we will simply state that whenever the player dies, for whatever the reason, the character will respawn back at the last saved checkpoint. There are two different approaches that we could take to this problem. The first would be to destroy the character when the player dies and then to create a new instance of the character object at whatever point in the game world we want. This seems like a viable option and it can be done, however, in order to do it we will need to have a game controller system or some other system in place that will be responsible for destroying and creating the player objects as well as keeping track of how many lives the player has remaining, among other things.

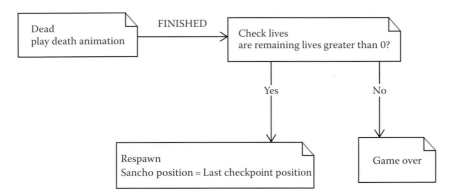

FIG 8.3 The respawn player state machine design.

An easier approach would be to simply move the current player after their death animation has completed and perhaps a reasonable amount of time has passed. We would also want to take into account whether the player has any Sancho lives remaining or not prior to respawning the player. If the player does not have any lives remaining, then the game should end, otherwise it will be OK for Sancho to respawn back at the last saved checkpoint. At any rate, those are implementation issues to worry about when we get there, although by considering these while we are designing the system, it will give us a solid running start at the implementation of this process as soon as we get to it. Figure 8.3 depicts the state machine that will be responsible for repositioning the player back at the spawn point. In this case, we will not destroy and recreate but will go ahead and move the character to where the last activated checkpoint is located at.

8.3.3 Sancho and Water

This example is derived from the needs of the story. The story, and as a result the game itself, needs the player to stay within the confines of the game world that we have created. In the last chapter, we created boundaries around the island in order to keep the player from falling off of the terrain and that addressed our needs at the time. Although, one of the other issues we addressed in that chapter was that the environment needs to direct the player through the world in the manner that the designer wants the player to go through the level. Keeping this in mind, what we are going to do is to kill the character when the player wanders out into the deeper part of the ocean under the pretext that Sancho cannot swim. Likewise, we do not want the player to bypass our bridges by running over the river so we will incorporate the same Sancho cannot swim rationale into interactions with the river. This still leaves one possibility open: the player can stay in the shallow part of the ocean and run around the mouth of the rivers into the other areas of the map. To counter this, we will employ another collider and this time blame the death of Sancho on the rapid current of the river pushing him out to sea where he still cannot swim. We could actually extend this one so that instead of a collider, we create a physics force that pushes the character out to the

321

deeper part of the ocean surrounding the island. With these basic ideas in mind, we can break this apart into a less cluttered state machine list.

- When the player collides with the deep part of the ocean:
  - Kill the player character.
  - Respawn the player character.
- When the player collides with the rivers around the bridges:
  - Kill the player character.
  - Respawn the player character.
- When the player collides with the mouth of the rivers in the ocean:
  - Kill the player character.
  - Respawn the player character.

Notice that throughout these, the player can be killed and respawned, but we have not addressed how many lives the player gets to have other than to mention that it was an issue to be concerned with during the respawning state machine. Granted that the design for respawning Sancho does indicate the checking for remaining lives, but it was not our goal at that time to design the complete life management system, this is being saved for an exercise at the end of the chapter. This detailed list of the state machine allows us to derive the state machine depicted in Figure 8.4. An interesting note is that we could have done it with only one state to handle all three of the different types of collisions possible (see Figure 8.5 as an example). Let's take a moment to look at these two different approaches more closely.

In the example of the first design (Figure 8.4), the system is entirely self-contained. So, the system takes care of detecting a collision and determines what to do as a result of the collision. We could continue to expand on this design to incorporate other no-no places that we do not want the player to go simply by

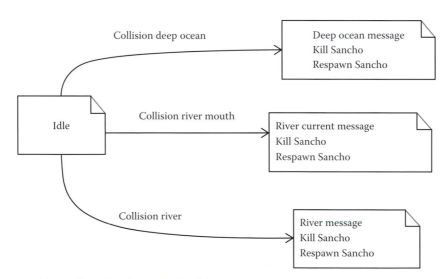

FIG 8.4 The state machine controlling collisions between Sancho and the water.

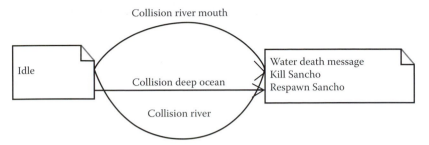

FIG 8.5 A simplified two-state version of the water collision system.

adding more collision detections, more transitions, and more target states. The second example, found in Figure 8.5, does not actually know what was hit; all it knows is that it has been triggered to do something. The warning message to be displayed to the player is a variable that is set by whatever state machine actually detected the collision. The advantage here is that this is much smaller and easier to maintain, at least within this view. However, in order for this system to work, we would have to move the actual collision detection off to other parts of the state machines within the player controller system thereby making the whole system more difficult to fully understand and build upon. By dividing them out as we have in Figure 8.4, we can utilize different audio or UI events when the player collides with the water death objects. To do this with Figure 8.5, we will need to have the various objects that we collide with setting variables that will determine which audio and which UI elements to display; it will just be easier for us to keep everything in one consolidated state machine and run the logic through as we have in Figure 8.4.

8.3.4 Sancho's Collection System

Our final example is going to be the ability of Sancho to collect various things within the game. We are going to start with having him collect sheep so that they can be delivered to the pen inside of the town. But this system could be abstracted out to allow us to use it for other animals within the game as well. This can then serve as the foundation for an inventory collection system in which the player can run around and gather other items to bring back to the town. The animals can follow Sancho around, but the other things will need to be put into his inventory, perhaps using Dapple as a pack donkey, to return them to the town. Our basic approach to this can be seen in the following list:

- Set the number of items he needs to find, if necessary.
- When Sancho collides with a sheep and still needs to find sheep:
  - Check to see if he has already gathered that sheep:
    - If he has then ignore the collision.
    - If he has not then:
      - Add the sheep to the collection of found sheep.
      - Set the sheep to follow Sancho around the world.
      - Add one to the number that he has found.

By introducing the maximum number of sheep that Sancho will be required to find, we are creating a victory condition for the player, that is, the player knows when they have completed that specific quest. We do not want the player wandering aimlessly around wondering if there are still more sheep to be found. This will also allow us to put more sheep than necessary into the game world to make it easier for the player to find the sheep. This is going to be important if we allow the sheep to wander around and possibly get themselves stuck in some part of the game map. We are going to have the found sheep follow Sancho around the game world rather than just have them disappear in a beeping noise with the counter of found sheep increasing by one. This will give the illusion of Sancho gathering and herding the sheep into the town, which would be for a more interesting game-play experience. If we are going to allow the sheep to follow Sancho around, then we will to have to incorporate a method for Sancho to get rid of those sheep.

- When Sancho enters into the sheep pen or collides with gate:
  - Any sheep that are with him will stay behind in the pen and stop following him.

We now have a basic guideline for both the collecting and the delivering stages of this system. Building the state machines themselves will result in systems that are shown in Figure 8.6. Notice

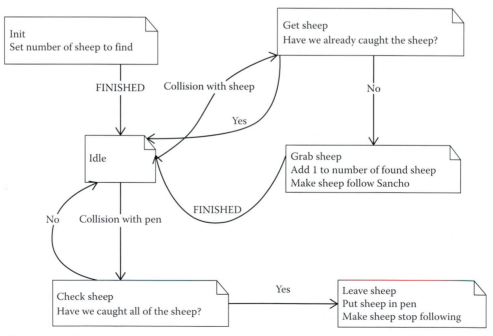

FIG 8.6 The state machine for collecting and delivering sheep.

that in this design we have incorporated both of our descriptions for a collection system into one state machine to make it easier to maintain and debug this system. This could be modified later by creating the item that we are looking for as a variable and then setting this state machine to trigger on that variable, but that is an implementation concept that we are coming to.

8.4 Implementing Our Mechanics

After completing the design work on the systems that we are going to add to our project, we will have a good understanding of how these systems work and where we need to add them into the developing game. Looking through the designs that we have constructed, most of the procedures resemble the ones that we have already used in other state machines that should make the implementation easier to complete. One of the things that gets overlooked when learning programming is that we continue to use the same methods as the core building blocks on more complex functionalities that we want to add. Before we go off looking for a new action that will do everything we want in one go, we need to look carefully at our design work and see how the pieces fit together, especially if we can reuse skills that we already understand and just put them together slightly differently.

Download
You can find the starting scene for this chapter in the complete project package on the companion website, the scene name is: "Chapter8_part1."

8.4.1 The Checkpoint System

For the checkpoint system, before we construct the logic of it, we will have to build something to serve as a visible marker for the checkpoint itself. This can be any kind of object that is sitting in the world and in some way drawing attention to itself so that the player notices it. For our version, we are going to make a rotating quad that will have an image of Sancho on it. In order to construct this, be sure to grab the checkpoint texture file from the companion website. Once we have that image downloaded, we will review some of the work from the last chapter by creating a new material to use and then construct the quad shape we will use for the checkpoint and get it rotating in our game world.

Download
Get the "checkpoint.tga" file from this chapter's section of the resources on the companion website.

1. Import the checkpoint.tga file into your project, the Materials folder would be a good location.
2. Create a new material by left-clicking on the Create drop down (directly beneath the word Project in the Project pane) and selecting Material from the drop-down menu.
3. Name the new material checkpoint_mat.
4. For the Shader of the Material, click Standard and select Legacy Shaders → Transparent → Cutout → Diffuse from the drop-down menu.
5. Drag the checkpoint.tga file from the Project pane and onto the Diffuse texture location inside of this new material.
6. Add a quad to the current scene: GameObject → 3D Object → Quad.
7. Change the name of the quad to be checkpoint.
8. Add the checkpoint_mat material to the quad by dragging it onto the quad from the Project pane.
9. Position and scale the checkpoint object so that it fits nicely into the initial entrance into the town on the island (see Figure 8.7).
10. Remove the default Mesh collider on the Quad.
11. Add a Sphere (or Box) collider to the quad).
12. This is the original 10 and then numbering of steps continues from here.
13. Create a duplicate of the checkpoint object by selecting it in the Hierarchy panel and pressing CTRL-D.
14. Rotate the new checkpoint object 180° on the Y-axis. For instance, in our example the original checkpoint object was at an angle of 106 on the Y-axis, therefore the new checkpoint object should be 286° on the Y-axis (180 + 106).
15. Remove the sphere collider component from the new checkpoint object.
16. Make this new checkpoint object a child of the original checkpoint object.
17. Select the Is Trigger check box for the Sphere collider component of the original checkpoint object.
18. Change the tag of the object to be Checkpoint; you will have to add a new tag.
19. Add a finite state machine (FSM) to this main checkpoint object and name the FSM Rotation.
    a. Rename State 1 to be Rotate.
    b. Add a Rotate action to this state.
    c. Set the Y Angle rotation value to be 8, leave all other settings at their default as shown in Figure 8.8.

Now that we have an object out in our game world that will serve as a checkpoint object for Sancho to run into, we are ready to get the functionality going for the checkpoint itself. But, before we do that, we will touch on a couple of things from the checkpoint object. The first thing to notice is that we created two checkpoint objects and parented them. This is because the materials and textures on them are only visible from the

FIG 8.7 The checkpoint object positioned and scaled in the game world.

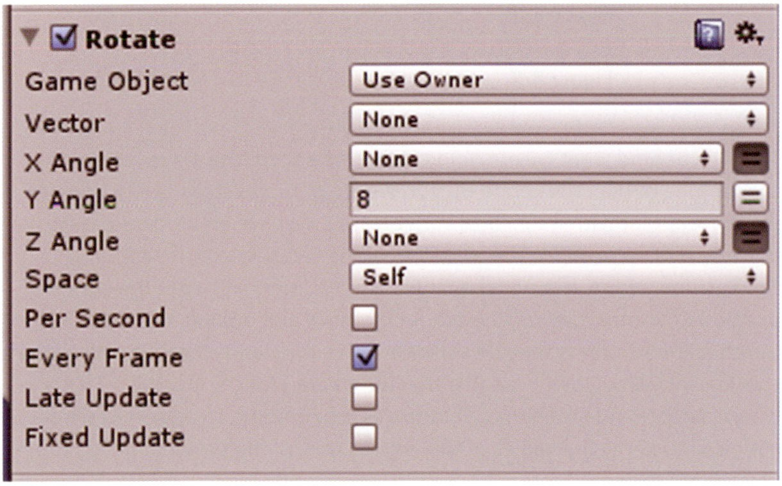

▼ ☑ **Rotate**		🛈 ⚙▾
Game Object	Use Owner	↕
Vector	None	↕
X Angle	None	↕ ≣
Y Angle	8	≡
Z Angle	None	↕ ≣
Space	Self	↕
Per Second	☐	
Every Frame	☑	
Late Update	☐	
Fixed Update	☐	

FIG 8.8 The Rotate action within the checkpoint object.

normal side of the object. The normal side of an object is defined as the side that light bounces off. If we do not have light entering our eye then we cannot see something, the same principle is at work with the cameras within a video game. When the camera was on the normal side of the object, we could see the texture, however, when the object had rotated around we could not see the object. Therefore, to solve this problem, we simply duplicated the object and flipped it around so that the copy would have its normal going in the opposite direction as the original object thereby eliminating the side that was invisible. We could have also solved this problem by creating a double-sided material by utilizing one of the other Shader types within Unity, specifically the Nature → Tress Soft Occlusion

Leaves shader. We are now ready to move on and get the checkpoint collision system working.

1. Select Sancho in the Hierarchy panel.
   a. Create a new FSM named Checkpoints.
      i. Change State 1 to Idle.
      ii. Add a new state named Store Location.
      iii. Add a new event named checkpoint trigger.
      iv. Add a new Vector3 variable named checkpoint location.
      v. Add a new GameObject variable named checkpoint.
      vi. Select the Idle state.
         A. Add the checkpoint trigger Transition and connect it to the Store Location state.
         B. Add a Trigger Event action and use the settings shown in Figure 8.9.
      vii. Select the Store Location state.
         A. Add a FINISHED transition event and connect it to the Idle state.
         B. Add a Get Position action and use the settings in Figure 8.10.
         C. Add a Destroy Object action and use the settings in Figure 8.10.

The idea behind what we are doing is that whenever the player enters the trigger area of the checkpoint object, we are going to store the location of that checkpoint within the local variable that we have created and name the checkpoint location. The grabbing of the location is done with the Get Position action, but notice that we have changed it to get the current position of another object; the other object we are looking at is specifically the checkpoint object that we collided with earlier and stored it within that checkpoint GameObject variable that we created for this purpose. This is where a good understanding of variables is beginning to pay off as *we* do not need to know the values of the various things; the *program* needs to know what they are.

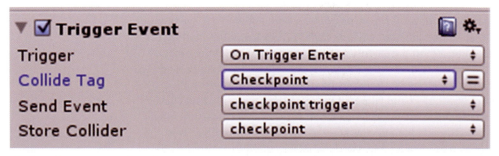

FIG 8.9 The Trigger Event action settings for the Checkpoint system.

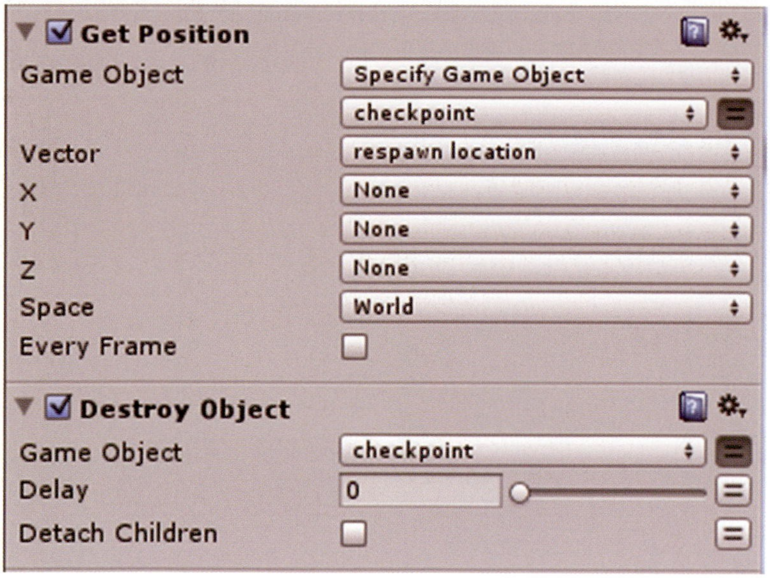

FIG 8.10 Settings for the Get Position state.

Once we have grabbed and stored that position, which is a Vector3 value, we can go ahead and get rid of the Checkpoint object that we just collided with. We are accomplishing this with the Destroy Object action, which requires that we specify which object it is that we want to destroy. There is an alternative action called Destroy Self that can be used to destroy the object that the state machine is attached to.

When we run this to test it, the new system appears to be working correctly as the checkpoint object that is rotating happily does disappear once we collide with the trigger around it. But, just to verify, we would like to take it a step further and make sure that the position of the checkpoint is indeed being stored correctly. Ideally, we would wait until we have set up the respawning system for testing, but then on the off chance that it did not work we would not know if it was broken in the new respawning system or if it was broken within this system grabbing the position of the checkpoint.

In order to test it, we will select the checkpoint object in the Hierarchy panel and take note of the Position vector that is within the Transform component of that object. With that value noted, we will go ahead and run the game again and go find that checkpoint to collide with it again. After the checkpoint object disappears from the scene and while the game is still running, open the PlayMaker editor making sure that Sancho is the selected object within the Hierarchy panel. Select the Checkpoints FSM that we just created from the state machine drop-down list. Select the Variables tab and check the value of the respawn location variable, the values should match the earlier value we saw for the Checkpoint object itself as shown in Figure 8.11. Now that we know for sure that this system is working the

329

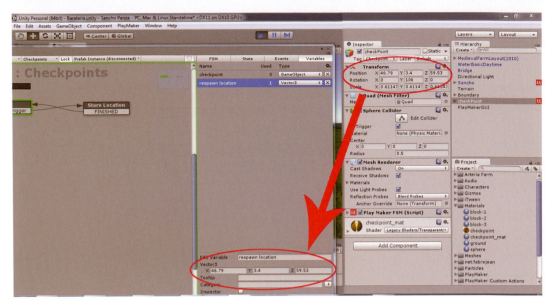

FIG 8.11 Verifying the value of the respawn location variable.

way that we need it to, we are definitely ready to move on. Any problems we run into next will not be within this system but will be errors or bugs introduced by the new system making debugging an easier process.

8.4.2 Sancho and Water

Like we did for the checkpoint system, we will have to add some things to the current scene in order for this system to work as designed. However, we can begin with the boundaries that are already in place surrounding the island. We will use those boundaries for the deep part of the ocean where Sancho dies and returns to his spawn point. The actual respawning system will not be developed until the next system, so for now we will initialize the killing of the player and display a message to the console that Sancho has drowned. Eventually, the message to the console will be replaced by a message to the user interface system, which we will be developing in an upcoming chapter. Our first step will be to change the tags of the cubes we are using as the boundary objects to Deep Ocean. With the tags altered, we are ready to set up the collision within Sancho for this.

1. Select the Sancho object in the Hierarchy panel.
    a. Add a new FSM to Sancho named Water Collision.
    b. Change State 1 to Idle.
    c. Add a new state named Deep Ocean.
    d. Add a new event named Drowning and an event named River Current.

FIG 8.12 Collision Event properties for the Deep Ocean.

e. Select the Idle state.
   i. Add the Drowning transition and connect it to Deep Ocean state.
   ii. Add a Collision Event and set its properties to those of Figure 8.12.
f. Select the Deep Ocean state.
   i. Add a FINISHED transition and connect it to Idle.
   ii. Add a Debug Log action and use the settings in Figure 8.13.
      A. For Text, we have used "Sancho cannot swim and has drowned."
   iii. Add a Set FSM Bool action and use the settings in Figure 8.13.
   iv. Add a Set FSM Int action and use the settings in Figure 8.13.

We have seen all of these actions before, especially when constructing the damage system for the spider earlier. However, we have added one new action in the Debug Log action. There are many times that it is useful to spit something out to the log or console window just to make sure things are going the way that we think that they should be; for instance, our output to the Console window is depicted in Figure 8.14. We can use such techniques for temporary placeholders of eventual clean output to the user. We have three different levels that we can send our message to as follows: Info, Warning, and Error. Essentially, the difference is going to be which icon is displayed next to the text within the Console window. The Text property is the message that we want displayed to the Console. We could have used a convert to string action prior to this one to grab a variable and put its value into a string that could then be spit out through this Text property. The final setting is the option to put it in the Log file only or to put it to the Unity Log Window, which is the Console pane.

For the remaining collisions that we want with this system, we will need to add some collision or trigger boxes to the areas that we want the collisions to be detected and to occur. We will begin this process by adding a 3D Game Object cube to our scene and placing it at the mouth of one of the rivers (see Figure 8.15). Once the cube is in place, we will go

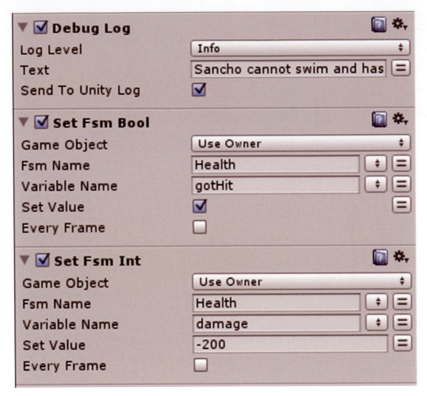

FIG 8.13 The Deep Ocean state actions and properties.

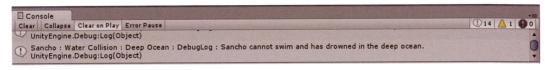

FIG 8.14 The log message being displayed in the Console window.

ahead and change its tag to be River Current, set the Collider Is Trigger check box to be turned on, and turn off the Mesh Renderer component of the object. Then we will be ready to implement the collisions for this new object.

1. Select the Sancho game object.
   a. Select the Water Collision FSM.
      i. Add a new state named River Mouth.
      ii. Select the Idle state.
         A. Add the River Current transition event and connect it to the River Mouth state.
         B. Add a Trigger Event action.
            I. Set Collider Tag to River Current.
            II. Set Send Event to River Current.

FIG 8.15 The placement of the collision cube at the mouth of a river.

C. Select the Deep Ocean state.
    I.   Hold down the SHIFT key and select each of the three actions.
    II. Select the small gear icon in the top right corner of one of the actions (see Figure 8.16).
    III. Select the Copy Selected Actions from the drop-down menu.
D. Select the River Mouth state.
    I.   Right-click in the action panel and select Past Actions.
    II. Change the text in the Debug Log to read: "Sancho got stuck in the current of the river and has drowned."

This system is essentially identical to what we previously constructed for the collisions with the deep ocean. All we need to do is to copy the cube that we are using to the other two river mouths so that we will have the collisions configured for all three of the river mouths coming out of the river. The last component of this system is going to be left as an exercise for the end of the chapter.

8.4.3 Respawning Sancho

In order to respawn Sancho, we will need to move him from wherever he is currently located to wherever it is that we want him to be respawned; generally speaking, this should be the last checkpoint that he crossed and the location was saved. However, we do have one unique situation to correct and that is the odd case of Sancho being killed before the player

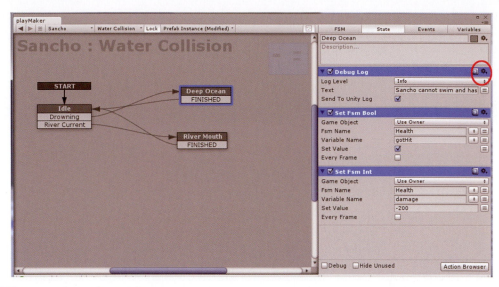

FIG 8.16 Gear icon in the top right corner of actions.

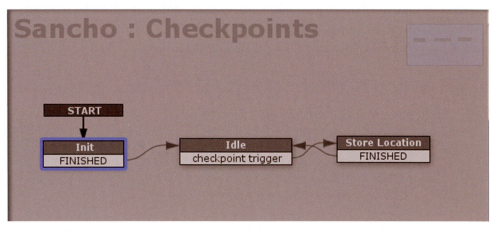

FIG 8.17 The modified Checkpoints state machine.

has managed to find a checkpoint and activate it. In order to cover this, we are going to modify our Checkpoints state machine from earlier to match the one depicted in Figure 8.17. We are going to add a new state to this machine named Init.

1. Select the Init state.
   a. Add a FINISHED transition event and connect the event to the Idle state.
   b. Right-click on the Init state and select Set as Start State.
   c. Add a Get Position action to the state.
      i. Leave Game Object as Use Owner.
      ii. Set Vector to respawn location variable.

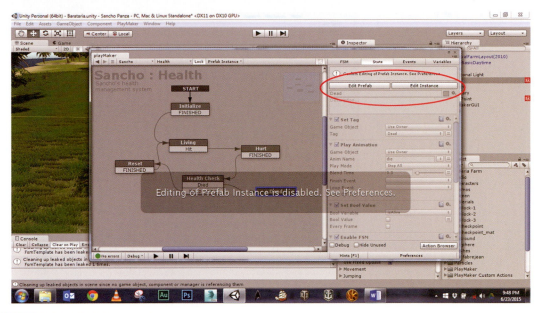

FIG 8.18 The Editing Prefab Instance warning message.

This new state that we have added takes the starting position of Sancho and stores it into the respawn location variable. This is a safety net so that if the player dies before discovering a checkpoint, Sancho will respawn back to this initial starting location that we have dropped Sancho into to begin the level. The other element in this was the Set as Start State option that we used in order to make the newly created state the default starting state for the machine. This is a nice feature to be aware of; in that way, if we need to make a different state as the starting state, we can easily modify the starting state for any state machine that we have created.

We are now going to look at how we can modify an FSM that we had created much earlier and that is actually part of the Prefab of Sancho that we made at that time. The ideal location for our respawning mechanism is going to be within the Health system that we have already created, this would also be a good location to add some life logic for keeping track of how many lives the player has. We will go ahead and select the Health FSM and as soon as we do notice that a warning message appears as displayed in Figure 8.18. This warning is letting us know that we cannot edit Prefabbed parts of our Sancho object when we have the Sancho instance selected. It is perfectly fine to add new things to our instance in our scene, as we have been doing; however, to alter any of the core prefab parts, PlayMaker will require that we edit the prefab itself. We can bypass this by changing the settings, but this is a good safety message as we are learning our way around PlayMaker to make sure that we do not accidently make a serious change that disrupts the prefab itself.

Consider it from this perspective, if we are changing one of the core prefab state machines, then it stands to reason that we will most likely want that change to cascade through all instances of this object. However, if we are only editing the

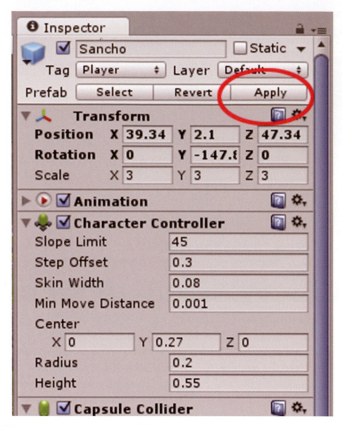

FIG 8.19 Using the Apply button to update a Prefab.

instance, then the changes will only exist within the instance we just changed and not the prefab itself. We have two methods of solving this issue. The first is to confirm that we want to edit the default prefab FSM within the instance by selecting the Edit Instance button, highlighted in Figure 8.18. Or, we can solve this by updating our prefab object of Sancho with the changes that we have currently made to our instance by clicking the Apply button located near the top of the Inspector panel when the instance of Sancho is selected (see Figure 8.19).

> **Note**
> Objects in the Hierarchy panel are *instances* and objects in the Project pane can be *prefabs*. When we add a prefab to a scene, we create an instance of that prefab and still have the prefab available for other scenes or to even add more of the same prefab to the current scene, for instance, adding multiple sheep into our scene.

With the prefab updated with our new changes, which also means all other scenes using this Sancho prefab have been updated with the new version of Sancho as well, we can select the prefab from the Project pane → Prefabs → Sancho and open the PlayMaker editor to make changes to the prefab itself.

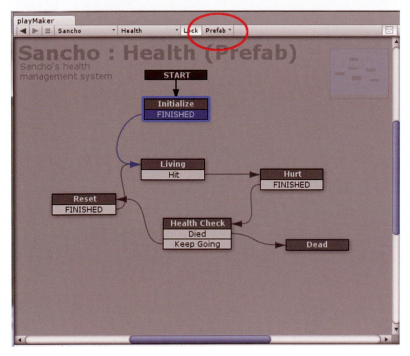

FIG 8.20 The location in the PlayMaker Editor that will specify the Prefab or Prefab Instance.

We can be sure that we are editing the Prefab instead of the Prefab Instance by noticing whether PlayMaker specifies the object as a Prefab or not. For instance, the state machine depicted in Figure 8.20 is from the Prefab object as PlayMaker is noting within the highlighted circle. Now that we are working with the Prefab object and have gotten rid of the warning message from PlayMaker that stopped us earlier, we will modify the Health FSM so that Sancho will respawn to the correct location after he dies.

1. Create a new Vector3 variable named respawnPoint.
2. Create a new state named Respawn.
3. Select the Dead state.
   a. Add a FINISHED transition and connect it to the Respawn state.
   b. Disable all of the actions within the Dead state except for the Play Animation action.
4. Select the Respawn state.
   a. Add a FINISHED transition and connect it to the Reset state, Figure 8.21 depicts the state machine.
   b. Add a Get FSM Vector3.
      i. FSM Name is Checkpoints.
      ii. Variable Name is respawn location.
      iii. Store Value is respawnPoint.
   c. Add a Set Position action.
      i. Vector is respawnPoint.

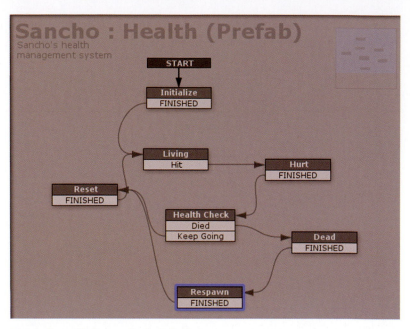

FIG 8.21 The modified state machine for the Health system.

We have seen all of these actions previously or at least discussed them, so we are fairly comfortable with the actions that are being used here. But, what we did with the Dead state is something that we should take a moment to consider before moving past. All of the actions that are in the Dead state will be needed, eventually. The key to understanding what happened here is that this state was only to be reached when Sancho is dead or when he has no more lives left. Once Sancho is dead, he cannot respawn. For the exercise requiring the construction of a life system, it gets placed into this area that we are working on here. Specifically, when the player dies, we want to play the death animation where we currently are. But after that is finished, we want to evaluate how many lives the player has left, if they have no more lives left then we want to go on and do all of the actions that we just disabled, we want Sancho to be entirely dead. However, if the player still has lives left, we would want to decrease the number of remaining lives and then go on and respawn the player wherever they are supposed to be and get the Health system back up and running. For our goal at hand, respawning Sancho, we have completed the task and it is working as we want it to, the life system is an exercise at the end of the chapter, just remember the hints that we just discussed when working on it.

8.4.4 Sancho's Collection System

The last example that we will build together in this chapter will be Sancho's collection system which can be easily modified for use with other types of collectible objects. In this case, we are going to build a sheep-collecting system for one of his first quests in which he must find the sheep wandering outside of the town and get them returned to a sheep pen within the town.

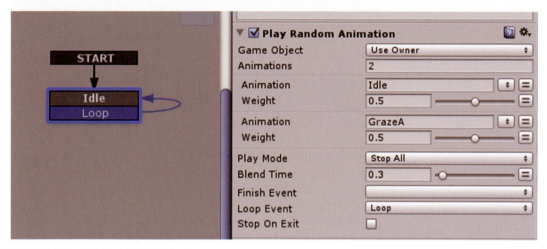

FIG 8.22 The Waiting FSM for the fluffy sheep prefab.

Go ahead and add one of the Fluffy Sheep models that we configured back in the characters chapter with all of its animations. Figure 8.22 gives an overview of the state machine that we will build for the idling sheep, and we will name this FSM Waiting. We will begin by getting the sheep all set up to handle collisions. Add a Box Collider component to the sheep and set the Is Trigger to on. We are now ready to add on to the Waiting FSM for the sheep to get some more behavior from it.

1. Select the Fluffy Sheep instance that has been added to the scene.
   a. Create the Waiting FSM as depicted in Figure 8.22.
   b. Add a new state named Follow and a new state named Move.
   c. Add the variables and events from Table 8.3.
   d. Select the Idle state.
      i. Remove the Loop transition event.
      ii. Remove the call to the Loop event from the Play Random Animation action.
      iii. Add the Start Follow transition event and connect it to the Follow state.
      iv. Add a Bool Test action.
         A. Bool Variable is Follow.
         B. Is True is the Start Follow event.
         C. Every Frame is checked.
   e. Select the Follow state.
      i. Add the Go Move transition event and connect it to the Move state.
      ii. Add a Play Animation action and play the Idle animation.
      iii. Add a Get Distance action.
         A. Target is Follow Target (the variable).
         B. Store Result is Distance (the variable).
         C. Every Frame is checked.

TABLE 8.3 Required Events and Variables for the Fluffy Sheep to Follow Sancho Around

Events	Variables and Types
Go Move	Distance → Float
Start Follow	Follow → Bool
Stop Follow	Follow Target → Game Object

      iv. Add a Compare Float action.
          A. Float 1 is Distance.
          B. Float 2 is 3.
          C. Greater Than is the Go Move event.
          D. Every Frame is checked.
   f. Select the Move state.
      i. Add the Stop Follow transition event and connect it with the Follow state.
     ii. Add a Play Animation action and play the Walk animation.
    iii. Add a Smooth Look At action.
          A. Target Object is Follow Target.
          B. Ignore Vertical is checked.
     iv. Add a Move Toward action.
          A. Target Object is Follow Target.
          B. Ignore Vertical is checked.
          C. Max Speed is 1.25.
          D. Finish Distance is 3.
          E. Finish Event is Stop Follow.

We have used these actions in the construction of the AI system for the spider, so there is nothing new here except the way that we have pieced this construction together. What we are doing is having this system get turned on, Follow Boolean being set to true, whenever Sancho triggers the collision with the sheep. At that point, the sheep will see how far away from Sancho it is. If it is more than 3 units away, then it will turn to face Sancho and move toward him until it is within 3 units of him. Otherwise, the sheep will just stand there and play its idle animation. We can go ahead and create a Prefab of this sheep by dragging it from our Hierarchy panel down into the Prefabs folder of the Project pane. This will allow us to have this sheep available in other scenes as well if need be. Now that we have the sheep ready to follow Sancho around the world, we will get Sancho's system put together to trigger this behavior.

1. Select the Sancho instance in the Hierarchy view.
2. Create a new FSM named Collecting.
   a. Add the variables and events depicted in Table 8.4.
   b. Rename State 1 to Idle.
   c. Add states named Follow Me, All Sheep, and Found Count.
      i. Connect the states with the events as shown in Figure 8.23.

d. Select the Idle state.
   i. Add a Trigger Event action.
     A. Trigger is On Trigger Enter.
     B. Collide Tag is sheep.
     C. Send Event is Got Sheep.
     D. Store Collider is Target.
e. Select the Found Count state.
   i. Add a Get FSM Bool action.
     A. Game Object is Target (Specify Game Object).
     B. FSM Name is Waiting.
     C. Variable Name is Follow.
     D. Store Value is beenFound.
   ii. Add a Bool Test action.
     A. Bool Variable is beenFound.
     B. Is True is Skip (transition event).
   iii. Add an Int Add action.
     A. Int Variable is numSheep.
     B. Add is 1.
   iv. Add an Int Compare action.
     A. Integer 1 is numSheep.
     B. Integer 2 is findSheep.
     C. Equal is the Got Sheep transition event.
f. Select the All Sheep state.
   i. Add a Debug Log action and set the text to "found all the sheep."
   ii. Make sure Send To Unity Log is checked.
g. Select the Follow Me state.
   i. Add a Set FSM Bool action.
     A. Game Object is Target (Specify Game Object).
     B. FSM Name is Waiting.
     C. Variable Name is Follow.
     D. Set Value is checked.
   ii. Add a Set FSM Game Object action.
     A. Game Object is Target (Specify Game Object).
     B. FSM Name is Waiting.
     C. Variable Name is Follow Target.
     D. Set Value is Sancho (selected from the Scene/Hierarchy view).

TABLE 8.4 Events and Variables Needed in Sancho for the Sheep Collection System

Events	Variables and Types
Got Sheep	beenFound → Bool
Skip	findSheep → Int (set to 2)
	numSheep → Int
	Target → GameObject

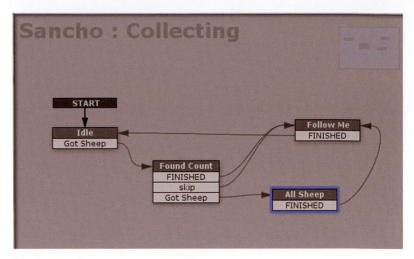

FIG 8.23 The FINISHED layout for the Collecting FSM.

We have seen these actions before as well or have at least seen actions closely resembling them so that we may not need to explain each one in detail. There are a couple of things that we should mention at this point about the FSM Name and Variable Name properties. It was necessary to type in both the FSM name and the variable name when configuring those. This is because we are using a variable to specify which object we want to set variable values of. Since it is a variable that means that while we are developing the state machine, the drop-down menus will not work because PlayMaker does not know what the variable is going to be filled with once the game is running. Sure, we know that it should be a sheep object, but PlayMaker does not know that. When typing in the name of the state machine and the variable name, pay attention to spelling and capitalization as these must exactly match that which we have inside of the sheep.

Another thing to point out is the general flow of the logic. While we are using actions that we have seen before, we should make sure that the logical construction that we have built here makes sense. To begin when we collide with a sheep, we entered into the Found Sheep state. The purpose of this state is to increase the number of sheep that we have found if the one that we just collided with was one that we had not already accounted for. As the sheep follow us, they will stop when they are near, and Sancho can go collide with them again at that point in time. If that were to happen, then the sheep he is colliding with would have the Follow Boolean variable set to true. Since we are grabbing that value inside the Collecting state machine, if it is true, we are skipping out of the rest of the actions inside of that specific state, otherwise we will drop down to the next action in the list, which is where we handle the counting of the sheep.

With that comparison out of the way, we know that the sheep we just hit has not been accounted for before; if it has been hit before, then we are no longer inside of this state—we have transitioned out of it. What we will do next is to add one to our current number of found sheep and compare that to the number of sheep that we are trying to find. If those two numbers match, then we will transition over to the event with the Debug Log action in it. This action is really just a placeholder for the moment, as eventually we will want some UI stuff going on here, but we will have the state in place and ready to have those new UI actions added to it at that point in time. Notice that we did not need to worry about transitioning to the Follow Me state as we are having the FINISHED transition event take care of that for us. The only way we get to have a FINISHED transition event fired by the state we are in is in the condition that the current number of found sheep does not match the number of sheep that we are looking for, in which case execution will drop down to the next action and since there is no other action the system fires a FINISHED transition event that we are handling in this state.

> **Note**
> Remember that actions are executed sequentially from top to bottom in the list of actions for a state. If we have something that is triggering an event, then we will not proceed to the following actions in the list if that event does get triggered, for instance, in a Compare action.

We can now test this and make sure that when Sancho runs up to the sheep that it will follow us around, delivery of the sheep to a pen is being saved for an exercise at the end of this chapter based upon our earlier design work with it. Also, make sure to add more sheep to your scene and ensure that we get the message displayed in the console window after we have successfully collected the specified number of sheep. If your sheep does not follow your Sancho around, double-check the following:

- Make sure the sheep is tagged as sheep.
- Make sure the tag we are looking for in the trigger event of Sancho is what the sheep is tagged as, double-check spelling and capitalization.
- Make sure the Is Trigger box is checked on the sheep's collider, we are using a box collider on ours.
- Make sure that the Every Frame check boxes are checked for both the Idle and Follow states inside of the sheep.
- Make sure that the Set FSM Bool and Set FSM Game Object actions are configured correctly from our list earlier.

8.5 Summary

We are now at the point where we have something that is playable and can be shown to other people. The player of our Sancho game can run around and collect sheep and return them to the pen in order to complete the first quest of the story line. We also introduced a system to enhance our level boundaries such that Sancho can be drowned by going too far into the water and respawn back at a point of our choosing. As can be seen from the examples that we constructed, implementing game mechanics within our games is no more complex than any of the programming work we have done up to this point. All it takes is for us to make sure we understand what we want to do through the design stage prior to trying to implement anything. Now that we see the importance of the mechanics in our games and not only the core mechanics but the balancing mechanics as well, we are now ready to begin putting some finishing touches on our game project. However, take some time to work through the exercises adding more mechanics and also take a stab at adding some of your own designs to the game as well. It is in the process of scripting for game mechanics that we will really stretch ourselves as programmers and as designers, both of which mean that we are stretching ourselves as game developers.

> **Download**
> You can find the final scene for this chapter in the complete project package on the companion website, the scene name is: "Chapter8_part2."

Vocabulary

Game mechanic
Core mechanic
Balancing mechanic
Story mechanic
Victory condition
Loss condition
System mechanic
Catch-up mechanic

Review Quiz

1. What is the difference between a core mechanic and a balancing mechanic?
2. Why are balancing mechanics added and tweaked during play testing of the game?
3. Why can't core game mechanics be protected by copyright law?
4. Why is it important for developers to play a wide variety of games?
5. Why is it best to have other people play test your game design?

Exercises

1. Play a game of your choice paying particular attention to the mechanics of the game. Write down the mechanics that are used in the game, specifically:
   a. What are the core mechanics?
   b. What, if any, are the balancing mechanics?
   c. What, if any, are the story mechanics?
   d. What, are the victory/loss conditions?
2. Given the additions to the project from this chapter, the player still has an infinite number of lives with which to play. Add a system to the game so that the player only has three lives and after the third life is lost the character does not respawn; double-check the discussion on the respawning system for hints on this one.
3. Create a system in which the player can go find the lost donkey, Dapple, and after finding the donkey it will follow the player around wherever they go.
4. Add the necessary pieces and state machines for the river system so that the player cannot run across the rivers instead of using the bridges.
5. Implement the system that will drop the sheep off into one of the pens once Sancho has brought them back to the pen.
   a. HINT: Knowing when to leave the sheep should be pretty straightforward, but where will you put the sheep? Think about the waypoints we used with the spider or even the respawn system of Sancho.

Design Document

In this addition to the Sancho Panza design document, we have added the logical components of some of the mechanics for our game as was discussed over the course of this chapter.

> **Download**
> Updated version of the Sancho Panza design document can be downloaded from the companion website: "DesignDocument_chapter8."

Consider your design document that you have been working on and add the following to it:

1. Create designs for the following elements of your game concept:
   a. Core mechanics, what are the basic rules of the game.
   b. System mechanics, how will the player interact with the game.
   c. Story mechanics, will there be any special rules needed to stitch the story into the game and make it a viable component of game play.
   d. Victory/loss conditions, how does the player win or lose the game, which should have been considered with the initial work on the design document.

SECTION III
Bringing It Together

CHAPTER 9

Audio

Audio is a surprisingly deceptive aspect of game production. It is easy to think that the audio will not take long at all to do and that we will not have any trouble getting the sounds and music that we want. However, there are copyright laws that we have to be very aware of while developing our games. In this chapter, we will not only look at how to use audio but also how to get audio as there are a wide range of sources that we can utilize. It is the audio that begins to bring the polish to our game projects and really consolidates the rest of the work into a unified setting. However, misuse of our audio can also be a major setback to the project as we lose the effect that we are trying to accomplish within the game. Audio is a ton of fun to play around with, and as we start adding these features into our game, the game seems to launch itself to a whole other level.

- How Is Audio Used in Games?
- Types of Audio
- Finding Audio
- Introduction to Editing Audio with Audacity
- Audio within Unity
- Accessing Audio through PlayMaker

9.1 How Audio Is Used in Games

Audio within video games essentially comes in three different varieties: music, ambience, and effects. While we will look at each individually, it is important to realize that they all work together to create a unified audio experience for the game player. The audio that we select for each use must be carefully considered in order to make sure that it blends with our other audio in the game, but also to make sure that it blends well with the story, theme, and environments that we have already constructed. While it is possible to break rules and expectations to get a desired response from the player, or just to keep the player on their toes, we need to know and understand those rules before we start breaking them. As a rough example, in our current project, Sancho is in a rather cheery, outdoorsy type of environment at the start of the game. Granted, all of the people have left and it is somewhat empty, but still there is no sense of ominous foreboding within the start of the game. Based on this, the music that we select to go with the start of the game should also have an open and somewhat lighthearted feel to it.

Unity can import the following audio formats for use as audio sources within our projects: aif, wav, mp3, and ogg. Unity will also support tracker modules, which are similar to MIDI files in that they can contain multiple instruments and scoring information, in the following formats: it, s3m, xm, and mod. Generally speaking, unless you have a leaning toward music and audio, you will only need the general audio formats that were first mentioned and will not need to worry about the Tracker modules, though it is nice to know that they are supported if and when you decide to advance your audio skills and knowledge. We will look at importing audio clips into our project later in this chapter.

9.1.1 Music

Music within video games serves the same purpose as the soundtrack does within a movie. With the music we can set the mood and feeling of a scene within a level. As the player explores the level that they are within, music can be utilized to build tension or to provide a soothing backdrop depending on the situation. We can approach these different situations with either looping or adaptive music. How music is used within a game is largely defined by the genre of the game as well. For instance, in exploratory or adventure style games, the player may be wandering a certain area for quite some time and as developers we have no control over when the player gets to a certain point in the level making these types of games more adapted to a score or instrumental type of music background. On the other hand, in a fighting game the very structure of the games is such that each level is a fight, making them more easily adapted to traditional vocal music tracks. Also, a racing game puts the player into a vehicle where we are used to a radio existing and the music being of the typical rock or pop variety and less of a movie soundtrack.

Looping music is an audio track that will play and then restart back at the beginning when it has finished continuously; you can think of this in the same way as having your favorite mp3 set on repeat in your player. The problem with using a looping music track for an entire level is that most musical scores have an inner personality, they have peaks and they have valleys. Each individual track of music is intended to provide the listener with a journey in some way. An example of looping music could be a nice country exploration track playing while Sancho is running through the forest looking for sheep, but then switching to something with a little more beat to it when he comes back into the town. One of the tracks can have a very open and natural feel, while the town track feels more busy and bustling and active. Both tracks can be played independently and they will loop as long as Sancho stays within the given environment.

Adaptive music, on the other hand, is intended to adjust to where and what the player is currently doing. It is music that will change as the player works through the environment. This is more than just switching to a different looping track of music, however. With the example from the looping music, we just switched our audio track to a different one, but with adaptive music the switch is smoother, using transition tracks to actually blend from the one to the other. Figure 9.1 depicts a rough diagram of the difference in these two approaches. Adaptive music does loop just as the looping music does; however, the individual pieces of the adaptive system will be shorter since we may need to transition to something else at any given moment.

Whether we select to utilize fixed looping or adaptive music is a decision that we need to make fairly early as it has a strong impact on the types of music that we need to either look for or create on our own. When it comes to creating our own music, if you are a musician (or know one) then the potential of creating your own musical scores for your games grows exponentially; however, if you are not a musician then you are limited to the music that others have created. Generally speaking, people very rarely release their music for use free of charge, so if we are searching for free music we will have to limit ourselves to the ones that come the closest to what we would like to have.

Another option, for those that are musically inclined but may not play instruments, is to look for and invest in some precomposed snippets of scores such as Pro Scores from Video Copilot (https://www.videocopilot.net/products/proscores). This provides a collection of music that can then be layered together in an audio editing program to create a musical composition of your choosing. This is a lot of fun to play around with, though it is definitely not a quick answer to creating a musical score for your game. Then again, when it comes to music within your game there really is no quick fix. Table 9.1 presents the types of music that we would like to find to throw into our project. When considering the music that you would like in your game, try to describe it as best you can; even if you are the only one that really "gets" what you are describing, you still need to put in the effort to think about and describe what you would like.

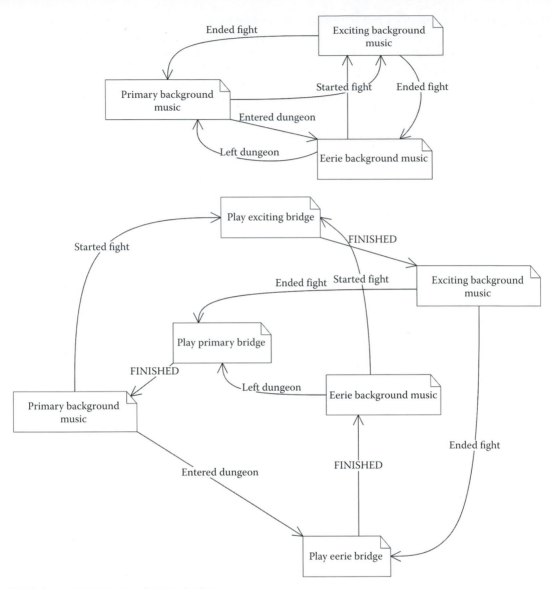

FIG 9.1 Looping music at top versus adaptive music at bottom.

9.1.2 Ambience

Ambience is the background noise of an environment. This is the sound of cars driving past your house, or the sounds of chickens clucking on a farm, or the sound of the ocean waves near the beach of Barataria. Without these ambient noises, our environment seems dead, we might see the water moving, but without the sound of the water moving we are missing a huge part of the experience. At first glance it seems as though the addition of the ambient sounds would not really make that much of a difference, however they bring the environment to life around

TABLE 9.1 The Different Types of Music for the Game

Location	Sound and Feeling
Main menu	Something light with an upbeat feel that gives the idea of an adventure, but not an ominous kind of thing.
Town	The town is empty and abandoned, something that is haunting but not eerie or spooky, just a feeling of emptiness and loneliness.
Surrounding pastures	The pastures are brightly lit and friendly places with lost animals, something upbeat and light that brings an open feeling.
Forest	The forest is a dense and hostile place with many spiders and skeletons and bad things, need something that heightens tension in this area to keep the player on edge.
Fighting	When in combat with a spider, the music needs to be fast and the action paced to work with the tension of the battle, but it should not be ominous as we want the player to win the fights.

the player. We need to be careful, however, that we do not bring in too much ambient noise and turn our environment into a cacophony of sound that assaults the player. For instance, we can have the sounds of crickets, birds, sheep bleating, rustling breeze, and donkeys braying as an ambient noise for our forest around the town. But if we keep adding to this, then it becomes way too noisy and the illusion of the environment that we are trying to create is destroyed. Also, with ambient sounds, they should not all play at one time or even play in the same order or in a specific pattern. It is best to have some basic looping track for the ambience, maybe the sound of a breeze blowing, and then to randomly insert extra sounds here and there. Another thing to consider with relation to ambient audio is how loud it is in comparison to where the player is within the level. The sound of the ocean should not necessarily be audible throughout the whole island but should be heard along the beach. At the same time, the sounds of creaking doors from the town should not be heard at the beach but should be heard within the town itself. When constructing ambient audio, we need to consider the different types of sounds that we might want to have within our environments as well as the different types of sounds that might exist in a similar real-world counterpart for our environment similar to Table 9.2.

TABLE 9.2 Potential List of Sounds to Use for an Ambient Audio System

Location	Types of Sounds
Rivers	Bubbling water, flowing river, birds, fish jumping
Beach	Surf, waves, breeze, seagulls
Town	Creaking shutters, breeze, creaking doors, scurrying mice
Forest	Mostly still to enhance the darkness of the forest
Pastures	Breeze, birds, animals

9.1.3 Sound Events

Sound events provide direct feedback to the user for various occurrences during game play. When the user hovers the mouse over a button or when the user clicks the button we can provide not only visual cues to the player (changing the color of the button for instance) but also audio cues for the player. Audio can also be applied to other distinct events within the game such as the sound of a footstep or the sound of a punch hitting a spider. All of these are used to not only bring those events to life but also to help notify the player of what is occurring within the video game. A simple example of this is the sound of tires squealing when going around a corner too fast in a racing game; this simple audio effect is informing the player that they need to be careful before they end up putting the car into the wall and having other bad things happen to them. While ambient sounds are tied to the environment and make audio that seems reasonable given the visual cues of the environment around the player, sound events are tied directly to the actions of the player giving the action a depth and meaning within the world. As a general rule nearly every event that the player can initiate while interacting with the game world should have some type of audio file associated with it as presented in Table 9.3.

9.2 Finding Audio

There are many places and methods for getting audio for your game project. However, taking your favorite band's CD and ripping the audio from it to use as background music is not a good option as that will lead to a copyright violation. While learning about game development we can get away with a lot of things because we are doing noncommercial or educational work. But, at some point we will want to transition over into doing commercial work and when we do so we will bring any bad habits that we have taught ourselves over into this commercial side of things. With this goal in mind, we are going to go ahead and approach our noncommercial project as though this were a game to be sold for profit and focus on obtaining legal audio that we can use. For this purpose, we will be using two primary sources for all of our audio: the Unity Asset store and the free sounds website at: freesound.org. As you continue to work on your own projects and to expand your own library of usable assets, keep in mind that you can record audio files using a microphone or even your cell phone and that you can also purchase very large and professional sound effect libraries from sources such as Sound Ideas (sound-ideas.com).

TABLE 9.3 Possible Sound Effects That We May Want

Footsteps—grass	Mooing cows	Sancho idles	Sheep are found
Footsteps—wood	Animal footsteps	Mouse over button	Donkey bray
Footsteps—rock	Hitting spider	Mouse clicks button	Donkey idle
Footsteps—leaves	Being bit by spider	Spider walks	Collection complete
Footsteps—water	Sancho dies	Spider charges	Sancho jumps
Bleating sheep	Sancho respawns	Sheep pen closes	

TABLE 9.4 List of Audio and Sources for Our Examples

Source	Audio	Use
Freesound.org	Nature → Sheep bleat outdoors By Yuval	Noise for our sheep
Freesound.org	River & Woods Ambience → Flowing river in the woods By CastleofSamples	Sound of a flowing river
Unity Asset Store	The Fantasy Music Collection (STARTER) By John Leonard French	Nice music tracks
Unity Asset Store	Authentic Early Medieval Ages Pack (FREE) By Marma	Time period music
Unity Asset Store	GUI Button SFX Pack C.R.Faith Music	Noises for the UI
Freesound.org	Footsteps_Grass.wav By kMoon	Walking on grass
Freesound.org	Footsteps → Fun with a water puddle By hintringer	Walking in water
Freesound.org	Stone Steps By Phil25	Walking on the stone in town
Freesound.org	GreenCouch Fieldrecordings → Beach Waves Medium.wav By GreenCouch	Sound of the surf
Unity Asset Store	EPIC ARSENAL—Essential Elements Free Epic Sounds and Effects	General UI and system sounds
Freesound.org	Bird Chirps By shw489	Interesting bird sounds
Freesound.org	Breeze.wav By keweldog	A breeze blowing

Just ensure that the creator of the audio you are using has licensed the work to you to use royalty free in your projects. Table 9.4 provides a detailed list of the audio that we will be using for our examples within this chapter.

Note
The Creative Commons License is one that generally gives you the right to use and alter files as you see fit even within a commercial context. Freesound.org has most of their audio files under this license, just double-check the license the developer has put their work under before making any assumptions.

Download
The audio files that the creators allowed to be redistributed have been included in a zip file in the resources section of the companion website: "audio.zip."

9.3 Introduction to Audacity

Many times when you find an audio file to use for a sound effect, the file will actually contain several different versions of the effect, for instance, the bleating sheep audio file from the last section. We would prefer to break these types of files up into individual audio files and to do this we can use a tool called Audacity. Audacity is a powerful and free sound editing tool that we can use to record, construct, and edit audio files. As far as recording, we can utilize Audacity to record any audio through a microphone. Another interesting option is to install an app on your smartphone that allows recording through it as well. Through either one of these approaches you can get a wide range of audio files that you have created and as a result can use however you want. An important thing to consider with audio is that we can use the same audio file for different sound effects. Audacity can be obtained from http://sourceforge.net/projects/audacity/, and Figure 9.2 displays the default user interface for this application.

The first section of Figure 9.2 depicts the control buttons that are used in order to play, pause, stop, skip forward/backward, and record audio. The space bar can also be used to play and pause rather than always having to move the mouse up to the control buttons in this section. Section 9.2 holds the modes that we can use to interact with our audio files once they are loaded within Audacity. We can use this to switch to mark mode to mark an in and out

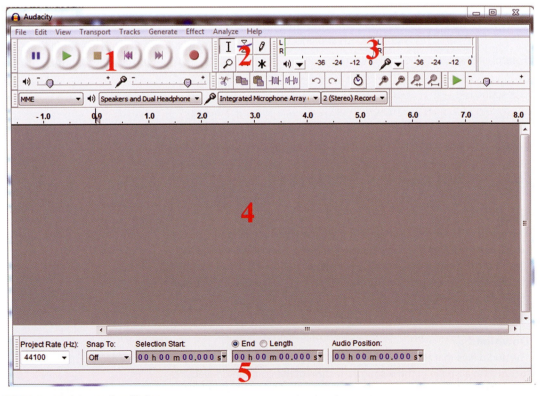

FIG 9.2 The default user interface of Audacity.

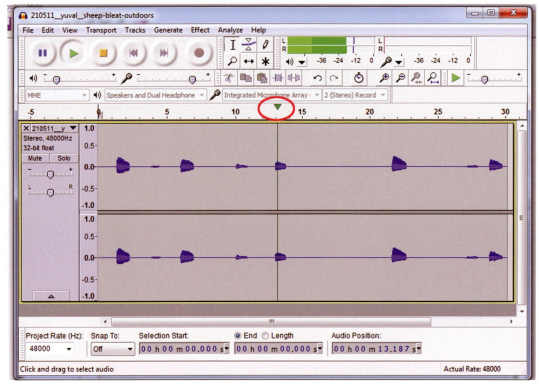

FIG 9.3 Audacity while playing an audio file, note the audio levels and the green play head.

location within the track; we will see this in our upcoming example, or we can switch to zoom mode to zoom in and out to get a better feel of the waveform. The third section contains graphical displays of the levels within the recording, with peak levels being marked by a blue line as can be seen in Figure 9.3. The fourth section is the waveform viewer which will depict our audio file in its waveform once we load one in. It is in this pane that we can directly work with the audio file utilizing the different modes from above. Finally, Section 5 is used to indicate the in and out times for our selections, shown in the first two time boxes, and the actual position of the green play head (see Figure 9.3 the play head is circled), shown in the third time box labeled "Audio Position."

9.3.1 Cutting Up an Audio File

We will now edit the bleating sheep file that we got earlier in order to have several different bleating sheep sounds that we can then randomly play at various times, think about the random animations that we worked with earlier in the book. We will begin by loading the bleating sheep file, either using File → Open or simply drag the file onto the Audacity editor pane. When you do so, you will get a warning message as shown in Figure 9.4. This message is essentially telling us that if we were to edit the original file and then save over that original file we could never go back to the original file and therefore Audacity believes it would be best if we saved a copy of the

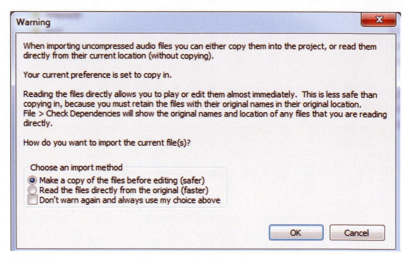

FIG 9.4 Warning message generated by Audacity when loading a file.

file and edited that instead of the original. While we have never run into any issues with Audacity and our audio files, it is always better safe than sorry when it comes to assets and the workflow pipeline for game development; as a result we will stay with that default recommendation of Audacity and after agreeing we will have an audio file ready to edit as can be seen in Figure 9.5.

Before we start editing the file too much, we will take a moment to see what we know about this file. We can tell that there are eight different bleating sheep sounds within this one audio file, see Figure 9.6 in case the eight sheep did not jump out when looking at the waveform. We can also see that this track is stereo, it has a left and a right audio channel. The left is the top waveform and the bottom waveform belongs to the right channel. It is not necessary that the left and right channels match identically as these two do, however. The controls to the left of the waveforms allow us to pan our audio, give more strength to one side over the other, as well as to increase or decrease the gain level of the audio file. When creating selection regions within Audacity, we can either use the mouse to click and drag a selection range or use the arrow keys while pressing the SHIFT key to create selection regions, see the video on using Audacity for more information. Once we have created a selection range within Audacity, playing the audio file will only play the region that has been selected; this can help us fine tune and tweak our selection ranges in conjunction with the zoom mode to get a close look at the boundary areas. Now that we have the very basics of the Audacity sound editor, we are ready to get to work and chop up this file.

Video
This chapter's folder on the companion website contains a video depicting a visual walkthrough of the Audacity user interface and some of its features and tools: "Using Audacity."

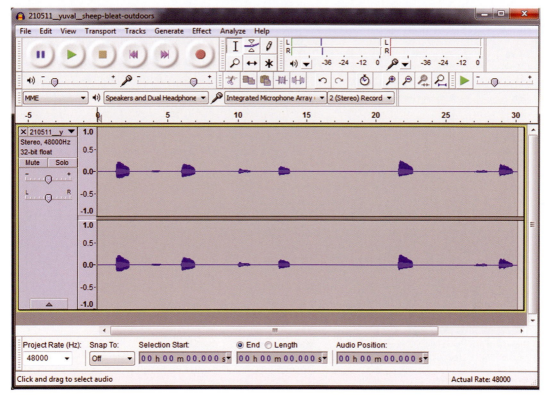

FIG 9.5 The Editor pane after loading an audio file.

1. Create a selection around the first of the bleating sheep noises in the editor, see Figure 9.7.
2. Select File → Export Selected Audio.
   a. Save the file as a WAV (Microsoft) signed 16 bit PCM, see Figure 9.8.
   b. Rename the file to sheep_bleat_01.
   c. Skip the Edit Metadata window by clicking OK when it opens.
3. Repeat this process for the remaining bleating sheep.

The process of exporting audio from one file and into another one is a pretty straightforward affair. A quick word of caution when doing this revolves around the selection stage when using the arrow keys. The arrows keys are oftentimes the easier approach to use when making selections; however, if your selection range extends beyond the audio that you are after pressing the opposite arrow key extends the other side of the range, it does not shrink the range back up as shown in Figure 9.9. When the range extends beyond the audio that we want, it is best to use the mouse to bring it back in and then tweak with the arrows if need be. The mouse cursor will change to a pointing finger when it nears the border of the range indicating that we can click and drag the boundary. With a little practice creating selections within Audacity will become second nature very quickly.

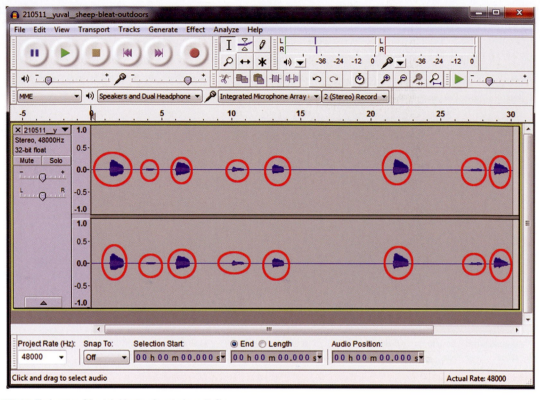

FIG 9.6 The location of the eight bleating sheep in the audio file.

> **Note**
> When using the arrow keys for selections in Audacity, the left arrow will always move the left border (starting border) to the left, and the right arrow will always move the right border (ending border) to the right.

9.3.2 Applying Effects to Audio

For our next example, we will look at some of the effects that are available within Audacity which will allow us to tweak and change audio more than just cutting sounds out of it. We are going to create the introductory narration audio file that was used in our chapter on story to introduce the backstory to the player at the start of the game. For this, one of my kids is going to read the narration while using a microphone to record the sound into Audacity, but you can download the original audio file from the companion website. Once we have the audio recorded, we can begin to play around with it. To create a recording, make sure to plug a microphone into your computer and click the red circle record button on Audacity. When finished, click the yellow square stop button to stop the recording. We recommend leaving a few seconds of silence at the start and end of any recording that you make.

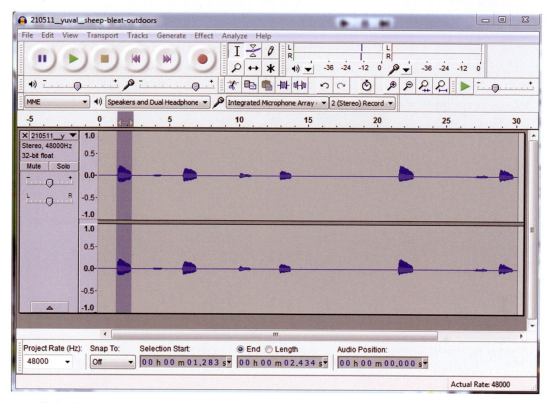

FIG 9.7 The first bleating sheep is selected within Audacity.

FIG 9.8 The Export Audio dialogue box in Audacity.

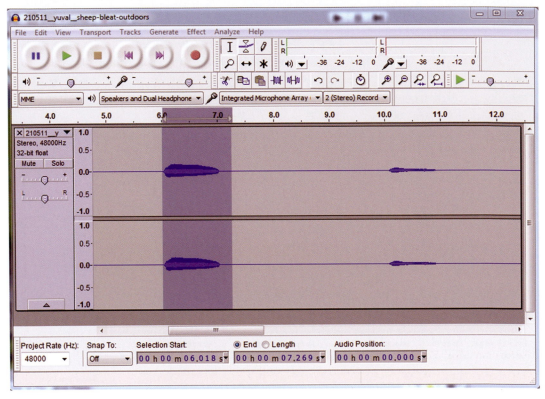

FIG 9.9 The selection range has extended past the desired audio.

Download
You can download the original audio recording of the introductory narration from the resources section on the companion website: "intro_narration_original.wav."

Note
While specialized microphones may be purchased, we use a standard cell phone headset with a microphone that is plugged into a splitter adapter to split the microphone and speaker signals before plugging into the computer—though there are many other solutions available.

1. Load the intro_narration_original file into Audacity.
2. Select the empty space at the beginning of the recording from 0.0 to 2.0.
3. Select Effect → Noise Removal.
   a. Click the Get Noise Profile button.
   b. Cancel the Noise Removal tool.
   c. Press CTRL-A to select the whole audio file.

d. Return to the Noise Removal tool.

e. Change Noise Reduction (dB) to 48.

f. Change Sensitivity (dB) to 5.

g. Click OK.

4. Select the opening of the audio file that was used for the Noise Profile and delete that section, we no longer need it.

5. Reselect the whole audio file and use Effect → Change Pitch.

a. Set Percent Change to −9, keep the other settings at default and click OK.

6. Select Effect → Compressor and keep the default settings, click OK to apply the effect.

7. Select Effect → Reverb.

a. Set Room Size (%) to 10.

b. Set Predelay (ms) to 1.

c. Set Reverberance (%) to 30.

d. Set Damping (%) to 30.

e. Leave other settings at default and click OK.

8. Select the section of blank audio at the end of the file and delete it.

9. Export the file as intro_narration_backstory.

After loading the audio file, our first step is to clean it up a little bit. It is very common for there to be some type of background noise or clicking sounds within a homemade recording. The Noise Removal tool is one approach to eliminating this, in our case we were specifically after getting rid of or at least minimizing the clicking sounds generated by the microphone hitting his shirt as he was recording the audio. Before we can remove noise, we must provide the tool with a sample of that background noise, which is the Noise Profile. While that sample does not directly contain the offensive clicks, it does provide the other ambient noises of the room that are helpful in cleaning up this recording.

The Change Pitch effect can be used to lower or raise the pitch of a recording, or section of a recording. In our case, we wanted to drop his voice down some and get closer to a movie kind of voice-over during the trailers of movies, particular the cheesy action movies of the 1980s. The more we drop the pitch, however, the more the voice seems to drag, so there is a balancing act to how far down we are willing to let it go.

After changing the pitch of the recording, we are going to bring in the compressor to give the audio a little more body and depth. The idea of the compressor is to be able to increase volume without having the audio start clipping. Audio clipping is created when the audio being played is at the maximum audio level that it can be; clipping is something that we want to avoid as it does not sound very good. Generally speaking, when it comes to increasing the volume of an audio we consider increasing the gain, but what that does is to raise all frequencies within the source the same amount and will usually introduce clipping. The compressor, on the other hand, will increase the frequencies by an average amount thereby avoiding the clipping but also giving the source a deeper presence, which was part of our goal on this one.

Our final step in this process is to add some room reverb to this file and give it a nice big feel to it. Reverb can be used to give a recording a more natural sound by simulating the way that audio behaves in different environments. This is to say that reverb governs how audio might echo and reflect off of different surfaces of the surrounding environment. For our purposes, we just wanted to get the reverb to give the recording a little more depth and also a presence with the soft echo behind it but did not want it to be too overpowering.

With our modifications done to the file, we can get rid of the slight excess at the end and go ahead and export it out. Of course, we already have the final exported version of the file in our project, anyway. After exporting the audio file back out, we have obtained the narration audio that was originally used earlier. There are many effects available within Audacity and are documented within the Audacity manual found at http://manual.audacityteam.org.

9.3.3 Adjusting Volume Levels

Before we leave this section, we will do one more very quick example of something that is a common need when dealing with audio in a video game, getting our audio sources to be of the same or similar volume levels. Consider the music folk tune found in the Authentic Medieval Ages Audio collection in comparison to the tracks Dangerous Dungeon and Tavern Lively found within the Fantasy Music Collection. The ones in the Fantasy Music Collection are louder than the Folk Tune. Since we will eventually be using these three tracks as part of our background music system, we will get them more balanced.

1. Select the Tavern Lively track in the Project view.
   a. Right-click on Tavern Lively and then select "Show in explorer." A new window will open with the file visible.
2. Open the Tavern Lively track within Audacity.
3. Select Effect → Amplify.
4. For Amplification set the value to –10 dB.
5. Export the file as Tavern Lively—Adjusted.
6. Repeat the process for the Dangerous Dungeon track.

9.4 Audio in Unity

The first step to using audio within Unity is to get it imported into our project. We have previously imported audio files into our project, but did not look at the properties that these Audio Clips have once they have been imported. We have already mentioned the audio formats that are supported by Unity and as long as our audio file is one of those formats we

FIG 9.10 The new folder structure for the Audio folder of our project.

will be able to work with it just fine. When an audio file has been imported into Unity it becomes an audio clip which can then be dropped into an Audio Source component to play the audio within a project. Before getting too far ahead of ourselves, we are going to go ahead and clean up our Audio folder within our project by embedding some new folders as shown in Figure 9.10. Audio, like any of the other assets, is going to become very confusing if we do not organize our files to make them easier to find within our project. After creating the folders, we have moved the music and UI sources (obtained from the Asset Store as listed earlier) into the appropriate folders and moved our introductory narration over to the Voices folder as well. We can go ahead and import our bleating sheep and other audio files at this point in time.

Figure 9.11 displays the Inspector window for an audio file that has been imported into Unity. The first check box allows the audio to be forced into a single channel of sound rather than dual channel stereo output. The next option will allow loading of an audio clip in the background, as opposed to the primary thread being used by the game within the CPU of the system. The default for this option is off as Unity prefers to load all audio clips before starting to play a level and this approach would be best to guarantee that we do not try to play an audio clip that has not yet loaded into memory. The final check box is to preload the audio data, which is the default setting, and indicates that this audio clip will be loaded up before the scene actually begins to play. If we have many large audio files in a scene, the loading of all of these files can be cause for delay on starting the scene. Following the check boxes, we are greeted with some drop-down selection menus that have been detailed in Table 9.5.

FIG 9.11 The properties of an Audio object imported into Unity.

An Audio Source component must be added to any object that we want audio to be produced by. We can even create an empty object and add an Audio Source to it, for instance, for ambient sound. This Audio Source is going to specify what audio file we want to play as well as provide some settings for the playback of the audio. While the Audio Source component is the source of the audio, or the speakers of the audio, within the game world, an Audio Listener component is the player's microphone, or ears, within the game world. There can be many different Audio Source components within a given scene; however, there can only be one Audio Listener component in the scene. The Audio Listener is what Unity uses to determine the effects of 3D audio while the player is moving around within the game world. As a general rule, the Audio Listener is added to the primary camera in the scene as that is both the player's eyes and a reasonable location to put the player's ears within the virtual world. An Audio Source component can play two types of audio in our games: 3D and 2D.

9.4.1 2D Audio

Download
You can find the starting scene for this chapter in the complete project package on the companion website, the scene name is: "Chapter9_part1."

TABLE 9.5 The Audio Clip Drop-Down Menu Selections

Option	Use
Load Type: Decompress on Load	The source audio is decompressed into memory as soon as it is loaded. Best used for small files to prevent the overhead of decompressing them during playback.
Load Type: Compressed in Memory	After the source is loaded into memory it will stay in its compressed format. Best used for larger files where the decompressed version would take up too much memory.
Load Type: Streaming	This approach will decode sounds while playing and will utilize the least amount of memory as the sources are not loaded until needed.
Compression Format: PCM	Highest quality of compression but will create larger file sizes so it would best be used by small sound effects.
Compression Format: Vorbis	This is the middle ground with files smaller than the PCM but larger than ADPCM. Similar impact to the quality of the audio as well.
Compression Format: ADPCM	Best used with small files that are played many, many times. Creates much smaller files and less CPU usage.
Sample Rate Setting: Preserve Sample Rate	Keeps the default sample rate of the audio source.
Sample Rate Setting: Optimize Sample Rate	This will optimize to the highest frequency that has been analyzed internally.
Sample Rate Setting: Override Sample Rate	This will override any default sample rate information from the source file.

As a simple example to explore these settings, we will go ahead and add an Audio Source component to the bridge that is crossing over the river and get our river ambient audio working, it may be necessary to disable any boundary systems that were created in the previous chapter if they are blocking our access to the bridge. 2D audio is the simpler of the two varieties, though it shares many of the same properties as the 3D audio, as shown in Figure 9.12. The AudioClip property is the actual audio that will be played by this Audio Source, by default it is blank. We can either specify an AudioClip directly within the Audio Source or we can specify an audio clip to play within our PlayMaker script, which we will do later. For the Output, we can either send the sound directly to an Audio Listener component, which is generally what we will want, or we can have it sent to an Audio Mixer and apply some effects to it similar to what we did in Audacity.

The Mute check box allows us to prevent a sound from being heard without stopping or pausing its playback. A potential example of this use would be if Sancho could stuff his ears with cotton while running around. When the ears are stuffed, then we could mute the audio but keep them playing so that whenever the player removes the cotton from Sancho's ears the audio becomes audible again from the point that it should be at. This would be very different than stopping and restarting the audio at the beginning or

FIG 9.12 The shared audio properties of 2D and 3D audio.

even pausing and then resuming the audio from the same location. The three bypass check boxes allow us to skip over any processing that might be done to audio files and instead send this Audio Source straight to its target without any in-game modifications to it. The final two check boxes allow us to have the audio automatically start playing when the object becomes active; this assumes that an AudioClip has been specified for the Audio Source otherwise there will be nothing to play. Then we can set the audio to be a looping audio, something very useful for ambient or music tracks.

The final section of settings allows us to alter the priority of the Audio Clip. Most games will have multiple sounds occurring at any one time and through this Priority slider, we can specify how important a particular audio is: 0 is most important and 256 would be the least important. Volume allows us to decrease the volume of the Audio Source; we say decrease because the volume cannot be increased above 1 which is the maximum volume level within the audio file itself. If you have an audio file that is too quiet within your game world and you need to get it louder, bring the audio file into Audacity and increase it within there with the available effects for what you need done. The only other setting that we need to concern ourselves with at the moment is the Spatial Blend setting. This one allows us to specify whether the audio source is a 2D or a 3D audio. 2D is best suited for game music or other types of audio that should be the same audio level through the entire scene. 3D, on the other hand, is best suited for ambient audio or sounds that should be heard differently depending on the location of the listener.

9.4.2 3D Audio

The difference between 3D and 2D audio is that 2D audio is the same throughout the whole level, whereas 3D audio behaves differently depending on where the listener is in relation to the Audio Source. Figure 9.13 displays the settings that are available for a 3D audio component. The Doppler Level defines how much of a Doppler effect to apply to the audio source, a value of 0 would indicate no effect. Doppler effect governs the way that sound behaves as we move closer or further away from it, generally at a high velocity. As the listener moves in relation to the source, the wave of the audio becomes either longer or shorter which in turn impacts the pitch of the audio itself.

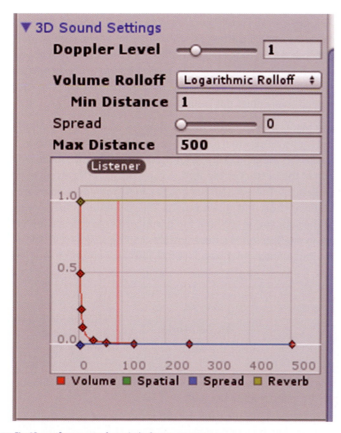

FIG 9.13 The 3D specific properties for an Audio Source component.

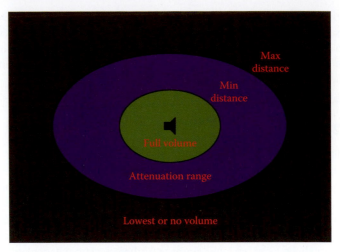

FIG 9.14 Graphical representation of attenuation of an audio signal.

The min and max distance properties are used to control the radius of a circle around the source of the audio that governs the attenuation of the signal as shown in Figure 9.14. Attenuation refers to the decay of the signal. If the listener is closer than min distance to the source then the audio will be at full volume. As the listener moves away from the source, the audio will gradually decay while the listener is still within the attenuation range. Once the listener has gotten to the max distance from the source then there is no more attenuation of the signal and it will continue to play at whatever volume it would have dropped down to by the time the max distance has been reached, many times this volume setting is 0.

The Volume Rolloff drop-down menu allows us to select a default algorithm for how the audio attenuates. The options that we have available are described in Table 9.6 and graphically shown in Figure 9.15. The graph at the bottom of the settings also displays the attenuation of the source signal. The curve of the graph can be manipulated manually by grabbing anchors and moving them. This allows us to specify how the falloff of the audio occurs. Within the graph we can also see where the listener is in relation to the source and this can be very beneficial when we are trying to fine tune the audio of various aspects within our level,

TABLE 9.6 The Volume Falloff Algorithms Available in Unity

Volume Rolloff	How It Works
Logarithmic	Very loud when close, however, the audio very rapidly drops in volume level becoming too quiet to hear in a short distance traveled from the source.
Linear	The drop off in volume occurs at a constant and smooth rate. It stays louder longer than does the logarithmic falloff.
Custom	Starts with a default ease-in and ease-out type of tangent for the audio volumes and can then be modified to best fit the needs.

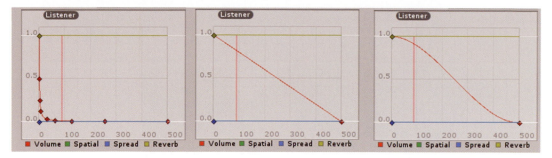

FIG 9.15 The three different falloff algorithms: Logarithmic, Linear, and Custom.

especially dealing with ambient noises. Many times, we may start with one of the default falloff algorithms and then manually tweak it to get exactly what we want.

9.4.3 Playing Ambient Audio

We are going to create an ambient audio track for our river system utilizing the Audio Source component that was just added to the bridge to finalize the concepts of the 3D audio source. Our goal here is to have the river sounds when we are on the bridge be their loudest but for the audio to fade as we move away from the bridge. We should be able to hear the river when we are close to the bridge but it should not be as loud as if we were standing on the bridge directly above the river, although if we are at the start of the bridge it should be fairly loud as well.

1. Add the river ambient sound downloaded earlier to the AudioClip property of the Audio Source.
2. Leave Play an Awake checked and check Loop.
3. Set the Spatial Blend to 3D (1).
4. Set the Volume Rolloff to Linear Rolloff.
5. Set the Max Distance to 50.
6. Play the game to test these starting settings and run Sancho toward the bridge.
7. Note Figure 9.16:
   a. The blue circle in the Scene view shows the max distance of the audio.
   b. The falloff graph shows that Sancho is currently standing close to 30 units from the source (he is the black smudge immediately to the left of the green arrow head in the Scene view).
   c. Try rotating the character from left to right, notice how the audio shifts from right to left speaker as needed. Now run onto the bridge and note the same effect, why is this happening and should it happen?
   d. Move toward the edge of the bridge, how far away from the source is the listener at that point?

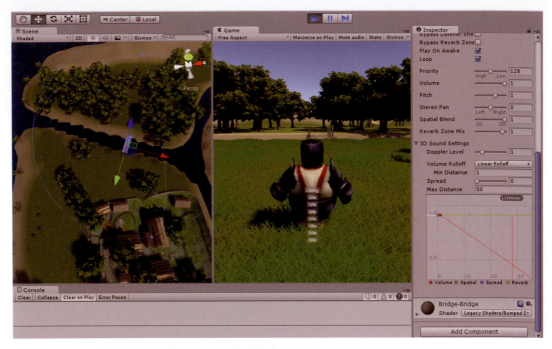

FIG 9.16 Sancho has neared the river and the Scene view shows the Audio Source's range.

Our ambient audio is working, though we came out of the play test with a couple of questions to consider as we tweak this to get it the way we really want it to be. The first thing that we notice is that even with a simple audio like this, our level feels so much better already. Onto the questions that we posed, we will begin with the last, as can be seen in Figure 9.17, the edge of the bridge is roughly 10 units from the Audio Source. We need to know this because it seems reasonable that the sound of the river really should be just as loud if we are standing immediately on the edge of it as if we were standing directly over the middle of it, there really should not be any attenuation at the edge of the river. But if we notice the graph shown in Figure 9.17, the volume has already attenuated at this point to roughly 75% of the original volume level, this is not so good for us. To fix this we will shift the Min Distance from 1 to 10 by changing the value of Min Distance. We could also do this by grabbing the red diamond that indicates the min distance inside of the graph and move it around to wherever we want. Figure 9.18 shows how this diamond has moved with the change of the Min Distance value.

> **Note**
> When adjusting the falloff curves, linear can only adjust the min and max values, the rest cannot be adjusted because by definition the falloff forms a straight line from the min to the max value.

FIG 9.17 Sancho standing at the edge of the bridge.

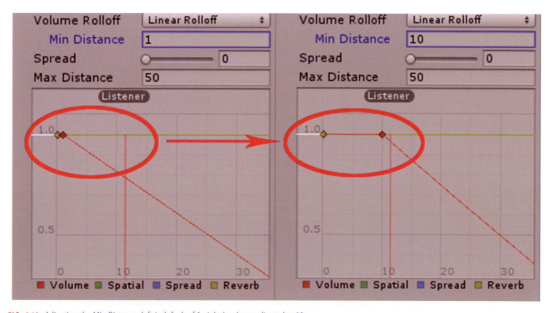

FIG 9.18 Adjusting the Min Distance, left is default of 1, right has been adjusted to 10.

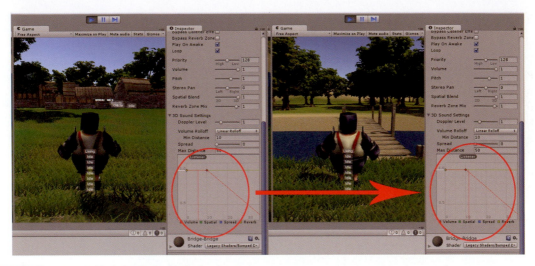

FIG 9.19 The movement of the Audio Listener when Sancho rotates.

We will now return to the first question that we considered when putting this together. The audio seemed to be rotating more than it should when we had Sancho standing on the bridge. If we consider this, regardless of which way Sancho turns, he should be completely surrounded by the audio of the river. While this has been partly cleared up by moving the min distance out further, hopefully you noticed something very interesting during your play test. Namely, once Sancho was on the bridge and we started to rotate Sancho, or for that matter wherever Sancho is, did you notice that the distance the Listener was from the Source kept changing within the graph (this is shown in Figure 9.19)? But if Sancho is not moving closer to or further away from the source, then why was this occurring? The answer to this riddle is found in the position of the Audio Listener component. Currently, it is stored within the Main Camera that is a child of Sancho. When Sancho rotates, the camera moves as well to maintain the same perspective on the character, this was part of the character controller system that we constructed. However, the Audio Listener should not be moving like that, rather, we should move the Audio Listener component onto Sancho to eliminate that odd fluctuation that we were getting while standing on the bridge. We have now analyzed our simple play test of the river's ambient audio system and are ready to make the fixes that we have discovered and try it again.

1. Stop the game.
2. Change the Min Distance value from 1 to 10.
3. Select the Main Camera object within Sancho and remove the Audio Listener component.
4. Select Sancho and add an Audio Listener component.
5. Click the Apply button at the top of the Sancho instance to apply these changes to the Sancho prefab object as well.
6. Test again, notice that rotating does not change the distance of the Listener from the Source.

9.4.4 Playing Background Music

Now that we have some ambient audio playing for our river, we are going to put in a background music track for our level as well. When we get into PlayMaker we will take a look at how we can change the music track that is playing within a state machine, but for now we will go ahead and set a basic track to play for the whole level. Make sure that the music packs from the Unity Asset Store in Table 9.4 have been downloaded and imported into your project; they should have already been moved into the Music folder within the project's Audio folder. We have many options to select from for our pasture/exploration music track; we are going to go with the Folk Tune found within the Authentic Medieval Ages Audio collection that was obtained from the Asset Store.

- Add a new 3D Object → Cube to the scene.
  - Name it Music and attach it to the Sancho object.
  - Change the position of the Music object to 0, 0, 0, if it is not already.
  - Disable the Mesh Renderer component.
- Add an Audio Source component.
  - Put folk tune into the AudioClip property.
  - Set Spatial Blend to 2D (0).
  - Set the Priority to 0.
  - Set Loop to checked.
  - Change the Volume level to 0.3.
- Play and test.

Now, when we run the game we have a nice background track playing that matches our goals for the background music of the pasture area. When you do play test, make sure to run over by the river and double-check the sound levels, this music file is much louder than the river so we can either adjust them in Audacity (as we did with the music tracks earlier) or we can just lower the volume of the music here within the Audio Source. You want to make sure that the music does not overpower the ambience and that the ambience does not overpower the music, they should blend well together. Our approach of lowering the volume level is working very well at the moment, but we do need to be aware of the potential issues that can arise by relying on adjusting volumes rather than setting all audio to same volume levels.

9.5 Using PlayMaker to Play Audio

As we have just seen, we can create quite of bit of noise within our games without having to do any scripting of any kind. However, as we have also seen, we can only go so far before we will have to develop some behaviors with scripting, or in our case state machines inside of PlayMaker. We are going to explore three different types of systems which will be remarkably similar. As we are nearing the end of our exploration of Unity and PlayMaker, we are

FIG 9.20 Logical structure of audio systems within PlayMaker.

beginning to notice there is a tremendous amount of interactivity we can create with essentially reusable actions or at the very least reusable logic but different sets of actions themselves. All three of our examples will share the basic logical structure, as can be seen in Figure 9.20, the differences will be found in how we will trigger the events and where we will be placing the state machines. Once these examples are understood, we can construct nearly any audio response system we want within our games.

9.5.1 Background Music

We will modify our background music system so that different tracks will be played in different locations; Table 9.7 presents our layout for this. The idea behind this will be to create trigger areas that when the player enters into those regions the Audio Clip that is being played by the Music object will change to the appropriate audio file. To make this system easier to manage and expand into other levels, we will also create Inspector level variables to store the Audio Clips, that way we can easily change and assign the appropriate audio at the Inspector level rather than having to return to the state machine to make any changes.

1. Add a trigger region for the town.
    a. Create a 3D Object → Cube.
        i.   Rename the Cube to Town Trigger.
        ii. Give the object a Tag of Town (will have to create a new tag).
        iii. Position it on the town and resize it to cover the town, see Figure 9.21.
        iv. Disable the Mesh Renderer.
        v.   Switch the Box Collider to a Trigger (turn Is Trigger on).

TABLE 9.7 The Different Music and Their Trigger Zones

Music Title	Region
Tavern Lively—Adjusted The Fantasy Music Collection	Default background music, to be played when exploring the pasture or beach areas.
Folk Tune Authentic Medieval Ages Audio	Plays while the player is within the town on the island.
Dangerous Dungeon—Adjusted The Fantasy Music Collection	To be played when the player crosses over the bridge and enters into the forested area.

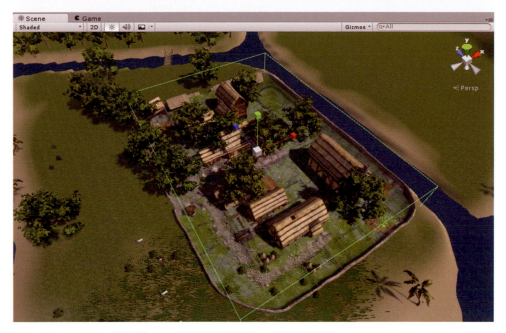

FIG 9.21 The trigger region for the town on the island.

2. Select the Music object attached to Sancho.
   a. Change the default AudioClip to none.
   b. Add a Rigid Body component (Physics → Rigid Body).
      i. Turn off Use Gravity.
      ii. Turn on Is Kinematic.
   c. Open the PlayMaker editor and add an FSM named Music Controller.
      i. Add the variables and events listed in Table 9.8; make sure all the variables are set to be Inspector level variables.
      ii. Change State 1 to Exploration.
      iii. Add a state named Mournful.
      iv. Select the Exploration state.
         A. Add the Play Mournful event and connect it to the Mournful state.
         B. Add a Set Audio Clip action.
            I. Audio Clip should be exploration.
         C. Add an Audio Play action.
            I. Set Volume to the volumeLevel variable.
         D. Add a Trigger Event action.
            I. Collide Tag should be Town.
            II. Send Event should be Play Mournful.
         E. Add a Trigger Event action.
            I. Collide Tag should be Forest.
            II. Send Event should be Play Exciting.

TABLE 9.8 The Events and Variables for the Music Controller State Machine

Events	Variables and Types
Play Exploration	exploration → Object → Unity Engine → AudioClip
Play Exciting	exciting → Object → Unity Engine → AudioClip
Play Mournful	mournful → Object → Unity Engine → AudioClip
	volumeLevel → Float

    v. Select Mournful state.
        A. Add the Play Exploration event and connect it to the Exploration state.
        B. Add a Set Audio Clip action.
            I. Audio Clip should be mournful.
        C. Add an Audio Play action.
            I. Set Volume to the volumeLevel variable.
        D. Add a Trigger Event action.
            I. Trigger should be On Trigger Exit.
           II. Collide Tag should be Town.
          III. Send Event should be Play Exploration.
          IV. Close the PlayMaker editor and set the Inspector variables for the Music object as shown in Figure 9.22.

Note
When adding variables of type Object, remember that we set the type of Object it is after the variable has been added to the list.

Notice that with the new music controller system we have built one of the first things to do was to remove the music being played automatically so that we could have the state machine govern what would be played and when to play it. It was also necessary for us to add the Rigid Body component to our Music object in order for the system to recognize when a collision, or in this case trigger, event occurs and send such an event to the object for processing. Other than that, the controller system utilizes two of PlayMaker's audio actions: Set Audio Clip and Audio Play.

At first glance, it would seem as though we could use the Audio Play action all by itself, but the One Shot Clip property defines which Audio Clip to play one time. Once the Audio Clip defined by One Shot Clip is finished playing, it does not loop back to the beginning regardless of what the Audio Source components are set for. Now, we could force it to restart by using the FINISHED Event property to call an event that loops back to this state to restart the music. However, the issue with that approach is twofold. On the one hand, it is a rather cumbersome and ugly approach to getting it to work. On the other hand, it will introduce another event and transition into our state machine and will not

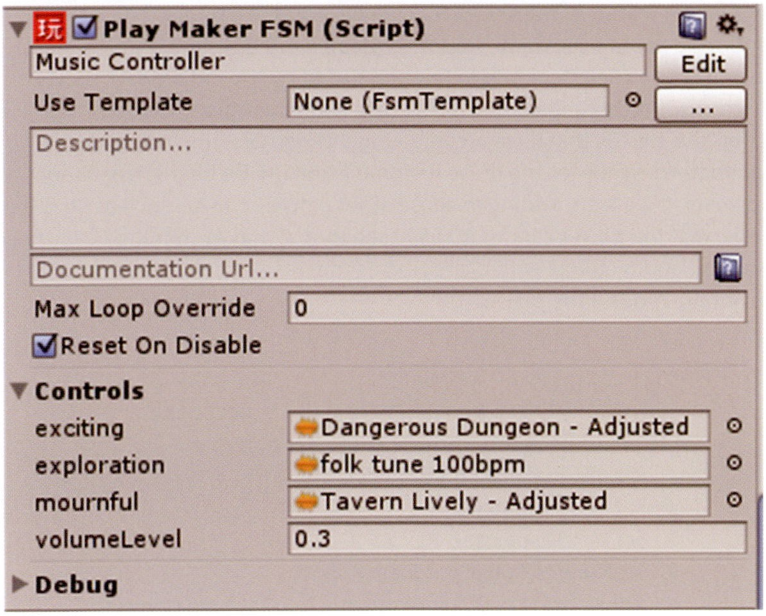

FIG 9.22 The Inspector variable settings for the Music object.

decrease the number of actions we need to use. The reason the action number would stay the same is that we would have to add an Audio Stop action to each state to stop any currently playing audio before starting up a new one. So, in the situation of transitions to a new region, the old music will continue to play with the new music playing at the same time, unless that Audio Stop action is used to stop the old music before starting the new music. Another potential solution to the problem would have been to use the Set Audio Loop action, but we still would have had to have the Audio Stop action anyway.

The Set Audio Clip property is used to define the AudioClip that is used by the Audio Source component. This is different from the One Shot Clip in that we can now still use the Looping property that is established as part of the Audio Source component so that the music will cleanly loop without any other processing overhead by our controller state machine. Another advantage here is that we will not need to worry about stopping the playing music because the music is running off of the Audio Source component properties more directly and once we change the Audio Clip that is within that Audio Source it can no longer play the music. The One Shot Clip property of the Audio Play action is best used for sound effects or other short audio things as we will discover in our next example.

9.5.2 Ambient Sounds

We have already seen one style of ambient sound system in the one that we constructed for the rivers. However, ambient sounds can also be applied to an object within the game world as opposed to the whole region. For instance, the sheep that we have put out into our game world, we could have them randomly bleat every now and then creating an ambient noise effect, but being generated by the individual objects themselves rather than being generated within a region. The real difference here is that if we are injecting a sheep bleating noise, then it would make sense for the noise to come from and be heard near sheep. However, if we were adding in some other ambient noise, such as chirping birds, that the player cannot actually see then it makes sense to keep those ambient audio effects within a region as the unseen noise makers could be anywhere around the player.

1. Select the Fluffy Sheep prefab object in the Project pane.
   a. Add an Audio Source component to the object.
      i. Set the Spatial Blend to 1 (3D).
      ii. Set Min Distance to 0.
      iii. Set Max Distance to 10.
      iv. Set Volume Rolloff to Linear Rolloff.
      v. Adjust the Max Distance until the blue sphere covers the region as well as possible, keep in mind that at the areas that will play other audio and therefore not need to be covered, our setting is 45 and is shown in Figure 9.23.
2. Open the PlayMaker editor and create a new FSM named Bleating.
   a. Create the events and variables listed in Table 9.9.
      i. For the sounds array set the size to eight and insert the bleating sheep audio files created earlier into their slots, see Figure 9.23.
   b. Change State 1 to Check and add a Play Something state and a Pause state.
   c. Select the Check state.
      i. Add the Go Play event and connect it to Play Something.
      ii. Add the Go Wait event and connect it to Pause.
      iii. Add a Random Float action.
         A. Store Result should be num.
      iv. Add a Float Compare action.
         A. Float 1 should be num.
         B. Float 2 should be 0.4.
         C. Equal should be Go Wait.
         D. Less Than should be Go Play.
         E. Greater Than should be Go Wait.
   d. Select the Pause state.
      i. Add a FINISHED event and connect it to Check.
      ii. Add a Random Wait action.
         A. Min should be 1.
         B. Max should be 5.
         C. Real Time should be checked.

e. Select the Play Something state.
    i. Add a FINISHED event and connect it to Check.
    ii. Add an Array Get Random action.
        A. Array should be sounds.
        B. Store Value should be playSound.
    iii. Add an Audio Play action.
        A. One Shot Clip should be playSound.

This system is working by picking a random number between 0 and 1 and then comparing that random value to some arbitrary value that we have selected, currently this is 0.4. The higher this value the more often we will get sheep noises and the lower the value the less often. The interesting thing about this random component of the system is the addition of the

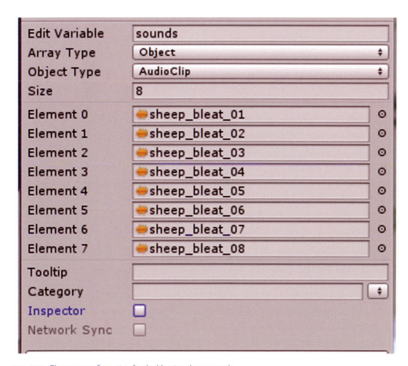

FIG 9.23 The array configuration for the bleating sheep sounds.

TABLE 9.9 The Events and Variables for the Bleating of the Sheep

Events	Variables and Types
Go Play	playSound → Object → Unity Engine → AudioClip
Go Wait	sounds → Array → Object → Unity Engine → AudioClip
	num → Float

Pause state. This is done to prevent a max loop count error from occurring. Remember, things inside the game are running at frames not at a real-time system. What this means is that if the check for a random number failed then on the next frame it would loop back and do it again. You can see that if our threshold value, the 0.4 in this example, is low enough then it is going to take a while before we trigger a transition, at least awhile in terms of frames but not in terms of human time. So to sidestep this checking every frame we have introduced the Pause state. If the check for a random value fails then we go to the Pause state and sit there for a random real-time amount of seconds before trying to pass our play sound test again.

Once the test is passed and control is handed off to the Play Something state, we reach into the array of Audio Clips that we have and pick one of them at random, any one it does not matter which one. After selecting that random Audio Clip, we assign it to our temporary playSound variable. Currently, PlayMaker does not allow us to drop the array item directly into an Audio Play action even though the array is an Audio Clip data type, this has to do with how PlayMaker is handling arrays internally and really does not concern us other than to recognize that we will have to drop that randomly selected Audio Clip from within the array into a single variable of type Audio Clip for everything to play well together and work as it should. This same random construction could be added to the river to introduce some random splashes or frogs or whatever we would like, with one caveat. The random system will have to be added to its own empty object with its own Audio Source component and then attached to the river ambient audio object. This is because the way that the system recognizes when an Audio Clip has finished playing, that is, how to get out of the Play Something state, is to look at the Audio Component and see if it is still playing. On the river ambient system it will still be playing that looping river sound we put on it and as a result the Play Something state will never directly finish.

9.5.3 Effects for Events

We are going to create a couple of different event audio setups from which we can then derive any type of audio event that we may want in the future. The first example will be some kind of audio to go with the collisions of the rotating checkpoints to indicate to the player that the system knows they just hit the checkpoint. The other example will be some footsteps for Sancho as he runs around the world. We will begin with the checkpoint system, when Sancho collides with the checkpoint we want to play an audio clip.

1. Select the Checkpoints state machine within Sancho.
   a. Add a checkpointAudio variable of type AudioClip to it, make the variable Inspector level.
   b. Add a volumeLevel variable of type Float and make it Inspector level.

As can be seen in the example, adding sound effects to events within a game is a very straightforward process using actions that we have already used before. It is also important to note that we do not, generally speaking, need to add any more states or events to our state machine. Usually, the logic is already in place for handling the collisions and doing something as a result of the collision all we need to do is to drop in an Audio Play action with the settings we would like to use within the appropriate state and we have added audio to it.

Our next example, however, is going to involve a little bit of construction on our part. We are going to combine what we learned when we created the music controller system with what we now know as a result of our sound events and ambient systems to create a footstep system for Sancho. We have two approaches on how we can construct a footstep system, as shown in Figure 9.24. The collision-based system makes more sense and seems to be a more reasonable approach to generating these footsteps; however, we need to ask ourselves if we really need the system to be doing extra collision detection for our audio. Ultimately, this is going to come down to the degree of exactness that your game project requires as getting the timing perfect can be very difficult. We have already created two footstep sound files that can be used for this example; they were derived from the footstep audio files listed earlier and then edited within Audacity to get just one sound

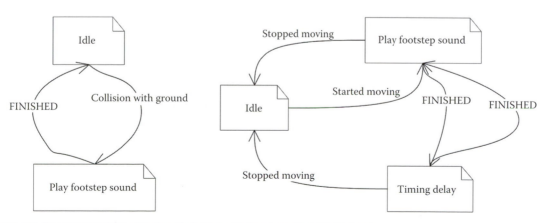

FIG 9.24 The system on the left is collision based for footsteps while the system on the right is time based.

from each. We could expand this by getting the other footstep sounds from the original file and then playing a random footstep noise each time.

Download
The footstep audio files used in the following example can be obtained from this chapter's folder on the companion website: "example_footsteps.zip."

1. Select the Sancho prefab object in the Project pane.
   a. Add a new FSM to it named Footsteps.
   b. Add the events and variables defined in Table 9.10.
      i. For the time variable give it a default value of 0.27 and make it Inspector visible so that you can edit it during runtime to get a smooth timing.
      ii. At the moment set the sound variable to be footstep_grass_01 from the audio files downloaded earlier from the companion website.
   c. Change State 1 to Standing Still and add a state named Walking and another state named Pause.
   d. Select the Standing Still state.
      i. Add a Go Move transition and connect it to the Walking state.
      ii. Add a Get FSM Float action.
         A. FSM Name should be Movement.
         B. Variable Name should be speed.
         C. Every Frame should be checked.
      iii. Add a Float Compare action.
         A. Float 1 should be speed.
         B. Float 2 should be 0.05 (roughly).
         C. Greater Than should be Go Move.
         D. Every Frame should be checked.
   e. Select the Walking state.
      i. Add a Stop Moving event and connect it to the Standing Still state.
      ii. Add a FINISHED event and connect it to the Pause state.
      iii. Add a Get FSM Float action.
         A. FSM Name should be Movement.
         B. Variable Name should be speed.
         C. Every Frame should NOT be checked.
      iv. Add a Float Compare action.
         A. Float 1 should be speed.
         B. Float 2 should be 0.05 (roughly).
         C. Less Than should be Stop Moving.
         D. Every Frame should NOT be checked.
      v. Add an Audio Play action.
         A. Volume should be 0.2 (roughly).
         B. One Shot Clip should be sound.

TABLE 9.10 The Events and Variables needed for the Timed Foostep FSM

Events	Variables and Types
Go Move	sound → Object → Unity Engine → AudioClip
Stop Moving	delay → Float
	speed → Float

<blockquote>

    f. Select the Pause state.

        i. Add a Stop Moving event and connect it to the Standing Still state.

       ii. Add a FINISHED event and connect it to the Walking state.

     iii. Add a Get FSM Float action.

          A. FSM Name should be Movement.

          B. Variable Name should be speed.

          C. Every Frame should NOT be checked.

     iv. Add a Float Compare action.

          A. Float 1 should be speed.

          B. Float 2 should be 0.05 (roughly).

          C. Less Than should be Stop Moving.

          D. Every Frame should NOT be checked.

      v. Add a Wait action.

          A. Time should be delay.

          B. Real Time should be checked.

</blockquote>

This system works by playing an Audio Clip, the grass footsteps one, whenever the player is moving. We can determine if the player is moving or not by looking at the value of the moveSpeed variable that is within the Movement state machine and is derived from the magnitude of the movement vector we were able to get from the Vertical input axis. Since we know that we are moving, we can go ahead and play our footstep sound effect then pause before playing it again. As it turns out 0.27 seconds of delay works out fairly well for the way that Sancho is moving on our test machine, your value may need to be tweaked depending on the movement velocity that you may have Sancho set for. This is a fairly simple system to construct and understand how it works without adding another collision detection for the processor to have to be calculating every frame and potentially slowing things down. Admittedly the collision detection overhead on this particular game would be negligible, but it is still a good idea to consider these things anyway. The only thing left for this system is to have it change footstep sounds based upon where the player is.

<blockquote>

1. Select the Music object attached to the Sancho prefab in the Project pane.

    a. Add the following variables to the Music Controller FSM:

        i. grass_footstep → Object → Unity Engine → Audio Clip.

          A. Default value of footstep_grass_01.

</blockquote>

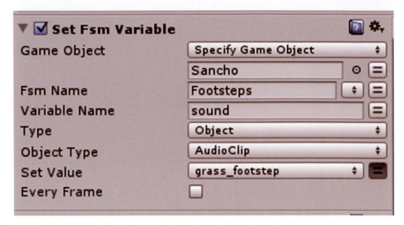

> ii. stone_footstep → Object → Unity Engine → Audio Clip.
>   A. Default value of footstep_stone_01.
> b. Select the Exploration state.
>   i. Add a Set FSM Variable action and see Figure 9.25 for the settings, note that the Variable Name will need to be typed in so make sure it is spelled and capitalized the same as the variable name that you used in the Footsteps state machine. Also, drag Sancho from the Project pane onto the line for Sancho under Specify Game Object.
> c. Select the Mournful state.
>   i. Repeat the process with the Set FSM Variable action but this time use stone_footstep for the Set Value property.

Our footstep system can be expanded to incorporate any other audio zone that we might decide to add, or for that matter our Music Controller could be renamed to be Sound Zone Controller and then we can add an ocean region to it that will only alter the Footsteps variable value without changing the background music that is being played.

9.6 Summary

In this chapter, we looked at how Unity plays audio files and how we can get these audio files to play when we want through the use of PlayMaker. Adding the ability to play audio and music to our game has turned out to be a fairly simple process, once we were able to find the audio files that we wanted to use. We were also able to randomize some audio elements. As mentioned at the beginning of this chapter, audio is oftentimes overlooked by developers as something that will be easy to do later, but it is often more time consuming than we had planned, as finding the perfect sound for a specific use in our project is not as straightforward as we had hoped. When it comes to audio, always remember that most of your time will be spent trying to find the audio sources that you would like to use and then getting them prepped for use in your game. Setting up the behavior scripts for the audio to respond to various in-game events generally does not take too long, although getting the 3D properties just right can take a fair amount of tweaking. However, now that we have added audio to our project and have gotten it tweaked into our environment and game events, the world of Barataria is really beginning to come alive and is developing a feeling for itself.

Download
You can find the final scene for this chapter in the complete project package on the companion website, the scene name is: "Chapter9_part2."

Vocabulary

Tracker module
Looping music
Adaptive music
Ambient audio
Sound effects
Creative commons license
Play head
Reverb
Pitch
Gain
Clipping
Amplify
Audio Clip
Audio Source
Audio Listener
2D Audio
3D Audio
Doppler effect
Linear rolloff
Logarithmic rolloff
Attenuation

Review Quiz

1. What audio formats does Unity support?
2. What is the challenge with using adaptive music in your game projects?
3. What is Audacity used for?

4. Why does Unity only allow one Audio Listener in a scene?
5. What are the three volume rolloffs supported by Unity?
6. What is the purpose of the Min and Max Distance properties with 3D audio?
7. Which PlayMaker action can be used to play an Audio Clip?
8. Which PlayMaker action can be used to stop an Audio Source that is playing?
9. Which Play Maker action can be used to change the AudioClip property of an attached Audio Source component?

Exercises

1. Try to find some other sources for audio than those that were mentioned in the chapter, what are the advantages and disadvantages of the new sources you have found?
2. Finish the Music Controller system by adding a trigger region for the bridge and forest area and get it working with the system that was already created for the town.
3. Using the provided water footstep file, create a region in the ocean that the player gets watery footsteps instead of the pasture ones.
   a. HINT: Use the Music Controller as hinted at in the last section of the chapter and maybe switch based on a collision with the water object, we do not need to worry about transitioning to any of the other sound zones when we are colliding with the water in the ocean, why?
4. Find an audio file to use to alert the player of when they have collected a sheep and get that sound working in the game.
5. Add an audio file for when Sancho swings his fist and also when he bonks with his belly.
6. Add an audio file for when Sancho jumps.
7. Bring a spider into the level and put him on the bridge. Disable his patrolling behavior. Add Sound for the spider's actions of noticing Sancho, attacking Sancho, and being killed by Sancho. Likewise, add noise to Sancho for when he gets hit by the spider, when he gets killed, and when he respawns.

Design Document

In this addition to the Sancho Panza design document, we have detailed the audio files that we will need, or would like to have, within the game project. We have also specified what would cause the audio to play as well as where certain audio regions would exist within the game world.

Consider your design document that you have been working on thus far and add the following to it:

1. Describe the type of music that you would like to incorporate into your game project and the various regions you would want the music playing. Pay special attention to the mood and feeling that you are trying to get across. At this point it is OK to list real songs to help other people understand the sound that you are looking for in your music.
2. Create a list of sound event effects that you may need in your game project. It is better to have too many than not enough. Consider the following:
   a. What actions can the player perform?
   b. What UI elements will be in the game?
   c. What other characters are in the game and what can they do?
3. Create a list of audio that you would like to be able to incorporate as an ambient audio system, consider the various regions and levels of your game and what you would like those areas to sound like.

CHAPTER 10

The User Interface

The user interface, or UI, is the primary means by which the player receives secondary information from a game. In this chapter, we will look at how Unity handles the graphical user interface, or GUI, in a game project and how we can leverage this to display information for the player. While it is possible to play a game based solely on what the player can see from the camera's perspective of the game world, at some point in time we will need to implement menu systems or scoring systems or life systems or even short text messages to the player. The creation of GUIs can be a very fun and rewarding experience as your game projects will begin to develop some polish to them through this process. We will also look at some basic principles for the design of our interface systems; as it turns out, there are some interesting ideas that we can utilize to make our interfaces better and easier to use for the player, which is our primary goal— focusing on the needs of the player while playing our game.

- Types of User Interfaces
- User Interface Design
- User Interface Implementation within Unity
- Updating the User Interface through PlayMaker

10.1 The Types of User Interfaces

Every game has different needs from its user interface system. This basically says that every game does not need to have every type of UI within the project, but only the ones that are beneficial to that specific game. At their core, the purpose of graphical UIs is to either get information *from* the player or to get information *to* the player. As a general rule, the information exchange is not a part of game play per se but adds to and enhances the game play that is within the game. Essentially, we have two types of graphical UIs that we use in video games: menu-based systems and heads-up display (HUD) systems.

10.1.1 Menu-Based Systems

Menu-based systems serve the purpose of getting information and input from the player. While there are some exceptions in providing for player input through an overlay system, generally speaking we rely on menu systems and their equivalent for getting input from the player. Menu-based systems are generally comprised of input components for the player to use such as buttons, sliders, and text boxes. An obvious use of such a system would be the main menu of a game from which the player may select to play or quit the game, and any other options that may be presented. The whole purpose of the interface is to find out what it is that the player wants to do. For the MMO player we can see another use of a menu-based system within a crafting interface. From one of these, the player is able to select which object they want to craft, how many they want to craft, and then either start the process or cancel and return to the game. Many times when menu systems are utilized, they exist outside of the game world itself, that is to say that they are not a direct part of the game world itself, but extensions of it. Menu-based systems are usually drawn in a 2D style and can easily be designed within a 2D graphics program such as Photoshop or Illustrator. However, there is a trend to migrate these traditional menu systems away from the standard 2D approach into a 3D type of interface. This move toward 3D menu systems not only allows the menus to be more appealing and active graphically, but they can also make it easier to blur the line between menu and game and push these menu systems into feeling more a part of the immersive game world rather than something outside of the game.

10.1.2 Heads-Up Display Systems and Overlays

The primary goal of a heads-up display (HUD) or overlay interface is to get information to the player about the current condition of the game. If we do not let the player know what is going on within the game that they are playing they are very likely to move on to other games. The information that a player needs to know can vary from how fast a car is traveling in a racing game to how many lives the player has remaining in an action–adventure game such as Sancho Panza. These HUD systems are generally created as overlays that sit on top of the game world itself. Generally speaking, HUD systems are 2D as an overlay over the game world. However, it is possible to embed an interface into the game world making it an integral component of the game itself and still relay relevant and timely information to the player. An example of this difference would be a numerical display of a car's current speed on the bottom-right corner of the screen, a HUD overlay, versus a working speedometer on the dashboard console that the player can see while driving the car, an embedded HUD overlay.

10.2 User Interface Design

When it comes to the design of the UI for video games, they really have their roots in a field of Computer Science called human computer interaction (HCI). The goal of this specific branch of study is to not only understand how we as people interact with computers, but also how that interaction can be improved and made more intuitive. True UI involves more than just what is displayed on the screen, the software (SW) interface system, but it also involves how the user *physically* interacts with the computer system, the hardware (HW) interface. We are not going to look into the physical interaction in this chapter as we are limited to the HW that has already been developed for use in our game projects. The study of developing HW for use as an interface is well beyond an introductory topic, therefore so we will not touch on it here other than to mention some of the different types as shown in Table 10.1. It is important to be aware of these different HW interfaces when designing our game, as mentioned during the chapter on the design document, as there are major differences between utilizing a virtual reality system and a traditional computer monitor.

TABLE 10.1 Different Types of Hardware Interface Systems

Hardware Interface	Example	Pros	Cons
Virtual reality headset	Oculus Rift, Morpheus	Immersive 3D environment, intuitive visualization	Text very hard to read, less room for UI elements
Motion tracking camera	Kinect	Intuitive motion system, immersive interface mechanism	Requires specific motions, may not recognize quick movements
Motion tracking sensors	Hydra Razer, Nintendo WII controllers	Intuitive interface, utilize more fine-tuned motions than cameras	Requires space to perform the needed actions
Keyboard/Mouse	Any laptop or PC	Readily available	Awkward to use in some games, not ergonomic
Game controller	Xbox 360 controller	Large base of experienced users	Requires memorization of button sequences
Voice recognition	Microphone	Immersion method of issuing commands	Speech recognition has a way to go, yet

FIG 10.1 Ergonomic evolution of game controllers.

Another factor to consider with HW interfaces is the ergonomics of the device in question. Ergonomics refers to how the HW fits or blends with the person using it. A more ergonomic piece of HW will in turn be easier and more intuitive for the user to use. An example of this can be seen in the evolution of game controllers; consider the boxy controller of the original Nintendo Entertainment System and the later version found on the Nintendo GameCube, the original could dig into the palms and be uncomfortable after some time spent playing (not that I actually remember that stopping any of us from playing, we just kept boxes of band aids nearby). However, the later controller with the GameCube fits the hand more comfortably and was much easier to use with the layout of the buttons (Figure 10.1).

The SW interface systems, on the other hand, have a different set of issues that we need to consider when creating them. The GUI system should be a natural and intuitive extension of the game-play experience on the screen and we need to pay attention to how this system is working. As we develop the UI we are going to have to be striving for the Goldilocks effect, which is to say finding the perfect middle ground between too much of something and not enough of that something. The something that we are referring to can be any of the following: text, color, fonts, images, or buttons. At its core, a UI is there to provide information to the user without interfering the user playing the game or accomplishing their current task within the game.

10.2.1 HUD Design

There are two primary things to consider when constructing our HUD overlay systems. The first is how the GUI exists within the game world, or even if it does at all. Erik Fagerholt and Magnus Lorentzon have done extensive work on the design of an interface system and how it is linked into both the narrative and the game play of the game. In their work, *Beyond the HUD: User Interfaces for Increased Player Immersion in FPS Games*, they explore the different uses of SW interfaces and created four distinct categories, as described in Table 10.2. While it is not necessary for us to

TABLE 10.2 Different Approaches to Providing Information to a Player through the Graphical User Interface System

UI Element	How Used	Example
Diegetic	UI elements exist within and are a part of the actual game world	Car dashboard in a racing game, HUD for a flight simulator, in-helmet HUD for a space-based game
Nondiegetic	UI elements that are not attached to any object within the game world and are not extensions of the world, traditional UI elements	Chat interface for an MMO game, character names appearing above the avatar, display of a weapon selection and amount of ammo remaining
Spatial	Elements that fit within the game world but are not a natural part of the game world itself	Placement of text on objects to provide information to player, waypoint trail to follow in a game that leads to a goal
Meta	UI elements that do not fit within the game world itself but are a natural extension of the game world	Red flashing screen when player is shot, the speedometer separate from dashboard in a racing game

create a list of which UI elements are going to be from which category, it is important to be aware of how the UI can be used to both immerse the player and to remove the player from the game. Creating a game with only diegetic interface elements seems like a great idea as it will be completely immersive and everything is a direct part of the game world the player is interacting with. However, that type of interface will eliminate the possibility of a mini-map with radar informing the player of the potential location of any baddies on the current level. It will also eliminate the capability of displaying a score or a character name, unless we are developing a game in which the player is wearing an augmented reality device.

The other aspect of HUD that we should be aware of is what and how we are giving to the player. If we think back to the chapter on story and the backstory that we created for our game project, while we have a great desire to dump all of that information onto the player so that they can know all of the hard work we put into this project, it is not necessary for the player to know all of that in order to play and enjoy the game. However, it is not only whether the player needs to know the information or not, but it also how easy it is for the player to get the information or perform the task that they need. Figure 10.2 provides two different mock-ups of a HUD overlay for our Sancho Panza project. As we create initial designs for these interfaces, we need to consider what the player *needs* to know which very likely may not be the same as what we *want* them to know. In the mock-ups of Figure 10.2, the left version depicts what we might like them to know whereas the version on the right provides only the information that the player actually needs at the moment while they are playing. The difference here is quite noticeable and is not always as obvious as it may seem. When laying out your GUI overlays, always consider each element from the point of view of the player and what they actually need to know as they are playing the game. Also, when doing mock-ups of your interface system, it

FIG 10.2 Different HUD overlay mock-ups, the one on the left has too much information.

is not necessary to have final graphics in place, the goal is to get a general idea of what you want to accomplish.

Consider the example of a crafting system within an MMO, we essentially have three ways that we can approach such a system. The first one we can give the player a text-based list of the items that they can craft and let them click whatever it is they want to craft. In the second, we can provide the user with a graphical representation of the ingredients that they need for the current recipe and allow them to select and drag those ingredients into available slots. For the third option, we can provide the player with a recipe book of things that they can craft from which they can see what ingredients are needed and within the crafting window itself allow the player to search through all of their ingredients to add the ones that they will need for a recipe they are currently constructing. The first example is the easiest to use, we display what the player can do and allow them to select it. However, this approach removes the immersion as the player does not feel as though they are involved in the crafting per se. In the second approach, the player has to add the ingredients needed based upon the recipe that they have selected. This one is more immersive as the player is involved with adding the ingredients and is also an intuitive approach making it a good middle ground option. The last option is cumbersome as the player will need to either remember or write down the ingredients listed in their recipe book so that they can find them when they are inside of the actual crafting window. While this may be the most immersive of the options, displaying all recipes and ingredients whether they can be made and are relevant or not, it is a far more awkward system for the player to have to use.

The other things that we need to consider when constructing our interface systems are entirely cosmetic. As game developers we have an innate desire to do something different, to create new and cool things. However, when it comes to UI design we need to make sure that it is not a stumbling block preventing the player from playing and enjoying our great creations.

FIG 10.3 UI mock-ups for Sancho, the left one does not blend as the right one does.

Regardless of our favorite colors or favorite fonts, the needs of the game players playing must come first when we design these GUI elements. Therefore, we should consider the colors and fonts that are being used by the interface and ask ourselves the following questions:

- Do they fight with each other?
- Do they fight with the game immersion and environment?
- Are they legible?
- Are they placed in easy-to-spot locations?

These concepts are demonstrated in Figure 10.3, which shows two different GUI designs that we could potentially use with our Sancho Panza project. In this straightforward example, we can see how the placement, styles, and colors selected for our interfaces can have an enormous impact on the interface itself. A good rule of thumb is to ask others what they think of your designs and actually be willing to listen to them regardless of your personal opinion on the subject. Try not to marry your ideas immediately, give them a chance to grow and mature before committing to them so completely that other things must be constructed around them. The idea for this game and the main character and overall appearance came before the concepts of the UI system, therefore any developed GUI must blend and work with what has already been decided on rather than bending the previous work to match the UI.

10.2.2 Menu Design

These same principles can and should be applied to the design of menu systems for our games. The difference with menu systems is that the focus is not on what the player needs to know, but what the player needs to be able to do from the current menu. While it may be necessary that the player possess certain knowledge in order to accomplish the task at hand, we must make sure that the player can do what they need to from the given menu.

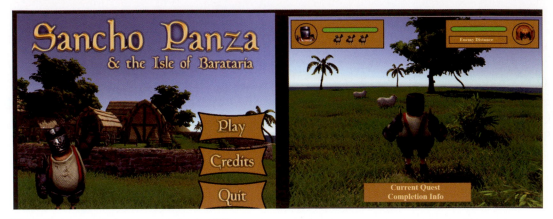

FIG 10.4 Final mock-ups for the main menu and in-game HUD.

For instance, we could create a main menu in which the player has the following capabilities:

- Start a new game
- Load a saved game
- Exit the game
- Adjust the music volume
- Adjust the sound effects volume
- Change the screen resolution
- Change the mouse sensitivity
- Change the default controls
- View the credits for the game

As you might imagine, such a main menu screen would be too crowded. It would be much better to off load the adjustment options to a different menu, perhaps one named Options, and in their place on the main menu add a button labeled Options that will load this new menu. Once again, this may seem obvious to those that have been playing games for a while, but as we have a desire to change things and be creative we must keep in mind that there are certain expectations the players will have coming in to our game and if we change things up too much we are liable to lose them as players due to the oddity or complexity of our GUI schemes that we employ. Based on these concepts of interface design, Figure 10.4 provides a mock-up of both our main menu and HUD system that we will construct for the game. Both of these designs will provide us with some flexibility when we construct them to tweak and modify in the game, although we will use these as a foundation from which to build.

10.2.3 Basics of Color Theory

We have briefly mentioned colors and fonts and we would be remise if we did not at least touch on the basics of color theory. While it is completely acceptable to just wing our color choices based on what looks good or feels right given the project that we are working on, there are times that it may be useful to dive a little deeper into the selection of colors for our interface systems and to at least be aware that there is a wealth of work and information we can draw upon. To begin, color theory at its core is a structure or rule set for the color and how the various colors are related to each other. Figure 10.5 depicts a color wheel in which many of the colors are shown in relation to other colors. Colors are divided into three distinct groups: primary, secondary, and tertiary. With primary colors we have our three essential color pigments that can then be blended to form more colors. Through the blending of the primary colors we will form the secondary colors. Finally, when we blend a secondary and primary color we end up with a tertiary color that is generally a hyphenated name indicating the original sources of the colors; Table 10.3 lists the essential primary, secondary, and tertiary colors. Notice that our list of colors does not incorporate the vastness of colors that we see in the world around us or can even grab from a box of Crayola crayons.

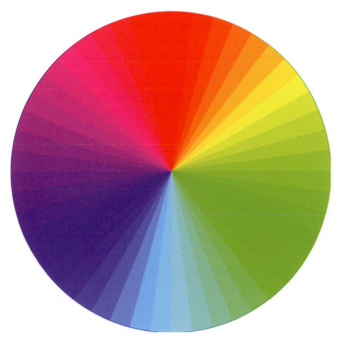

FIG 10.5 A basic color wheel.

TABLE 10.3 The Three Categories of Color

Color Type	Colors
Primary	Red, yellow, blue
Secondary	Orange, green, purple (violet)
Tertiary	Red-orange, yellow-orange, yellow-green, blue-green, blue-purple, red-purple

Note

It is important to point out that computers utilize an additive color system and the real world uses a subtractive color system. In addition, computers utilize RGB (Red, Green, and Blue) as their primary colors rather than the Red, Yellow, and Blue of traditional art. For example, to create yellow we would add red and green together and end up with yellow when working with colors in a computer. However, the basics of color theory hold true for either system.

As we develop our interfaces and overlays, the colors that we utilize should harmonize and blend, both with the environment and the game and also with each other within the interface design. We essentially have two approaches to achieving this color harmony. The first is to use colors that are neighbors to each other on the color wheel; this approach would be using analogous colors. When doing an analogous color scheme, we will need to use three colors that are neighbors of each other as shown in Figure 10.6. We could also select our colors by choosing complementary colors which would be colors that are opposite to each other on the color wheel. These two approaches provide simple techniques that we can leverage when selecting colors for our UI components.

Another aspect to be aware of with colors as we design our interfaces is the temperature and emotional connectivity of those colors. Figure 10.7 displays

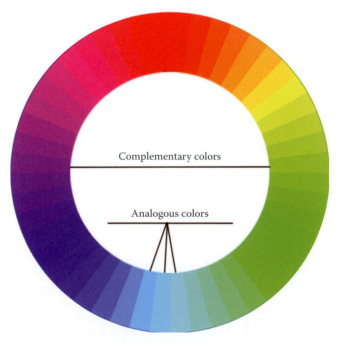

FIG 10.6 Analogous and complementary color section.

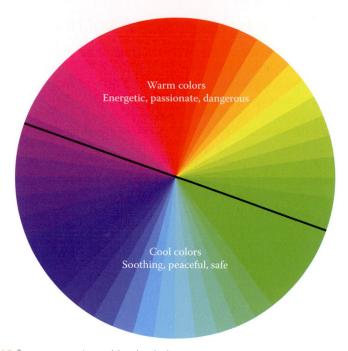

FIG 10.7 Temperature, emotions, and the color wheel.

the full color wheel from earlier with added temperature labels. These color temperatures can be extremely beneficial when designing the lighting for an environment; by using cooler colors, we will create a more subdued environment reminiscent of night time and would even help to set the stage for an eerie scene as well. The hotter colors will create a more festive feeling game world along the lines of day time. We can use these temperatures to help a player key in on information within the interface that is vital to know by using hotter colors, and information that is less important to focus on can be presented with cooler colors. Another aspect of the color temperature will impact how soothing the interface overlay is for the player; by using only hot colors throughout the interface, it will become a very tiring experience for the player as there is nothing soothing, the whole interface screams for our sudden and immediate attention.

While these temperatures are useful, they also tie into an emotional response from us when we see them. Looking at Figure 10.7 again we can also notice the emotional labels associated with colors. We can create a feeling of threat or hostility by using red or similar coloring within our interface. For instance, the circle border around the image of the enemy could be red and the player will pick up on the angry intention of that representation. It is interesting to note that the same red color for anger and hostility can also bring about ideas of romance and passion; it all depends on the setting in which the colors are used. Combining this overview of color theory with the needs of our interface systems, we can move on to the actual construction of these within the Unity game engine.

10.3 The User Interface System of Unity

With the release of Unity 4.6, Unity has shifted from the traditional UI system that was employed to one that has been labeled uGUI. The primary difference between the original UI system and uGUI is that the first one was programming based and the new version is visually based. To clarify this, with the old interface system, the objects (buttons, sliders, text labels, etc.) were all placed in the scene through scripted behavior. So, in order to construct an interface it was necessary to be familiar with scripting and programming which made it much more difficult for artistically minded content developers to construct the interfaces for their game projects. On the other hand, uGUI is visually based utilizing a WYSIWYG (What You See Is What You Get, pronounced "wizeewig") approach that allows content-focused developers to build the interfaces for the games by dragging and dropping elements where they want them to be on the screen. This has streamlined development on the interfaces quite a bit by making it a more intuitive process. Throughout this section, we will explore the components of this new Unity system while constructing the interfaces that we have designed in the previous section.

> **Download**
> Be sure to download the collection of assets from this chapter's folder on the companion website in order to be able to complete the examples in the following sections and unzip the folder on your hard drive once you have it: "gui_assets.zip."

10.3.1 Building Blocks of uGUI

When constructing an interface, whether menu or HUD, the components of the interface are all placed on a Canvas object. We can think of the canvas in the same way that a painter would view a canvas, all of our UI elements will be placed somewhere on a canvas, just as all of the painting for a specific work of art would be placed on a painter's canvas. The Canvas itself is a Game Object within our game scene and as a result can be moved and repositioned how we want and where the canvas goes, the elements that are attached to it will go also. Canvases can also be rendered, drawn, and displayed by the camera, in different ways as listed in Table 10.4. These different rendering modes for the Canvas object allow us to create UI elements that are better suited for specific needs within the game.

Just as other Game Objects within a scene have a Transform component, a Canvas object also has a Transform component named a Rect Transform, though it has been modified to suit the specific needs of a Canvas. The difference is that the Rect Transform not only contains position, scale, and rotation information but also anchor points and size information. The sizing allows us to specify a height and width for the Canvas, or for other UI elements that have a Rect Transform (see Figure 10.8), without changing the scale of the object. Anchor points allow us to freeze an edge

TABLE 10.4 The Render Modes of a Canvas Game Object

Render Mode	Description	Example Use
Screen Space—Overlay	This mode is a more traditional interface system in that it is rendered on top of everything else in the scene. If the screen resolution changes, the Canvas will automatically adjust as well	Score, health bar
Screen Space—Camera	Very similar to the Overlay mode, except here the Canvas is set at a given distance from a camera. Generally, the camera used is not the same as the main game view camera, as the camera used for this overlay is only used to render the Canvas and its elements, not the rest of the scene. The Canvas can be drawn in 3D or 2D based on the render mode of the camera itself (perspective or orthographic)	Dialogue system, inventory system, mini-map
World Space	Will cause the Canvas to act just like the other Game Objects that are within the scene. Can manually set the size with the Rect Transform property. UI elements will appear behind or in front of other Game Objects based on 3D placement in the world	Names over characters in game, speedometer on a car dashboard

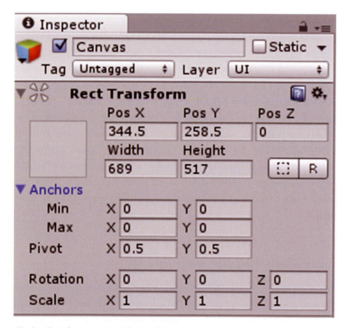

FIG 10.8 The Rect Transform component for a UI element.

of the Canvas to a part of the screen so that even if the screen resolution changes, the Canvas will stay relatively the same. If we anchor a Canvas object in the center of a screen at a resolution of 1024×768 then in-game change the resolution to 800×600, the anchored Canvas will shift to stay in the center of the new screen as much as possible. UI elements also have a Pivot point that we can specify and it is from this pivot point that all rotations and resizings would be relative to, it is difficult to explain in plain text the anchor points within the Rect Transform, be sure to take a look at the video found on the companion website for a more in-depth look at this component. With our previous work, the pivot point of the meshes was defined from within the 3D application that was used to create the models and could not be altered here within Unity.

Note
The properties of the Rect Transform for a Canvas object can only be manually altered if the Render Mode is set to World Space for that Canvas. Otherwise the values are set by the Canvas itself automatically and based upon the screen resolution.

Video
Watch the video in the chapters section of the companion website for an overview of the Rect Transform component with A specific focus on anchor points: "Rect Transform."

The Canvas forms the base that we build the remainder of the UI on. We can have more than one Canvas within each scene as well so it is not necessary for us to figure out how to fit everything onto one Canvas. We can put UI elements onto the Canvas that will serve to provide information to the player which the Unity manual refers to as Visual Components or we can get information from the player utilizing Interaction Components. Table 10.5 provides a list of the different types of components that we have as a part of the uGUI system. Some of these we have already seen from our exploration with a dialogue system during the chapter on story development and integration. From these components, we can construct the interfaces that we will need for our game project.

10.3.2 Constructing the Main Menu

Using the main menu mock-up from earlier in this chapter, we are going to go ahead and construct the full menu within Unity. We will begin doing this by creating a new scene (File → New Scene) then immediately saving the scene as Main Menu (File → Save Scene As). Before we get into constructing the menu, we need to make sure that our scene is configured for what we will need. Considering that we are constructing a main menu, we will have no use for the 3D perspective camera or for the skybox that is in the scene, though we will need the light as without light we will not be able to see anything. We are also going to go ahead and import all of our assets into our project in the beginning so that we can continue to move at a steady pace through the development and not have to go get more content (with the exception

TABLE 10.5 The Different Types of UI Components in Unity

Component Type	UI Component	Use
Visual	Panel	Group components within a Canvas.
Interaction	Button	Allows the user to make a selection by clicking and responds to a single click from the user.
Visual	Text	Displays text-based information to the user and can also be used as a label for other components such as the text label on a button.
Visual	Image	Used to display a 2D image that is in sprite format and contains custom formatting options specific to an image. This is used for the vast majority of the times we want to put a picture into our UI.
Visual	Raw Image	Used to display a 2D image that is in a texture format, should only be used in rare situations when the Image component does not cover what is needed.
Interaction	Slider	Similar to the scrollbar except that the value range can be specified by a script to be between any values, for instance, the number of bots in a level.
Interaction	Scrollbar	Decimal value from 0 to 1 that allows the user to make a percentage selection, consider sound volume level.
Interaction	Toggle	Check box to turn something on/off, useful for enabling/disabling features.
Interaction	Input Field	Gets text information from the user, input can come from a keyboard or other character selection device.
Visual	Canvas	Primary parent for a set of components.
Interaction	Event System	Primary controller object for managing user input, this will be added automatically to the scene when a Canvas is added.

of Fonts). With these goals in mind, we will go ahead and get the scene configured for our menu.

1. Select the Main Camera
   a. Change the Y Position from 1 to 0
   b. Change Projection from Perspective to Orthographic
2. In the Scene Editor click the 2D button (see Figure 10.9) to switch from 3D to 2D mode
3. Eliminate the default Skybox
   a. Select Window → Lighting
   b. Select the small circle icon for the Skybox and change it to None
4. Create a new folder in the Project folder named UI Images
   a. Import everything from the UI Images folder from the compressed asset file downloaded from the companion website earlier
5. Import everything from the UI Audio folder into the Audio folder of the project. The UI Audio folder is from the compressed asset folder downloaded from the companion website earlier
   a. For the Textures, be sure to change their Texture Type from Texture to Sprite (2D and UI)

405

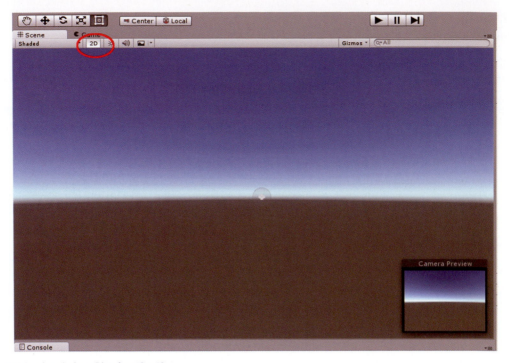

FIG 10.9 Switching the Scene Editor from 3D to 2D.

Skyboxes are materials that are rendered around an entire scene with the goal of creating the illusion of a sky being within the game world. Since we are building a main menu only, we do not need the skybox, so have gotten rid of it. While these changes were relatively minor to this main camera, if we do them at the beginning we are less likely to forget things later, as the final version of this scene will contain two different cameras one for viewing the GUI we are getting ready to add and the other for viewing Sancho in our world. uGUI elements are drawn on top of other Game Objects, so in order to see our GUI and any Game Objects that we might want visible it will be necessary for us to use different cameras, or be very aware of this rendering system when we design the UI to begin with, for instance, when we construct the HUD overlay system in the next section. Now, it is true that we could have just as easily left the skybox in the scene; however, it is not going to be visible anyway.

Finally, notice that the imported image files were switched from the default Texture Type to the Sprite Texture Type. The reason for this is that when using the Image UI object, it requires that the images we assign to it be of type Sprite. Essentially, a texture is the whole image whereas a sprite may only be a portion of the image within the file. As it turns out, each one of our image files only contains one sprite, however, we could have packed more sprites into each image file if we had wanted to. This would have allowed us to define the rectangle surrounding each one of the sprites located within the overall image file. After making the changes to the Inspector properties of the image file, do not forget to click the Apply button to update and commit those changes. With the assets in place that we will need and the scene is prepared for a menu as opposed to a standard 3D scene, we are ready to begin the construction of the menu itself.

1. Add a Canvas object to the scene, GameObject → UI → Canvas
   a. Make the following changes to the Canvas Scaler (Script) component:
      i. UI Scale Mode should be Scale with Screen Size
      ii. Reference Resolution should be 1024×768
2. Add an Image object to the Canvas
   a. Right-click Canvas and select UI → Image
   b. Change name of the object to Background
   c. Change the Source Image to Sancho Main Menu
   d. Click the Set Native Size button
3. Add an Image object to the Canvas
   a. Change the name of the object to Title
   b. Change Source Image to Sancho Panza, found within the UI Images folder
   c. Click the Set Native Size
   d. Position the Title object in the Scene Editor near the top middle of the screen
   e. Change the Anchor points from Center to Top Center
4. Repeat Step 3 for a Subtitle object, using the Barataria image, place the image below the Title as depicted in the mock-up
5. Add a Button object to the Canvas
   a. Click the triangle next to the button to access its attached children and delete the Text object
   b. Rename the Button object to be Play Button
   c. Change the Source Image to play btn
   d. Click Set Native Size
   e. In Rect Transform mode, grab the Blue anchors at the edge of the bounding box and resize the button to better fit (either larger or smaller, depending on your screen size and resolution)
      i. Hold down the SHIFT key while resizing the button to force Unity to do a uniform resize, meaning it keeps the aspect ratio. This also causes Unity to resize with the center point of the object as the reference pivot point
   f. Reposition this button along the right-hand side of the screen as depicted in the mock-up
   g. Change the Anchor points from Center to Bottom Right
   h. Change the Highlighted Color, see Figure 10.10, to a nice yellow
6. Copy the Play Button
   a. Change the name to Credits Button
   b. Change Source Image to credits btn
   c. Move the Credits Button down as needed
7. Repeat Step 6 for the Quit Button using the quit btn image

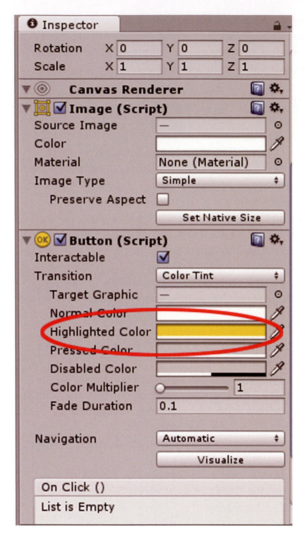

We began by adding a new Canvas to our scene as it is required for the uGUI system. UI objects added to the Canvas are rendered as though they are layers, that is to say that something listed after an element will be rendered after, the previous object. As an example, move the Title object in the Hierarchy panel so that it is above the Background object; notice that the Title is no longer visible as the Background object is rendered after the Title object is. This is an important concept to keep in mind as it means that we can layer UI elements on top of each other to get specific desired results out of the system. With the Canvas object that we added we changed the Canvas Scaler property so that the children of the Canvas object will scale appropriately if and when the screen resolution changes; this is a wonderful feature as it means less work for us when porting to other devices such as mobile and it also means it will be easier for us to allow the user to change resolutions if we want such a feature in our game. We have specified a reference resolution of 1024 × 768 as that is our default resolution that we are setting for the game and also the resolution of the image that we are utilizing as a background for our main menu. This is an easy component to overlook, and this is all that is needed in order to have the remainder of our UI objects scale correctly with resolution changes to our game, assuming that we have the anchor points of the other objects set correctly.

After adding the Canvas object, we added an Image object that we named as the Background. Within this object the background image for the main menu is loaded and displayed. During that process notice that we needed to resize this object to match the size of the actual image that we are using and the Set Native Size button was the easiest and quickest way to get that size correct. When setting Anchor points for objects within a Canvas it is best to set them in relation to the nearest side or we can also leave them to the default center. Keep in mind that the Anchor points determine what part of the UI object stay put, although with our scaling system we are using it will still scale, but stays in a relative position to that Anchor point.

The final item of interest on the initial Background object was to change the Alpha from the default setting up to 255. What this has done is to remove any transparency on this object, not on the image itself but on the overall object. Remember, UI elements can be layered on top of each other and therefore at times it might be advantageous to have the last rendered component slightly transparent so that the underlying layers are visible, something we will utilize with a portion of our HUD overlay later. However, notice that with the Alpha set to the default midwaypoint the Background image is dim and not very vibrant, we wanted the image to be brighter and crisper, therefore bumping the Alpha up to its maximum value has given us a solid background image. For the Title and Subtitle image objects, the same basic procedure was followed that we used on the Background image object with the exception of having to manually place where we wanted things. When moving UI objects around the scene, make sure that the Scene editor is in Rect Transform mode as depicted in Figure 10.11.

Placing the Button objects is very similar to the work that we did on the Image objects already, just one thing to note on this process. Keep the Game window at whatever resolution it is at until after you have finished with the initial sizing and positioning of the buttons. Working with these objects may seem a little overwhelming at first, but it quickly becomes second nature and the whole process becomes far more intuitive and natural. Whenever learning a new skill,

FIG 10.11 Rect Transform mode for the Scene editor.

TABLE 10.6 Available States for Button UI Objects

State	Description
Normal color	The standard state when the button is active, but the mouse is not on it and it has not already been clicked.
Highlighted color	Whenever the mouse enters into the area defined by the button this state is triggered and this color tint will be applied to the button. This is a good method of letting the player know that they can click on this if they wish to.
Pressed color	If the user has clicked this button, we can provide a visual cue to the player so that they know through this color tint, for instance, that the music can be on or off and the button with the pressed color (probably darker) is the one that is currently selected.
Disabled color	We can disable buttons and this color will allow a visual cue to the player that this button is not a viable option, consider the grayed-out buttons we often see in menus.

the first time is sometimes a little rough, stick with the uGUI system and it will become second nature very quickly. Remember to always be in Rect Transform mode whenever you are resizing or moving a UI object around the scene. The Button objects, unlike the Image objects, have multiple states that they can exist in to define the color tinting that is applied to the button, these states are summarized in Table 10.6. Currently, we have overlaid a nice and bright yellow color on our Button image so that when the mouse passes over the button the player knows that they can click on this button if they want to.

In our main menu mock-up, we placed a Sancho object into the scene with the intention of giving the scene a little bit of life. We can obtain this life in the scene by animating Sancho as he stands there and waits for the user to click one of the buttons and launch the game. Go ahead and add a Sancho object from the Project pane into our scene and position him at 0, 0, 0. Notice that as soon as we did this, we lost our main menu in the Game window as the camera tied to the Sancho object has taken over for us, so we will need to make some adjustments. Be careful as we adjust Sancho for this scene to not Apply our changes to the Prefab object as these changes are not needed in the rest of the game, they are only going to be needed for this main menu screen.

1. Click the triangle to see the objects attached to Sancho
   a. Remove Music
   b. Remove Journal
   c. Remove Narrator
   d. Remove Main Camera
2. Select the Sancho object to see his Inspector properties
   a. Disable all of the PlayMaker components as well as the (see Figure 10.12)
      i. Capsule Collider
      ii. Character Motor
      iii. Audio Listener
      iv. Audio Source
      v. Turn on Play Automatically in the Animation component

FIG 10.12 Modified Sancho game object.

3. Select the Canvas object
   a. Change Render Mode to Screen Space → Camera
   b. Assign Main Camera to the Render Camera
4. Use the Move, Scale, and Rotation modes to position Sancho as shown in the mock-up or in Figure 10.13

We have added Sancho to our scene began by removing all of the parts that we are not going to need for this version of Sancho, which turns out to be an awful lot of what we have already done in the previous chapters. We also had to reposition him to better fit the spot that was allotted for him and while it is true that earlier we said not to scale meshes but to change the scale factor instead, for this one situation there is nothing wrong with breaking the rules to make it easier for us, as long as we do not apply these changes to the prefab and therefore throughout the rest of our game. The interesting aspect, at this stage,

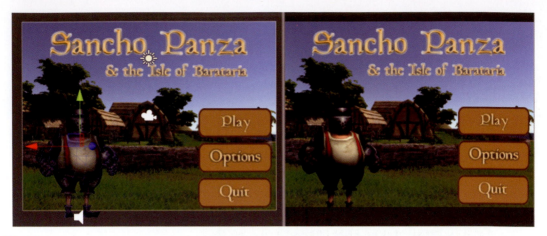

FIG 10.13 The final position of Sancho and view of the main menu as it stands at this point.

was that we could not actually see Sancho at first until after we changed the Render Mode of the Canvas object. As long as it was set to Screen Space → Overlay, the Canvas was rendered on top of everything else that is in the scene, this will be useful for our HUD overlay, but for this main menu with a nontransparent background image that caused problems. Therefore, by changing it to be rendered to a specific camera, Sancho became visible and could be seen as long as his Z value is between that of the Camera (−10) and that of the Canvas (90) and the starting Z value of 0 is definitely between those two numbers. We can now run the game and see our wonderful main menu in action with idling Sancho watching us expectantly and if we resize the Game window then everything scales with it as it should; this is a very good start to this menu and when we get to the PlayMaker section we will add some functionality to it.

10.3.3 Constructing the HUD Overlay

Recall our basic mock-up for the HUD overlay that we plan to utilize within the game play of our project. For the construction of this overlay, we will begin with the information box in the top left-hand corner that has Sancho's current health and his number of remaining lives. This box will also contain a picture of Sancho's head so that the player will be able to visually recognize that the information being displayed is for Sancho and not for some other character on the screen. We have already imported all of the image files that we will need and set them to be Sprite (2D and UI). The images that we will use in this stage of development will be: Character Info, Health Bar, Sancho Head, and Sancho Life. We are going to use images for the representation of the number of lives that Sancho has remaining, specifically a little picture of Sancho with his hand up in the air. Make sure to load the Barataria scene that we were working with prior to the construction of the main menu. With our preliminary pieces in place we are ready to begin.

1. Add a Canvas to the scene and change the name to HUD Overlay.
   a. Make sure that the UI Scale Mode is set to Scale With Screen Size and Reference Resolution is 1024 × 768.
2. Add an Image UI object to the Canvas and change the name to Sancho Info.
   a. Change the Source Image to Character Info.
   b. Click Set Native Size and turn on Preserve Aspect Ratio.
   c. Resize and reposition the object as necessary so that it fits well in the top left corner of the Game view.
   d. Change the Anchor point to Top Left Corner.
3. Add an Image UI object to the Sancho Info object name it Sancho Head.
   a. Change Source Image to Sancho Head.
   b. Resize, reposition, and change Anchor point to Middle Left.
4. Add an Image UI object to the Sancho Info object name it Sancho Health.
   a. Change Source Image to Health Bar.
   b. Resize, reposition, and change Anchor point to Middle Center.
   c. Select the Color bar beneath the Source Image and change the color to Green.
5. Add an Image UI object to the Sancho Info object name it Life 1.
   a. Change Source Image to Sancho Life.
   b. Resize, reposition, and change Anchor point Center.
6. Duplicate Life 1 two times to create Life 2 and Life 3.
   a. Reposition the images as needed.
7. Figure 10.14 depicts the final hierarchy layout for these objects and Figure 10.15 shows the final positioning of these objects within the Game view.

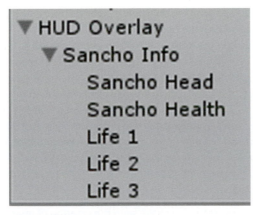

FIG 10.14 Hierarchy relationships of the Sancho Info UI overlay.

FIG 10.15 Final positioning and arranging of Sancho Info UI overlay in Game view.

The construction of our HUD overlay was built off of the knowledge that we gained when constructing the main menu system from the previous section. This time, we did not do a Camera Overlay for the Render Mode of the Canvas, however. Keeping the Render Mode of the Canvas to the default of Screen Overlay allows the Canvas to lay on top of the whole screen, whatever the size of the screen. Keeping in mind that our HUD system is just going to put some UI elements in specific places on the screen and attempt to not be obtrusive, the Screen Overlay is the best option for us as we can utilize only the portions of the Canvas that we will specifically need.

The images that we created were created in the same process as the Images for the Main Menu system; the only new aspect in these steps was the use of the Color property for the health bar that we have created. The original health bar image is white, with some transparency around it; this color was selected with the end goal of allowing us to change the color of the health bar within Unity as opposed to being stuck with one color. Also, when changing the Color property of an Image object, keep in mind that what we are really doing is applying a tint of that color to whatever the image is. In the case of a white image, which means that we are applying a new color tint to a white background or changing the color to that new color tint. However, if we apply a tint to the info box itself, we get that tint overlay on top of whatever colors are actually within the image; see Figure 10.16 for a demonstration of this difference.

Other than this new feature, we have seen the creation of Images and manipulation of both their position and Anchor points during the work on

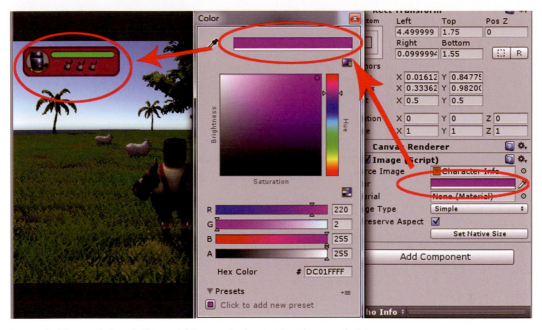

FIG 10.16 Applying a purple tint to the Character Info image, notice the output is not the same as the tint.

the main menu. Our Sancho Info box is now laid out the way that we would like it to be and it scales very well with new resolutions; the functionality of changing the health bar and the lives will come when we add PlayMaker to these systems. Our next step will be to get the quest journal that we had thrown together real quick in an earlier chapter functioning as a proper member of our new HUD overlay; before continuing, be sure to download the font file found at the companion website.

Download
Download the "roger-white_milwich.zip" file from this chapter's folder at the companion website. This is the font created by Roger White that we will be using for text in our UI; it is the same font that was used for the creation of the image files that have been used previously in this chapter.

1. Select the Sancho object in the Hierarchy.
   a. Delete the Journal object that we created earlier and attached to him. When you do this, there will be a warning message that we are losing the Prefab connection, see Figure 10.17, just click Continue.
   b. Click the Apply button on the Sancho object to apply our changes to the prefab itself, the Sancho object in the Hierarchy should return to a blue color now.
2. Create a new folder in the Project panel and name the folder Fonts.
   a. Import the "MILWICH_ font" that was downloaded before beginning these steps.

FIG 10.17 The Prefab warning dialogue that appears when moving objects out of a prefabbed asset.

3. Create an Image UI object and attach it to the HUD Overlay.
   a. Rename the Image object to Quest Info.
   b. Change Source Image to Quest Box.
   c. Change the Alpha transparency value to around 175.
   d. Position the object near Sancho's feet, something like Figure 10.18.
   e. Change the Anchor points to Middle Bottom.
4. Create a Text UI object and attach it to Quest Info.
   a. Change the name from Text to Quest Display.
   b. Provide some sample text for testing, we are using:
      i. This is a test quest.
      ii. Found 0 of 7 things.
   c. Select the Font property and change it to MILWICH_.
   d. Change Font Style to Bold so that the text stands out a little sharper.
   e. Leave Font Size at the default value and change Line Spacing to 3.
   f. Change the Alignment of the Text to be Centered, see Figure 10.19.
   g. Click the check box for Best Fit.
   h. Change the Color property, we are using a reddish-maroon kind of color.
   i. Reposition the text object within the Quest Display for best fit.
   j. Change the Anchor points to Center.

We now have our Quest Display system in place and ready to be dynamically updated when Sancho is given a quest to complete during the course of the game. The Image object that we used as part of this process was simply there to provide a background for the text to show up against. Dropping the Alpha value down has added some transparency into the image so that it does not stand out as sharply; however, this is a personal decision and if you prefer yours without the transparency then by all means set the Alpha back up to 255.

The Text object is new, granted we used it very quickly in an earlier chapter, but here we have done a fair amount of changing and tweaking. Our main goal with the changes that were made was to make sure that

FIG 10.18 Positioning of the Quest Info object beneath Sancho.

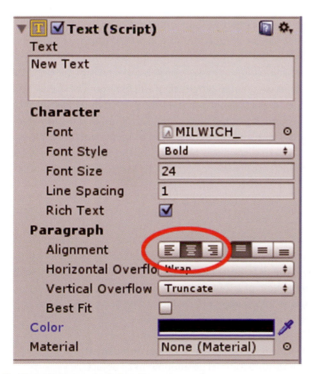

FIG 10.19 The Alignment properties for the Text object.

the text will rescale with the rest of the game if the resolution of the game display were to change. When dealing with fonts and font sizes, rescaling can sometimes be something of a nightmare; however, Unity has streamlined this whole process for us by handling all of the number crunching in the background. The key was to use the Best Fit option for the text. With this property turned on, Unity will actually ignore the properties that we have specified as Font Size. In other words, Unity will dynamically determine the best Font Size for the text to fit within the bounding box of the Text object. But, Line Spacing will need to be specified by us, to see this in action you are encouraged to change the Line Spacing value and see how it impacts the text whereas the Font Size has no impact on the final display. Our Quest Info system is now in place and ready for PlayMaker to send it some new information to display. Notice that this is a cleaner system than the one that we had hacked together in our chapter on story. We will get both of these to update dynamically when we come to the PlayMaker section of this chapter; the addition of the enemy info box for the HUD Overlay is being left as an exercise for the end of the chapter.

10.3.4 Polishing the Dialogue Work

In one of our earlier chapters we throw together a hasty dialogue system in order to demonstrate methods of bringing story into our game projects. This time we are going to rework that dialogue system so that we can take advantage of the uGUI tools that are available to us and correct many of the frustrating issues that we had with our first take at dialogue in our game project. We will import the Teresa prefab object into our Barataria scene and place her somewhere within the town or perhaps just outside of the town. If you did not make a prefab object of her, load the Chapter 6 Test scene that we created where all of the dialogue work was done before and drag the Teresa object from the Hierarchy panel down into the Project panel (make sure to put her in our Prefabs folder) and then we can reload the Barataria scene and drop the prefab of Teresa into here. We will begin by creating the UI system for the dialogue and then in our PlayMaker section we will make some corrections to Teresa to bring the whole system together.

1. Add a Canvas object to the scene and name it Dialogue Overlay.
   a. Set the Sort Order (beneath the Canvas Render Mode) to 1.
   b. Set the UI Scale Mode to Scale with Screen Size and default resolution of 1024×768.
2. Attach an Image object to Dialogue Overlay.
   a. Rename the image to Dialogue Box.
   b. Change Source Image to Quest Box.
   c. Resize and reposition this box to dominate the screen, see Figure 10.19 for final positioning of UI objects.

FIG 10.20 The final positioning of all the UI elements for the Dialogue system.

3. Attach an Image object to Dialogue Box.
   a. Rename the image to Speaker Image.
   b. Position the image near the top left corner of Dialogue Box.
   c. The default size is fine.
4. Attach a Text UI object to Dialogue Box.
   a. Rename the text to Speaker Name.
   b. Provide some sample testing text.
   c. Position to the right of Speaker Image (see Figure 10.20).
   d. Change the Font to MILWICH_.
   e. Change the Font Style to Bold and Italic.
   f. Turn on Best Fit.
   g. Change the Color to a nice bright green (0, 255, 0).
5. Attach another Text UI object to Dialogue Box.
   a. Rename the object to Speaker Words.
   b. Provide some sample testing text.
   c. Change the Font to MILWICH_.
   d. Change the Line Spacing to 3.
   e. Position the object below Speaker Image and Speaker Name.
   f. Resize the text box so that it takes up quite a bit of room within the Dialogue Box; remember this is where all of the spoken words from the speaker will be displayed.
   g. Change the Alignment to Center.
   h. Turn on Best Fit.
6. Add a Button UI object to Dialogue Box.
   a. Rename the object to Response 1.
   b. Change Source Image to Quest Box.
   c. Resize and reposition the Button as necessary to match Figure 10.20.
   d. Change the Highlighted Color to a bright yellow or some other color that you like.

e. Click the triangle next to the Button to access the attached Text child object.
  i. Provide some sample testing text.
  ii. Change the Font to MILWICH_.
  iii. Change the Line Spacing to 3.
  iv. Change the Alignment to Center.
  v. Turn on Best Fit.
7. Duplicate Response 1 and rename the new copy to Response 2.
  a. Reposition Response 2 below the first button.

There is only one new option that we are using in this dialogue system that we have not used in our previous UI work: the Sort Order on the Canvas. The Sort Order for the Canvas tells Unity which order to render multiple Canvases at runtime. The rendering will occur starting at the lower numbers and rendering new Canvases on top until it has gone through all of the values in the Sort Order. This is allowing us to render this Dialogue Canvas on top of the current HUD Overlay that is already on the screen. This is very easy to implement and provides a very nice capability for when we want various Canvases rendered in different sequences for whatever effects we may be trying to accomplish. You may have noticed that when this was rendered, by playing the game, that we can still see the display from PlayMaker listing which state each object is in. This display is OK for now as it is not impacting performance in anyway and we will be turning off all of those FSM displays soon enough. We are leaving them in there for now for testing purposes as it helps to know what state a given object is in while trying to do some testing of our FSMs.

Other than that, we have seen all of these properties with our previous UI work. With our Dialogue system now in place and ready to be brought to life by PlayMaker, we will go ahead and disable this Canvas so that it is no longer visible, just select Dialogue Overlay in the Hierarchy and then click the check box next to the Canvas component as shown in Figure 10.21. We will enable this Canvas component through PlayMaker while the game is running whenever we need this Canvas to display dialogue.

10.4 Updating the User Interface with PlayMaker

We have completed our preliminary work with the UI systems in that we have them set up the way we would like and they are displaying within the game. The buttons are also responding to the user by changing colors when the mouse cursor passes over them, but any functionality beyond that is simply not there until we create some FSMs within PlayMaker to add the behaviors that we want. We will focus on providing the necessary behavior systems to the three UI elements that we have constructed. If you have not done so already, you will need to add a Spider asset into the scene (near the bridge to guard it would be a good location) so that we can configure and test the

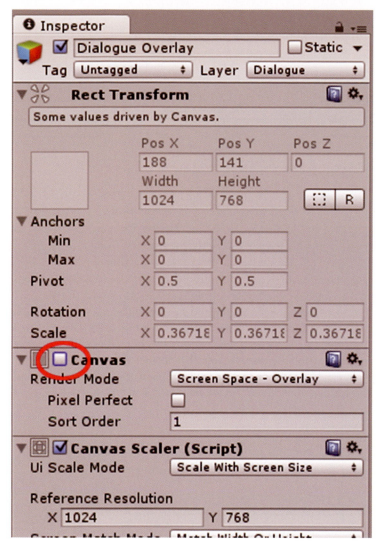

FIG 10.21 Disabling the Dialogue Overlay system.

health system of Sancho, the life system we can test by running out into the water and drowning. Other than that, we will need to remove some of the work that we did in a previous chapter with the dialogue system, but most of that will be modification rather than full on removal. We will begin with the Main Menu then move on to the HUD Overlay with Sancho's info box and wrap this chapter up with the Dialogue system and some further updating to the Quest Info object within the HUD Overlay.

10.4.1 Responses on the Main Menu

We have already done some basic work with button responders in the previous chapter with the hacked together dialogue system. We will be

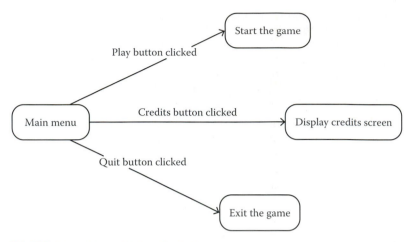

FIG 10.22 A design diagram of the logical flow for the main menu system.

utilizing the same approach here as responding to a button click is always done the same way; the whole question is what you do with the button responses, or more specifically how do we want the game to respond when the user makes a specific selection. For our main menu, we have provided the user with three options that they can select from, these are diagrammed in Figure 10.22. In order for us to launch a new scene, we will need to bring in a new PlayMaker action that we have not used previously, though there will be some minor fiddling that we will need to do for it to work.

> **Note**
>
> If you are missing the uGUI Button On Click Event in the next section be sure to download it using the Ecosystem updater:
>
> - Select PlayMaker → Addons → Ecosystem.
> - In the search box enter "u gui button on click."
> - Download and add the only action that will appear in the search results.
>
> If you are missing the Ecosystem updater, double-check the steps on downloading and installing it found in the chapter introducing Unity and PlayMaker (Chapter 3).

> 1. Create an empty game object and name it Menu Controller.
>   a. Add an Audio Source component to this object.
> 2. With Menu Controller selected open the PlayMaker editor.
>   a. Add an FSM and change its name to Mouse Responder.
>   b. Change State 1 to Idle.
>   c. Create two new states named: Exit and Play.
>   d. Create two custom events: Play Clicked and Quit Clicked.

e. Select the Idle state.
    i. Add the Play Clicked event and connect it to the Play state.
    ii. Add the Quit Clicked event and connect it to the Exit state.
    iii. Add a uGUI Button On Click Event.
        A. Change Game Object to Specify Game Object.
        B. Drag the Play Button from the Hierarchy onto the red None selection field, see Figure 10.23.
        C. Change Send Event to Play Clicked.
    iv. Repeat the process for the Quit Button using the appropriate button and event.
f. Select the Play state.
    i. Add an Audio Play action to play a button clicking noise from the audio assets we imported during the Audio chapter.
    ii. Add a Wait action to wait for the duration of the Audio file that you have selected, ours is 1 second long so the Wait action is 1 for Time with Real Time Checked.
    iii. Add a Load Level action.
        A. For the Level Name type in the name of the game level, in our case it is "Barataria" make sure it is spelled and capitalized the same as in the Project pane.
g. Select the Exit state.
    i. Add an Audio Play action to play a button clicking noise from the audio assets we imported during the Audio chapter.
    ii. Add a Wait action to wait for the duration of the Audio file that you have selected, ours is 1 second long so the Wait action is 1 for Time with Real Time Checked.
    iii. Add an Application Quit action to this state.

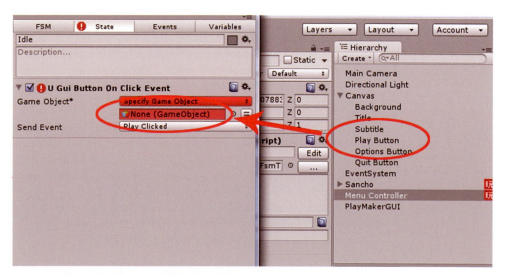

FIG 10.23 Assigning the Play Button to the Button On Click Event action.

The uGUI Button On Click Event action is developed for the sole purpose of responding to the user clicking on one of the uGUI Button UI objects that are available within Unity. It is possible to put this action within an FSM found on the Button object itself, however, by creating one master controller object such as we have, there is one centralized location to look for any errors and also to add any updates to the work later. This central approach can be very beneficial when constructing the internal control mechanisms for a game and since it is utilizing an empty object we do not have to worry about it being visible somewhere within the game and it will be easy to find by searching through the game objects listed in the scene hierarchy.

We will begin our exploration with the Play state and its new action Load Level. However, before we get to the Load Level action notice the Wait action that is being used to force the execution of our actions within this state to pause long enough for our button clicking sound to finish playing. Remember, if the button click sound that you select is not loud enough, or too long or whatever, you can load it up within Audacity and make some corrections to it then export it back out and into your game project. Also, you can find the duration of the Audio by selecting it in the Project pane and viewing its properties in the preview pane of the Inspector panel (Figure 10.24).

The Load Level action will allow us to specify a level for Unity to load. When entering the Level Name to load it is vital that the name entered matches exactly with the name of the level that we want to load, we can see the name of the level that we want to load by looking through the Project panel and reading the scene names. Generally speaking, the process of loading a level involves loading a new scene into memory and then deleting the current scene once the load is complete. However, there are a couple of interesting properties to look at that define how the loading of a new scene behaves.

The first of these is the Additive option, which will load the new level without removing the current level. This allows us to load new content into our current level; this is a good technique if we have a huge world and we want to load new sections into the current scene when the player nears the boundaries.

The other option is the Async check box which will load the new level in the background which means that we could continue playing within the current level or we could add a loading progress bar to the current level. Once a traditional load level has begun, the current level will no longer do any updating until the new level is ready to take its place, so by using the Async option we could avoid this and still have the current level functional. We could also combine both of these options and load a scene in the background that will then be added to the current scene.

There are a couple of things to keep in mind when dealing with scenes and loading them. They use memory. That may seem like a simple

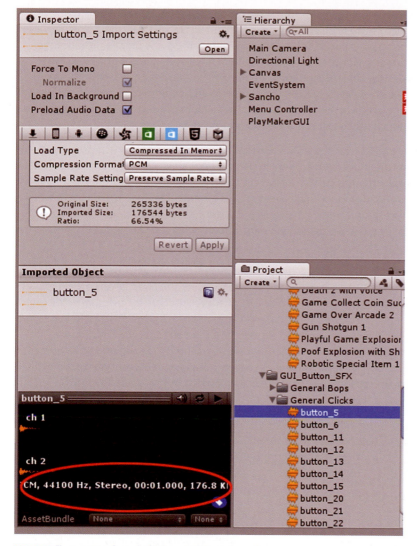

FIG 10.24 The properties of an audio file shown in the Inspector panel.

statement; however, many beginning game developers will overlook this situation and end up with games that require huge amounts of memory that can only run on specialized systems. If we are to port our game project over to a mobile device, we have to be very aware of the memory that is available to us on such a device and recognize that we may not be able to load huge virtual worlds that dynamically load into memory for the players to explore. There is also the potential case of having memory leaks occur with scenes being loaded using any of these other techniques.

The last option of interest for us with the Load Level action is to have the object initiating the scene change to either be destroyed or not be destroyed.

Remember our earlier discussion about controller objects within game scenes. These objects can do more than just handle user input; they can also be responsible for storing data relevant to the game play, for instance the player's name or the current health of the player. When we use the Don't Destroy On Load option, that object will not be destroyed when the new scene is loaded, you can think of this as an Additive scene load of adding the new scene to the current object that is not being destroyed. At the moment we are leaving all of these options turned off.

For the Exit state, we used a new action that has only one purpose and that is to quit a currently running game. There are no properties or options that we can set to customize how this thing behaves; any customization that we want done would have to be performed before we use this action. As an example, rather than going straight to the Exit state, we could have popped up a question to verify if that is what the user actually wants to do or not.

Before we are able to test this menu system, we will have to edit the build settings for our project. The way that the Load Level commands work is that they look at the list of scenes that are included with the build settings for the project to find the level to be loaded. The action does not go through the Project folder to find the correct scene. This means that we can have many scenes that we are using for testing and development but only include the scenes that we actually need in our game project build settings. To configure these settings follow the following procedures:

1. Select File → Build Settings
   a. Drag the scenes from the Project panel into the Scenes In Build list box.
   b. Be sure that the first scene you want loaded is at the top of the list, see Figure 10.25.

With these steps out of the way, we can go ahead and test our project to make sure that it works. For our first test, we will launch the project the way that we have been by pressing the Play button at the top of the button controls within Unity itself and this will launch the game within our Game view. When we click the Play button on our Main Menu, we get the button clicking noise that we want and then after a brief pause the main level of our game does load; however, it may appear to be quite a bit darker than it was when we were playing it before. This is a bug within the new Global Illumination system and will be patched soon there is no doubt. The built version of the project will display the lighting correctly it is only when the scene is loaded within the in-editor game view that the lighting is darkened; we can correct this by changing the following setting for the Barataria scene (or any scene for that matter): Windows → Lighting → Lightmap Tab → Uncheck the Auto check box and then click the Build button, see Figure 10.26. Once this has been

FIG 10.25 The list of scenes to include in the build of the project.

completed a new folder will be created within the Scenes folder for each scene that we are creating the lightmap snapshots for as shown in Figure 10.27.

The Quit button cannot test within the Unity editor; however, if we go ahead and create a full build of our game we can test to make sure that the Quit button is working as we had intended it to. Creating a test build can be done with just a couple of mouse clicks so that we can verify that the quit button is working as we would like it to.

1. Select File → Build Settings.
2. Click the Build button at the bottom of the dialogue.
3. Browse to a location to save the executable file, generally we create a folder called Builds that is within the root folder of our Project (in this case the Sancho Panza folder).
4. Provide a file name for the build.
5. Click the Save button.

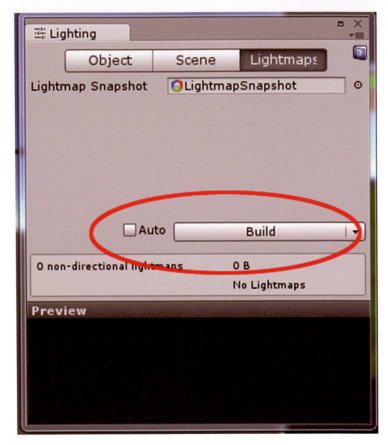

FIG 10.26 Creating a Lightmap snapshot for our scenes.

6. After the build is complete, double-click the new executable file to launch the game.
7. Select a screen resolution for testing the game, see Figure 10.28.
8. Once the game loads, click the Quit button to verify that the game will exit.
   a. WARNING: Do not click the Play button as we currently have no way to get back out of the game.

After doing our preliminary testing, we can see that the game does exit as we want it to and we can also see that we can start the game when clicking on the play button. Although, if we are testing this by running the built version of the game, we ran into a fun little problem in that once the game has loaded into Barataria we cannot exit the game, though hopefully everyone heeded the warning in the steps and did not actually test the Play button. We can remedy this by adding a controller object into the Barataria scene

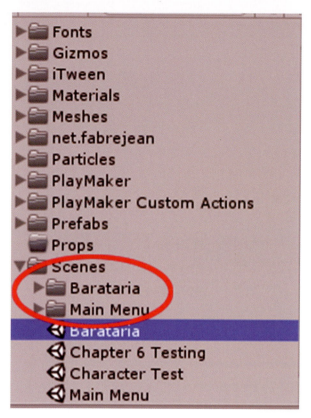

FIG 10.27 New folders that store the lightmap snapshots for each scene.

that is sitting there listening for the Escape (ESC) key to be pressed and when it is pressed the game exits out or returns to the main menu. This solution is demonstrated in the following steps.

1. Load the Barataria scene.
2. Add an empty Game Object and rename it to Game Controller.
3. Open the PlayMaker editor.
   a. Add an FSM and rename it to Exit Menu (or Pause Menu).
   b. Create a custom event named Escape Pressed.
   c. Rename State 1 to Idle.
   d. Add a new state named Exit and select this state.
      i. Add an Application Quit action.
   e. Select the Idle state.
      i. Add the Escape Pressed event and connect it to the Exit state.
      ii. Add a Get Key Down action.
         A. Select Escape from the drop-down menu for Key.
         B. Select Escape Pressed as the Send Event.

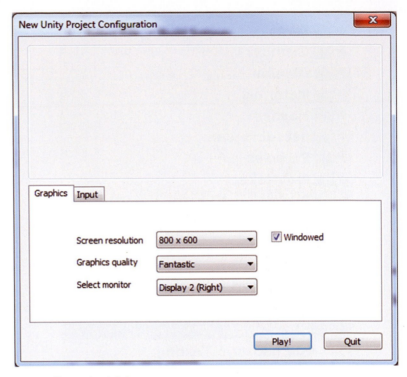

FIG 10.28 The game launch dialogue screen.

10.4.2 Updating the Overlay

We will begin the process of updating the HUD Overlay by getting it to correctly display the number of lives that Sancho has remaining. After getting the life display to work correctly we will have Sancho get beat up by a Spider and get the Health bar to decrease appropriately. To begin with the life display on the overlay, we will start with the life management system that was added to the health system of Sancho as an exercise in one of the previous chapters. The solution of which is depicted in Figure 10.29. Also, a new variable was introduced to keep track of the number of lives that the player has left, this variable is of type int and we named our variable lives. The essential logic in this structure is outlined as follows:

- When the player's health reaches 0 the player will die.
  - Play the death animation.
  - Disable all of the movement animations for Sancho.
  - Subtract 1 from the current number of lives.
- Check the current number of lives.
  - If the number of lives is above 0 then the player can respawn.
  - Otherwise the player is dead and the game is over.

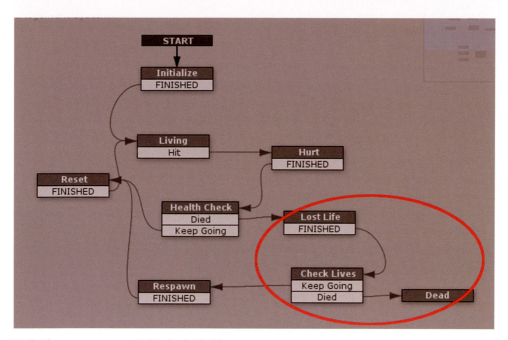

FIG 10.29 The life management system added into Sancho's Health system.

Our basic approach to updating the life display in the HUD is going to be to display the appropriate number of life images as diagrammed in Figure 10.30. Notice that within this design structure, we will only have to disable one of the life images each time. The reason for this is that in order for Sancho to be down to only 1 life, as an example, that would require that the last run through this part of the state machine Sancho was at 2 lives. Since he was at 2 lives last time and we turned off the third life image the last time, then this time when Sancho is down to 1 life we know that we only have to turn

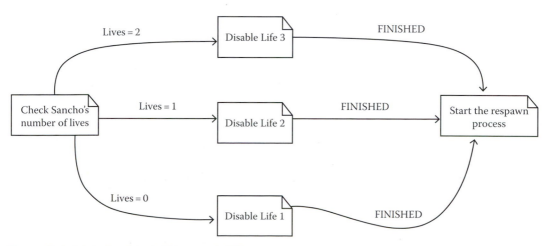

FIG 10.30 The logic design for updating the life images on the HUD.

of the second life image as the third is already disabled from the previous run through this design.

1. Make sure that you are within the Health FSM for Sancho.
2. Add three new events: 0 Lives, 1 Life, and 2 Lives.
3. Create a new state named Update HUD.
4. Connect the Keep Going event from Check Lives to Update HUD.
5. Create three more states named: Lives 2, Lives 1, and Lives 0.
   a. Add a FINISHED event to each of these and connect to the Respawn state.
6. Within the Update HUD state add the three new events and connect them to the appropriate state, see Figure 10.31 for an overview of this placement.
7. Select the Update HUD state.
   a. Add an Int Compare action.
      i. Integer 1 should be the lives variable.
      ii. Integer 2 should be 2.
      iii. Equal is the 2 Lives event.
   b. Add another Int Compare action.
      i. Integer 1 is the lives variable again.
      ii. Integer 2 is 1.
      iii. Equal is the 1 Life event.
      iv. Less than is the 0 Lives event.
8. Select the Lives 2 state.
   a. Drag the Life 3 Image UI object from the Hierarchy panel into the Actions panel of the state.
   b. Select Set Property from the pop-up menu that will appear when releasing the object.
   c. Select active from the drop-down menu for property.
9. Repeat step 8 for the Life 2 and Life 1 Image UI objects in the scene.

To test this system, we can take Sancho and run out into the water until he drowns and see if the number of displayed life images changes within the HUD overlay. Every action that we are using within this new addition to the state machine, we have used in previous states for other purposes. At this point we can really begin to see how these actions are forming the building blocks of the behaviors for our games. We are using the same actions that we have before, but are putting them together in different sequences or with different values to get the desired results. The trick to becoming a good programmer is recognizing that every program is constructed of the same building blocks it is just a case of how we put those pieces together, understanding the underlying logical flow is absolutely vital, and by this point in the book we are starting to put the pieces together in our minds. Eventually, we will add more actions to our knowledge base as our programming skills continue to grow and improve through practice.

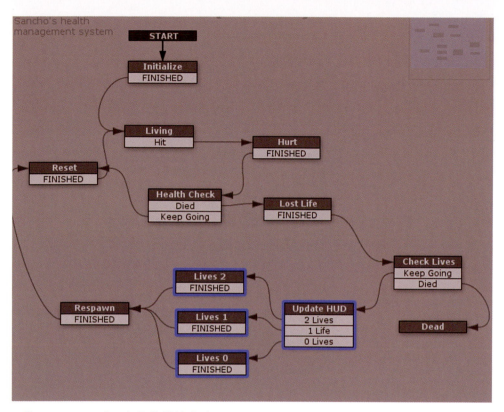

FIG 10.31 The new states inserted into the Health FSM for Sancho.

Next on our list for the HUD Overlay system will be to get the health bar of Sancho to decrease as he is attacked by an enemy, in this case, a spider. Earlier in the book you were challenged to place a spider on the bridge to act as a guard and respond to Sancho's presence. The focus at the time was adding audio elements to the spider and its reactions as well as modifying the prefab slightly for our purposes by disabling the patrolling system (which can be turned back on at any time that we want that behavior put back in). We will go ahead and play with the spider because it is already hungry to hurt Sancho if it can. It may be easier for construction and testing to either move Sancho closer to the spider or move the spider closer to Sancho, either one will save us time during testing.

Before we jump into PlayMaker we are going to consider what it is that we want done. The health bar that we have displayed in the HUD, we want to work as a percentage bar. Therefore, a fully healthy Sancho will have the health bar all the way up and green, a half healthy Sancho will have the health bar halfway down to the left and yellow and a sickly Sancho will have the health bar nearly all the way down to the left and red. This is a common scheme in games that use health bars, but to make sure we can see a visualization of this in Figure 10.32.

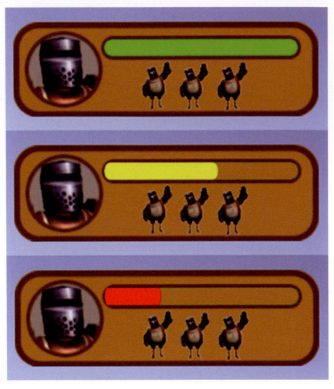

FIG 10.32 The Health bar of Sancho in action.

Note

By this point your Barataria Hierarchy panel may be starting to get a little complex and difficult to manage. There are a couple of things that can help us manage this Hierarchy panel as our scenes get more and more complex. The first is the search bar at the top, we can enter what object we are looking for and objects matching that criteria will be the only ones to show up in the Hierarchy panel. The second option is to use Empty Game Objects as folders for categories of game objects also shown in Figure 10.33. Be aware, set your empty objects to 0, 0, 0 especially when nesting UI objects.

It turns out that the Image UI object already has a way to do what we want built-in, we just need to take a look at these options. Select the Sancho Health UI object that we created earlier and change the Image Type from Simple to Filled, see Figure 10.34. A Filled Image Type is one that we can change how much of the image is visible. We can modify the fill of the image either horizontally, vertically, or radially. Our Health Bar is horizontal, so utilizing a Horizontal Fill Method will allow us to change how much of the image is visible based upon the Fill Origin which we

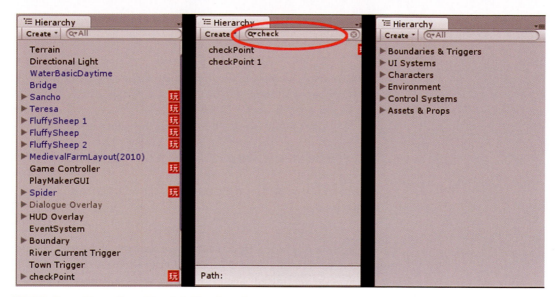

will set to Left. Now, if you adjust the Fill Amount slider you will be able to see the health bar image fill to the appropriate amount based on the Fill Amount.

We now know what we want to change within Unity, but before jumping into PlayMaker we need to consider how we are going to get these changes to occur. As we have seen earlier, it is much easier if we take our time and design our solutions before actually trying to implement them, this becomes even more important when we are editing state machines. Before we start adding or removing things from our state machines, we need to take a few moments to consider exactly how we want the new system to function without worrying about exactly how that is done within PlayMaker.

- After Sancho has gotten hurt by something update the health bar.
  - Change the fill amount to be the same as Sancho's new health.
  - If Sancho's health is below 66% change the color of the bar to yellow.
  - If Sancho's health is below 33% change the color of the bar to red.
- After Sancho has died reset the color and fill amount on the health bar.

Following on our text-based list we see that we want the fill amount for the health bar to be set to the value of Sancho's health whenever Sancho gets injured. However, we created Sancho's health as an int and those are whole numbers only. As we played with the fill amount property we noticed that it was not whole numbers but rather values between 0.0 and 1.0 or a float value. When using a value between 0 and 1 this is oftentimes referred to as a *normalized value* which is to say that the value has been converted to a value between either all on (1) or all off (0). An example of this would be if we normalized our color values so that a completely red color would be 1, 0, 0 rather than 255, 0, 0 (using RGB values). The easiest way to normalize a value is to divide the current value by the maximum that it could be, for instance, 255 divided by 255 would be 1, or in the case of a health bar 80 divided by 100 would be 0.8. A full diagram of this system can be seen in Figure 10.35 which helps us to visualize these changes that we are getting ready to make.

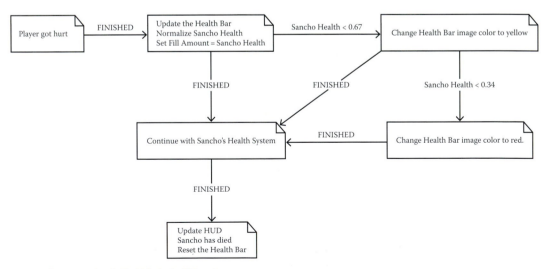

FIG 10.35 Design to update the Health Bar in the HUD overlay.

1. Select the Health FSM within Sancho.
   a. If you have not done so previously, set the maxHealth variable to 100.
   b. Add a new variable of type float named healthBar.
   c. Add a new event named Change Health Color.
   d. Create three new states named Update Health Bar, Yellow Health Bar, and Red Health Bar, see Figure 10.36 for these new states.
   e. Connect the FINISHED event from the Hurt state to the Update Health Bar state, see Figure 10.36 for this placement.
   f. Select the Update Health Bar state.
      i. Add a FINISHED event and connect it to the Health Check state.
      ii. Add a Change Health Color event and connect it to the Yellow Health Bar state.
      iii. Add a Convert Int To Float action.
         A. Int Variable is health.
         B. Float Variable is healthBar.
      iv. Add a Float Divide action.
         A. Float Variable is healthBar.
         B. Divide By is 100.
      v. Click the Lock button along the top, see Figure 10.36.
         A. Find and select the Image (Script) component within the Sancho Health UI object from the Hierarchy panel.
            I. Drag this component into the Action panel for PlayMaker.
               – Select Set Property from the pop-out menu that appears when releasing the mouse.
               – Select fillAmount from the Property drop-down menu.
               – Select the healthBar variable for the Set Value.
      vi. Add a Float Compare action.
         A. Select healthBar for Float 1.
         B. Enter 0.67 for Float 2.
         C. Set the Less Than event to Change Health Color.
         D. See Figure 10.36 for the final construction of this state.
   g. Select the Yellow Health Bar state.
      i. Add a FINISHED event and connect it to the Health Check state.
      ii. Add a Change Health Color event and connect it to the Red Health Bar state.
      iii. Repeat dragging of the Image (Script) component from the Sancho Health object into this Action panel.
         A. Select Set Property.
         B. Select color → color for Property.
         C. Select a Yellow color for Set Value.

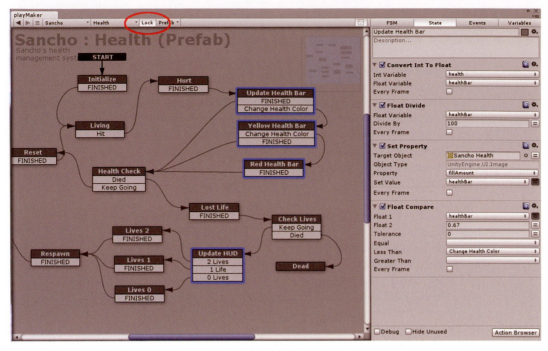

FIG 10.36 Lock selection in the PlayMaker editor and overview of the modified Health System.

iv. Add a Float Compare action.
 A. Set healthBar to Float 1.
 B. Set 0.34 for Float 2.
 C. Less Than Event should be Change Health Color.
h. Select the Red Health Bar state.
 i. Add a FINISHED event and connect it to the Health Check state.
 ii. Repeat dragging of the Image (Script) component from the Sancho Health object into this Action panel.
 A. Select Set Property.
 B. Select color → color for Property.
 C. Select a Red color for Set Value.
i. Select the Update HUD state.
 i. Add a Set Property action to set the fillAmount property for Image (Script) of Sancho Health to 1.
 ii. Add a Set Property action to set the color property for Image (Script) of Sancho Health to green, see Figure 10.37.

The truly tricky part of this sequence of actions is getting that Set Property action to work exactly the way that we would like it to. By turning on the Lock feature in the PlayMaker editor, we are able to click around the Hierarchy, or Project for that matter, and select other objects without having the focus of the PlayMaker editor window change. This way we can actually select the

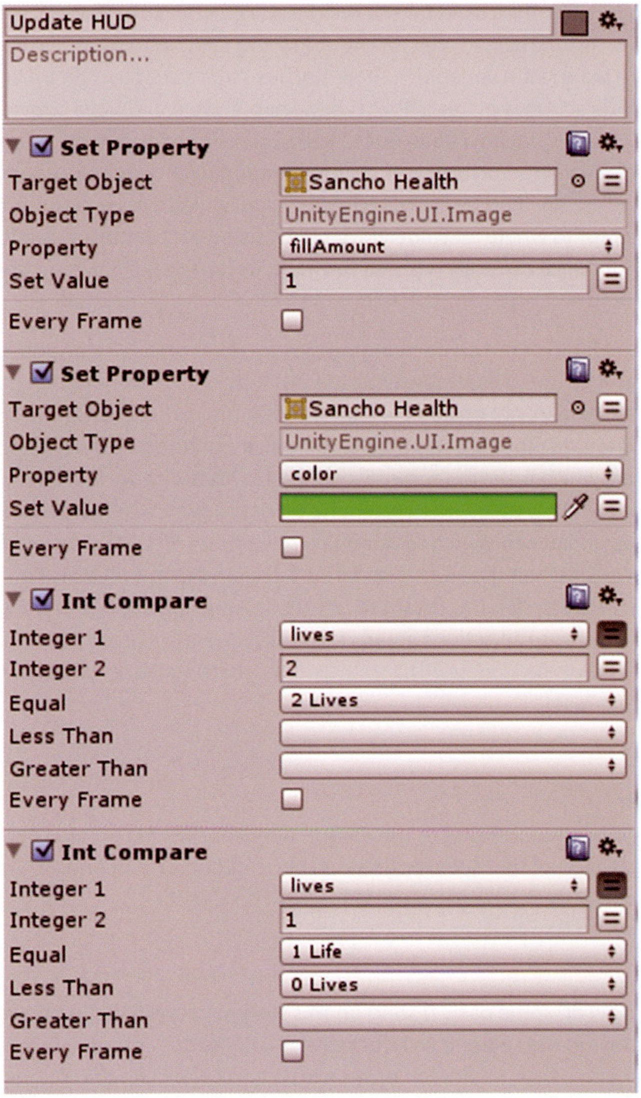

FIG 10.37 The modified Update HUD state.

Sancho Health object and grab a component out of it. The key here is that we are wanting to change a property, or set a property value, for that specific component, not for the object itself. Once we are able to drag that into our Actions pane, we can get the exact property that we are wanting to change and get it set to whatever value that we want. This is an easily overlooked feature of PlayMaker, being able to directly set the properties of components like this and the key to it is using the Lock button and also dragging that component into our Action pane.

The normalization of the health value for Sancho so that it can be used by the fill amount property is done by utilizing the Float Divide action and dividing by 100. 100 is used for the divide by value because that is the maximum health that we are currently allowing Sancho to have. We cannot insert the maxHealth variable in there because that variable is an int and the Float Divide action requires a float type variable. We could have converted the maxHealth value to a float, but to keep this as brief as possible we just hard coded a value. You are strongly encouraged to change this around so that we are dividing by the maxHealth value, which can be changed in the Inspector to whatever value we want. By using that value instead it will always normalize correctly without having to return to our FSM and change this value.

Finally, the flow for our color changing system relies on a fall through kind of logical structure. The best way to see this flow is if we were to reverse the Float Compare actions that we are using in the various states. To begin, if the current health is greater than 0.66 then keep the current color of the health bar, which is the default color of green. Otherwise we will change the color to yellow unless the current health is below 0.34 at which point we will go ahead and switch to our final color of red. All of this is reset to the default values when the HUD is updated after Sancho has died and before he actually respawns. It is important to get those resetting actions at the top of that state because all actions are performed sequentially from top to bottom and if we leave the Update HUD state before resetting those values then they will not get reset.

Video

A video has been posted to the companion website that provides a visual walk through of the steps for getting the updating of Sancho's HUD to work correctly, it is named: "Updating Sancho Health."

We can now do some basic testing on this system and will that when we charge toward the spider it will notice us and come get us and with each of its attacks on us our Health Bar drops a little and even changes color at the appropriate times. Our HUD overlay is now updating based upon actions that are occurring during game play.

10.4.3 Integrating the Dialogue System

For our final section, we will modify the original dialogue system to work with our much cleaner system in the new UI that we have constructed over the course of this chapter. We will begin by placing Teresa into our scene, if she is not already in there, and put her somewhere over by the entrance into the town on the island. In this example we will demonstrate the changes needed for Teresa, or any other dialogue object, and how we can update our quest information to keep the player properly informed as to what they should be doing. We will begin by reviewing the previous work on the dialogue system for Teresa.

Within the Teresa object we had placed a Canvas object to serve as the temporary UI for the dialogue. The thinking at the time was that by attaching it to Teresa the dialogue would display wherever Teresa is and while this did work and is a very strong option, we now have a different dialogue system in place within our HUD overlay. There are two advantages to switching to our new system, the first is that any object can use it that wants to. And the second advantage is that it turns out to be much cleaner than what we had done with Teresa; it is easier to read and easier to interact with. Based on this, we will go ahead and delete the Canvas object that is currently attached to Teresa then we would only have to switch over the object references within the PlayMaker state machines for Teresa and everything should work just as it did before.

1. Select the Teresa object from the Hierarchy and open the PlayMaker Editor.
2. Reassign all of the variables as shown in Figure 10.38.
3. Notice that we have created a new variable named speaker_image, this variable is of type Object → Unity Engine → UI → Image.
4. In the Start state for Teresa's Starting Dialogue FSM add a Set Property action.
   a. Target Object is speaker_image.
   b. Property is Sprite → Sprite.
   c. Select the Teresa Head image from the UI Images folder.

With the new assignments for the variables within our dialogue system from previously, it now works just as it did before, except better as it is easier to read and easier to see and generally easier to interact with. Through the use of those variables that we created in our earlier chapter and the careful design work we did when constructing this conversation system, bringing it into a new scene did not involve too much work. We did make one addition to our state machine, we have added a picture of Teresa to the dialogue just in case the player forgets who he is talking to. Now we need to connect this updated system with the new Quest Journal on our HUD Overlay. For this, we will return to the Collecting state machine that we constructed within Sancho for handling the collection of sheep.

1. Create a new event named Start Sheep Quest.
2. Create the variables listed in Table 10.7.
3. Create a new state named No Quest.
4. Right-click this new state and select Set as Start State to make it the new start state.
5. Add the Start Sheep Quest transition event to the No Quest State.
6. Connect the Start Sheep Quest transition to the Sheep Quest state.

FIG 10.38 The new variable values for Teresa.

7. Select the No Quest state.
   a. Add a Bool Test action.
      i. Bool Variable is isSheepQuest.
      ii. Is True is Start Sheep Quest.
      iii. Every Frame should be checked.
   b. Add a Set Property action.
      i. Target Object is quest_display.
      ii. Property is text.
      iii. Set Value is "Go find Teresa."
8. Select the Sheep Quest state.
   a. Add a Convert Int to String action.
      i. Int Variable is findSheep.
      ii. String Variable is need_text.
   b. Add a Convert Int to String action.
      i. Int Variable is numSheep.
      ii. String Variable is found_text.
   c. Add a Build String action.
      i. String Parts is 5.
      ii. Element 0 is "Found."
      iii. Element 1 is found_text.
      iv. Element 2 is "of."
      v. Element 3 is need_text.
      vi. Element 4 is "sheep."
      vii. For separator hit the space bar to put a space between each one of the elements.
      viii. Store Result is quest_text.
   d. Add a Set Property action.
      i. Target Object is quest_display.
      ii. Property is text.
      iii. Set Value is quest_text.
9. Select the All Sheep state.
   a. Remove the Debug Log action.
   b. Add a Set String Value action.
      i. String Variable is quest_text.
      ii. String Value is "Return the sheep to the pen."
   c. Add a Set Property action.
      i. Target Object is quest_display.
      ii. Property is text.
      iii. Set Value is quest_text.

While it was necessary for us to add quite a few new variables to this previously created state machine, we did not need to do too many other modifications to it. We began by switching the default starting state to be No Quest where we can set the default message to appear in the Quest Display for the player, in this case the default is "Go find Teresa." This message will be displayed to the player whenever they have completed a quest to remind

TABLE 10.7 The New Variables Needed in the Collecting FSM of Sancho

Variable Name	Variable Type	Variable Purpose
found_text	String	The number of sheep currently found as a string.
isSheepQuest	Bool	Whether or not we are on the sheep quest.
need_text	String	The number of sheep we need to find as a string.
quest_display	Object → Unity Engine → UI → Text	The Text UI object that we will be displaying quest information to.
quest_text	String	The string that we will display to the user with quest information.

them to go back to her and get a new quest for the reclaiming of Barataria. We can add other Boolean variables into this state to launch into other quests for the player to engage in, such as the Go Find Dapple quest that the player is actually assigned by Teresa at the moment. For testing purposes, we will go ahead and turn the isSheepQuest variable to True so that we can verify that this does indeed work. Beyond this, we have added the actions to convert the current number of sheep found and the number of sheep needed to be found into Strings and then constructed a string message to display on the screen to the player. Finally, once the player has found the sheep, we are going to change the quest message to inform the player that they need to get the sheep back to the pen in town. Before testing this system, be sure to assign the value for quest_display in the Inspector. This quest can be triggered at the end of a conversation with Teresa in which Teresa will reach over and turn the isSheepQuest, or isDappleQuest for that matter, Bool variable to true and off it will go. Also, notice that with this construction the sheep will not follow Sancho unless he is actually on that quest.

> **Video**
>
> To help with the modification of the quest journal for the sheep quest, we have created a video named "Sheep Quest UI" that can be found on the companion website, as some of these variables can be a bit tricky to deal with.

10.5 Summary

Throughout this chapter, we have seen the power of the new uGUI system included with Unity 5. This graphical approach to creating UIs makes it much quicker and more intuitive to put together the systems that we want. Also, through the graphical construction, it is a lot easier to bring the visions of the interfaces to life as we want them to be. We also looked at how we can use these tools to construct different types of interface systems ranging from menu-based systems with our main menu and also our dialogue system to the HUD overlays that we constructed for the main game play of our project. As we have seen, UIs can be a lot of fun to construct though they do often involve utilizing 2D assets that have been created outside of Unity, generally speaking, Photoshop is the tool of choice for these activities (see the companion website for a video demonstrating the use of Photoshop for the creation of UI elements that were used in this chapter). Through the techniques that we looked at in this chapter, we can construct more complex interface systems that respond to different types of dynamic information through FSMs within PlayMaker.

Download
You can find the finished scenes for this chapter in the complete project package on the companion website, the scene name is: "Chapter10_final."

Vocabulary

Hardware interface
Software interface
Virtual reality
HCI
Ergonomics
UI
GUI
HUD
Diegetic UI
Nondiegetic UI
Meta UI
Spatial UI
Menu-based systems
Color theory
Primary color
Secondary color
Tertiary color
Analogous colors
Complementary colors
uGUI
Rect transform
Canvas UI object
Text UI object
Button UI object
Image UI object
Normalize value

Review Quiz

1. What are the differences between a menu-based system and a heads-up display?
2. What are the advantages and disadvantages of a motion camera system and a motion sensor system?

3. Why is uGUI easier to use for content-based creation than the traditional Unity UI system?
4. Why does a Button UI Object contain a child Text UI Object by default?
5. What is the advantage of using images that have been colored white for UI elements within Unity?
6. If a treasure chest in the game world can hold 15 objects and it currently contains 8, what would the normalized value be for how full it is if we wanted to display this fullness as a vertical image bar?

Exercises

1. Create a loading game text box that is displayed once the player clicks the Play button on the Main Menu.
2. Using the techniques to construct the info box for Sancho Panza, construct a similar info box for the Spider object guarding the bridge across the river.
3. CHALLENGE: See if you can come up with a way to abstract this spider info box so that it can be shared by any other enemy assets that are encountered by Sancho during game play, you will find the graphics that you need for this already imported in your project from when the graphic assets were imported earlier in this chapter.
   a. HINT: Consider the work that we did with the dialogue system. Construct the spider info box as a part of the HUD Overlay just as we did for Sancho. Disable the object by default and when the Spider detects Sancho and begins a charge at him, turn on this info box. With the box turned on, use a PlayMaker FSM inside of the Spider to set the image of the info box to belong to the spider and also to set the health to be that of the spider. When the spider dies, disable this info box. With this done, we could use these same steps for any other object to utilize this info box.
4. Create some new quests for Sancho to complete and get them working with our dialogue system and also with the quest display system.
5. Add a splash screen of your design to the project, it does not need to be anything fancy at this point as the graphics can be modified at a later point, utilize the following basic logic:
   a. When the splash screen starts have it display your design and play an audio fanfare of your selection for a few seconds then automatically launch the main menu.
   b. You could create a looping system by having the main menu return to the splash screen after a few minutes of the player not selecting any of the buttons.
6. Create the Credits menu screen with a button to return to the main menu.
7. Using what you have learned from the Main Menu and also from the Dialogue system, construct a new dialogue system to appear when the player clicks to quit the game asking the player if they are sure they want to quit. If yes, then go ahead and exit, otherwise return to the main menu.

8. Add a pop-up message that appears when the player runs into deep water and provide a text message to the player as to why they are losing a life, perhaps something like "I cannot swim." While we are at that, we can go ahead and remove the text message that we were displaying to the console window on this event.

Design Document

In this addition to the Sancho Panza design document, we have added our design ideas for the menu systems as well as the HUD displays within the game.

Download
The updated version of the *Sancho Panza* design document can be downloaded from the companion website as: "DesignDocument_chapter10."

Consider your design document that you have been working on thus far and add the following to it:

1. Design a main menu mock-up for your game project.
    a. Consider what the player can do from the main menu.
2. Design a HUD overlay for your game project.
    a. Consider what information needs to be displayed to the player.
3. What other UI systems will you need in your project?
    a. Create mock-ups for any of these other systems.

CHAPTER 11

Testing, Tweaking, and Publishing

We are nearing the end of our introduction to game development, and Sancho Panza is almost ready to be let out of the house. In this chapter, we will look at three distinct yet interrelated topics: testing, tweaking, and publishing. We will look at the wealth of options that Unity provides for us to build our game projects so that others may be able to enjoy and possibly even buy them. However, before we get too excited about getting our game into the hands of gamers everywhere, we will need to spend some serious time testing it and even though we have done some testing during the whole development process, we need to go into more depth and discover how to test a game. With our game nearly completed, we cannot go back and rebuild it just to add a new feature or two; however, if those new ideas will fit within the framework of what we have already done, then there is nothing wrong with making a tweak here and there, or even polishing up some of the work that we have done to iron out the kinks. We will explore all of these topics throughout this chapter.

- What Is Testing?
- How to Approach Testing
- Finding and Tracking Bugs
- Tweaking the Game
- Supported Build Platforms
- Building and Publishing Projects

11.1 What Is Testing?

Testing a game is more than just playing a game. At first glance it is easy for us to think that we can test our game simply by playing it and discovering what does not work within the game. There are three distinct approaches that we will look at with regard to testing: play-through testing, unit testing, and break testing. These each serve different purposes and will require different approaches to successfully test our game to ensure that it is ready to get out in the general public. Another piece to consider in regard to testing is who does the testing. For some of the testing, we as developers can go ahead and do the testing ourselves, however for other parts of testing we will really need someone that has not been working on the game to take a look at it with a fresh pair of eyes, so to speak, and see what they discover. We will begin our look at testing by getting our project ready and exploring bugs.

To get our project ready for others, or even us, to better test it, we are going to turn off those PlayMaker state labels that have been showing up in the game. Until now, they have been beneficial for the testing and building that we have been doing, but now that we are going to get serious about testing we need to get these off the screen. One reason to get these off the screen is to make sure that no one thinks they are bugs; for instance, in Figure 11.1 we can see that labels are appearing in front of the dialogue box containing our conversation with Teresa. It is only natural to assume that it is a bug since from a player's perspective there should not be any white text like this in front of the dialogue box. Another reason to get rid of these labels is that they do clutter the space somewhat and make it more difficult for us to see details within the game during game play.

Elimination of the state labels during game play can be done by disabling the PlayMakerGUI (Script) Component within the PlayMakerGUI Game Object that is located within the current scene as shown in Figure 11.2. Ofcourse this means that we will have to go to any other scenes, such as the Main Menu, and disable the PlayMakerGUI (Script) component in there as well. However, disabling this one component is quicker and easier than going through each individual Game Object and manually turning off the PlayMaker state labeling system. If we were to disable the Game Object itself, rather than just

FIG 11.1 The various state labels blowing through our dialogue box with Teresa.

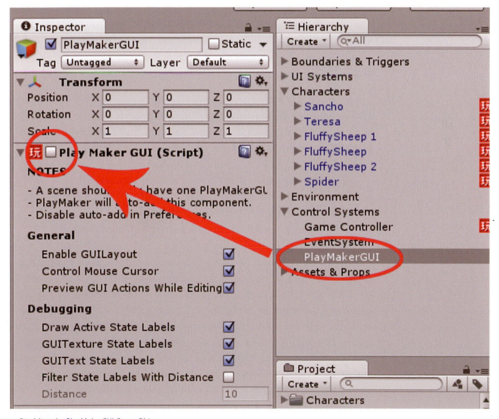

FIG 11.2 Disabling the PlayMakerGUI Game Object.

the component within the Game Object, then there is a strong possibility that PlayMaker will add that Game Object back into the scene because it will not detect the Game Object there, after all it is disabled. Generally speaking, this should not happen, but if we were to update the PlayMaker files we are using in our project it would definitely happen. With this disabled, we will no longer see those white text labels throughout our game world and are now ready to advance to hunting some bugs.

11.1.1 Hunting Bugs

The ultimate goal of play testing is to find and discover any bugs that may be hidden within the game and to help tweak and polish the game for final release. A bug can be a flaw in the game that causes the system to behave incorrectly; we might even say the system behaves unexpectedly. A bug is always caused by a flaw within our programming logic. Notice that we are not saying an error in our programming logic, because technically speaking an error in our logic would actually prevent the game from running. Code errors, syntax errors, or PlayMaker errors are detected by the compiler when getting the game ready to run and are then displayed with the red exclamation point in the Console as we have encountered at various times during this project. A bug, rather than being an error, is a flaw in the logic that we have constructed. Something to keep in mind with computer software, including games, is that it only does what it has been told to do or programmed to do. We can expand on this to recognize that any bug in the game is the computer doing exactly what we told it to do, but apparently what we *thought* we were telling it to do and what we *did* tell it to do are not the same thing.

When testers encounter a bug, in whichever testing stage they are in, the bug needs to be documented and the tester needs to ensure that they understand what is going on. When documenting a bug the following guidelines should be followed:

- Provide a screenshot of the bug or a video capture of it.
- Describe in detail what the bug is, focusing on what went wrong.
- Describe in detail what you did to cause the bug.
- Does the bug happen every time you try to make it happen?

The idea that a picture is worth a thousand words makes a screenshot or video capture of the bug in action absolutely vital. Trying to verbally describe what the screen looks like is nowhere near as effective as taking a quick screen capture of the bug in action and then using Photoshop or something to circle and highlight the areas that have bugged out in the game. The description of what caused the bug is more important than we may first realize. Remember that as testers we are looking at bugs from the player's perspective not from the developer's perspective. Sure, as a developer we may have no idea why the game is behaving as it is, but as a player we should absolutely know that when we do X in situation Y the game will always do Z. We can test this, we can verify this, and then we can tell the developers this. Now, the developers can look at doing X in situation Y and try to figure out what is happening.

Keep in mind that testing our game project needs to be a thorough and procedural process in which we focus on certain types of bugs or certain aspects of the game in order to find any bugs that may be hiding in there. It is very possible, even likely, that a couple of bugs here and there will slip through our testing process and still live within the game that we ultimately release. While it is important to try to find as many bugs as possible, it is equally important to recognize that some are going to slip through the cracks, but we can fix them later through game patches or updates.

11.1.2 Play-Through Testing

Play-through testing is playing through a game from start to finish with the goal of making sure that the game can be completed. While conducting a play-through test, any side quests or side goals of the game are not tested. For instance, a play-through test of *Super Mario Bros.* would not involve gathering all of the coins and exploring as many of the warp pipes as possible, it would be a blaze through the game from start to finish. With Sancho Panza, a play-through test would be going right through the game without exploring the whole island, because the whole island is not necessary for completion of the game. For instance, while conducting a play-through test it is very possible that the testers would never discover that Sancho dies if he goes too far out into the ocean, as going out there is not relevant to completing the game.

When conducting this type of a test, it is best to use people that are familiar with the game as we need them to blow through the game as quickly as possible just to verify that the game does work and that it can be completed. Someone that has never seen the game would not be a very good selection for a play-through tester as they do not necessarily know the quickest way through the game. It is also important to note that while doing this we cannot utilize any cheats or disable any settings and features. It would be much easier to do a play-through test if we disabled Sancho's health system so that we did not need to worry about him getting hurt and causing a delay as we respawn and run back to where we were. At first glance, it seems as though this would actually help with a play-through test, but what if there is an issue with a challenge later in the game in which Sancho does not get damaged by something that should be hurting him, this should be discovered by a play-through as we want to guarantee that the game can be completed as intended, which also means challenging to the player through the main game play as intended.

When we think of testing a game, we generally mean play-through testing. However, as we have seen this type of testing is not just about playing the game, the focus is to make sure that the game can be completed in a direct manner. So much of what we do while playing games is not relevant to play-through testing. All of the exploring, wandering, crafting, and gathering that we might do during a game, if they are not directly required in order to complete the game do not need to be tested during a play-through test.

During a play-through test, it is not necessary to make sure that all of the checkpoints on the island of Barataria work or that the player cannot sneak past any artificial boundaries to get to other areas of the map. The only purpose of play-through testing is to make sure that the player can begin the game and complete the game by doing exactly what is required to complete the game, all of the other stuff gets picked up in our other testing categories.

11.1.3 Unit Testing

Where play-through testing focuses on the start to finish game, unit testing focuses on individual chunks or units of the game. This is best done by breaking the game apart into chunks to test. We have been doing this, to an extent, during much of our development process thus far. As we would design a solution and implement the given design we would then test it. For instance, if I press the space bar does Sancho jump? If the answer is "yes" then that individual unit is considered to be working correctly. For unit testing we must test each possibility and each situation to make sure that it works as intended, this can be a very tedious process. Consider, for example, if we are working on a fantasy RPG game and silver weapons are required to kill certain creatures we will need to test each silver weapon on the various types of creatures that are supposed to be hurt by them. But, to go with that, we will also need to test all of the nonsilver weapons to make sure that they do not hurt these creatures. This would come down to a few hours of doing nothing but finding and attacking these creature types with all of the different weapons to make sure the correct ones work and that the others do not. Only after every weapon has been tested with the werewolf and verified to work correctly could we call that unit tested and verified and move on to the next silver weapon creature. As can be seen from this example, unit testing is less about playing the game and more about making sure that each part of the game works as it is supposed to. When it comes to unit testing, to-do lists become our best friend as they help us stay on track and also guarantee that when a particular unit is tested and verified it has actually been tested thoroughly. Another example of unit testing is providing a diagram of a dialogue system to the testers and having them verify that the dialogue in the game works as it was diagrammed to do so making sure that the correct options are displayed at the correct times with the correct responses from the other characters. Some aspects of the unit testing were already completed as we developed each individual unit; for instance, after completing the "go find Dapple" conversation system, we should have tested it to make sure that each option appeared when it should and led to the appropriate response by Teresa.

There is an interesting thing about unit testing in regards to the construction system within the Unity game engine. If our prefabs have been constructed correctly and work as they should, then whenever that prefab is used again it will work correctly as well. For instance, it is not necessary for us to test every individual sheep that is placed in the game to verify that they follow Sancho as desired. The reason for this is that the sheep are instances of the prefab object so if the prefab is working correctly and if we have properly utilized those prefabs in the creation of our other sheep (specifically in the addition of our other sheep into the scene) then there is no reason that the other sheep will not work correctly. The same thing goes when using tags for our collision systems, as long as every object is properly tagged then they should work correctly within the state machines that govern their collision behavior. But, this is the whole point of unit testing, to verify that everything is added to the scene correctly and that everything does have the proper tag. It is easy to skip over unit testing working under the assumption that it worked correctly when we developed it; however, unit testing is a method of double-checking ourselves and making sure that we did not overlook something such as accidentally retagging one of the sheep to something else. The best approach to this topic is to give your testers a list of things that you want them to test and let them go verify that they work correctly.

We are going to create a unit list of the sheep quest system and test it to make sure that it is working as desired. We have already tested for the basics during development in that if we collide with a sheep it will follow us, so we know that is working. However, what other things could we test to be able to validate this complete unit?

- Can the player collect sheep before getting the quest?
- Can the player collect more than the required number of sheep?
- Do the sheep follow Sancho over a long distance?
- Do the sheep get lost?

After thoroughly testing this unit system we have found that it does work but we are also getting some odd behavior out of it. For instance, if the player goes out to the beach or even into the water, the sheep will follow as they are supposed to, but they float in the air, as can be seen in Figure 11.3. This bug is

FIG 11.3 It is the super floating or flying sheep.

caused, from the player's perspective, by collecting a sheep so that it will follow us and then running out into the ocean. It is also caused by collecting the sheep and then running to an area of the island that is lower than where the sheep was originally located at and collected from. Remember, testing is about figuring out what causes the bug from the player's perspective and reporting that to the developers. As testers we should not be trying to solve the problem for the developers just telling them what it is, the fact that in this case we are both tester and developer does not mean that we should alter this too drastically.

We have also discovered that if we run through the town or around the town, the sheep pass right through the walls of the town and keep following Sancho. This can be seen in Figure 11.4. We have documented the cause of this problem as collecting the sheep and then running away in such a way as to put an obstacle between us and the following sheep. When this occurs the sheep just walk right through the obstacle. As developers, we may already know the solution to this, or the cause within the game, but as players we do not know what the solution is, only how to make the bug happen.

Finally, during unit testing this, we noticed that if we run out into the ocean and die, the sheep will continue to follow Sancho, it will take them awhile to return to where Sancho is located at his given new location after respawning. Whether this is something that we want to change or not is entirely up to us as the developers of the project. But as testers of the project, it is our responsibility to document this kind of behavior. If we as the player found the behavior to be odd, then perhaps that type of behavior system is a detraction from playability and fun. This is something that could be brought up with

FIG 11.4 Sheep that ignores walls and other buildings.

other testers to get their feedback on this aspect of the game and decide how to proceed from there.

11.1.4 Break Testing

The goal of break testing is to intentionally try to break the game. This is the most difficult type of testing for the developers themselves to do. The reasoning for this is that we are so familiar with the game and the systems that we have constructed that we will naturally play the game within those systems and rule structures. It is very difficult for us to think of things other than what the game is programmed to do to try. The best break testers are those that have not played the game before, or at the very least have not been involved in the actual development of the game. This is because they will come to the game and immediately start trying to do things that we as developers have not even considered. There are a couple of different approaches that can be taken when conducting this type of testing. One of these is to simply let people play the game and see what happens. It is interesting how many things gamers will come up with to try within your game project that never even occurred to you to consider during development.

For an example of break testing, we will return to our sheep quest that we worked with on the unit test in the last section and see if we can break that system somehow. Before we begin, we can try to come up with some off-the-wall type of things just to try and see how the game will respond, such as

- What happens to the sheep if Sancho dies?
- Can we get the sheep stuck on something or someplace?

Beyond this we turn our testers loose with the goal of breaking this quest system and see what they come up with. Notice that both of the questions that we have proposed as possibilities that could *break* this aspect of the game were already discovered during our unit testing in the previous section. This showcases how there is an overlap between these types of testing procedures that we work on within our game projects. Another approach to this is that we can explain the quest to the player so that they know what they are *supposed* to do and then tell them to *break* it; in the case of my kids, this is one of their favorite things to do. We will need people to think outside of the box on this one and just try off the wall stuff to see if they can break the game that we have constructed. One of the most common things that crop up from break testing will be map holes, which allow a player to slip through the map at certain places and get to locations that we are not wanting them to get to. These are fixed by looking very closely at our colliders on objects and also at the boundary systems that we create to surround the player and keep them in the regions we want.

11.2 Fixing and Tweaking

After having explored some of the types of testing and applying them to our Sancho Panza project, we have discovered a couple of bugs that will need to be fixed and also a couple of issues that should be tweaked in some way for smoother game play. In the following sections, we will go through solutions to the documented bugs found earlier in this chapter. When fixing bugs, it is important that we turn the game loose to the testers again and have them verify that the solution works. The verification process involves repeating the steps that initially caused the bug to occur and then trying to see if we can get it to occur through some other means.

There is another aspect of validation testing though and that is testing the other parts of the game to make sure that our fix for this one problem did not go off and break some other part of the game. For the bugs that we will be working on that should not be a problem; however, the more complex and interdependent the game system becomes the more likely that a seemingly minor change in one location will cascade into a major change elsewhere.

11.2.1 Fixing the Following Sheep

Our game testers have sent us some issues involving the sheep following Sancho around. To recap, the first issue is that once a sheep has been collected, if Sancho wanders to a part of the island map that is lower vertically than where the sheep was found, the sheep will float in the air. We are now ready to put our developer's hat back on and as soon as we do so we recognize that gravity is not acting on the sheep. This is a result of constructing our initial character systems on a flat surface and not unit testing for gravitational forces at that point in time. As the project continued to develop this just fell through the cracks, granted in this situation it was intentionally allowed to fall through the cracks to serve as a teaching tool for debugging our project. With the Sancho character, gravity was handled by the CharacterMotor script that we added in order to add jumping to our game. As a result of adding that script, we got gravity for free without necessarily trying to get it. We can verify this by raising Sancho vertically off of the ground of the island and starting the game, notice he falls down to the ground. Based on that, we will need to try something different.

Gravity is a part of the physics system within Unity. This system can be added to a Game Object by adding a Rigidbody component, which can be found in the Physics section of components. Figure 11.5 displays the default properties of a Rigidbody component. We have provided a description of each of these properties in Table 11.1. For our needs with this project, we are going to keep all of the values on their default setting, though we will tinker with the Rotation Constraints by hitting the check boxes to turn all of them on to get a feel for how they work since the Constraints can be an easily overlooked aspect of the component and yet have an enormous impact on the behavior.

After adding a Rigidbody component and enabling the Rotation Constraints, we will need to add a collider component to this sheep

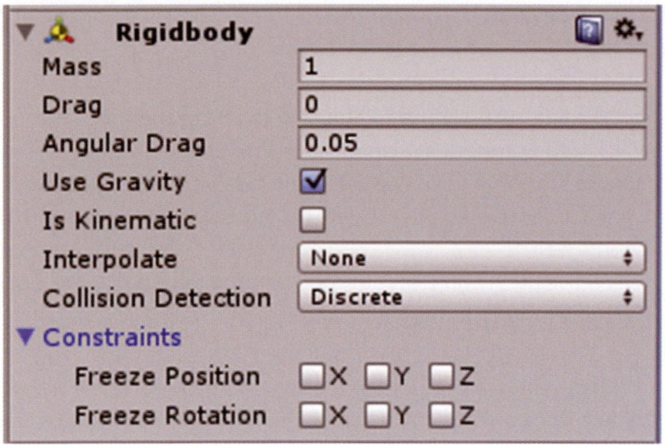

FIG 11.5 The properties of a Rigidbody component.

TABLE 11.1 The Properties of a Rigidbody Component

Property	Purpose
Mass	Defines how massive an object is.
Drag	Amount of air resistance to apply to the object.
Angular Drag	How much air resistance impacts rotation of the object.
Use Gravity	Toggle to use gravity on the object or not.
Is Kinematic	Toggle to use the physics system or not, if Is Kinematic is turned on then the object only moves based on the scripted movement, not on the physics interactions with the environment.
Interpolate	Different methods of how the movement occurs as a result of the Rigidbody, experiment with the other settings to try to smooth out any movement that is too jerky during runtime.
Collision Detection	Fast-moving objects will pass through each other without registering a collision, these settings can be changed for faster-moving objects, Continuous Dynamic is best for these.
Constraints	Disable movement or rotation that is a result of physics interactions with this object.

object as well. Notice that we already have a collider object attached to it; however, this one is set as a Trigger which means that it will allow objects to pass through it. With the trigger turned on and the Rigidbody added, during game execution the sheep object will drop through the ground and keep on falling forever. The gravity is working correctly; however, there is no collider to prevent the sheep from passing through the ground, this is the reason for adding a second collider to our sheep. We could convert our current collider back to a regular collider by removing the Trigger option; however, then the collider will prevent the player from being able to run through to collect the sheep. How we want this to behave is entirely up to us as the game developers, but for this example, we will go ahead and add in a secondary collider object on the sheep.

1. Select the FluffySheep prefab object in the Project panel.
    a. Click Add Component → Physics → Box Collider.
    b. Change the Y value of the Center property to raise the collider so that it is centered on the sheep, for our example a value of 0.55 works well.
    c. Decrease the X and Z part of the Size property so that the Collider is smaller than the Trigger is, values of 0.5 seem to work fairly well.

To begin, when we add a Collider component to an object it will be centered around that object's pivot point, which in the case of the sheep (and most animated characters) is going to be on the ground between their feet. If we leave our collider there, then the sheep will be floating above the ground because the collider will be hitting the ground quite a bit below where the sheep is actually located at. The other part that we have changed is the size of the collider; if we leave it at 1 then it will completely overlap the Trigger volume and thereby defeat the whole purpose of having a separate collider box from the trigger. The Y value is fine at 1, but the X and Z define the box around the sheep and dropping it to 0.5 gets a very tight box that snugs up against the sides of the sheep very well.

We are now ready to do a quick unit test on these changes before sending it back to the testers for verification testing. Remember, we intentionally checked the Freeze Rotation boxes to be able to see how these impact the behavior of the physics system on the object. We will go find a sheep and get it to follow us back down toward the ocean to replicate the bug that had been reported. Figure 11.6 shows what occurs now. The sheep is doing much better than it was before; however, it seems as though it is standing on a hidden platform that is extending out from the surface of the island. As it turns out, that is exactly what it is doing, that hidden platform is the collider box as shown in Figure 11.7. What is occurring here is that the Rigidbody is creating a gravitational pull on the sheep bringing it down to the surface of the land; however, since we have frozen the rotation, the box collider stays in its original orientation. If we unfreeze those Rotation Constraints, we will notice that the sheep will nicely fall onto the surface of the incline just as we would like it to. This brings up an interesting situation with different shapes of colliders; for instance, a spherical collider will roll down this incline as though it were a ball, perhaps good if we want Jill to tumble down the hill, but we do not want our sheep to do that at all. By getting this collision system to work correctly, we have also fixed the issue of the sheep running straight through a wall or other obstacle.

11.3 Building the Game

In this section, we will look at the various stages of development that a video game passes through while exploring the many options that Unity provides for us to create executable versions for various platforms. We must build

FIG 11.6 The invisible platform beneath the sheep.

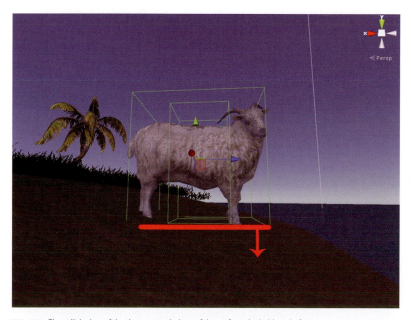

FIG 11.7 The collider box of the sheep extended out of the surface, the hidden platform.

our game for others to be able to play it outside of the Unity game engine, which would be necessary for other people to be able to play our game. We will conclude this section with a step-by-step example of building a game project with Unity. For our example build of the Sancho Panza project, we are going to construct a Windows Standalone that will be ready to be published and distributed for others to play. Through this we will also take a look at most of the settings for building this version of the project. These settings are shared across the different platforms that we can construct a deliverable for.

11.3.1 Game Development Life Cycle

The life cycle of a game project defines the various stages that a game passes through and what it is capable of at those points. For instance, as people we have a life cycle similar to baby, toddler, child, teen, young adult, adult, elderly, and dead. Granted the last stage is not one that we look forward to but it is a part of the life cycle that we experience. As a baby, there are things that I cannot do, such as drive a car. In game development our projects pass through a very similar set of stages during their lifetime. Table 11.2 depicts the stages of a game project. Notice that each stage has very unique expectations from it and we need to be careful to not expect too much from an alpha version of a game. Every project

TABLE 11.2 The Life Cycle for a Game Project

Stage	Deliverables	Purpose
Concept	High-Concept Document	Basic outline of the game idea, this is the elevator speech for the game, just the facts.
	Design Document	Full documentation for the game idea and how to build the game.
Development	Alpha	Initial playable version of the game, this is proof of concept of basic game mechanics, generally has rudimentary graphics and no audio.
	Beta	Most graphics and audio are in place, game is fully playable on the main storyline with some side quests and other elements still in development.
	Gold	Game is ready for release, any bugs still in at this point in time will have to be repaired via patches following release. This version of the game is packaged and sent to distributors.
Testing	Bug Reports	Testers work with the Alpha and Beta versions of the game trying to find bugs and issue bug reports to the developers for fixes.
Release	Patch	Once the game is released, we can continue to fix known bugs or new bugs reported by players through patches that we develop and release for the game.
	DLC	New content can be released as downloadable content (DLC) that players can purchase to add new content and life to the game. As developers we can utilize DLCs to add life to our games following its release.
	Abandonware	There comes a point in time when there will be no further DLCs for the project, no more patches, no more support, and the game itself will not be available for sale through mainstream channels. At this point, the developers have abandoned the game, though they still hold the intellectual property rights to the game (copyright).

that we work on will go through this same life cycle, although some of them may have an untimely death as they are cut off before growing to full maturity.

> **Note**
> We are never completely done with a game until it has been abandoned either by us or by our company. As long as the game is still out there and being supported, we are working with it to some extent; however, there comes a point in time where continuing to maintain the game is no longer a viable option and it might be best to let the game go to the great console in the sky.

Within each of the stages of a game's life, there are deliverables. A deliverable is a product of some type; it is something that is produced and created during that stage and can then be given to someone else. While testing and development are technically listed as distinct stages, they work very closely together as we have seen in this chapter.

11.3.2 Build Options in Unity

Unity provides us with a wide range of platforms that we can build our games for. Our first thought when glancing through a list like the one shown in Table 11.3, is that we will just go ahead and build it for all of the platforms, this way more people can get and play our game, which would be good. Well, not all platforms will be a good fit for our game; not to mention that way back when we were working on our initial design document for our project, we selected a couple of platforms that we were going to target and we had specific reasons to go after those platforms. Generally speaking, it is best to stay with the target platforms that we selected in the beginning, although if another platform is similar, such as Android and iOS which are both mobile platforms and as such fairly similar, then it would be a good idea to build a release version of the game for these platforms as well. The initial platform selection dialogue box is pictured in Figure 11.8.

It is important to recognize that some of these build platforms have specific requirements that we need to be aware of if we are intending to

TABLE 11.3 The Range of Target Platforms That Unity Can Create Release Builds For

Unity Web Player	OSX Standalone	Linux Standalone	Windows Standalone
iOS	Android	BlackBerry	Tizen
Windows Store	Windows Phone 8	WebGL	Samsung TV
Xbox One	PS3	PS Vita	PS4
Xbox 360			

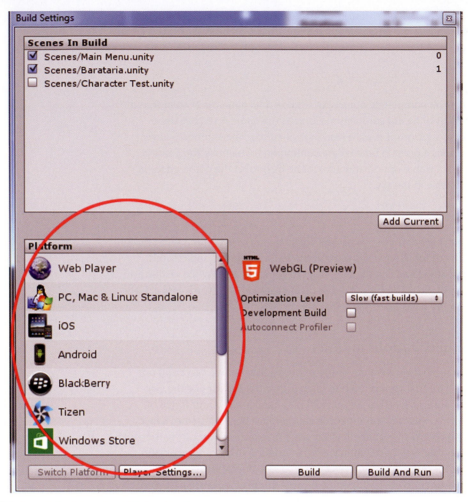

Platform selection dialogue box within the build settings.

target those systems. For instance, building for OSX or iOS will require an Apple computer to do the building on. It will also be necessary to have a developer account with the Apple Store. Unity Web Player is another one with unique needs. Originally, this was a wonderful method of delivering content through a web browser to our players; however, Google Chrome has since stopped allowing the Netscape Plugin Application Programming Interface (NPAPI) framework that the Unity Web Player plugin uses, a framework that other plugins use as well, which in turn rules out a potential group of players for our games. As a result, Unity Web Player is probably not a great choice if we want to deliver our content via a browser, unless we are going to require our users to use a specific browser. With Unity 5, though, we can build for WebGL, though this is still new and there are some issues with it, but this option has an extremely promising future.

Note

If you are interested in creating a build with WebGL and PlayMaker, it will be necessary to change your version of PlayMaker to the NACL version, depending on the release versions. To perform this change, find the PlayMakerNACL.unitypackage file located within the PlayMaker → Versions folder of the Project pane and double-click the package to import it. You will need to confirm any update and overwrite warnings that appear. If you want to revert to the original version of PlayMaker, import the PlaymakerDefault.unitypackage file located in PlayMaker → Versions.

11.3.3 Creating a Stand-Alone Build

We will begin our sample build by opening the Build Settings dialogue through File → Build Settings. We looked at this dialogue briefly in the last chapter while testing the ability to load another level from the main menu. Be sure to add both the Main Menu scene and the Barataria scene to our Scenes In Build section, as shown in Figure 11.9. Notice that the Main Menu scene is at the top of the list of scenes to include and that it is numbered as 0. Remember from our discussion of arrays that within computers numbering begins at 0. Whichever level is at number 0 in our build list will be the level that is loaded by default once the game launches, in our case, the Main Menu is where we want the player to be sent to first.

Before we build our game, we need to take a look at the game-player settings, which are the specific settings for each platform build of our game. Each target platform can have different values for these settings and they all share the same general settings that can be utilized. The settings that are available for the players are as follows: resolution, icon, splash image, and other settings. In order to access the settings for the players, we need to select the Player Settings button as shown in Figure 11.9 earlier with the Build Settings dialogue. While the various players have these same settings and can have different values for each, Figure 11.10 shows the settings that are shared across all of the platforms and are therefore the same regardless of the build target selected. These properties are self-explanatory in that they are the name of the game, name of the developer, and icons for the game and the cursor. The only one a little different is the Cursor Hotspot, which will define, in pixels, the bounding box that forms the hotspot for the default cursor. We will go ahead and configure these shared properties.

Download

Be sure to download the new assets that will be used for finishing the build of our game from the companion website in the folder for this chapter: "buildAssets.zip." Import the image files to the UI Images folder that we created in the last chapter.

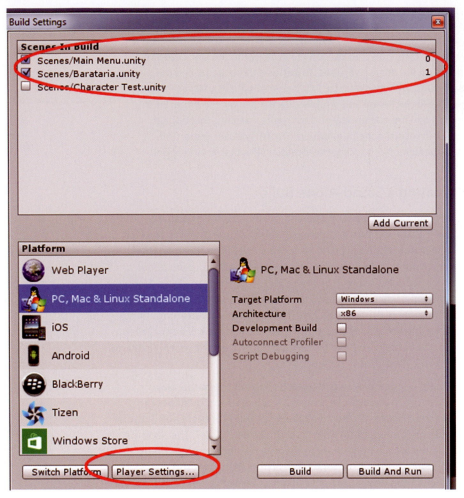

FIG 11.9 The Build Settings that we will use for our Windows Standalone build.

1. Change the Company Name to your name or the name of some studio you would like to be.
2. Change the Product Name to "Sancho Panza & The Isle of Barataria."
3. Change the Default Icon to either the Sancho Head or the Sancho Life image, whichever you like.
4. Change the Default Cursor to the cursor image file imported to the project from the downloaded assets.

All we have done thus far is to make some basic changes to ensure that the proper game name is displayed, including some minor graphical changes, such as the icon and cursor. You can now run the game within the editor to see the new cursor in action; it was very easy to change the image for the cursor in our game. While the cursor is working within the editor inside of Unity, in order for it to work correctly once we build the project, we will need

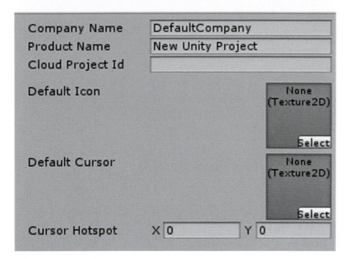

FIG 11.10 The shared Player Setting properties.

to make sure that the Texture Type for the Cursor image file is set to Cursor in the drop-down menu of the Inspector properties for that image file. We will move on to the resolution settings as shown in Figure 11.11. We will make the following changes to these settings:

1. Turn off the check box on Default Is Native Resolution.
2. For the Default Screen Sizes, use 1024 for the Width and 768 for the Height.
3. Change the Display Resolution Dialogue to Disabled.

In these steps we have turned off the dialogue window that appeared when we ran the game in the last chapter asking what screen resolution we would like to run the game at. In a future version of the game, we could rearrange our main menu to provide for an Options page in which the user could select a resolution to run the game from within the game, however using the default dialogue box is an approach that we have opted to bypass. Also, we have forced the game to run at the full screen resolution that we have specified. The default setting of Native Resolution means that the game will run at whatever resolution the player's computer is set too, generally speaking we can do this just fine, however as an example we thought it beneficial to demonstrate how to specify the resolution that the system was actually built for.

The next Player Setting section is for the Icon for the game. If you remember we have already specified a Default Icon for the game earlier, Sancho's head, however, we could provide a different icon for the stand-alone version of the game if we wanted to differentiate it in some way from the other platforms. Notice that Unity has already populated the various icon sizes with versions of our Sancho head scaled to the appropriate size, for our purposes we are good with the settings in the Icon section.

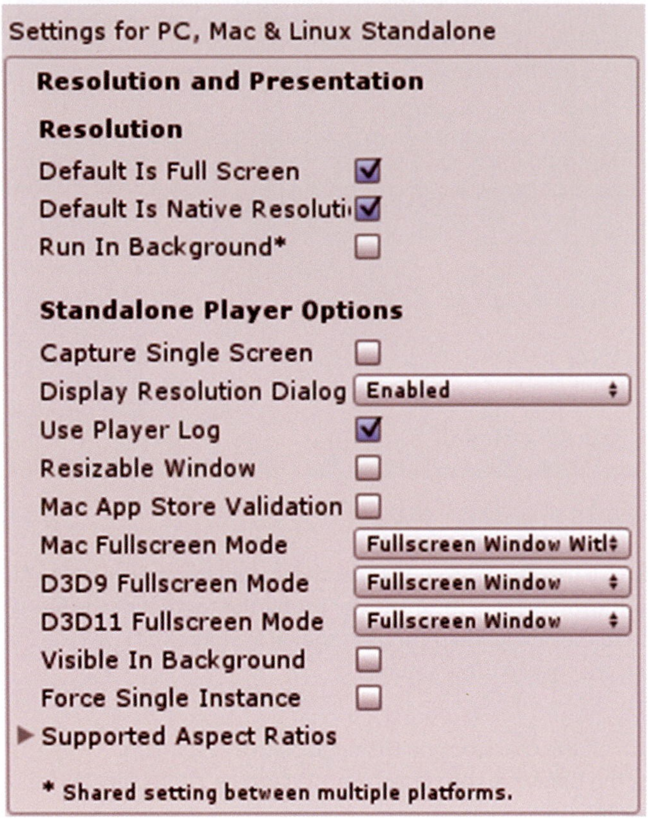

FIG 11.11 The Resolution Settings page.

Following the Icon section is the section for the Splash Image. A Splash Image is an image that is displayed as the game is loading. With the Personal Edition of Unity 5 that we have been using, we do not have the option to disable the Unity Splash Screen, though if we had purchased a license we could disable this. For us, we do not really see a reason to disable the Unity splash screen as we have no problem with people knowing which engine we used to create the game. The only thing we can change in this section, as shown in Figure 11.12 is the Config Dialog Banner image. Since we have disabled the Config Dialog box in an earlier section, there is no point in worrying about this image; however, this image would appear at the top of the Config Dialogue box of you were to decide to implement an image.

While we are on the topic of splash screens, many people get frustrated because they feel that Unity 5 will not allow them to display a custom splash screen, for instance, a brief video of the studio name. We can create this same effect by putting a different scene at number 0, let's call this new scene Company Splash Screen, and when the game loads it will display this "splash screen." Within this scene add an empty Game Object and give it a PlayMaker finite state machine (FSM) that will pause for however long it takes to play the company name animation and then transition to a state

FIG 11.12 The Splash Image icon settings section.

that will use the Load Level action to load the Main Menu scene, actually this exercise was presented in the last chapter.

The final section to look at is the Other Settings area shown in Figure 11.13. As a general rule these are performance settings and generally best left at their default values. With that said, the Rendering Path setting determines the quality of lighting and shadows as far as the real-time rendering system is concerned. Forward is the default which is good for lighting though not so great for real-time shadows. Deferred Lighting is the best for both light and shadows; however, it will slow your game down tremendously. Vertex Lighting is the worst for lighting with no shadows. Generally speaking, stay with Forward unless your shadows are not working correctly or you are targeting slower systems.

The Color Space setting determines which type of color space to use for rendering; we are mentioning this in case you are interested in exploring development with Oculus Rift devices as we have noted times when switching this has impacted the quality of the graphics displayed within the device. The default values for the other settings should work just fine for nearly all project builds, but full documentation on these settings may be found in the Unity Manual at http://docs.unity3d.com/Manual/class-PlayerSettingsStandalone.html.

Now that we have all of our Player Settings configured for the Standalone build we are ready to return to the Build Settings dialogue and start the build process. Select the Build button then browse to a folder where you want to save the build of the project. We like to keep all of our builds within a folder named Builds that is inside of our Project folder, though not inside of the Assets folder which is the folder that shows up within the Project Pane of the Unity editor. After selecting a folder give the game a name, we are going with Sancho Beta Build click Save and wait for the build to complete. The process of building the project will take a few minutes to complete, depending on your computer; however, once it has finished you will be able to browse to the folder where the build was saved and it should be similar to Figure 11.14, notice the icon being applied to our game's executable file. To distribute this game to other people they will need to have both the executable file and

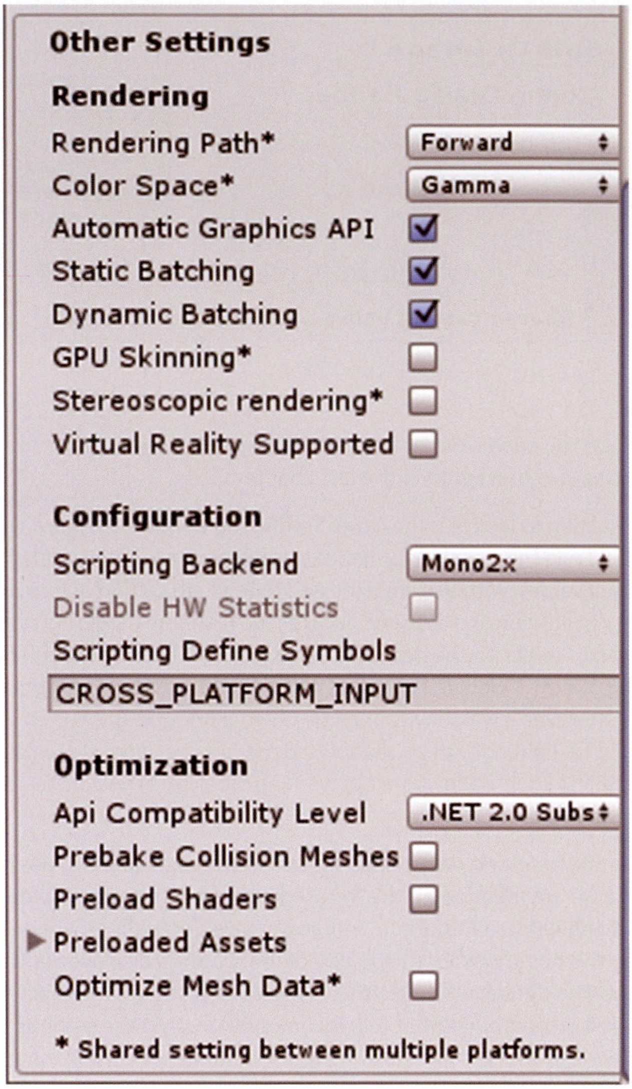

Other Settings

Rendering

Rendering Path*	Forward ⇕
Color Space*	Gamma ⇕
Automatic Graphics API	☑
Static Batching	☑
Dynamic Batching	☑
GPU Skinning*	☐
Stereoscopic rendering*	☐
Virtual Reality Supported	☐

Configuration

Scripting Backend	Mono2x ⇕
Disable HW Statistics	☐
Scripting Define Symbols	
CROSS_PLATFORM_INPUT	

Optimization

Api Compatibility Level	.NET 2.0 Subs⇕
Prebake Collision Meshes	☐
Preload Shaders	☐
▶ Preloaded Assets	
Optimize Mesh Data*	☐

* Shared setting between multiple platforms.

FIG 11.13 The Other Settings section for the Player Settings.

the folder that is suffixed with _Data, in our case "Sancho Beta Build_Data." We are now ready to get this game in the hands of more players and testers.

11.4 Summary

Throughout this chapter we have explored what play testing is and how we should approach it with our game projects. As a result of the play testing that was conducted, we discovered some bugs within the project that were then fixed by properly determining what caused the bug to occur. We were also able to discover some aspects of the game that could be improved upon with a couple of quick tweaks, or in some cases, with a little more work, to make

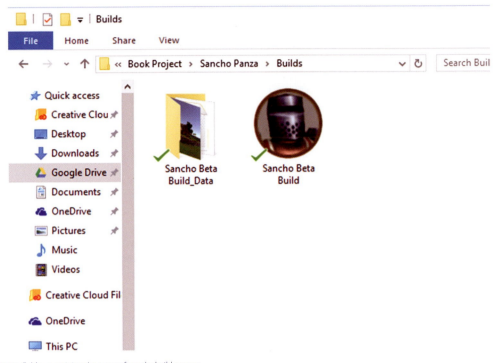

FIG 11.14 Folder containing the output from the build process.

the final product more playable and hopefully more fun. Finally, we looked into all the options that are currently available for building our game projects within Unity. This ability to develop our game in this engine and then deploy it to multiple platforms is a very powerful and useful feature, which makes it easier for us to port our games to other systems and expand not only our player base but also the game's availability. Throughout this book, we have focused on one specific game project while laying the foundation for building a completely different project through our design document that we have written. While Sancho Panza is a solid starting point, we really should add more features to the game and create a deeper complexity of interaction and storytelling for the player to explore; however, as an introduction to game development the project has served our purposes admirably. We hope that you have enjoyed this journey into game development as much as we have and look forward to playing and seeing your amazing creations which will be soon to come. Never stop playing, never stop learning, and never stop developing.

Vocabulary

Testing
Bug
Game build
Alpha

Beta
Gold
Patch
DLC
Abandonware
Play-through testing
Unit testing
Break testing
WebGL
Unity Web Player
Standalone

Review Quiz

1. What is the difference between the Web Player and WebGL?
2. How are unit testing and break testing different?
3. Why do you think that play testing is viewed as "just playing the game?"
4. Why do you think that we should have such a methodical approach to testing?

Exercises

1. Do some research and find out what would be needed to build and publish games for:
    a. Xbox One
    b. PS4
    c. Linux
    d. Windows Phone 8
2. Continue to test your game, especially your solutions to exercises throughout this book and solve any bugs:
    a. Find the bugs and document what causes them.
    b. Develop a methodical procedure to troubleshooting the bugs as a developer.
3. Have a friend or two play your game, see if they can break it.
4. In consultation with your play testers, what tweaks could you make to your project to make it more playable or more fun?
5. Do some online research and find out the necessary requirements to be a game tester for a game studio.

Design Document

Our design document was completed in the last chapter. Though you may want to take the opportunity to look back over what you have written and make any changes based upon what we have learned throughout this book. You should now be ready to take on your own projects; you will encounter questions along the way, do not be afraid to ask them and do not allow them to stop you.

Index

A

AAA Studios, 6–7
Abadonware, 462–463
Abstraction, 170
Achievers, Bartle player type, 5
Action–adventure games, 232
    game mechanic design, 319
    HUD, 392
    Sancho Panza project, 317
Action games, 14–15, 227
Adaptive music *vs.* looping, 350–352
Adding grass, environments
    billboards, 296
    brush size, 299
    bush free, 300
    detail mesh, 296, 299–300
    healthy and dry color, 297
    LOD, 299
    noise spread property, 296–297
    Paint Details tool, 296–297
    prefab object, 301
    property dialogue, 296, 298
    Render mode, 299
    3D shrubs, 296
    wind settings section, 299
Adding trees, environments
    approaches, 292
    brush size, 290
    color variation, 292
    random height setting, 290
    random tree rotation, 292
    unity, 289
Adding water, 288–289
Additive option, 424
Add terrain texture, 285
Advanced Spider Patrol, 180
Adventure games, 11–12
AI, *see* Artificial intelligence
Albedo, 58
Allies, 220–221
Ally, 95
Alpha game versions, 462
Ambient audio system
    array configuration for, 380–381
    audio listener, 374
    beating sheep sounds, 381
    looping track, 353
    min distance value, 372–373
    potential listing of, 353

    sound, cacophony of, 353
    3D audio source, 371–372
American gamers, 4
Analogous colors, 400
Animations, 111, 115, 118–119, 129
Antagonist, 96
Approaching the cave, 221
Area lights, 307
Aristotle and the greeks
    characters
        fatal flaw, 214
        intricate relationship, 215
        motivations and desires, 214
        tragedy, quality of, 214
    diction, 215
    melody, 216
    plot
        beginning, 212
        catharsis, 213
        cause-and-effect manner, 213
        challenging task, 214
        Freytag triangle, 213
        Hollywood 3-Act story
            structure, 212–213
        knowledge discovery, 214
        Lord of the Rings, 212
        middle stage, 213
        potential plot twists, 214
        resolution, 213
        tension and emotional
            investment, 213
        tragedy, 212
        unity, concept of, 212
    poetics, 211
    spectacle, 216
    theater and drama, 211
    thought, 215
    tragedy, six parts of, 211
Array, 173–174, 198–199
Array Get action, 176
Arteria3D medieval farm, 301
Artificial boundaries, 265
Artificial confines, 223
Artificial intelligence (AI), 319
Assassin's Creed IV: Black Flag, 14
Assets package, 280–281
Async check box, 424
Attack and health states
    FSM value, 194
    gotHit Boolean variable, 195

    Jaws_collider object, 195
    Sancho's health management,
        194–195
    spider collider object, 194
    trick, 194
AttackRange, 171
Attack state, 197
Attenuation, 370
Audacity, 233
    adjusting volume levels, 364
    applying effects
        amplify, 364
        audio clipping, 363
        Change Pitch effect, 363
        gain level, 363
        narration audio file, 360
        Noise Removal tool, 363
        room reverb, 364
    audio position, 357
    default UI, 356
    editing an audio file, 357–360
    sound editing tool, 356
Audio
    Audacity, 356–357
        adjusting volume levels, 364
        applying effects, 360–364
        cutting up an audio file,
            357–360
    finding of, 354–355
    in games
        ambience, 352–354
        music, 350–352
        sound events, 354
    PlayMaker, 375–376
        ambient sounds, 379–382
        background music, 376–379
        effects for events, 382–386
    in Unity, 364–366
        ambient audio, 371–374
        background music, 375
        3D audio, 369–371
        2D audio, 366–369
AudioClip property, 367–368
Audio editing program, 351
Audio listener, 233, 374
Audio Play action, 378–379
Audio source, 233, 235
Audio Stop action, 378–379
Authentic Medieval Ages Audio,
    364, 375

B

Background music
  PlayMaker
    audio actions, 378
    Inspector variable
      settings, 379
    music controller state
      machine, 377–378
    trigger zones, 376–377
  in Unity, 375
Backstory, 207
  information, 232–233
  revelation, 224
Balance mechanics, 316
Barataria, 269
Bartle player types, 5
Beating sheep sounds, 381; *see also*
    Audio
  array configuration for, 380–381
  events and variables, 381
Bejeweled 3, 18
Beta game versions, 462
Billboards, 296
Black box functions, 170
*The Book of Unwritten Tales: The Critter
    Chronicles* (KING Art), 11–12
Bool variable, 243, 247
Boss battles, 231, 262
Bounce, 56
Boundaries, 307–310
Boundary conditions, 153, 176; *see
    also* Scripted behavior
Break testing, 457
Broadleaf trees, 294
Brush falloff, 275
Brush size, 275, 299
Bubble Pop, 18
Bug hunting
  in game, 452
  screenshot/video capture of, 452
Bugs, 196
Building blocks, 260
Button UI objects
  available states for, 410
  image objects, 409
  PlayMaker, 422

C

Call of Duty, 13
Call to adventure, 219
Canvas component
  deactivate, 250, 252
  dialogue system, 420
  main menu, 408
  Rect Transform, 402–404

Capitalism Plus, 16
Capsule Game Object, 188
Casual gamer, 4–5
Catch-up mechanics, 316
Cathartic experience, 228
Central conflict, 226–227
Change Pitch effect, 363
Character data, 152
Characters; *see also* 3D assets
  Aristotle and the Greeks,
    214–215
  asset design, 102–104
  building blocks, 206
  controller, 121–122
  design, 99–102
  game types
    information, 98–99
    merchants, 97–98
    quest giver, 98
  requirement, 90–91
  traditional character types
    ally, 95
    herald, 95
    hero, 93
    The Lord of the Rings, 92
    mentor, 94–95
    shadow, 93–94
    shapeshifter, 96
    threshold guardian, 96–97
    trickster, 95–96
Chat Mapper, 230
Checkpoint system
  game mechanic design
    action–adventure
      games, 319
    positions of, 319
    state machine layout, 320
  mechanics, implementation of
    collision system, 328
    companion website, 325
    GameObject variable, 328
    game world, 326–327
    get location state,
      328–329
    materials and textures, 326
    respawn location variable,
      329–330
    rotate action, 326–327
    trigger event action
      settings, 328
Choose Your Own Adventure, 228
Chorus, 216
Chunks, 302–303
Civilization V, 15
Climactic conflict, 205, 221
Collider component, 54, 460–461
Collision, 185, 187

Color space setting, 469
Color theory
  analogous and complementary
    color section, 400
  categories of, 399
  color wheel, 398–399, 401
  interface systems, selection
    of, 399
  temperature and emotions,
    400–401
  UI components, 400
  Unity game engine, 401
Color variation, 292
Complementary colors, 400
Complex assets, 200
Complexity, 207
Computer-controlled Sim, 159
Concept art, 102
The Controller
  abstraction, 170
  attackRange, 171
  black box functions, 170
  detection range, 171
  distance, 170
  events and variables, spider
    controller, 168
  Find Closest action, 170
  float compare action, 171
  FSM, 168
  patrol, 170
  PlayMaker, 168–169
  Sancho, 169
  targetAlive Bool variable, 171
Controller state machine, 181, 184
Controller systems, 317
Copyright law, 225, 318
Core mechanics, 204
  examples of, 314–315
  hide and seek, 314
  Sancho Panza project, 314
Costumes, 216
Creative Commons License, 349
Creativity, 206, 238
CrossPlatformInput, 279
Cursor Hotspot, 465

D

Data structure, 173
Debug Log action, 343
Decision-making process, 152,
  158–159
Deepest water point, 277–278
Descriptive design, 27–28
Design document
  game audio, 36–37
  game characters, 33–34

game concept, 30–33
game idea, 24
game interface, 37
game story, 34–35
game world, 35–36
logical design *vs.* descriptive
design, 27–28
methods of, 26–27
mission and vision, 28–29
requirement, 25–26
software development, 24
Design work, mechanics
checkpoint system, 319–320
respawn Sancho, 320–321
Sancho and water, 321–322
Sancho's collection system,
323–325
Destroy Object action, 329
Detail Mesh, 296, 299–300
Dialogue
character
backstory narration, 239
basic detection system, 243
Bool variable, 243, 247
canvas, final version of,
245, 248
collider settings, 240, 242
custom events and
variables, 250
detection and firing system,
240–241
Ecosystem package browser,
246, 249
elements and components,
244, 247
final layout, 251, 253
Find Dapple, 255
FSM, 239
functional conversation
system, 254
Game Object action, 255
Inspector variables, 250–251
PlayMaker state machine, 239
Sancho *vs.* Teresa, 238, 241
scale tool, 247
starter conversation, 238, 241
starting dialogue FSM, 246, 250
unity GUI system, 246
wrap and overflow, 245, 248
story design
Chat Mapper, 230
hobo-type character, 230
Microsoft Office, 230
needs, 228
NPC, 228
response system, 229
trees, 229–230

system
canvas component, 420
overlay system, 420–421
PlayMaker, 418
uGUI tools, advantage of, 418
Dialogue system integration,
PlayMaker
Boolean variables, 444
Sancho, FSM of, 441, 444
Teresa, variable values for,
440–442
Dialogue trees, 229–230
Diction, Aristotle and the Greeks, 215
Diegetic UI, 394–395
Diffuse map, 304–305
Digital media and video games, 318
Directional lights, 307, 309
DLC, *see* Downloadable content
Donkey Kong, 12, 94, 157
Don't Destroy On Load option, 426
Doppler effect, 369
Downloadable content (DLC), 462
Dungeons & Dragons, 11

E

Ecosystem, 82–84
Ecosystem package browser,
246, 249
Editing, audio file
audio exporting, 359
bleating sheep sounds, 357, 361
editor pane, 358–359
eight bleating sheep file, 358, 360
export audio dialogue, 359, 361
warning message, 357–358
Edit terrain texture, 285
Empty game objects, 172–173, 179
Enemies, 220–221
Enemy agent, 156
Entertainment Software
Association, 4
Entertainment Software Rating
Board (ESRB) rating
system, 31, 33
Environment
boundaries, 307–310
for games
challenging the player,
264–265
controlling the player,
261–263
final design, 265–268
informing the player, 263–264
imported assets, 301–306
lighting, 307
for stories, 260–261

terrain dressing, standard
content
grass, 296–301
painting textures, 279–287
trees, 289–295
water, 287–289
Unity, creating the terrain
collider, 273–274
height tools, 274–279
settings, 271–273
Ergonomics, 394
Escape (ESC) key, 429
Europa Universalis IV, 15
Event audio setups
Audacity, 383–384
Audio Play action, 383
checkpoint, 382
collision-based system, 383–384
Events and variables, 340–341
Evolutionary systems
computer-controlled Sim, 159
decision-making process, 159
genetic algorithms, 160
merchant character, 161
potential evolutionary decision
process, 159–160
The Sims, 159, 161
video game character, 160
Expert systems
Donkey Kong, 157
limiting factors, 157
real-world situations, 156
specific state, transition to, 157
strategy games, 156
Explorers, Bartle player type, 5
External conflict, 207–208

F

Falloff, 274–275
Fallout, 11
Fantasy Music Collection, 364
Farmville, 4, 6
FBX file, 104
The Fellowship of the Ring, 221
FIFA, 17
Final design, environments
artificial boundaries, 265
assets, list of, 267–268
Finding Dapple, 267
Hollywood 3-Act structure, 266
isle of Barataria, 265–266
level progression, 266–267
natural boundary, 265
Final tweaks, NPC
array, 198–199
attack state, 197

bugs, 196
FSM, 199
game object, 199
global transition event, 197
hard coding, 198
Jaws_Collider object, 196
keys, 196
moving state, 199
patrolling state, modified version
        of, 198
PlayMaker, global event check
        box, 196, 198
play testing, 196
Find Closest action, 170, 192
Finding Dapple, 255, 267
FINISHED layout, 340–341, 343
FinishRange variable, 173
Finite state machine (FSM), 127,
        141–142, 168, 194, 199
    events and variables, 384–385
    PlayMaker, 468
    properties for, 386
Finite state machines, 239
Fixing and tweaking
    Sancho Panza project, 457
    sheep following, 458–460
Flexibility, 206, 238
Float, 134
    compare action, 171
    Divide action, 439–440
Fluffy sheep models
    events and variables, 340
    Waiting FSM, 339
Follow Boolean variable, 342
Football Manager, 17
Friction, 56
FSM, *see* Finite state machine
Functional conversation system, 254

G

Game
    audio, 36–37
    characters, 33–34
    concept, 30–33
    developer
        industry, 8–10
        skills and jobs, 8–9
    development life cycle
        deliverable, 463
        stages of, 462
    idea, 24
    interface, 37
    story, 34–35
    testing
        break testing, 457
        characterMotor script, 458

collider component, 460–461
    goal of, 452
    gravity, 459
    hunting bugs, 452–453
    invisible platform, 460–461
    play-through testing, 453–454
    Rigidbody component,
        458–459
    unit testing, 454–457
types
    action games, 14–15
    adventure games, 11–12
    MMO games, 18–19
    platformer games, 12–13
    puzzle games, 18
    role-playing games, 10–11
    shooter games, 13–14
    simulation games, 16–17
    sports games, 17
    strategy games, 15–16
window, 409
world, 35–36
GameCube, 394
Game mechanics; *see also* Mechanics
    categories of
        balance, 316
        core, 314–315
        story, 316–317
        system, 317
        victory and loss conditions,
            315–316
    internal rules, 314
Game Object
    game testing, 450, 452
    sprite texture type, 406
    uGUI elements, 406
Game Object action, 183, 255
Game-play components, 317
Game-play-specific elements, 225
Gamification, 4, 16
Genres, 10, 12–15, 17–18
Get Distance action, 182
Get Next waypoint state, 175, 177
Global Illumination system, 426
Global transition event, 197
Gold deliverables, 462
Goldilocks effect, 394
Good *vs.* evil, 210, 223, 226
Google Earth, 269
GotHit Boolean variable, 195
GotHit variable, 191
Graphical user interface (GUI), 236
    main menu, Unity, 406
    SW interface system, 394
Graphics, 216
Grass borders, 287
GrassHillAlbedo texture, 285

Guard agent, 154–155
GUI, *see* Graphical user interface

H

Hard-coded values, 198
Hard-core gamer, 4–5
Hardware (HW) interface system
    ergonomic evolution, 394
    game controllers, 394
    types of, 393
HCI, *see* Human computer interaction
Heads-up display systems (HUD)
    action–adventure game, 392
    design of
        aspects, 395
        crafting system, 396
        diegetic interface
            elements, 395
        GUI systems, 394–395
        mock-ups, 395–396
        Sancho, UI mock-ups for, 397
    dialogue system integration, 441
    goal of, 392
    life display, 430
    logic design, 431
    menu design, 398
    overlay *vs.* working
        speedometer, 393
        alignment properties, text
            object, 416–417
        color property, 414
        difference demonstration,
            414–415
        game view, 413–414
        hierarchy relationships, 413
        mock-up, 412
        prefab warning dialogue,
            415–416
        Quest Info system, 416–418
Height value, 272
Herald, 95
Hero, 93
The Hero with a Thousand Faces,
        192, 217
Hidden barriers, 263
Himalayas, 274
Hobo-type character, 230
Hollywood 3-Act structure, 205,
        218, 266
HUD systems, *see* Heads-up display
        systems
Human computer interaction
        (HCI), 393
HW interface system, *see* Hardware
        interface system
Hybrid genre, 15, 17

I

Image objects, 409
Image UI object, 416, 434, 441
Imported assets
    Arteria3D medieval farm, 301
    chunks, 302–303
    diffuse map, 304–305
    graphical continuity, 305
    legacy shaders, 304
    Mesh Collider component, 306
    Mesh Renderer component, 306
    modular approach, 302
    normal maps, 303–305
    Sancho, sizing test of, 303–304
    sizing purposes, 303
    standard shader, 304–305
    3D modeling application, 302
    town or environment, 302
Index variable, 175, 177
Indie Studio, 6–7
Indoor environments, 310
Informational character, 98
Input manager, 126, 131
Insane asylum, 155
Inspector check box, 173
Inspector panel, 54
Inspector variables, 250–251
Intellectual protection law, 225
Interactive fiction, 12
Internal conflict, 207
Internal *vs.* external conflict,
    207–208
Isle of Barataria, 265–266

J

Jagged height transitions, 276
Jarring experience, 260
Jaws_Collider object, 195–196
Joseph Campbell, return of
    approaching the cave, 221
    call to adventure, 219
    crossing the threshold, 220
    meeting the mentor, 220
    ordeal, 221
    ordinary world, 219
    refusal of the call, 219
    resurrection, 222
    return with Elixir, 222
    reward, 221
    road back, 222
    tests, allies, and enemies,
        220–221
Journal systems, 255
Journey of the Hero, 217–218
Jungian approach, 217

K

Killers, Bartle player type, 5
Knight, 110

L

L.A. Noir, 317
Legacy shaders, 304
*The Legend of Zelda: The Wind
    Waker,* 219
Level of detail (LOD), 299
Level progression, 266–267
Lighting, environment, 307
Linear rolloff, 371
Load level action, 425
Logarithmic rolloff, 370–371
Logical design *vs.* descriptive design,
    27–28
Looping music *vs.* adaptive, 350–352
The Lord of the Rings, 162
Loss conditions; *see also* Mechanics
    definition of, 315
    types of, 315–316
    zero-sum game, 315
Love triangle, 208–209, 226–227

M

Madden, 17
Main menu
    PlayMaker
        audio file, properties of,
            424–425
        click event action, 423
        ESC key, 429
        game launch dialogue
            screen, 430
        lightmap snapshot, 426–428
        Play button, 426
        Quit button, 427
        scenes, list of, 426–427
        uGUI Button, 424
    Unity
        Alpha change, 409
        canvas scaler property, 408
        highlighted color option,
            407–408
        Sancho object, 410
        skyboxes, 406
        3D perspective camera, 404
        view of, 411–412
Map holes, 262
Mario Kart series, 316
Mass place trees button, 292
Mathematical behavior modeling
    attack state, 158
    decision process, 157
    re-engage, 158–159
    same time, scene and
        tweaking, 159
    sentry guard, 158
    strict patterns, 157
    traditional scripted events,
        comparison of, 158–159
The Matrix, 220
Mechanics
    designing of
        checkpoint system, 319–320
        respawn Sancho, 320–321
        Sancho and water, 321–322
        Sancho's collection system,
            323–325
    game
        balance, 316
        core, 314–315
        story, 316–317
        system, 317
        victory and loss conditions,
            315–316
    implementation of
        checkpoint system,
            325–330
        respawn Sancho, 333–338
        Sancho and water, 330–333
        Sancho's collection system,
            338–343
    origin of, 317–318
Meeting the mentor, 220
Melody, Aristotle and the
    Greeks, 216
Mentor, 94–95, 220
Menu-based systems, 392
Menu design
    final mock-ups, 398
    game HUD, 398
    principles of, 397
Mesh Collider component, 306
Mesh Filter part, 54
Mesh Renderer component,
    172, 306
Metaphor, 215
Meta UI, 394–395
Microsoft Flight Simulator X, 16
Microsoft Office, 230
Mission statement, 28–29
MMO games, 18–19
Modified Sancho game object,
    410–411
Modified update HUD, 438–439
Modular approach, 302
Mortal Kombat, 15
Moving state, 177, 199
Multiplayer game, 316
Multi-user dungeons (MUDs), 5

Music
  controller, 386
  types of, 351, 353
  within video games
    instrumental type of, 350
    looping *vs.* adaptive, 350–351
    vocal tracks, 350
Musical component, tragedy, 216
Music controller state machine,
        377–378

N

Natural boundary, 265
Netscape Plugin Application
        Programming Interface
        (NPAPI), 464
Neverwinter Nights, 25
A New Hope, 260
Nintendo Entertainment System, 394
Noise Removal tool, 363
Noise spread property, 296–297
Nondiegetic UI, 394–395
Non-player characters (NPC), artificial
        intelligence (AI), 228, 230
  definition, 152
  designing threshold guardian,
        162–167
  implementing threshold
        guardian
    attack and health states,
        connecting, 194–195
    attacking the player, 184–190
    controller, 168–171
    final tweaks, 196–199
    hurting the player, 190–193
    patrolling, 171–180
    spotting the player, 180–184
  prefabs, 199–200
  selecting an, 161–162
  types
    evolutionary systems,
        159–161
    expert systems, 156–157
    mathematical behavior
        modeling, 157–159
    random behavior, 154–156
    scripted behavior, 152–154
Non-zero-sum game, 315
Normalized value, 436, 440
Normal maps, 303–305
NPAPI, *see* Netscape Plugin
        Application Programming
        Interface
NPC, *see* Non-player characters
        (NPC), artificial
        intelligence (AI)

O

Object-oriented programming, 77
Oculus Rift Virtual reality (VR)
        headset, 317
One Shot Clip, 379
Opacity, 275, 281
Ordeal, 221
Ordinary world, 219; *see also* Joseph
        Campbell, return of
Outdoor environments, 310
Overlay interface; *see also* Heads-up
        display systems
  design, 436
  filled image type, 434–435
  hierarchy panel, 434–435
  inserted new states, 432–433
  life display, 430
  lock selection, 438
  logical flow, 432
  logic design, 431
  modified update HUD, 438–439
  normalized value, 436
  Sancho's Health system, 430–431,
        433–434
  vs. working speedometer, 393
    alignment properties, text
        object, 416–417
    color property, 414
    difference demonstration,
        414–415
    game view, 413–414
    hierarchy relationships, 413
    mock-up, 412
    prefab warning dialogue,
        415–416
    Quest Info system, 416–418

P

Pac-Man, 12, 94, 128
Pads, 110
Paint Details tool, 296–297
Paint Height, 275
Paint Tree terrain editing tool,
        290–291
Palm trees, 293–294
Park Baseball, 17
Particular state machine, 175
Patch deliverables, 462
Patrolling
  array, 173–174
  array get action, 176
  basic skeleton of, 174
  boundary conditions, 176
  data structure, 173
  empty game objects, 172–173, 179

finishRange variable, 173
Get Next Waypoint state, 175, 177
hierarchy panel, 179
index variable, 175, 177
Inspector check box, 173
Inspector, starting settings, 180
logical flow, array, 177–178
Mesh Renderer component, 172
move toward action, 179
moving state, 177
particular state machine, 175
primary approaches, 171
scripted patrol mechanism,
        171–172
second approach, 171
smooth look at action, 177–178
variables and single event,
        173, 175
vertical check box, 178
waypoint system, 172
Patrol state, 181–182
Photoshop, 452
PhysicsMaterials, 47
Pitfalls, 273
Pivot point, meshes, 404
Place Trees tool, 289–290, 295
Platformer games, 12–13
Player, 4–5
  attacking
    animation, 185
    capsule game object, 188
    collision, 185, 187
    controller state machine, 184
    health system, 190
    hit state, 189
    next frame button, 187
    random wait action, 185
    Sancho, 186
    spider, child objects, 186–187
    transition event, 190
    trigger events, 189
    unity, 189–190
  challenging, 264–265
  controlling
    boss battles, 262
    character, 262
    geography, 263
    hidden barriers, 263
    location and actions, 263
    map holes, 262
    natural boundaries, 263
    Sancho Panza control
        system, 261
  hurting
    Boolean variables, 191
    damage variable, 190
    dead state, 193

Find Closest action, 192
float compare, 193
global event, 192
gotHit variable, 191
health state machine, events and variables, 190
living state, 192
PlayMaker, 190–191
set tag action, 192
states and transitions, 190–191
informing
color scheme, 264
environment, 263
mini-map, 264
quest-type items, 264
spotting
animation, 184
attack state, 182
controller state machine, 181
Game Object action, 183
Get Distance action, 182
patrol state, 181–182
PlayMaker editor window, 181
pursue state, 182–183
Sancho, 180
spider, 181
tweaking, 181, 184
waypoint navigation, 183
Player *vs.* environment (PvE), 5
Player *vs.* player (PvP), 5
Play head, 351
PlayMaker, 153, 168–169, 190–191
ambient sounds, 379–382
audio systems
logical structure of, 375
to play audio, 375
background music, 376–379
character control systems
input through unity, 126
response system, 123–125
dialogue system integration
Boolean variables, 444
HUD overlay, 441
Sancho, FSM of, 441, 444
Teresa, variable values for, 440–442
effects for events, 382–386
game testing, 450, 452
installing, 60–62
interface, 63–65
mechanics, 335–336, 342, 420–421
overlay, HUD
design, 436
filled image type, 434–435
inserted new states, 432–433

life display, 430
lock selection, 438
logical flow, 432
modified update HUD, 438–439
Sancho's Health system, 430–431, 433–434
response on main menu
audio file, properties of, 424–425
click event action, 423
ESC key, 429
game launch dialogue screen, 430
lightmap snapshot, 426–428
Play button, 426
Quit button, 427
uGUI Button, 424
spider asset, 420
UI elements, 419
using
default action browser in, 74
editor, 71–72
FINISHED state, 82
inside of, 70
Inspector pane, 71, 73
instantiating an object, 77
Set Material Color action, 75, 78
sphere Game Object, 76
state label, 81
state machine, 71
3D game, 70
PlayMakerGUI Game Object, 450–451
PlayMaker state machine, 239
Playtesting, 318
Play-through testing, 453–454
Plot
Aristotle and the Greeks, 212–214
building blocks, 209
events, 231
Point lights, 307
Position vector, 329
Prefabs, 199–200
Primary color, 399–400
Primary conflict, 205, 207–208, 223, 260
Professional water asset, 288
Props, 216
Pursue state, 182–183
Puzzle games, 18

Q

Quest display system, 416–417, 443
Quest-type items, 264

R

Raise/Lower Terrain tool, 276
Random behavior
computer characters, 155
decision, 154
enemy agent, 156
guard agent, 154–155
insane asylum, 155
Sancho, idle animation of, 154
solo decision-making mechanism, 155
state machine, 156
Tic-Tac-Toe game, 155
twist, scripted behavior, 155–156
Random element, 162
Random height setting, 290
Random tree height check box, 295
Random tree rotation, 292
Random wait action, 185
Real-time strategy game, 15–16
Real-world situations, 156
Rect Transform
canvas component, 402–404
main menu, 409
properties of, 402–404
uGUI, 402–403
Re-engage, 158–159
Refresh button, 295
Refusal of the call, 219
Render mode, 299, 414
Respawning Sancho
checkpoint, 333
game mechanic design
action–adventure genre, 320
state machine design, 321
mechanics, implementation of, 333
Response system, 229
Rigidbody component, 458–459
Role-playing games, 10–11
Room reverb, 364
Rotate action, 139–140
Rudimentary skeleton, 163

S

Sancho and water
game mechanic design
advantage of, 323
collision control, 322–323
example of, 321
simplified two-state version of, 322–323
mechanics, implementation of
apply button, 336
boundary objects, 330

collision event properties, 331
deep ocean state actions, 331–333
gear icon, 333–334
health system, modified state machine of, 337–338
modified checkpoints state machine, 334
PlayMaker editor, 337
prefab of, 335–336
Sancho Panza control system, 261
Sancho Panza project, 256
  action–adventure elements, 317
  checkpoint system, 318
  core mechanics, 314
  final position of, 412
  fixing and tweaking, 457
  hierarchy relationships, 413
  HUD, 395
  mechanics design, 319
  Sancho, Health bar of, 433–434
  UI mock-ups for, 397
Sancho's collection system
  game mechanic design
    basic approach, 323
    collecting and delivering sheep, 324
    state machine for, 324
    victory condition, 324
  mechanics, implementation of
    FINISHED layout, 340–341, 343
    fluffy sheep models, 339
    Follow Boolean variable, 342
    sheep-collecting system, 338
    Waiting FSM, 339
Sancho's health management, 194–195, 430–431, 433–434
Sancho vs.Teresa, 238, 241
SandAlbedo, 284–285
Scenes, 59
Scripted behavior
  computer opponent, 154
  PlayMaker, 153
  predictable nature, 154
  security guard, 153
  state diagram, 153
  state machine, 152, 154
Scripted patrol mechanism, 171–172
Secondary color, 399–400
Self-serving, 207
Sentry guard, 158
Setting and backstory
  animations, 226
  asset creation, 226
  character models, 226
  copyright law, 225

game-play-specific elements, 225
  intellectual protection law, 225
Setting building blocks, 206
Shadow, 93–94
Shapeshifter, 96
Sheep collection system, 340–341
Sheep plot event, 265
Shooter games, 13–14
The Sims franchise, 315
Simulation games, 16–17
Skyrim, 11
Smooth Height, 276
Smooth look at action, 177–178
Socializers, Bartle player type, 5
Software (SW) interface system, 393
Sonic the Hedgehog, 228, 315
Sound effect libraries, 354–355
Sound events, 354
Space property, 135
Spatial blend setting, 368
Spatial UI, 394–395
Spectacle, Aristotle and the Greeks, 216
SpeedTree, 289
Spider collider object, 194
Splash screen, 468
Sports games, 17
Spot lights, 307
Stand-alone build, 465–467
Standard shader, 304–305
Standard trees, 290–291
Starter conversation, 238
Starting dialogue variables, 251
Star Trek:The Next Generation, 152
State machines
  approach, 68
  building, 68
  camera follows Sancho, 145–147
  complex version of, 66
  concept of, 65
  core component of, 66
  define, 65
  development, 67
  jumping Sancho
    capability of, 140
    characterMotor script component, 142–143
    FSM, 141–142
    property actions, 144–145
  rotating Sancho, 138–140
  Sancho
    Add Event textbox, 130–131
    C# scripting, 127
    data types, use, 135
    design work, 127
    editor window, 127
    FINISHED event, 130

FINISHED Move Forward state, 132–133
    gear selection icon, 133–134
    knight object, inspector panel, 136–137
    Pac-Man, 128
    play random animation action, properties for, 129
    and renamed, 128
    scene—notice, 135–136
  technology, 69
Stories, 260
Story
  Aristotle and the Greeks
    characters, 214–215
    diction, 215
    melody, 216
    plot, 212–214
    spectacle, 216
    thought, 215
  building blocks of
    characters, 206
    plot, 209
    problem, 206–209
    setting, 206–207
    solution, 209–210
    theme, 210–211
  definition, 204
  design
    characters, 224
    dialogue, 228–231
    plot, 227
    problem, 226–227
    setting and backstory, 225–226
    solution, 228
    theme, 223–224
  game, putting into the
    character dialogue, 238–255
    journal systems, 255
    voice-over narration, 232–235
    written text, 235–238
  Joseph Campbell, return of
    approaching the cave, 221
    call to adventure, 219
    crossing the threshold, 220
    meeting the mentor, 220
    ordeal, 221
    ordinary world, 219
    refusal of the call, 219
    resurrection, 222
    return with Elixir, 222
    reward, 221
    road back, 222
    tests, allies, and enemies, 220–221
  purpose of, 204–205
  telling, 205

Story-centric game, 227
Story information, 231
Story mechanics
    game, component of, 316
    rules, 316
    victory conditions, 317
Strategy games, 15–16
Street Fighter, 15
Strict patterns, 157
Stumbling block, 223
Super Mario Bros, 30, 453
Super Mario Galaxy, 13
Super Mario World, 227
SW interface system, *see* Software
            interface system
System mechanics
    kinect device, 317
    VR headset, 317

T

TargetAlive Bool variable, 171
TargetAlive variables, 171
Target audience, 30
Target platform, 31
Team Fortress 2, 13–14
Terrain, 269
    resolution, 271
    size, 272
    textures, 288
Terrain dressing, standard content
    assets, 279
    CrossPlatformInput, 279
    painting textures
        add terrain texture
            dialogue, 284
        assets package, 280–281
        asset store, 279
        opacity setting, 281
        paint texture settings, 281, 283
        SandAlbedo, 284–285
        target strength setting, 281
        tileable and nontileable
            texture, 280, 283
        2D graphics program, 280
    standard environment asset
        package, 280
Tertiary color, 399
Tests, 220–221
Text UI object, 396, 416
Texture maps, 103–104, 107
Theme, building blocks, 210–211
Thought, Aristotle and the Greeks, 215
3D assets
    importing
        animation list, 104, 107
        knight.zip archive file, 107

new asset option, 107
project pane, 107, 109
Sancho folder, 109–110
test scene, 107
to player controllable assets,
    120–122
settings for importing
    animations, 111, 115
    clip creation, 117
    inspector pane, 120
    model, 111, 113
    rig, 111–112
    wrapping modes, 117, 119
3D audio system
    AudioClip property, 367
    Doppler effect, 369
    graphical representation of, 370
    shared audio properties of,
        367–369
    volume rolloff drop-down menu,
        370–371
3D Game Object, 331, 333
Three-dimensional space, 272
3D menu systems, 392
3D mesh, 102–103
3D perspective camera, 404
3D shape, 54
Threshold guardian, 96–97
    designing
        attacking process, 164–165
        collision response system,
            165–166
        controller state machine, 164
        fleshed-out character, 162
        health state machine, 166
        logical flow, 166
        The Lord of the Rings, 162
        nasty attacks, 164
        patrol system, potential
            design layout, 164
        primary controller
            system, 164
        pursue finite state machine,
            164–165
        rudimentary skeleton, 163
        Sancho, 162
        spider object, 162–163
    implementing
        attack and health states,
            connecting, 194–195
        attacking the player, 184–190
        controller, 168–171
        final tweaks, 196–199
        hurting the player, 190–193
        patrolling, 171–180
        spotting the player, 180–184
Tic-Tac-Toe game, 155

Tileable and nontileable texture,
    280, 283
Tracker modules, 350
Transition, 65–68
Transition event, 190
Tree density, 290
Trees, graphical quality of, 295
Trickster, 95–96
Trigger events, 189
Turn-based strategy game, 15
2D arcade space shooter game,
    318–319
2D audio system
    AudioClip property, 367–368
    Mute check box, 367
    shared audio properties of,
        367–368
2-day game development
    camp, 318
2D graphics program, 392
Types of games, 10; *see also* Genres

U

UI, *see* User interface
Unified audio, 350
    ambient, 371–374
    audio clip drop-down menu
        selections, 364–365, 367
    background music, 375
    folder structure, 365
    properties of, 365–366
    3D audio, 369–371
    tracker modules, 350
    2D audio, 366–369
Unit testing
    dialogue system, 454
    double-checking, 455
    individual chunks, 454
    sheep quest system, 455–456
    super floating/flying sheep, 455
    Unity game engine, 454
Unity
    Barataria, 269
    building options
        platform selection dialogue
            box, 463–464
        target platforms, 463
        video game development,
            463
    character controller system, 270
    collider, 273–274
        collision object, 273
        data property, 273
        physics materials, 273
        properties of, 273
    Google Earth, 269

height tools, 274–279
  brushes section, 274
  buttons, 274
  deepest water point, 277–278
  falloff, 274–275
  flatten button, 278
  Himalayas, 274
  noisy and smooth terrain
    feature set, 276
  opacity, 275
  Paint Height, 275
  Raise/Lower Terrain tool, 276
  roughly sculpted island of
    Barataria, 277–278
  scaling, 277
  Smooth Height, 276
hierarchy panel, 269
importing assets in
  projects, 105–106
  3D assets, 107–111
inspector panel and tool options,
    270–271
installing, 42–43
interface
  create new project dialogue
    screen, 44–45
  default project wizard
    browser, 44
  scene and game views, 50
  Scene Editor, 48–49
  toolbar, 51–52
  Unity 5, standard asset
    packages, 46–47
Sancho prefab object, 270
settings, 271–273
  default terrain resolution, 271
  pitfalls, 273
  terrain editor, 271
using
  ecosystem, 83–84
  Game Objects, 53–55
  hierarchy view, 52
  Inspector panel, 53–54, 57
  mathematical algorithm, 57
  mouse event messages, 79
  navigating scene, 59
  Scene Editor view, 52
  test development scene, 52
  triggers and colliders, 56
Web Player, 464
world units, 272
Unity Creative Magazine, 224
Unity graphical user interface (uGUI)

building blocks of, 403–404
Game Objects, 403
Rect Transform, 402–403
UI components, 404–405
User interface (UI), 232
  design of, 393–394
    color theory, 398–402
    HUD, 394–397
    menu, 397–398
  PlayMaker, 420–421
    dialogue system integration,
      440–444
    overlay, HUD, 430–440
    response on main menu,
      421–430
  types of
    HUD, 392–393
    menu-based systems, 392
  Unity system, 402
    dialogue system, 418–420
    HUD overlay, 412–418
    main menu construction,
      404–412
    uGUI, building blocks,
      403–404
UV Unwrap, 102–103

V

Variable, 64–65, 136
Vector3, 135
Vector3 value, 329
Victory conditions; *see also*
    Mechanics
  definition of, 315
  types of, 315–316
  zero-sum game, 315
Video game; *see also* Music
  ambience, 352–354
  development
    life cycle of, 462–463
    stand-alone build, 465–470
    in Unity, building options,
      463–465
    Windows Standalone,
      461–462
  music, 350–352
  sound events, 354
Video game players in 2014, 4
Video gamer, 4
Video games, 261
Virtual reality (VR) headset, 317
Vision statement, 28–29

Visual components, 404
Voice-over narration
  action–adventure style
    game, 232
  Audacity, 233
  audio file, 233
  audio listener, 233
  audio source, 233, 235
  backstory information, 232–233
  information overload, 232
  narrator object, 234
  platformer, 232
VR headset, *see* Virtual reality
    headset

W

Waypoint system, 172
WebGL, 463–465
Windows Standalone build,
    465–466
  player settings, 469–470
  resolution settings page,
    467–468
  shared player setting
    properties, 467
  splash image, 468–469
Wind settings section, 299
World of Warcraft, 6
*The Writer's Journey: Mythic Structures
    for Writers,* 192
Written text
  canvas object
    position of, 236, 238
    properties of, 236–237
  GUI, 236
  minor issues, 238
  nonlinear story lines, 238
  potential solution, 235
  quest, 236
  story components, 237
  text object, 236, 239

X

Xbox, 472

Z

Zero-sum game, 208